AVID

READER

PRESS

When Women Lead

What They Achieve,

Why They Succeed,

and How We Can Learn from Them

Julia Boorstin

Avid Reader Press

New York   London   Toronto   Sydney   New Delhi

AVID READER PRESS
An Imprint of Simon & Schuster, Inc.
1230 Avenue of the Americas
New York, NY 10020

First Avid Reader Press trade paperback edition January 2024

AVID READER PRESS and colophon are trademarks of Simon & Schuster, Inc.

Simon & Schuster: Celebrating 100 Years of Publishing in 2024

For information about special discounts for bulk purchases, please contact Simon &
Schuster Special Sales at 1-866-506-1949 or business@simonandschuster.com.

The Simon & Schuster Speakers Bureau can bring authors to your live event. For
more information or to book an event, contact the Simon & Schuster Speakers
Bureau at 1-866-248-3049 or visit our website at www.simonspeakers.com.

Interior design by Ruth Lee-Mui

Manufactured in the United States of America

1   3   5   7   9   10   8   6   4   2

Library of Congress Cataloging-in-Publication Data is available.

ISBN 978-1-9821-6821-6
ISBN 978-1-9821-6822-3 (pbk)
ISBN 978-1-9821-6823-0 (ebook)

To my parents, Paul and Sharon,
who inspire me to pursue hard
things and instilled in me a
love of asking questions.

And to my husband and partner, Couper,
whose patience and co-parenting
made this book possible.

Contents

Introduction　　　　　　　　　　　　　　　　　　　1

I. How and Why Women Build Strong Companies　　23

1. Overcoming the Odds　　　　　　　　25
2. Building with Purpose　　　　　　　　53
3. Leading with Empathy　　　　　　　　81
4. Engineering Smart Teams　　　　　　117

II. Fixing Problems　　139

5. Reforming Broken Systems　　　　　　141
6. Embracing Change　　　　　　　　　170
7. Managing in Crisis　　　　　　　　　202

III. Creating New Patterns　　235

8. Defying CEO Archetypes　　　　　　237
9. Discovering Resilience　　　　　　　268
10. Creating New Communities　　　　　294
11. Defeating Bias with Data　　　　　　326

Epilogue: Learning Lessons　　　　　　357
Acknowledgments　　　　　　　　　　371
Notes　　　　　　　　　　　　　　　375
Index　　　　　　　　　　　　　　　417

"When you grow up, everything will be different."

I still remember my mother saying that when I was thirteen years old, squeezed between friends in the back seat of afternoon carpool. We had just heard Gloria Steinem speak at our school's annual women's history speaker series. It was an experience my mother saw as a rite of passage for me. She had marched against the Vietnam War and for civil rights, and proof of it sat on her desk: a photo of her younger self in a flower print minidress, flanked by her best friends holding picket signs. Drawn to the energy and potential in the women's rights movement, she had heard Steinem speak in the 1970s.

"We marched so you wouldn't have to," she said. "*My* parents told me my only two choices were teacher and nurse." (She chose teacher.) But now, she said, in this last decade of the millennium, opportunities would be unfolding before us. "You will be *captains of industry*! Women will be running companies! The halls of Congress will be full of women!" I rolled my eyes and looked out the window. Given the steady march toward progress, my mom's enthusiasm felt pointless and even embarrassing. "CEO!

Rocket scientist! Brain surgeon! Nothing will hold you back!" she continued. *Of course, Mom. I know.*

Eight years later, on the sixteenth floor of the Time Warner building in midtown Manhattan, I realized we had both been wrong.

It was my first day working at *Fortune* magazine. I was one of the last people hired before the stock market crash of 2000. A twenty-one-year-old Princeton graduate with a degree in history, I didn't have a single economics or accounting class on my transcript, but I had been an editor at *The Daily Princetonian*, and I came armed with writing samples from a class I'd taken with John McPhee. I also had done an assortment of internships at the White House and for the State Department's delegation to the Organization for Economic Co-operation and Development (OECD). I guess my new bosses figured I could learn how to analyze numbers, read SEC documents, and examine financial results. It was an assumption that was both refreshing (no outmoded stereotypes about girls and math here!) and also a little daunting (what's an S-1 again?).

That morning, a supervisor invited me into her office for an informal orientation, mainly to review corporate policies on expense accounts and explain the guidelines for pitching stories. "Oh, and your timing is so lucky," she added as we were wrapping up. "There was *just* a big sexual harassment settlement at Time Inc., so everyone"—she waved to the corridor of male editors—"will be on their best behavior."

I was stunned. That was 2000—long before the #MeToo era and broad recognition that the combination of lopsided workplace power dynamics and anything sexual could be toxic. Even the Monica Lewinsky scandal, which had broken into public view during my White House internship, had been viewed by many people (me included) as more a tawdry sex scandal than abusive workplace behavior. My reporter instincts had me itching to ask questions about the settlement, but they were questions I suddenly didn't feel comfortable asking. What kind of sexual harassment? What does "big settlement" even mean? Was it a victory that the men in this office would be slightly more nervous about—*about doing what, exactly?*

As I walked out of her office, past the warren of dark reporter cubbyholes, I saw the true male/female 50/50 split that I'd been accustomed to in high school and college. As I turned the corner to the row of midcareer writers, the men outnumbered the women, but not by much. Then I got to the rows of senior editors' offices. There was one belonging to the legendary female editor-at-large Carol Loomis. But the vast majority of senior editors were men. I considered the power ratio.

Later, when I asked an older female writer about the sexual harassment situation, she gave me no details. Instead, she advised me to follow a "Men-minus-two" rule: stay two drinks behind the male editors at postwork happy hours. "*Never* accuse anyone of sexual harassment," she warned. "Unless you're *guaranteed* to make enough money from the settlement that you'll never have to work again." To her it was an obvious statement of fact—that kind of accusation would make one unhirable. She was just being practical. But for me, it was a giant crack in the monolithic wall of confidence that my mother had built for me about my opportunities in an equitable world.

That was just the beginning. A few months later, during one interview, a mutual fund manager scoffed when I pressed him on his declining returns: How could such a "young woman" like me possibly have any informed questions about the subject? On another occasion, when Oracle CEO Larry Ellison and his senior executive team swept into the conference room for a cover story I was helping report, they asked me to get them coffee, assuming that I was a secretary. When I reported a story about twenty CEOs whose net worth had declined by more than $1 billion during the stock market downturn—all of them happened to be men—I received angry phone calls and emails from a number of them, questioning my math and accusing me of not understanding their businesses. The rule, rather than the exception, was for men to either sneer at or leer at young women like me.

While doing interviews with CEOs, analysts, and fund managers, I learned to expect a low simmer of condescension. I protected myself by donning an armor of boxy suits and chunky glasses (which I didn't really need). I decided I would be taken more seriously if I never discussed my personal life. I tried to minimize my natural girliness and turned myself into a financial reporting utility, studying S-1 IPO filings, annual reports, and analyst notes. I created a work identity: overprepared and calm. When an inappropriate comment made its way to me, I kept a guarded, neutral half smile on my face. Unlike my male peers, I didn't linger at after-work happy hours (I always stayed Men-minus-two). That workplace identity wasn't really me, but it worked for me.

One morning in 2003, my colleague Grainger David slumped into the chair next to my desk. Every day we traded professional strategies and intraoffice gossip, and he'd come to report on the tennis game he'd played with two senior editors the night before. If I were to run a gender workplace experiment, David would have made a perfect control set. He and I had graduated from Princeton together and started working at *Fortune* magazine within a few weeks of each other. Our academic backgrounds were remarkably similar (although he, unlike me, had taken Econ 101).

The tennis game, David told me, had led to cocktails and then to a larger discussion about his dream of covering the gold rush—the one *in Mongolia*. Sending a reporter and photographer abroad, especially somewhere like Mongolia, was an expensive investment for an atypical *Fortune* piece. Perhaps aided by his racquet skills, or the cocktails, he had convinced them, and it was happening.

What I saw was unconscious bias in action. The men who held the most power felt most comfortable hanging out with younger versions of themselves, which offered those young men exposure and opportunities for advancement. The hours David spent with our bosses on the court, or over bourbon, naturally led to comfort and kinship. That enabled him to informally explore what story angles and ideas might fit into the pages of *Fortune* (or which ones could be *made* to fit).

Though David's advantage was one freely given to young male reporters, I had a different kind of advantage that was the product of pure luck. I had happened to join *Fortune* at a moment when then-editor at large, Andy Serwer, had taken on new responsibilities at the magazine and also at CNN. As the youngest reporter on staff, I had been assigned the new—and, for my peers, *unique*—job of assisting Serwer as he churned out a regular column, a daily newsletter, and cover stories, while managing his daily appearances on CNN.

As a result of my daily access to Serwer's office, I had extraordinary visibility into the processes of a great reporter. Unlike my young female colleagues, I was the recipient of serendipitous mentorship by Serwer—with no tennis courts involved. And the fullest proof of my good fortune: Andy Serwer was, and remains, an exceedingly good guy.

What I learned by reporting for my mentor I channeled into my own pieces for the magazine. They included new takes on old, iconic companies such as Smucker's and Wrigley. I wrote essays about viral marketing campaigns and profiles of big business personalities, from the retail impresario and then-CEO of J.Crew, Mickey Drexler, to Whole Foods Market founder John Mackey.

Occasionally, reporters like me were invited to appear on *Fortune*'s then-sibling company's network, CNN, to discuss a business news story. About a year into my job at *Fortune*, I was asked by CNN to come on air to talk about an article I had written. It was my first experience on live TV, and by some miracle I didn't get nervous. It turned out that the workplace alter ego I had been cultivating (overpreparedness and a half smile) was highly portable to live television. CNN invited me back, and after a few months of regular appearances, I became a contributor with a thrice-weekly segment on CNN Headline News bearing the ungainly name *Street Talk with Julia Boorstin*.

After five years of appearing regularly on CNN while writing for *Fortune*, I was offered a job as an on-air reporter at CNBC, so I decided to leave print magazines for TV business news. There was, of course, something fundamentally different about delivering my stories on live television, especially when bias crept into the dynamic.

A few weeks before my wedding in 2007, I was doing a live segment on CNBC with a short-lived anchor on the network when he decided I was too bullish on Netflix. After I reported a story on the company's growth prospects, he fired at me with snide relish that my analysis was faulty and overly optimistic because my judgment was clouded. He said sarcastically, "You must be *really happy* in your personal life." This older man was belittling my ability as a journalist, implying that my life as a woman was interfering with my ability to do my job. Why was the identity I thought I had left safely at home being dragged into my work? And why was my colleague using it on CNBC's air to score points against me? The strange and random deployment of my "personal life" created a moment of cognitive dissonance for me: As soon as the words left my colleague's lips, I flinched, causing my earpiece to fall out of my ear. As the years wore on, I developed the ability to quickly respond to such affronts (I never again accidentally popped out an earpiece during a segment). The anchor soon left the network, and the last time I checked, Netflix turned out okay.

More often, though, such offenses happened off camera. There was that time I was strolling into a high-level private event at the Consumer Electronics Show with a male CEO and another CEO asked me if we were having an affair. And there was another time that a source of mine, whom I considered a friend, told me over dinner that I would be far more successful if I "got a boob job." Despite my saying clearly that the conversation was inappropriate, he spent the next forty-five minutes repeating and defending his argument before I could find a way to exit.

At first I struggled with that kind of objectification as an on-air personality. Had I brought this humiliation upon myself by choosing to report news in a medium that featured my appearance? Did that kind of invasion of my personal space come with the territory? The absurdity of the "boob job" comment was a turning point: I decided I loved my job too much to let that kind of stupid, painful interaction distract me.

I worked to ignore and forget those experiences and to focus on the freedom I had to pursue my interests at CNBC. I certainly wasn't living in the egalitarian utopia my mom had hoped for me, but over the years that type of offense became far less common. As I moved through the world of TV business news, I found I was adapting to it—and thriving in it.

My bosses encouraged me to be entrepreneurial and create new franchises and series, and I was again lucky to learn from and collaborate with smart colleagues, especially some women around my age. And I loved interviewing acclaimed leaders such as the Walt Disney Company CEO Bob Iger and Netflix CEO Reed Hastings and reporting on how they were transforming their companies and reinventing the business of entertainment.

Then, when I was thirty-three, I became pregnant with my first son. The protective "work identity" that I had so carefully cultivated was suddenly being colonized, and visibly so, by my personal one. Once I was "showing," the number of offensive incidents rose in apparent proportion to my growing belly. There were comments about how it would be impossible to continue my TV career once I had children. Many men I interviewed rubbed my belly before they sat down to clip on a microphone. Some even remarked on my breasts. Like millions of women before me, I was annoyed and scared about how this new identity could impact my career momentum.

As my pregnancy progressed, I discovered that my professional success often hinged on my ability to *not* flinch when men said (or did) inappropriate or offensive things. Luckily, I'd had a decade of practice. It turned out that playing the "role" of a twenty-one-year-old cub reporter in boxy blazers and Clark Kent glasses had been a protracted dress rehearsal for the big show—the gendered treatment that too often comes with pregnancy. *So how long are you going to keep doing this? You won't ever see your kids with your hours—you'll want to stay home.* Those comments could have felt like kryptonite, but with plenty of practice I developed a kind of force field. The barbs revealed everything about the biases of those men, I realized, and nothing about me. If some men felt so weird being interviewed by a woman with a giant pregnant belly that they felt compelled to make a comment, it was *their* problem, not mine.

Then there was maternity leave. After years of the breakneck pace of daily live television, I was suddenly away from my job for three solid months, completely unplugged and totally focused on my baby. I was surprised that I loved every minute of it. When my maternity leave was over, I packed up my breast pump and ice packs and squeezed into Spanx. I didn't know what to expect. Would my career still be there when I returned? In the same place where I had left it? And how would I feel about my work and that mythical work-life balance I'd heard so much about?

As it turned out, my career was still there and in roughly the same condition. But now, of course, there was a new, adorable demand on my time waiting for me when I got home every day. And a strange thing happened: however sleep deprived I was, it became something of a comfort to know that whatever small indignities befell the workplace "Julia Boorstin," there was another identity I could retreat to back at home. My growing family was now the most important thing in my life, so I wasn't as intimidated by my bosses or my interview subjects. Those stakes felt smaller in comparison. The minutiae didn't distract me and stress me out as much because I felt at my core that they were not as important as all the stuffy noses and baby milestones I worried about and relished. With my new priorities and time constraints, I focused my attention at work on the most important things. And so even with the new pressures of motherhood, my first year back from maternity leave was my most productive at CNBC to date: I reported a documentary on the future of television and started creating CNBC's annual Disruptor 50 list of startups.

Instead of feeling like the fact that I was a woman was something that I needed to overcome, it became a kind of superpower that gave me perspective and bolstered me in the most challenging situations.

As my self-perception changed, the world around me seemed to as well. More women were ascending to senior positions and occasionally reaching the typically male C-suite. A cultural inflection point came with the 2013 publication of Sheryl Sandberg's *Lean In: Women, Work, and the Will to Lead*. The book and the nonprofit built on its ideals sought to demystify the challenges of female corporate leadership and destigmatize accommodations that corporations could make for female employees— and encourage companies to make those accomodations. Sandberg represented a new kind of role model—both aggressive and feminine—and she started a conversation. The book provoked backlash for seeming most useful to white women in positions of privilege. But for me—and I was certainly in a position of privilege—it inspired a renewed commitment to actively seize professional opportunities.

In the years after I found my confidence as a working mom, I began to see more women around my age come into leadership roles, and I had a chance to interview some of them for CNBC. In addition to the slow rise of female corporate executives, I watched a proliferation of female entrepreneurs pursuing their passions. Over the course of countless interviews, I was struck by a unique approach to leadership many of these women were taking. I saw them solving problems and creating products they wanted or needed that didn't yet exist. They were finding opportunities in arenas that men had overlooked. From Bumble, which inverted the power dynamics of online dating, to the biotech company LanzaTech, which turns pollution into fuel, women were creating and leading some of the most disruptive and innovative businesses I covered for CNBC.

I also felt the result of all that slow progress in the workplaces I visited. In the corridors of corporations large and small, I found more breast-pumping rooms. At conferences I saw panels expanded to include more than a single, token woman. Even late-night tech conference poker games started to include female participants—not just female cocktail waitresses. While I was writing this book, *Fortune* magazine named its first female editor-in-chief. The pace of change was slow, and the path to gender equity is a very long one. But I increasingly noticed a range of women speaking up about the pressures, the obstacles, and the double standards—and succeeding despite all of those things.

To thrive against the odds, those women had to be remarkable. That's why I've devoted a book to telling their stories. By definition, they're exceptional.

One thing that has consistently impressed me most over my past twenty-odd years of business reporting is the way female leaders have been able to turn genuine grievance into entrepreneurial grit. I have been struck by how women have had to be far more scrappy, flexible, thick skinned, and innovative—and how the companies they have built have also taken on those characteristics. Women such as Sallie Krawcheck, CEO of the female-focused investing company Ellevest, who was ignominiously fired from one of the most powerful perches in finance. Or Shivani Siroya, who created Tala, a system for providing microloans to people in emerging markets who couldn't borrow money from banks. Or Aileen Lee, who cofounded the nonprofit All Raise to help women rise in the male-dominated VC world. Those women looked around and said, "Enough. I am going to start something new, and I'm going to do it myself." This is hardly the first wave of powerful female entrepreneurs—Estée Lauder founded her makeup line in 1946, Mrs. Fields Cookies was founded by Debbi Fields in 1977, Sara Blakely invented Spanx in 2000, Arianna Huffington launched the Huffington Post in 2005, and Oprah Winfrey and Martha Stewart have been at it for decades. But now a new breed of founder is taking the baton and formulating novel approaches to a wide range of industries.

In May 2019, I interviewed Rent the Runway founder and CEO Jennifer Hyman when her company had just been named number five on CNBC's Disruptor 50 list, which ranks fast-growing private companies that are challenging established industries. Hyman was nine months pregnant and was visiting the company's warehouse in New Jersey for the last time before her maternity leave. She ran through her plan: she would take four months off after giving birth, and during that time, the company's executive ranks would manage the launch of a new distribution center—without her. Sitting in the middle of Rent the Runway's dry-cleaning operations, plastic-sheathed dresses flying around us, I asked a routine question about whether recent IPO flops made her concerned about her company's own chances in the public markets. Hyman smiled, narrowed her eyes, and proceeded to dismantle the premise of my question. Those companies' challenges and balance sheets, she explained, were very different from hers. "As a female CEO, I haven't been given the permission, or the privilege, to lose a billion every quarter."

Hyman's umbrage, like her business cred, is well earned. In fact, female founders have consistently drawn less than 3 percent of all venture capital dollars, and it is VC funding that enabled companies such as Facebook, Google, and Airbnb to spend years losing money while growing.[1] (This is part of a broader lack of female representation in leadership across business: women comprised 8.8% of CEOs of the Fortune 500 as of May 2022, and represented just 24 percent of all roles in the C-suite, companies' most senior group of managers, as of 2021.)[2]

When those few female entrepreneurs *do* successfully raise venture funding, they generally raise less than half as much as their male counterparts. Indeed, the pressure of not being able to raise as much money as her male peers made Hyman focus *not* on driving growth—in order to cash in on the company with a sale or an IPO—but rather on operations. The condescension and gender bias she'd faced from venture capital investors had made her persistent and creative and taught her to do more with less. Now she felt empowered to shape the culture of the company she had cocreated so she *could* take maternity leave while her deep bench of (female) C-suite executives filled in.

It's not just that women are especially outnumbered in the world of startups; there's another reason why I'm interested in tech-driven companies such as The RealReal, a digital luxury consignment platform; Spring Health, a mental health care service for companies; and Insurify, an insurance comparison shopping platform. For the past thirty years, the technology industry has had more impact than any other sector on both business and society. It has encoded massive changes into the culture, transforming the way we communicate, work, travel, learn, and play. It has also produced tools—from Amazon Web Services to Dropbox to Slack—that are lowering the barriers to entry for new entrepreneurs, both male and female.

Tech entrepreneurs have an opportunity to turn a crazy idea into a game-changing institution when given the powerful boost of venture capital. It is from investments made by venture capital funds—some canny bets on a growing industry, some wild moonshots on industries that don't exist yet—that so much tech innovation emanates. That is the reason I am choosing to focus this book on the startup world. Because of the broad impact of tech companies, the headwinds faced by female tech entrepreneurs are particularly meaningful. With less access to venture capital, female founders face more barriers to building companies that could have a massive effect on the world.

I saw just how high the stakes can be for startups—companies such as Google and Uber influence how we live, work, and spend money— or they create new consumer sectors, as Rent the Runway and Airbnb have. Plus, through my reporting I understood how hard it can be for women to succeed in the powerful world of tech. But I didn't want this book to be a polemic against inequitable systems. Instead, I wanted to understand how some women had been able to become exceptions. I wanted to know how they had done it—and what we can all learn from them.

When I started reporting this book in early 2020, I flew up to Silicon Valley and interviewed more than a dozen venture capital investors about the female founders they'd backed. I heard stories about the resilience the women had demonstrated, how they'd managed to scale their companies despite fewer resources, and the obstacles they'd faced. I started calling up those female founders to ask about their fundraising challenges, what tactics they had used to scale disruptive ideas, and how they had managed to succeed against the odds.

On the afternoon of March 10, 2020, I was on my way to interview one of them, Beautycounter founder and then-CEO Gregg Renfrew, when I pulled over to read an urgent text from my children's elementary school: classes would be canceled for the foreseeable future due to covid-19. I finished the drive to Beautycounter's headquarters in Santa Monica and, feeling winded by the news, sat in the lobby, full of sleek glass bottles encasing the company's clean skin care and makeup lines. I looked at the notebook in my lap, full of questions that I had prepared weeks earlier. I'd been reading the reports that the World Health Organization was about to qualify covid-19 a global pandemic, and now it felt as though those scribbles were from another lifetime, on topics that were suddenly inconsequential.

As Renfrew greeted me in her airy office, with giant photos of her three children on the wall and a potted plant arching over her desk, I had the terrifying feeling that she would be the last person I would interview in person for a very long time. She immediately apologized for having pushed our meeting back. The company, she explained, had been in triage mode as it prepared for the total disintegration of its in-person business.

When we settled into the interview, Renfrew explained that the biggest challenge in her career wasn't when she'd pitched to VCs to raise money. It wasn't when she'd testified before Congress on the need for cosmetic safety regulations. It wasn't even the time she decided to discard a whole new line of products when they failed to live up to her company's high safety standards. Her toughest management decision, at that point, had been how to handle canceling the company's annual conference, which had been scheduled for the previous week in San Francisco. The top two thousand of the company's fifty thousand marketing consultants—the vast majority of them female—had planned to fly in to learn about the company's commitment to safe ingredients and to try its serums, sunscreens, and lipsticks in person.

Understandably, she feared what canceling might represent: the economy frozen, the inability to gather women in living rooms, where they could try—and buy—her products. She feared that there would be prolonged retail closures just as she was adding brick-and-mortar locations to her virtual business model. She feared that with the stock market in free fall, consumers' priorities would naturally shift away from beauty products.

But even then, Renfrew was thinking about how to adapt in the short term: creating online environments to train Beautycounter consultants and market new products to consumers. She also talked about the long-term stakes—not just returning a profit to her investors but keeping the business functioning at scale and those fifty thousand women earning an income. "Somebody's got to make these tough calls. As a leader I'm always having to make tough decisions," she said. "You're expected to be in high growth mode all the time, you're expected to meet the ever-changing demands of the consumer, and you're expected to be profitable simultaneously. All those things are really challenging to do." And now she was going to try to do those things in the midst of what was about to become a global pandemic.

After we concluded our interview, I drove away from the office on an eerily empty freeway, wondering if the quiet at rush hour was the opening scene of a world-changing story. The entire economy was about to come to a screeching halt. The following two weeks would see 10 million Americans file for jobless benefits, nearly the same number of people who had lost their jobs over the two-year-long recession of 2008–2009.[3]

I felt as though I was watching a weird economic experiment. Here I was, researching a book about the degree to which female entrepreneurs are more adaptable, versatile, cool-headed in their risk taking, and able to do more with less. Suddenly all those qualities would be put to the most extreme test that the global economy had faced since World War II.

Profiling successful female entrepreneurs such as Gregg Renfrew and enumerating their personal and professional qualities seemed like more than enough material for a book. As I conducted interviews, though, I realized that I needed better tools to understand their successes. So while I was interviewing these incredible women, I also searched for data and research that could help me categorize their approaches and understand why they had worked. Then I wanted to identify if these particular characteristics were more likely to be demonstrated by women. The stories I was hearing intersected with the research I was reading when I found studies that elucidated leaders' tactics or when I noticed a quality in a CEO that I had read about in an academic paper. It was the intersection of personal narratives and research that gave me a full understanding—not just of the special quality of a particular entrepreneur but of the broader lessons to be learned from her example.

In other words, the research helped me take atypical, seemingly inimitable women leaders and understand them as new, imitable archetypes.

It is the synthesis of these biographical stories and academic research that I hope will bring a new set of archetypes to life. They don't look or behave like the commonly held images of corporate America's suits (the imperious salt-and-pepper patriarch) or Silicon Valley's hoodies (the move-fast-and-break-things tech bro). These women possess such extraordinary characteristics that they are able to defy the odds and grow companies—and those companies tend to add value to both industry and society.

In the research and personal stories, I've found that women's strengths have often been overlooked or simply not associated with great leadership. There are a range of qualities I've found that women tend to possess that correlate with great leadership. They have a tendency to be more considerate of data in their risk assessment. They are also more likely to include varied perspectives in decision making and as a result are better at empathizing with both colleagues and customers. They often lead with vulnerability, a willingness to ignore expectations and to do things their own way. I found that these women frequently focus on achieving a greater purpose beyond profits, and are more likely to pursue social and environmental goals with a heightened sense of gratitude for their access and opportunity. Their approaches may have been overlooked, undervalued, or not associated with leadership for the simple reason that it is women who most often exhibit them.

To many women, the enumeration of sexist and misogynistic biases can seem thuddingly obvious and pointlessly demoralizing. My intention in highlighting inspirational stories and the characteristics women deploy is to be positive and forward looking. (My use of the terms *woman* and *female* is inclusive of anyone who identifies as that gender.)

My hope is that the strategies highlighted here can be a resource for anyone, of any gender, who is looking for modes of succeeding in business. I think those practical takeaways are possible, because I found them myself. In reporting this book I wasn't just testing hypotheses about female entrepreneurs—I was learning how to better navigate the world.

In the winter of 2020, the darkest period of the pandemic, I was lucky to be healthy and working from home, broadcasting on CNBC just feet away from my Zoom-schooled kids. I felt particularly grateful given the horrifying headlines about how women were most affected by the pandemic. Women were more likely to be laid off and quit in record numbers as they struggled to manage their children's online schooling and protect their family's health. During that time, I happened also to be poring over research on female leaders, who, even in nonpandemic circumstances, are subjected to an added set of stressors. As I made my way through dozens of academic studies, I found myself stuck on a particular pile of reports that detailed all the different ways women in business were judged more harshly. I struggled to figure out how I could organize that demoralizing research into a positive, practical framework. It all felt overwhelming and depressing.

But then I saw a use for all those data in my own professional life, when on CNBC on December 8, 2020, I interviewed Ann Sarnoff, who was then the CEO of WarnerMedia Studios and Networks Group. Warner Brothers had just made the controversial decision to release its next eighteen movies simultaneously on the company's HBO Max streaming platform and in theaters—without warning the filmmakers and actors, whose paydays, which were normally driven by theatrical box office revenues, would be affected. I asked Sarnoff to respond to the criticisms of the filmmaker Christopher Nolan and other Hollywood names and inquired about concessions the company would have to give to theater chains in order to simultaneously release films on HBO Max. I pressed her when she evaded questions.

After the interview, a PR executive called. "I thought you were kind of mean in that interview with Ann," he told me. "I mean, your tone just felt *really harsh.*"

Umbrage from PR flacks is a professional hazard of business reporting, but it can be harrowing because this kind of opprobrium often comes with a threat—implicit or explicit—of blocked access to an entire organization. (In TV reporting, executives' on-air participation is valuable currency.) My general strategy in these kinds of situations had always been to take a warm and upbeat tone and defuse the tension with a comment about what a great opportunity it was to address the headlines. Occasionally I would review a tape with colleagues and ask whether, in fact, I had pushed too hard. After more than twenty years at this, I know my stuff. And even when I'm tough, I think I'm fair. Executives continue to return my phone calls. The earth continues to spin.

But when it came to that particular call and that particular comment, I had all that research thrumming through my head. At that moment, one study conducted by my old employer, *Fortune* magazine, was particularly vivid. Called "The Abrasiveness Trap: High-Achieving Men and Women Are Described Differently in Reviews," it detailed the way women tend to be judged for their style and personality, whereas men are judged for their performance.[4] So when the PR exec told me I had been "mean," I heard that word in a way I hadn't before. "That's odd," I replied. "I thought I was incredibly fair." Then I blurted out, "Would you have given the same critique to one of my *male* colleagues?" There was an awkward silence. Then he said something surprising.

"Well, maybe I would expect it of *him*. I don't know." He sounded more reflective than chastened. "I'll think about it." Maybe he was admitting that I had a point. Or maybe *I* had scared *him* a little. Or maybe it was a bit of both.

In any case, it was empowering: I wasn't crazy for perceiving bias. The knowledge I had gained in my research helped me distinguish fair criticism about my performance from unfair criticism relating to my gender. In that moment, I could understand the word "mean" for what it was: a discomfort with my "unfeminine" tone rather than a genuine criticism of my performance. What was particularly interesting to me is that Sarnoff herself hadn't seemed to notice anything out of the ordinary. We emailed after the interview, and she later volunteered to join me for a fireside chat for a group of women executives in the entertainment industry. The following year she invited me to interview her on the Warner Brothers lot about the studio's postpandemic plans. At issue wasn't the reality of the exchange between two professional women on CNBC's air; at issue was a man's *perception* of that exchange.

As I conducted more research and interviews, I realized that although the data about ways in which women are judged more harshly can be discouraging, they can also be a valuable tool to empower women. Defining the shapes of an obstacle can naturally help you circumnavigate it. Understanding how leaders have handled tough situations and the science behind their strategies will, I hope, help others find ways to thrive in the face of adverse conditions.

Nearly two years after my first encounter with Gregg Renfrew, she was one of the last women I checked in with before this book went to print. Beautycounter was thriving. In the face of the adverse conditions of the pandemic, she had indeed figured out how to navigate the unforeseen challenges. In the year after our meeting, she had gone on what she called a listening tour, talking to more than a thousand of her consultants and customers. "In the absence of being able to physically gather to give someone a hug or just feel that energy, I just reached out and talked to people," she said. And conversations on Zoom, where anyone could raise a virtual hand, she said ended up feeling more intimate and effective than gathering hundreds of people in a room.

Despite her fears that afternoon in March 2020, in the following eighteen months the company introduced a range of new products that won awards, launched a new interactive shopping show on streaming video, and grew its ranks of sellers from fifty thousand to sixty-five thousand. "We've been able to anticipate and also focus on riding the wave of people caring about the health of their bodies and the health of the world," she said. The company revamped its packaging to be more environmentally friendly and introduced new cosmetics just in time for fresh demand for makeup. In April 2021, Beautycounter sold a majority stake to the Carlyle Group at a $1B valuation. (In January 2022, Renfrew stepped down from the role of CEO and became executive chair and chief brand officer.)

What to Expect in This Book

Renfrew was one of more than 120 women (plus some men!) I interviewed for this book. For reasons of space and narrative focus, there was unfortunately not room for all of them. In the chapters ahead you'll find profiles of women organized thematically, interwoven with relevant research.

The book is divided into three sections. The first focuses on how and why women tend to build strong companies, starting with the structural challenges they must overcome to raise venture capital and scale their businesses. Then I examine the impetus for women to structure their businesses in a more purpose-driven way. I take a broader look at these companies and how women use empathy and gratitude to solve big-picture problems for the long term. Then I delve into health care, one sector in which women are more likely to both start companies and be customers. The first section of the book concludes with a chapter looking at how women build smart teams by embracing a growth mindset and welcoming varied perspectives.

In the second section I look at how women tackle complex problems. I start by highlighting the stories of women who found success, chafed against their industries' male-orientation, and then used their expertise to reform them. The second chapter in the section takes a closer look at the transformation of one particular sector where women are the target customers—fashion. The third chapter shows three leaders trying to address seemingly insurmountable problems and to fix their organizations in the face of the most complex challenge of our time: the covid-19 pandemic.

The final section is focused on the new patterns that women leaders are creating to break free of old male-dominated systems. I start with a look at how underestimated characteristics—quietness and vulnerability—can provide a major leadership advantage. Then I examine the myriad ways women have cultivated resilience to overcome challenges, followed by a look at the new networks and communities women are forming to help one another grow and make gains in business. And finally, I look at how data are driving companies and investors to embrace diversity and change.

Though there is plenty of deeply discouraging research about double standards and lack of representation, writing this book gave me an overwhelming feeling of hope. I'm optimistic that these women and others like them—along with the data about the value of their leadership qualities—will make the business world a more equitable place. These companies show us how agile, fast growing, and resilient our economy can be when more women run things—and that reveals promise for our collective future.

My mother said, "By the time *you* grow up, you'll be able to do *anything*." When it comes to gender equity, conditions have not changed as much as she had hoped. The world right now looks nothing like what she expected. But maybe what she meant was that women of my generation would find new ways to do new things. From what I've learned in reporting this book, they are. We need those new approaches now more than ever.

Part I

How and Why Women Build Strong Companies

One

Overcoming the Odds

Follow the Money

In order to understand how exceptional the business leaders profiled in these pages are, it's important to understand the obstacles they faced before they got started. Nearly all of the women in this book share a crucial attribute: they've raised venture capital dollars. Venture capital investment is the magic ingredient that can turn an audacious technology-based idea into a world-changing institution. To quickly scale a tech startup or establish a new one, venture capitalists can pour tens of millions of dollars into it and not expect a return for a decade. Plus, they often join the boards of directors of nascent companies and provide mentorship, guidance, and access to a network of potential partners, suppliers, and even customers.

Venture capital firms pool funds from an array of sources: pension funds, financial institutions, and wealthy families. They then invest in startups beginning at the earliest stages of their life cycles—those first checks are called a *seed round*. Then, through Series A, B, and C rounds of fundraising, VCs provide companies millions of dollars with little expectation of near-term profitability—and hope for a return someday worth hundreds or even thousands of times their original investments. VCs don't just eliminate the pressure to generate revenue or profits as startups first launch. They can also provide even more capital after six or eight years to still-unprofitable companies in the hope that their continued support will make the company more valuable in the long run. Facebook, Uber, Airbnb, and Google spent years losing money and burning through venture capital before becoming the global behemoths they are today (and returning huge profits to their investors).

The $330 billion in VC capital invested in US companies in 2021 (a record) drives the innovation economy. It determines which ideas will become businesses that will transform the way we live and which entrepreneurs will become billionaires.[1] That's why it's so important to understand the deployment of these dollars. In securing this key ingredient to startup growth there is a gap between male and female entrepreneurs—and it is massive.

We hear a lot about the gender pay gap: women earn about 82 cents for every dollar men earn and Black women earn 63 cents for every dollar white men earn.[2] But those gaps are dwarfed by the gap in funding for startups. Between 2011 and 2020, startups with solely female founders secured an average of 3 percent of all venture capital funding globally. Soon after, that percentage declined: in 2021, female-founded companies in the United States drew 2 percent of venture capital dollars and 6.5 percent of VC deals. Those numbers show that the average funding round for a female-led company—the check size—is less than half as big as the average investment in a male-led one. Leadership teams with at least one male cofounder secured more funding: 15.6 percent of capital and 18.8 percent of deals in 2021.[3]

This means that startups *run entirely by men* brought home more than 82 percent of all capital and nearly 75 percent of all deals in 2021.

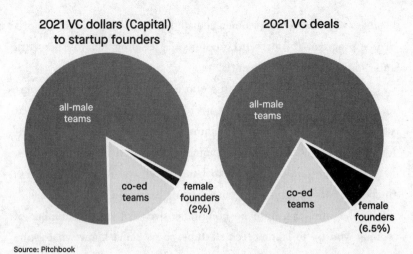

2021 VC dollars (Capital) to startup founders

2021 VC deals

all-male teams

co-ed teams

female founders (2%)

all-male teams

co-ed teams

female founders (6.5%)

Source: Pitchbook

So not only do all-male teams dominate the investment landscape, but each check they secure is, on average, bigger than the investments secured by coed or all-female teams.

The statistics are even more stunning for non-white founders. Just 1.2 percent of venture capital dollars and 2.1 percent of VC deals in the first half of 2021 were to Black startup founders, both male and female.[4] A 2020 study found that businesses led by Black and Latinx women CEOs drew 0.43 percent of VC investment in 2020, down from 0.67 percent over the prior two years.[5]

These kinds of harrowing statistics aren't just the domain of startups. Only 8.8% percent of Fortune 500 companies have a female CEO—and that's an all-time high. Of the more than two thousand companies that went public in the United States between 2013 and 2020, only eighteen, or 0.9 percent, had a female founder/CEO.[6]

The numbers are particularly shocking given that fully 42 percent of all small-business owners are women—and as of 2019, the number of women-owned businesses grew faster than the total amount of business growth.[7] Though women make up a slight minority (39 percent) of business school students, women actually outnumber men in bachelor's degree programs (57 percent), master's degree programs (60 percent), and PhD programs (52 percent).[8]

Some defenders of the status quo argue that, well, there are just many fewer women pitching startups to the VC community. Some even say VCs would *love* to invest in more female-led companies, but unfortunately, they just don't hear enough pitches from women founders. Maybe women just don't want to launch tech startups that need VC financing? Maybe they're too busy starting hair salons and bakeries?

To be sure, there are no comprehensive data on the number of women who *try* to launch tech startups, so we don't know what aspiring female entrepreneurs' success rate is raising money from VCs compared with their male counterparts. But there are some data points that give us a clue. In 2019, Silicon Valley Bank surveyed 1,400 startups and found that 28 percent of them had at least one female cofounder, a much higher percentage than the 12 percent of venture capital dollars that year that went to companies with a female cofounder.[9] This could indicate that companies with female leaders raise fewer dollars and do so less frequently or that they have a higher survival rate. Then there's that aforementioned fact that 42 percent of all small businesses in 2019 were owned by women, which seems to imply that women are trying to start companies at a greater rate than the rate that VCs invest in them. It seems that the population of women interested in creating startups exceeds the small percentage of women who get access to the benefits of the venture capital system.

All those statistics are what makes the women who have managed to raise financing and grow a business all the more remarkable.

If ever an entrepreneur understood the implications of the data about female founders, it is Snejina Zacharia. As she pitched her startup idea to venture capitalists in 2015, a peculiar question kept coming up. It had nothing to do with her educational background, her experience, the revenue growth and forecasts for her insurance comparison startup, Insurify, or the varieties of insurance products she envisioned offering.

The question that seemed to be on many investors' minds was something else entirely. "Do you have kids? How young are they?" they would ask. With a tight smile, she would answer (two, ages four and six). "You probably need to spend a lot of time with them," she recalled one of the investors saying. The questions didn't feel malicious; they were just totally irrelevant and a waste of the precious time she needed to present Insurify's business model. As she tried to lay out numbers to explain her company's potential, the people across from her too often seemed distracted by her personal life. *Okay*, she would think. *This is not going to go well.*

From the start, Zacharia was aware that she stood out in those meetings, and not just because she was frequently the only woman in the room. She has a high-pitched voice with a strong eastern European accent and a pale complexion that contrasts with her wavy reddish hair. Plus, her biography is untraditional for an entrepreneur pitching VCs. She grew up as Snejina Macheva in the 1990s in Sofia, Bulgaria, inside an opaque Communist information bubble (she changed her name when she got married). Her parents both held master's degrees and valued education, but her worldview was deeply provincial. As a child, she knew every other kid in the neighborhood surrounding her apartment and almost nobody beyond.

In the late 1980s, when she was ten and just coming into her own as a math prodigy, that Communist structure started to collapse. Determined to tap into the new opportunities of capitalism (and get out of financially depressed Bulgaria), young Snejina thrust herself into her schoolwork. With various scholarships given to students with the highest GPA, she earned a bachelor's and then a master's degree in economics from the University of National and World Economy in Sofia. The scholarships, however, didn't cover living expenses, so by her second year at the university, she was working full-time in the marketing department of a hotel chain.

In her next job, at a software company that processed e-commerce transactions, Snejina Macheva was introduced to the world of tech start-ups. That led to a job at another software company called Netage Solutions. At the company's Sofia office, she proved her skill set: she was highly organized, and she presented to management and negotiated with partner companies with ease and poise. In 2003, when the company was looking to expand in the United States, the eager executive volunteered to move to Boston. It was there, the following year, that she met her husband, an immigrant from Cyprus who had studied at MIT and was running a startup that used data to advise hedge funds.

In Boston, Zacharia followed her love of data to AMR, which was acquired by the global data research firm Gartner, which supplies thousands of companies with statistics on everything from supply chain strategies to technologies for health care, retail, and consumer goods companies. Zacharia's focus was building the supply chain business. She loved it. When her bosses decided it was too expensive to maintain local offices overseas, she proposed a plan to run the European business—and expand it—while based in Boston, by traveling extensively and using then-novel web-based virtual tools.

In 2011, seven years after joining the company, she asked her boss for a promotion. Her pay and title, she reasoned, should reflect the contributions she had made to her division's enormous growth. Her boss told her to wait one more year. She thought he felt threatened by her swift rise.

So Zacharia did what many high-achieving but frustrated professionals do when they hit a ceiling at their companies: she applied to business school to help her make the transition to become an entrepreneur. She was accepted to her first choice, the quant-heavy MIT Sloan School of Management. In 2012, she matriculated into its selective one-year Fellows program with 120 other midcareer executives. As a woman, she was in the minority—her class was 22 percent female.[10] As an aspiring first-time founder, she felt at a social disadvantage to other young entrepreneurs at MIT and so many nearby business schools. "I didn't go to high school or college with tons of other people that might work at great companies . . . that can potentially give you stronger foundations," she explained.

But she adapted. After putting her kids to bed, she would sneak out to Sloan networking events. She paid for a premium subscription to LinkedIn, sending "In-mails" to many MIT alumni and occasionally connecting with other immigrants with whom she felt a quick kinship. But compared to other aspiring entrepreneurs who had graduated from Harvard or Andover (or both), it still felt as though she was shooting at a much smaller target from much farther away.

One day while driving to an MIT event, the car in front of Zacharia slammed on its brakes, and she couldn't avoid smashing into it. As she dutifully swapped insurance information, she knew she would be considered the at-fault party and would lose her "reliable driver" status. When her insurance premium was raised, she called her broker to ask for advice on how to reduce it. The broker was unhelpful and didn't seem concerned that she could switch insurers. So she decided to figure out what to do herself. She set about getting quotes from other insurers. And she did it in the way that only a data-obsessed MBA student mother of two could: she made a detailed spreadsheet.

That was when Zacharia realized why her insurance agent didn't seem worried about losing her business. It was nearly impossible to sort through the thicket of premiums, deductibles, mileage limits, introductory offers, penalties, and rewards that each insurance company offered. It felt impossible to price the product accurately until one needed to use it. That frustrating lack of transparency reminded her of Communist-era Bulgaria. But it also meant that there was an opportunity.

She pulled out her notes from her class on entrepreneurship and in 2013 started putting together a business plan for the company she would call Insurify. By simply inputting your license plate number, she envisioned, you could see how much different offers would actually cost. It was like giving all her insurance customers their own mother-of-two business school student armed with Excel. When she and two classmates took the concept to the MIT $100K Entrepreneurship Competition, they were named semifinalists.

After graduation, Zacharia turned her attention to building Insurify into a working product, which meant she needed to raise about $2 million in a seed round. She brought on her husband as a cofounder and mined her premium LinkedIn account to contact investors who had a record of backing early-stage companies. She secured a dozen pitch meetings with VCs across the network she'd built at MIT and her husband's contacts as an entrepreneur.

It is in the seed round that the biases of venture capitalists are naturally at their most intense. Early-stage companies have little or no track record, so investors' decisions are based on factors that are mostly intangible. A seed round investment naturally becomes a bet on the entrepreneur and the idea. Of the twelve VC firms that gave Zacharia a first round of meetings, not one had a woman in the room. The investors directed many of their questions about the business to her husband or her male engineering lead—despite the fact that *she* was the CEO. Insurify had been her idea. It didn't seem as though they were trying to insult her; it just seemed like they assumed that she couldn't *really* be the boss.

Then there was that dreaded, repeated question. Zacharia was a high-achieving immigrant with multiple graduate degrees and a decade and a half of experience who was promising to organize a mass of hugely useful and practical data to give an opaque insurance system real transparency. But too often the people who could decide the fate of her company seemed more interested in her child-rearing strategies.

Zacharia was used to being the only woman in a room at all the companies where she'd worked. She had a playbook for a male-dominated world: she always wore suits—with pants, never skirts—and made sure to be as buttoned up as possible. But now, with her ambitions for Insurify on the line, she keenly felt the absence of other women. "They're really making a decision in the first ten seconds," she recalled. "Maybe one second—they're looking at you to decide if they feel like you're somebody that they can back. It's quite scary—it's all about how these men feel."

Pattern Matching

Zacharia was able to close a $2 million seed round—not from one of those VCs, but from a high net worth angel investor group in New York. Insurify quickly found traction with consumers and drove business to its partners. In 2020, she expanded the company from auto insurance into home, rental, and life. In 2021 Toyota partnered with Insurify to power its own insurance-shopping product. The company's track record enabled Zacharia to raise larger rounds, and each successive pitch process became easier and easier. In the years following those first painful pitch meetings, the company grew to serve over 5 million customers and by 2021 was consistently growing its revenue by 2 times every year. That fall she secured an additional $100 million, led by VC firms, along with the insurance giant Nationwide and the venture capital arm of MassMutual, bringing its total raised to $128 million.

Insurify, in its success, is an outlier. By some measures 70 percent of new businesses and 90 percent of venture-backed startups fail by their tenth year.[11] Zacharia's ability to raise money as a female CEO also makes her a rarity: Insurify's 2021 fundraise was among the 15.6 percent of VC dollars that year that went to companies with coed teams.

But at the seed stage, before Zacharia had any results to show investors, she was at a disadvantage because she wasn't a familiar type. At play in those VC offices was something behavioral psychologists call pattern matching, the process by which people try to predict future outcomes based on past patterns. Investors meet with hundreds of company founders every year. They want to invest in ideas and types of CEOs that have yielded successful investments in the past. But the instinct to find the familiar thing can create an echo chamber in which funding repeatedly goes to a group of homogeneous ideas and leaders. It also makes anything that deviates from that model hard to analyze; there is no pattern for comparison. When investors asked Zacharia about her child care challenges, it wasn't to insult her; they just had not encountered many female CEOs. They had no pattern to match.

In a 2013 *New York Times Magazine* profile of the influential startup incubator Y Combinator, its leader, Paul Graham, conceded, "I can be tricked by anyone who looks like Mark Zuckerberg. There was a guy once who we funded who was terrible. I said, 'How could he be bad? He looks like Zuckerberg!'" In another brazen admission of pattern matching that portends difficulties for an eastern European immigrant such as Zacharia, Graham told of a ranking of every Y Combinator company by its valuation: "You have to go far down the list to find a C.E.O. with a strong foreign accent . . . like 100th place," he told the reporter. "'You can sound like you're from Russia,' [Graham] said, in the voice of an evil Soviet henchman. 'It's just fine, as long as everyone can understand you.'"[12]

Because the risks of investing in startup ideas are so great, venture capitalists rely heavily on affinity and social connections to make their decisions. A 2021 survey by Harvard Business School professors of nearly nine hundred venture capitalists found that their assessment of a startup's *founder* was by far the most important factor in their investment decision making—more important than the business model, the industry, the market, or even the idea. A stunning 31 percent of those surveyed said they do not forecast *any* financials at all when they make an investment. And they reported that nearly two-thirds of all deal flow comes by referral from other investors, colleagues, and work acquaintances. Some of the survey's respondents seemed abashed by that fact and acknowledged to the professors that "the need to be plugged into certain networks can disadvantage entrepreneurs who aren't white men."[13]

This practice of pattern matching was likely a factor in the string of rejections all-male venture capital investors dealt to Karla Gallardo and

Shilpa Shah. The female team had résumés packed with top-tier business schools (Stanford and Berkeley) and blue-chip companies (Goldman Sachs, Apple, and the Walt Disney Company). With PowerPoints full of research and promising early demand for their first products, they were looking to raise about a million dollars in seed financing for Cuyana, a streamlined retail concept that would circumvent the traditional supply chain and tap into underutilized luxury-goods factories. The idea was to source from around the world a small selection of sustainable, well-made, classic pieces—starting with hats, knits, and leather goods—and sell them directly to consumers, with no middleman.

Gallardo grew up in Quito, Ecuador, in a family that didn't go shopping frequently. They waited until their annual trip to Miami. Her father, who worked in finance, would limit Gallardo's annual purchases to a few items that could fit into a small suitcase. She would wear them until she grew out of them. In 2001, when Gallardo moved to the United States from Ecuador to attend Brown University, she started going shopping with her new friends, who introduced her to Forever 21 and H&M. She was hooked. Fast fashion was her shopping equivalent of "the freshman 15." "It was basically an all-you-can-eat buffet when you're hungry," she said.

The sugar high left her with a closet crowded with cheap, empty-calorie items. It also led to an anxious Skype conversation with her dad about her credit card bill. "It was the most embarrassing, shameful moment for me when I realized that I had gotten lured by the rush of shopping that my parents were preventing us from doing all our lives," said Gallardo. "After that I started to think more consciously. So I started to try to figure out how to do what they wanted to teach me—how to purchase things that would last. The idea for Cuyana started simmering because I didn't have the access to the quality I wanted."

After graduating from Stanford Graduate School of Business, Gallardo was working in strategy for Apple's online store division when she borrowed twenty thousand dollars from her family to start producing and selling clothing and accessories. Cuyana's first two items—a Panama hat woven by women in Ecuador and an alpaca scarf from Peru—quickly sold out. At those early signs of traction, Gallardo felt it was time to find a complementary partner. She thought of her friend Shilpa Shah, a computer science major with a decade of experience in digital interface design. "I wanted to build a big business, and doing it alone felt lonely," she said.

Shah was then in her second year at Berkeley's Haas School of Business, the mother of a toddler and a two-month-old. She had supported her husband through his years in medical school and residency, and the couple had just made the switch for him to be the breadwinner while she completed business school. Shah didn't think of herself as being into fashion or even interested in being an entrepreneur, but when Gallardo approached her, the idea of Cuyana resonated and she wanted to take the plunge. Shah said it felt as though it was her turn: "It seemed to me that it would be really lame for me *not* to take a risk."

Together, the two women defined Cuyana's brand: their motto would be "fewer, better things" and the products would be the antithesis of fast fashion. They were allergic to the premise of luxury brands such as Louis Vuitton and Chanel, with their seasonal schedule of new products designed to get women to ignore the garments that were already crowding their closet and chase the newest style. And unlike those high-end brands, which emblazoned logos all over their wares, Cuyana's name would be nearly invisible. The products would be classic and long lasting. And they saw an opportunity in the fact that Prada and Burberry had moved part of their manufacturing to factories in Asia, leaving some smaller, high-end factories in Europe and Latin America sitting idle. Gallardo was aware of a similar situation in her native Ecuador. She had started to reach out to underutilized luxury factories there and elsewhere around the world to identify locations where she could produce just a few items in limited quantities and carefully manage the supply chain. By forgoing retail space and selling directly online, Cuyana could give women access to a simple leather bag or a cashmere sweater at not much more than wholesale price.

Gallardo and Shah knew that for their nascent e-commerce business to compete, they would need venture capital funding. They developed a pitch that detailed how they would use data to drive production and marketing and take advantage of opportunities in the supply chain. Shah recalled how painful it was to pitch their business to a series of male investors in 2012: "We're at this café, and we're telling this [VC] our story. Basically, after the first ten minutes, his eyes glazed over. And we still had to tell him about the company for another forty minutes, which is totally demoralizing when they're not even paying attention and there's nothing that you can do to bring them back on track."

Other investors listened and then told them to change their business model. During one pitch, an investor insisted that they should pivot to low-quality subscription clothes, to be more like one of his portfolio companies, a shoe subscription service fronted by Kim Kardashian called ShoeDazzle. (It was a subscription business that encouraged customers to buy things on a regular cadence, like the Columbia House CD model.) The suggestion of something so antithetical to their vision made it clear that he wasn't paying attention. They began to see that instead of trusting their experience as women and their research as entrepreneurs, the male investors thought they knew better.

"We'd be talking about consumers' needs not being met, and the VCs—all men—would say 'Well, my wife has a lot of handbags,'" Shah said. She and Gallardo knew that venture capital investors' wives could afford to spend thousands of dollars on a logoed handbag that signaled their wealth and status. Those women weren't the target demographic for Cuyana's simple, durable $200 bags. Young professional women, like Gallardo and Shah themselves, were.

Then there were the moments when male VCs would insist on bringing a woman into the room, thinking that surely only a woman could judge the value of Cuyana's approach. They would grab an assistant from the hallway to look at their designs, thinking they were doing the right thing, the smart thing, by focusing solely on the look and feel of the product. "Yeah, that was awkward," Shah recalled. "Of course, the product is quality, that's important. But we hadn't told them about the intelligence of the model yet." The VCs didn't realize that they were overlooking Gallardo and Shah's innovation in Cuyana's use of data to streamline production and minimize excess inventory. The wrong kind of pattern matching was at play. The founders didn't fit the mold of anything investors had seen before. And the VCs' instinct was to evaluate the appeal of those products rather than the economic efficiency of the business.

Shan-Lyn Ma, the CEO of the wedding planning and registry company Zola, faced a similar string of rejections from male investors when she was trying to raise her Series B round. During most of her pitches, investors questioned whether weddings were a big enough business. (An estimated $51 billion was spent in the United States on weddings in 2021.)[14] "The vast majority of investors I was pitching were white men who on average were much older than our target demographic—fifty or sixty years old and upwards," Ma recalled. "It was very hard to even get them mentally to the point of 'There is a problem to be solved and therefore an opportunity in solving the problem.'" Investors told Ma that their wives hadn't seemed to have any problems planning their weddings or suggested that they ask a female assistant for feedback.

For Shah and Gallardo there was an additional challenge in the fact that in the early 2010s, the retail industry as it had existed for decades was starting to fall apart. Amazon was growing in power, and its varied attempts to push into clothing retail were putting pressure on Macy's and other retailers to cut prices and deliver faster. Reports of retailers from Prada to Gap closing stores and failing to meet earnings estimates revealed an industry in turmoil. Malls were losing tenants as smaller chains shuttered and consumers shifted to shopping online. By all measures, the bar for starting a new retail brand seemed impossibly high. But amid so much disruption they saw an opportunity.

Gallardo's confidence grew once she noticed another industry trend: "The fast-fashion bubble was bursting. The consumer was tired of low quality and was aware of the economic damage [of low-cost clothing]," she said. "It was time to put to market a brand that delivered something different." Gallardo and Shah decided that Cuyana would start with just one new item every couple of months, with the plan to build out a curated online store. They would hold minimal inventory and could tweak their orders based on demand, instead of spreading themselves thin and launching dozens of products at once.

The concept was counterintuitive. How do you grow a business that is implicitly telling women to buy . . . less? The marketing, manufacturing, and sales would all be enabled by tech, unlike traditional retail concepts, which relied on foot traffic into stores. But as Gallardo and Shah pitched their idea, investors seemed stuck on the fact that retail concepts don't traditionally raise VC funding because they're not usually fast growing or profitable enough. In 2012, the first fifteen firms to which they presented Cuyana turned them down.

During that time, the cofounders were spending a lot of time scrolling through Pinterest. The then-nascent platform's algorithm worked by feeding its users things they might like based on images they and people they followed had "pinned," or saved. It was a good way to find and organize looks they liked. One day, while browsing through fashion and home decor on the platform, the founders came across an image titled "All Female Venture Capital Partners." The image contained a list of just nine names.

"We realized that we needed to change our investment strategy because the men we met didn't understand the problem," Shah recalled. "They didn't understand the need." Gallardo and Shah reached out to each of the nine women on the Pinterest list. One of them, Maha Ibrahim at Canaan, recognized the absence of Cuyana's types of products in the marketplace. In 2012 and 2013, she invested a total of $1.7 million in the company.

With financial backing and guidance from Ibrahim, Gallardo and

Shah started producing bags. They knew they would burn through the initial investment quickly if they tried to compete with traditional retail brands' big-budget marketing. So they fired their PR agency and started giving their bags away to holders of Instagram accounts with significant numbers of followers. Today, that strategy might seem obvious, but in 2013, Instagram was just a few years old, and leveraging the power of influencers was cutting edge. Cuyana quickly took off. They proved the opportunity in the market that so many men had overlooked. The company went on to raise more than $45 million, including from other female investors.

The Room Where It Happens

Cuyana's success illustrates a fact borne out by the statistics: male VCs are half as likely as female VCs to invest in female-founded companies.[15] To see more diversity in the leaders of startups, there needs to be diversity in the people who are deciding whether or not to fund them. Women represent a mere 13 percent of VC decision makers. If venture capital investing teams were more diverse, the leadership of funded startups would be more diverse, too.

Who are the people who work at VC funds? In 2019, 65 percent of VC firms did not have a single female partner with the decision-making power to write checks. That's progress from 2018, when that number was 85 percent.[16] In addition to the fact that 87 percent of VCs with investment-making power are men, they are 70 percent white, and they are mostly from a narrow educational background. A full 40 percent of investing partners went to either Harvard or Stanford, according to an analysis of 1,500 VCs by a partner at Equal Ventures.[17] That's not all. The investors are often former entrepreneurs who have sold a business and now want to spend their time with other like-minded entrepreneurs.

Indeed, the desire to maintain a fund's intimate, collegial culture is often used as an excuse for its homogeneity, says the longtime investor

Sonja Perkins. In 1996, at age twenty-nine, she was the youngest general partner to join Menlo Ventures. After working there for twenty-two years, she started her own fund and founded the all-women angel investing network Broadway Angels (more than 40 percent of her angel investments are in female-led companies and more than 12 percent in Black female entrepreneurs). She often hears from senior male venture capitalists that it's easier to get along with someone who "went to the same school as you, and you're already friends with, than someone who's different." She says one famous male venture capitalist told her that working for his venture capital fund felt just like being in his fraternity in college. Perkins says that investors don't pick companies based just on what they think will produce the highest returns but also on which entrepreneurs they want to spend time with.

There's another factor in play: VCs may get to pick only five or ten investments a year, with only two in ten showing any return.[18] That makes them want to control every factor they can, explained Canaan's Ibrahim. "What I can control, if I'm an investor, is what's familiar to me," she says. "It's going to be people that maybe have the same cultural background or the same school network, and that's just naturally going to lead to small groups of homogeneity."

It's a self-perpetuating cycle: Male investors are more likely to fund male CEOs. Male CEOs hire people similar to them to be their first employees and give them a piece of the company. When a company goes public or sells, those men make more money. That in turn gives them cash to seed the next early-stage startup, which will also likely be run by men. This cycle can continue without anyone ever intentionally trying to exclude women or overlook their ideas.

Many people I interviewed for this book pointed to the uniqueness of the VC world. Companies in other sectors, such as finance and retail, have diversified their employee base as they've grown, or they've changed their practices under pressure from public-market investors or consumers. But the intimate and long-term nature of venture capitalists' investments and the particular business model of their funds has enabled the industry to resist much change.

"It's not that the lack of diversity is pernicious—I mean, some of it is—but most of it is fully understandable . . . given the context of small groups and the level of risk that we're taking at the early stage," said Ibrahim. When she joined the firm about twenty years ago, she was the only woman at the table. Within about ten years, Canaan had become about 40 percent female and 47 percent immigrants or first-generation Americans. She attributes this in part to the fact that for several years she, a woman of Egyptian descent, took on the responsibility of hiring Canaan's tech investment team.

"Many in our industry really think that in order to hire a woman or person of color you have to lower standards," Perkins said. To combat that, her personal approach to expanding the white male-dominated venture capital field has been "not lowering standards but *changing* them." She said, "If your job specification to be a partner at a venture fund requires experience as a CEO and an engineering degree from an Ivy League school. . . . Well, very few women and people of color fit that profile. . . . So change the criteria to expand the pool. It's not the same thing as lowering your standards. It's just making them different." Perkins herself was hired as an investment analyst right out of college without an engineering degree or significant work experience and she has invested in several startups that reached billion-dollar valuations.

In fact, expanding the criteria for hiring into investing roles has been found to be financially beneficial for VCs. VC firms with diverse representation—both gender and race—are more likely to be among the top-performing funds, according to a study conducted by All Raise, a nonprofit founded in 2018 to increase the representation of women in venture capital and the tech startup ecosystem.[19] Another study found that VC firms that increased their proportion of women partner hires by 10 percent saw an average 1.5 percent increase in their overall fund returns annually. Plus, their funds had exits that were about 10 percent more profitable.[20]

I've laid out why VC firms would benefit from being more diverse and investing in more diverse startups. So why aren't they? The homogeneity of the VC industry can engender unconscious bias in the rooms where it happens: pitch meetings in the sparkling metal offices of venture capital investors on Sand Hill Road, running through Silicon Valley.

There are two main factors to consider. The first is how investors approach female founders. Even when women make it into the room, male and female entrepreneurs are simply asked different types of questions. Male entrepreneurs, for example, are more likely to be asked about potential gains—"hopes, accomplishments and advancement considerations." Female entrepreneurs are asked to explain losses "related to safety, responsibility and security considerations," according to "All In: Women in the VC Ecosystem," by PitchBook and All Raise. Even when male and female entrepreneurs are asked about the same topics, the nature of the conversation is different. Male entrepreneurs are more likely to be asked how they plan to acquire new customers, while women are more likely to be asked how they plan to retain the customers they already have, according to the PitchBook study.

The second factor lies in the way men and women respond to their respective lines of inquiry. Female founders "prefer to provide realistic projections of market opportunity and growth trajectory, while their male counterparts tend to overpromise, which has become what most investors expect to hear," according to the report.[21]

Zacharia told me that the findings of this study resonated with her. When pitching Insurify, she had wanted to be realistic: she focused on the financial opportunity in capturing even a small piece of the industry she wanted to transform. She explained how she could serve as a partner to the traditional insurance giants as well as the upstarts. Cuyana's founders were similarly interested in focusing on the company's financial strengths: its margins and low marketing costs. "You have to make the numbers work, and you have to show that they do. The only way you could take gender out of the equation, or any subjectivity, is if you could prove it," Shah explained. Instead of (rosy) projections, they shared the results of the early products they had introduced.

Those entrepreneurs' focus on tangible numbers may actually have been to their disadvantage. In Silicon Valley, adjectives matter. The venture capital industry is designed to pursue a handful of massive returns, which creates a bias for entrepreneurs who seem to be swinging hard for the fences. So *how* a person describes a business venture can make or break his or her ability to secure an investment in a home run–driven ecosystem such as venture capital. Bluster plays a key role in negotiations and valuations. Exaggerated potential can be read as "bullish expectations," "audacious goals," or "a vision to change the world." Indeed, investors actually *expect* entrepreneurs to inflate their expectations, with the understanding that the investors will discount them. One woman cited in the PitchBook study said that men take a confident posture and talk about their business "as they'd like to see it in a year," describing it as though it's that successful already. In contrast, women prefer to start small and overdeliver.[22] In an industry where investors hope to have a few outsized home runs rather than singles and doubles, the more "male" instinct to promise the moon is a huge advantage.

That was explained to Zola's Shan-Lyn Ma by a rare female VC among a panel of men. After making her pitch for simplifying wedding planning and registries, Ma cautiously approached the woman to ask her advice. "Look," Ma recalled the investor saying, "every male entrepreneur that comes in here bangs his fists on the table and swears that their company is going to be a multibillion-dollar business, and they have no doubt that it's absolutely going to be huge. . . . And while your pitch is very compelling, the fact that you are not banging your fist on the table and swearing there's absolutely no doubt that this is going to be a multibillion-dollar business, and everyone before you and after you does that, does raise an implicit question mark in our minds, even though we know that you may not feel as comfortable doing that." That conversation convinced Ma to be more emphatic about her confidence in her business's full potential.

If women are less likely to bluster, investors could write them off as unambitious. If they do secure an investment, they may do so on less favorable terms than their blustering male counterparts do. In other words, they may end up giving away more of their company in exchange for the investment. When it comes to startups, the gender gap extends far beyond the total investment dollars raised—to the gap in who *owns* shares of startups. Women own just 23 percent of founder and employee equity and only 20 percent of the people who have million-dollar-plus ownership stakes in startups are women, according to a report from Carta.[23] These factors create a vicious cycle in which women have fewer chances to earn millions of dollars from startups they work for and thus have fewer chances to then seed a new generation of female-led startups.[*]

With these many layers of unconscious bias at play, women are not securing the biggest checks. A "megaround" of financing is a $100 million investment round, the kind of money that can catapult a company into "unicorn" status—a valuation of $1 billion or more. When companies such as Uber, Airbnb, and Peloton raised more than $100 million in an investment round relatively early in their trajectory, it increased the expectation of an eventual huge IPO or sale, and it drew the attention of the media—and other investors. Investment rounds of this size are getting more common as companies wait longer to go public; between 2016

---

[*]The jobs women tend to hold also generally mean that they get a smaller piece of a company. One in eight CEOs raising funds is female, and CEOs get more than double the equity of the next-highest-compensated executive, according to Carta. Chief marketing officers, the executive role with the highest percentage of women, at 32 percent, have the lowest median equity award in the C-suite. In contrast, engineering employees have the highest average equity grants—more than double those of the employees in any other division. Women represent less than 20 percent of engineering teams. Carta attributes women's not holding the most profitable roles at startups in part to the fact that they don't start working at early-stage companies early enough. That could be due to the fact that there are more men working at tech companies, and therefore more of them could split off to found startups or the idea that women could be opting for more pay upfront rather than forgo pay for a chance at a huge windfall years down the line.

and 2018, the number of funding rounds worth $100 million more than doubled.[24] Still, women were less likely to get them. Companies with only male founders secured 85 percent (or 1,240) of these megarounds between 2019 and 2021, while companies with at least one woman on their founding team secured 205, or 14 percent, of rounds at that level, according to Crunchbase.[25]

The reality is that women rarely grow their companies to the size to be able to secure a $100 million funding round. That's in part because they suffer from less access to funds earlier in their startup's life cycle. Typically, the total number of deals funded for all companies drops between the seed round and the Series A round, as new products and services fail to gain traction; that's no surprise. But companies with at least one female founder see a bigger drop than male-founded companies do. Fifty-seven percent of women and 66 percent of men who complete a seed round go on to raise a Series A round. Looking at entrepreneurs who have completed a Series A round, 62 percent of female founders and 68 percent of male founders go on to complete a Series B.[26]

But something interesting happens once companies are mature enough for their Series C round. All Raise found in its analysis of 2018 PitchBook data that after completing a Series B round, a greater percentage of female founders than male founders (67 percent to 64 percent) go on to raise a Series C. And after raising a Series C, women and men are equally likely (62 percent of both groups) to raise a later round, according to All Raise's internal data.* All Raise's former CEO Pam Kostka explained why, at this level, female founders are just as likely as their male counterparts to raise money: "At that point, the economics of her business have taken over . . . and the merits of the business speak for itself. We think that [at the earlier stages] a lot more unintended bias comes in

---

*According to a 2019 All Raise analysis of 2018 PitchBook data provided directly to the author.

to influence that decision-making process." In contrast, investments in Series C funding rounds are made based on a proven track record.

That was certainly true for Cuyana. Once it had the numbers to prove its case, the business model could speak for itself. H.I.G. Capital, an investor that specializes in retail, saw the company's growth and avidly pursued it, investing $30 million in Cuyana's Series C round in 2019. With that news the company also announced that it was profitable. "We always viewed that the unit economics mattered, that we wanted to be profitable at first sale," said Shah. "We are much more fiscally conservative than most."

Doing More with Less

Fiscal responsibility is a common trait among female entrepreneurs. From 2011 to 2020, companies founded by women have consistently been sold or taken public—and paid back their investors—faster than those founded by men did. According to a 2020 PitchBook survey, the average for female founders was 6.7 years, nearly a year faster than the overall 7.5-year average for startups.[27] This could be the result of less access to capital or a preference for receiving guaranteed near-term payouts rather than waiting for bigger but riskier outcomes.*

In fact, much research over the last two decades has identified the advantages of female leadership. The first landmark study, called "Women Matter," came in 2007 from the global consulting firm McKinsey & Company. The firm measured and graded companies' performances in everything from direction and motivation to accountability and innovation.

---

*It's worth noting that female CEOs may be more focused on profitability because they have no other option. Without the safety net of additional financing—a situation many female-led businesses face—a startup is forced to find ways to operate profitably, much faster. If company managers feel that they can tap into venture capital resources—a situation male-led businesses are more likely to find themselves in—they're able to use their funding to drive growth at the expense of profits.

The study found that companies with three or more women in top management functions outperformed those without that level of female representation. Companies with women in senior management had much higher scores in direction, "articulating where the company is heading, how to get there, and aligning people," work environment, values, and "shaping employee interactions and fostering a shared understanding of values."

The advantages were more than just cultural. Companies with the most women on their management team had 48 percent higher earnings and 1.7 times the stock price growth over the prior two years. The bottom line: "Companies where women are most strongly represented at board or top-management level are also the companies that perform best."[28] McKinsey has continued the study annually, and there have since been a slew of similar reports from business schools and consulting firms explaining how every facet of business and every size company ultimately benefits from having women involved in leadership.

Other studies of mature public companies have found that female representation in senior roles has a measurable beneficial impact on financial performance. In the two years following a new CEO appointment, companies that appointed female chief executives saw their stock prices outperform those that appointed men by an average of 20 percent, according to S&P Global. Female chief financial officers also improve their companies' results, driving "more value appreciation, better defended profitability moats," and higher risk-adjusted returns for their firms.[29]

According to a *Harvard Business Review* study, there's also a tangible benefit to having women in the boardroom: better investment and acquisition decisions are made, and with less aggressive risk taking. The explanation: female board members help temper the overconfidence of male CEOs and push them to be more rational. "Female directors tend to be less conformist and more likely to express their independent views than male directors," the authors noted.[30]

A dozen years after the original study, a new report from McKinsey found that it's not just female-led teams but also racially diverse teams that are increasingly valuable to corporate performance. Companies that are more diverse (in the top 25 percent when it comes to diversity) are 24 percent more likely to deliver above-average profits. In every passing year, diversity has yielded a bigger boost: diverse companies were 21 percent more likely to have above-average profitability in 2018, up from 15 percent in 2014.

These findings about large, mature companies are also true for tech startups. In 2015, the venture capital firm First Round reported that ten years of data showed that investments in companies with a female founder had performed 63 percent better than investments in all-male founding teams.[31] In 2018, Boston Consulting Group studied 350 early-stage companies in a mentorship program and found that women-owned startups deliver twice as much per dollar invested. Yet the average startup founded or cofounded by women received $935,000, or less than half the $2.12 million the average male-founded company received. Over a five-year period, the women-owned companies generated more in revenue: for every dollar invested, 78 cents in revenue was earned, compared to the male-founded companies' 31 cents.[32]

Similarly, racially diverse founding teams—also a tiny minority—yielded outsized returns. Teams with at least one founder with a non-white perceived ethnicity earned 30 percent more on IPOs and acquisitions than all-white startup founding teams, according to a Kauffman Fellows study.[33] The study also found that diverse executive teams had an even greater advantage, yielding a 65 percent higher return than the all-white teams' returns.

Sonja Perkins said that the data reflect what she's found as an investor: "A diverse point of view is much more helpful for a diverse market." That thesis has been proven by the success of her female-led investments, ranging from Hint Water and The RealReal to Ellevest and UrbanSitter. "The white male market is small—about 30 percent of the US population—while the market for everyone else is 70 percent."

All of this adds up to one simple fact: in relying on pattern matching and overlooking female-created companies, investors are missing enormous investment opportunities. McKinsey quantified that missed opportunity. By its calculation in 2016, if women attained full gender equity, the United States could add up to $4.3 trillion in annual GDP in 2025.[34]

The results of these studies have not been hidden from the investing community. They've been repeatedly touted in headlines in the *Wall Street Journal*, in stories in *Fortune* and *Fast Company*, and in reports by me and my colleagues on CNBC. So if female-led companies have certain advantages, it would make sense for investors to find ways to identify and overcome their biases and back more of them. After some fifteen years of data showing that female leaders bring measurable value, it just isn't logical for such a small percentage of VC dollars to go to female founders. Bias must be deeply entrenched for investors to miss such a clear arbitrage opportunity and forgo those billions.

New Patterns

Despite this persistent irrationality, there are small but meaningful signs of progress toward more equity at tech companies. The software company Carta, which helps private companies manage their shares, reported that more companies are taking steps to bring on more diverse employees at the earliest stage, when they can be compensated with meaningful equity. The number of female-led unicorns (companies valued over $1 billion) hit a record of twenty-one in 2019, and the number continued to grow. In 2021, 83 companies founded by women achieved unicorn valuations, and companies with all-female or coed teams represented 12 percent of total new unicorns created.[35] The increase in the number of big companies being run by women means there's a larger set of high-profile women to serve as examples for the next generation. Those women are establishing new patterns of what successful entrepreneurs look like.

In the public markets—where Cuyana and Insurify hope to end up someday—there has been slow change. The number of companies with only female founders that have gone public grew steadily from six in 2019 to eleven in 2021, according to data pulled by Crunchbase. Looking more broadly at venture-backed startups with female CEOs, in 2021 there were a record nineteen venture capital–backed companies that went public with a female CEO, but because the total number of IPOs increased as well, those women represented just 5 percent of the total.[36]

Corporate boards are also adding more women and minorities. As of 2020, women accounted for 26.6 percent of board seats in the Fortune 500, up from less than 16 percent fifteen years earlier, according to Catalyst, a nonprofit consulting and research firm focused on women in the workplace.[37] Part of that growth is being driven by a California law passed in early 2018, which mandated that by the end of 2021, companies with six board members were required to have at least half of them be women (as of the paperback printing of this book, the law has been struck down by a federal district court and remains under appeal.).* It's not just that boards can help temper CEOs' overconfidence and improve corporate performance; they can also influence management to change corporate culture by supporting parental leave or by pushing to examine the fairness of pay and promotion practices.

Younger male entrepreneurs, too, are realizing the value in having a diverse team. Dana Settle, who cofounded venture capital firm Greycroft (and is an investor in Cuyana, along with many other female-founded companies including The RealReal, fashion brand Anine Bing, and probiotics company Seed), says it's increasingly rare to see an all-male founder team. "If we are pitched by an all-male team," Settle says, "they immediately acknowledge the deficit."

*Thanks to this law, over half of new board members named to companies based in California in 2021 were women, according to the California Partners Project.

They're not telling investors like Settle that they're working on their diversity just because they know the optics of an all-male company look bad. They tell her they're working on it because increasingly, they realize that they're missing out on financial rewards. The potential is not obscure, like the complex pricing of insurance products Zacharia worked to clarify. The data are clear.

Two

Building with Purpose

Great Power and Great Expectations

In the last chapter I described the myriad challenges women face in building startups. Silicon Valley's poor showing—consistently investing less than 3 percent of all VC dollars in female-led companies—looks worse when you compare its numbers to those of US small businesses, 42 percent of which are run by women.[1] Yet there is one particular kind of business in which women founders are represented in roughly equal numbers as men. This category isn't defined by industry or target customer but rather by the purpose of the enterprise.

Among businesses dedicated to achieving a social goal or impact, about half are founded by women. In fact, women are 20 percent more likely than men to create ventures with a social or environmental purpose.[2]*

---

*Women are about 1.2 times as likely as men to create ventures with a social or environmental purpose than economic-focused ones. Of the world's social entrepreneurs, an estimated 55 percent are male and 45 percent are female.

Why is that? When asked what drives them, women in general are more likely than men to say they're driven not just by financial success but also by a purpose that is not economic. Men, on the other hand, are more likely to say they're motivated by wanting to be their own boss and "achieving power," as the academics put it.[3,4] In 2017, 80 percent of female social entrepreneurs said generating value to society and the environment was more important than generating financial value; 66 percent of men said the same.[5] Most often, women are pursuing a purpose that involves helping the environment, which they tend to be far more concerned about than their male counterparts.[6]

The differences between men's and women's entrepreneurial sensibilities extend beyond their intentions to their reception in society. In 2016, Harvard Business School professor Laura Huang and INSEAD professor Matthew Lee gathered 224 MBA students for an experiment. They told the students that they were going to be listening to an audio recording that had been captured at a recent venture capital pitch competition. Based on what they heard, the students were asked how strongly they agreed with a series of questions about the company's potential for success: "This venture will grow to have 100+ employees at some point in the future," "This venture will be successful in getting the financial investment it needs to grow," and so on. What the students did not know was that it wasn't just another classroom exercise evaluating hypothetical business models. Though they were all listening to the same pitch, half were hearing the pitch delivered by a man; the other half, by a woman.[7]

Much has been written on the subject of bias against women in the workplace, so perhaps it's no surprise that those MBA students, a mix of men and women, tended to penalize the female speaker. They judged 53 percent of the startup pitches made by men positively and only 40 percent of the pitches made by women positively—even though they were judging exactly the same "company." The professors' explanation for the penalty to the female founders was a perceived "lack of fit" between female stereotypes and the expected (male) stereotypes of entrepreneurs.[8] But there was another part of this experiment. One group of students heard the pitch with one key revision: the business was designed to have a positive social impact. When the MBA students judged the social impact version of the company, the researchers found something astonishing: there was no longer any bias against women; the male presentation and the female presentation of the social impact pitch were rated exactly the same. "Social impact framing *reduces the discriminatory effects of gender bias*," the professors concluded.

The key to this rebalancing of gender perception could be attributed to one primary trait: warmth. Though both the male and female entrepreneurs were rated as warmer when their pitches were mission oriented, only the females saw a boost in their overall evaluations when they were seen as fulfilling the stereotype that women are warmer.[9] When warmth is seen as an asset in business (as it is in such purpose-driven companies), women benefit from that stereotype. For once, a bias worked *for* women rather than against them.

This gendered expectation that women will be both warmer and more focused on "giving back" is supported by studies that have nothing to do with entrepreneurship. Data show that women across all income brackets, cultures, and geographies donate to charity more than men do, participate in the nonprofit sector more than men do, and say that social impact plays into their investment decisions more than men do. In a 2016 lab experiment that examined how much money participants would give to others, women were more altruistic. But the study also found that women were expected to be even more altruistic than they actually were.[10] When it comes to helping others, women reach a higher standard than men. But they are held to an even higher standard.[11] All those data lead to something that the authors of the MBA students study concluded: that women entrepreneurs are more likely to get funding if they emphasize their social mission.[12]

One of those mission-oriented entrepreneurs is Christine Moseley. When she decided to found her purpose-driven company in 2015, she wasn't being opportunistic by taking an approach that would draw less antiwoman bias (the study of the MBA students hadn't yet been conducted). She was simply trying to fix what she saw as broken in the food and agriculture industry. Straight out of college in 2004, she went to work for the shipping company Maersk as a management trainee. The company had pioneered the standardization of shipping containers in the mid–twentieth century, an innovation that had led to a massive increase in efficiency in freight transportation. Yet between 2006 and 2008, when Moseley was a trainee based in Cape Town, the inefficiencies she saw in the region's trade alarmed her.

"I saw a lot of waste firsthand. Africa is one of the most resource-rich continents in the world, and yet they were struggling financially, partially because they were not selling and exporting everything that they could. It was *not* optimizing its resources," she said. As she traveled around the continent, she saw that was a widespread problem. While on a work trip in Zimbabwe, she was shocked to find massive unharvested sugarcane fields close to where Maersk's ships were docked in the port. Yet she knew from managing Zimbabwe's exports via Maersk that the country was exporting only low-value items such as wastepaper and scrap metal. "Why are they not shipping their excess sugarcane?" she remembered asking herself. Zimbabwe was one of the poorest countries in the world, yet its resources were not being captured and utilized. Then, when a chrome mine in Zambia broke down, there was no effort to pivot to another export. Trade stalled for months. "It boggled me that these African countries were facing so many problems, and yet there were so many opportunities that weren't being capitalized on. It made me really want to help—and I also saw the huge opportunity there."

That vision stuck with her even after she returned to the United States to attend business school at Wharton. She took her MBA to an organic juice and food startup based in New York, where she grew frustrated that its $13 healthy green juices were completely unaffordable for most Americans. The company couldn't bring its prices down, though—the ingredients costs were too high because it was buying perfect-looking organic produce to make the juices, and that was the only option available. She knew that billions of pounds of edible produce are wasted on US farms every year because the fruit or vegetables don't look unblemished or have a buyer, part of the 40 percent of all food that goes to waste.[13] So she left the company and moved from New York to Silicon Valley with a plan to start a company to solve the produce industry's efficiency problem.

That was why one day she found herself on a farm, standing in a sea of lettuce leaves as she watched workers bag romaine hearts. Moseley noticed a key flaw in the massive operation: the farmers were harvesting only the inner portion—the "heart"—of each head of lettuce, the part deemed suitable for grocery stores. That meant that up to 75 percent of the plant was being left to rot on the ground. "I just remember walking and stepping calf-deep on perfectly edible food that would have been perfect for the green juices I was just selling," she recalls. If her previous juice company had been able to buy those discarded romaine leaves, it would have provided valuable revenue to the farm and enabled the juices to be sold at a lower price.

The problem Moseley saw in all that wasted lettuce was the fault of consumers' and grocery stores' becoming pickier about how their produce looked. The reason the problem had not been solved—and ingredients for green juices remained so costly—was that farmers didn't have the tools to sell leftover produce efficiently. Farmers would try to get rid of extra inventory—exterior romaine leaves and produce too misshapen for grocery stores—by personally calling potential buyers. But they often either couldn't find a buyer fast enough or couldn't afford the cost of shipping the excess product in time, while it was still fresh. "The majority of farms are on the verge of bankruptcy, with very limited time and resources," Moseley said. "It's a perishable item, too; they don't have the time to spend hours on the phone calling around asking 'Do you want my ugly produce?'" But Moseley knew that there were plenty of companies that would want those leftover fruits and vegetables: in fact, there was a booming trend in plant-based items such as cauliflower-crust pizzas and sweet-potato chips. Though grocery stores may not want misshapen apples or too-small tomatoes, companies making juices, sauces, or dried snacks certainly wouldn't care about such aesthetic imperfections.

There was also the environmental impact: the kind of food waste that Moseley witnessed is estimated to contribute as much as 10 percent of global greenhouse gas emissions—nearly equal to all the emissions from India.[14] "We were in the middle of the drought in California. We have climate change and people were going hungry, and here I was looking out at acres and acres of just wasted perfectly edible food. . . . That was the moment I realized, 'I need to solve this, because if I don't do this, I don't know who will. This is urgent.'"

So in 2016, she launched the business-to-business marketplace Full Harvest, which helps farms sell imperfect and surplus produce to food and beverage companies that don't care what produce looks like.

She was excited, but her friends who worked in business treated her new enterprise with no small measure of condescension. To them, it sounded like a charity project. "They would say things like 'Oh, bless your bleeding heart' or 'Wait, you want to sell trash? Isn't that rotting produce? Is that even allowed?'" Moseley recalled. But she saw a very clear financial opportunity—a massive market in using technology to connect farmers with buyers. "I was like, 'I don't think you understand, this is a fifteen-billion-dollar-plus opportunity in the US alone. It's a resource efficiency problem. I can build a massive company—oh, and by the way, yes we can also save the world.' So I thought that it would be amazing to really prove that you can do well and do good at the same time—a true win-win."

Moseley was onto something; businesses pursuing a social good tend to be at least as profitable as regular enterprises. Indeed, in 2020 funds invested in public companies with an environmental, social, and governance (ESG) focus far outperformed traditional investments.[15]* A focus on social impact also helps with recruitment: purpose-oriented companies report 40 percent higher levels of workforce retention and 30 percent higher levels of innovation than their competitors do, according to a 2019 Deloitte report.[16] And social impact can, of course, help with marketing: a 2020 survey of more than eight thousand respondents found that consumers are four to six times as likely to buy from, trust, and defend companies with a strong purpose.[17]†

Today, the Full Harvest marketplace connects farmers with new buyers to sell produce of all shapes and sizes online, taking a percentage of each transaction. And it's yielding results. The company says that some farms are selling up to 30 percent more produce and have increased their profits by up to 12 percent. The utility of Full Harvest became much more urgent in 2020, when the covid-19 pandemic produced a demand shock as restaurant orders suddenly disappeared and grocery stores became the only food purchasers. Farmers began to rely on Full Harvest to adapt their business models. A surge in farmers needing to find new buyers for their produce increased the amount of produce in the marketplace fivefold. Because many farmers had excess produce that they had previously sold to food service companies, Full Harvest partnered with impacted suppliers and the nonprofits World Central Kitchen and Eat. Learn. Play. to box excess produce and deliver it to more than 250,000 food-insecure families during the pandemic.

Full Harvest was indeed doing good as it did well. In 2020, it

---

*Sixty-four percent of actively managed ESG funds beat their benchmarks, compared to just 49 percent of traditional funds, in the first three quarters of 2020, according to RBC Capital Markets.

†Efforts to achieve the United Nations' Sustainable Development Goals are projected to open up at least $12 trillion in market value and increase employment by up to 380 million jobs globally by 2030. The UN commission estimates that the business opportunities around energy are worth $4.3 trillion; improving cities, $3.7 trillion; agriculture, $2.3 trillion.

partnered with Danone, which created a yogurt line using "Full Harvest Verified Rescued Produce," and Full Harvest's revenue tripled between 2020 and 2021. It has drawn more than $33 million in funding from top tech- and agriculture tech–focused investors.

Proximity Breeds Insight

If social impact enterprises often outperform their peers, the question is: Why aren't there more of them? "There are a lot of markets that people in venture capital don't relate to," said Ulu Ventures' Miriam Rivera of the predominantly rich white male venture capital community. Rivera has found that industries such as, say, child care and fair payday lending are massively underfunded by venture capital. "Investors don't relate to the average American, and yet the problems those Americans face create huge markets. VCs pile onto markets that affect the one percent, and far too few are trying to figure out a better mousetrap for the ninety-nine percent." In other words, VC firms are more likely to relate to the $13 juice customer than to the struggling farmer.

This is not just a pet theory of Rivera's. Academic studies have found that people are typically more focused on helping victims of problems they're personally familiar with, a sort of philanthropic version of pattern matching.[18] Deborah Small, a University of Pennsylvania professor and the author of a chapter in *The Science of Giving: Experimental Approaches to the Study of Charity*, has found that "our personal relationships with people who have suffered from specific misfortunes shape which misfortunes we feel responsible for addressing."[19] Moseley wanted to help improve the food industry because, through her work, she felt close to the problems of the waste and environmental destruction that industry was causing.

One would be hard pressed to find an entrepreneur in the financial technology sector more proximate to the problem of lack of access to financial services than Sheena Allen. She grew up in the 1990s in Terry, Mississippi, a town of about a thousand people just south of Jackson.

She was smart, creative, and entrepreneurial—she earned money painting designs on her friends' shoes—and her parents urged her to be the first in their family to go to college. Allen was itching to get out of her small town but didn't have the role models or the resources to help her. "I had one uncle, Billy, who owned a flower shop—it was the most I knew about being an entrepreneur. Most people in my family had nine-to-fives or relied on government assistance due to not having a job or making below a living wage. Typically, what you see in that area was—maybe you go to a state school, you move back to your hometown, you marry someone from your hometown, and it's a cycle," she said.

"I remember even as early as middle school thinking *This is not what I want for my life—I know there's much more to the world.* My decision very early on was that I was not going to fall into that cycle." So she played varsity basketball and volleyball, graduated from high school with a 4.2 GPA, and earned a scholarship to the University of Southern Mississippi. Inspired by Mark Zuckerberg, she started working on a social network of her own during her freshman year and went on to double major in psychology and film with a minor in marketing. She developed a series of apps, first living in Silicon Valley before moving to Austin in 2013.

Then, one day in 2016, she was visiting her family back home in Terry when she noticed something at the local grocery store. "People were standing in line, [but] not to actually buy groceries; they were standing there because they were cashing checks," she recalled. She realized that she had forgotten how little access the members of her community had to basic financial services. Many of her friends and family were "unbanked"—without credit cards or checking accounts. What she saw in line at that store stood in stark contrast to what she'd experienced in Austin, where plenty of restaurants at the time wouldn't even accept cash.

"I said to myself, 'Sheena, you have an advantage—it's your privilege that you understand what it's like to be from a town that did not have proper access and fair access to opportunity in the financial world.' I also understood very well how to operate and build a company," she told me.

So she did. In 2018, she founded CapWay with the goal of offering financial services to the more than 7 million American households that don't have a bank account.[20]

Allen was accepted into the Y Combinator "accelerator" that invests in and fosters promising entrepreneurs. But she felt isolated as one of the few Black people in the program. And she had trouble getting those on the Silicon Valley tech scene to understand the market for, and mission of, CapWay. "I remember speaking with an investor at an event and being asked, did I make up the word *unbanked*?" Allen recalled. It was clearly a waste of both her time and theirs: "If you think I made up the word *unbanked*, you're clearly *not* going to write me a check." Luckily, she had a mentor who coached her on how to better translate her mission into terms of financial opportunity—terms the Silicon Valley investor class could understand. She finally secured a seed check and moved to Atlanta. She wanted to be far away from the Silicon Valley bubble and closer to the customers she would be serving.

She knew from her community in Mississippi that it wouldn't be enough to just hang out a sign and offer banking services to people who had never before had a bank account; she would need to meet them where they were and create an environment where they would feel comfortable. To earn their trust, she promoted her own outsider status. "People would say, 'I don't trust the banks because that's the Man,'" said Allen. "We've had people of every race—Black, white, Hispanic, immigrants—say, 'Hey! *You're* not the Man. I trust you because you're giving me something different.'" She also wanted CapWay to be user friendly, fit to the consumer. The app is bright and casual, with tabs for "Money Goals," "Send and Receive Money," and "Phunds," the company's financial literacy program. Allen said that she wanted the app to feel more like a social network than a banking platform, "because people aren't comfortable having serious financial conversations, but people will get on Facebook and tell the world every problem they're having."

In October 2021, CapWay partnered with Visa to offer a debit card with no hidden fees, overdraft charges, or minimum balance fees. Anyone can set personal savings and investing goals and a more public-facing version of money goals that acts as a GoFundMe alternative. Perhaps most important, CapWay provides free financial literacy programs, working with community organizations, schools, retailers and employers. In early 2022, the company partnered with Goodr, a startup that helps businesses donate food waste. When people pick up food from Goodr, CapWay offers them financial education. CapWay is also working with banking services to provide data on the impact of financial literacy programs, based on what it's seeing among its users. But this isn't bleeding-heart altruism; it's part of Allen's belief that there is a huge financial opportunity in serving overlooked customers. That opportunity was possible only because Allen's experience straddled two worlds: she could navigate the world of entrepreneurs and startups, but she also understood the needs of the overlooked and, yes, unbanked customer base.

Driven by Different Data

Shivani Siroya also felt as though she was part of two worlds. Growing up, she split her year between her parents' house in Brooklyn, where her mother ran a Medicare/Medicaid clinic, and her grandmother's house in western India. There Siroya spent her summers with children who didn't have her comfortable middle-class background. "We played with everyone, and it only occurred to me as I got older that one of the families that we were playing with was five people living in one bedroom," she said. "It didn't change how I felt about those kids. I knew at a very human level that we were all the same. But it was a realization of 'Oh, wait, they're not going to high school, they're not going off to college.'"

As was expected of her, Siroya did go off to college, followed by a turn at an investment bank before earning a master of public health in econometrics and health economics from Columbia University. She was working among some of the most privileged people in the world, but she often thought about those summers in India, where she had witnessed immense poverty up close. So in 2006, she took a job with the United Nations Population Fund. To help the organization understand what was preventing small business owners in India and Africa from making economic progress, she was assigned the task of interviewing 3,500 entrepreneurs, following them to work and the market, tallying their spending and saving habits. "It was walking in their shoes with them, seeing the frustrations and the struggles that they went through every day, seeing the fact that they loved running their businesses and why that was different than doing manual labor," Siroya said. She came to understand that they were stymied by something the developed world takes for granted: access to capital. Indeed, many of the entrepreneurs she tracked were too embarrassed by the state of their clothing to even enter a bank. Even if they did muster up the courage, banks were often wary of offering them loans because of the small business owners' lack of credit history and track record.

One day, a woman Siroya had been working with, Seema, needed money to support her jewelry shop, so Siroya took her into the bank. The bank would not loan to someone without any formal records, so Siroya offered to serve as Seema's guarantor. For Siroya, it wasn't a risky move; she knew Seema's "credit history" simply from observing her work. "She saves so much money, she's so particular about what days she buys her inventory, she shops around to get the best rates, she's sending her son to computer class, every box was checked for me," Siroya said. The loan officer told her, "I can do this for one person, but, Shivani, how many other people are you going to keep bringing in here?" Siroya took the question as a challenge rather than discouragement. "That's what got the wheels turning: 'Okay, if I really want to do this, how would I solve this?'" she said.

The traditional banking system didn't recognize the potential in those women. But Siroya did, and she started tackling the problem herself. She began to offer small loans to other small business owners in the communities she was researching for the United Nations. Not a single recipient failed to pay her back. In fact, the only difficulty Siroya occasionally encountered was in convincing the entrepreneurs to take her money. "At first they were skeptical, but then they actually started to realize I was just there to observe and understand how you use money, and they started to ask *me* questions," she said.

It became clear to her that trust didn't need to flow only from the lender to the lendee; it was a feedback loop. The small-business owners earned her trust by giving her visibility into their lives, and she earned theirs by going into their homes, sitting on the floor with them, eating the food they gave her, and, most crucially, *not* telling them what to do with the money she would be lending them. "Communities in these markets, they help each other, so there is that closeness. I just think that they were just shocked that I felt like that about them."

After Siroya wrapped up her research for the United Nations and returned to New York to take a banking job at Citigroup in 2008, she couldn't stop thinking about the people she had spent so much time with back in India. She was working at one of the biggest credit card issuers on the planet, yet a behemoth like Citi could never lend to the people she had lent to. She also understood that local banks couldn't possibly reach the people she'd interviewed unless their people spent hours traveling to rural areas. Even then there were more obstacles, including a lack of business records.

But she had observed different ways to prove creditworthiness and saw that there was a financial opportunity in lending to all those people who had reliably repaid her loans. So in 2011, she started crafting a business to re-create the informal data she had gathered to replace a traditional credit score. In 2012, she raised a seed round. In 2016, she renamed the company Tala. At the center of the company's lending methodology is a new kind of credit score. The score is calculated based on data from the one piece of technology that is ubiquitous, even in the poorest countries: the cell phone.

"We think of [cell phones] as 'daily life data.' It goes back to those interviews and thinking about what good proxies we can use. We have access to how much someone pays on their cell phone bill or how many remittances they're receiving, and that gives us a good sense of the consistency of inflows and outflows of cash," Siroya said. Other cell phone data are valuable as well; in Kenya, people who make calls at night, when mobile time is more expensive, tend to have more liquidity. The algorithm also considers behavioral data, such as how quickly someone completes an application, whether he or she reads the terms and conditions, and how many attempts it takes to answer a question. "It's not 'a one size fits all,' it's an ensemble of different categories and different things that can allow us to back into a methodology of credit scoring—and the likelihood they will pay back."

Eighty-five percent of people who download the Tala app receive a small loan within five minutes. If a loan is approved, a small fee is charged and $10 to $500 is sent instantly to the customer. Borrowers have a choice of repayment terms from just a few weeks to up to 120 days in some markets. If they don't repay the loan on time, there's no penalty levied or accruing interest; they simply won't get another loan from Tala. "Remember, people are not serving this customer," Siroya told me, "so for them, actually, not having access is actually like a penalty." Women are typically the most reliable borrowers of microfinance loans and represent between half and two-thirds of Tala's customers, depending on the market (on average, just 7 percent of female small-business owners in emerging markets have access to traditional capital sources).[21] The company also provides financial education to help people understand what they're capable of repaying, and although Tala often offers a smaller loan than an applicant requests, on occasion it will offer more, which a borrower can choose not to accept.

That mutual trust works: more than 90 percent of Tala's customers repay their loan and become recurring customers, which, Siroya said, creates a feedback loop of opportunity.[22]* "The first piece is to say, 'We

---

*In contrast, 17.4 percent of loans awarded by the US Small Business Administration from 2006 through 2015 went into default.

trust you enough to try this.' The second piece is 'You paid us back, now you've earned more of our trust. Now let's keep giving you higher loan sizes, lower interest rates, longer terms. Let's give you other products.' In Mexico we have a debit card, a savings product."

She calls this strategy *radical trust*, and it's not just about how Tala interacts with customers, it's also a cornerstone of her approach to managing Tala. Every day, she says, she aims to clearly outline expectations, understand her employees' capabilities, and give them the freedom to solve problems. What's good for Tala's customer base is also good for Siroya's management style. Hundreds of studies support self-determination theory, the idea that if people feel that what they are doing is of their own volition, they'll feel more motivation and passion at work, which will result in better performance.[23]

It seems to work for Siroya: when Tala launched in the Philippines, the product failed to catch on the way it had in India and Kenya. So she gave one of her employees the opportunity to move to the country for six months. "He walked in customers' shoes to understand where they're going to pick up money, to understand what they have access to," she recalled. "We went back to basics." He ultimately discovered that because 85 percent of the Philippine market is cash based, Tala's service would appeal only if integrated with remittance centers and retail chains to dispense paper money. Because Siroya gave the executive the trust and autonomy to explore the issue, Tala changed its strategy in the country.

Siroya's approach to management can also be described as "servant leadership." This management theory centers on the value of cooperating with colleagues and emphasizing stakeholders, humility, and lack of ego; when leaders prioritize and empower employees, the employees' performance improves. A 2005 study of CEOs found that those who adopt a philosophy of servant leadership have higher trust from their employees and generate higher trust in the organization.[24] Though men also employ servant leadership (FedEx's and Starbucks' founders, Fred Smith and Howard Schultz, have both said they adhere to it), women are found to have a particular advantage when they use this approach. A 2019 study by two business school professors found that its effects are stronger when implemented by women and are greatest when implemented within female-populated teams. (They determined that teams with more women responded to manager servant leadership, which resulted in stronger performance.)[25]

Though Siroya leads with an emphasis on serving others, Tala is a for-profit enterprise. There are plenty of nonprofits and NGOs that provide zero-interest loans, but Siroya, like Christine Moseley, wanted to create a self-sustaining business model, not a charity. She had seen firsthand at the United Nations that philanthropic dollars could be redirected from year to year, depending on earmarking of government aid for a particular trendy issue. For Tala to serve its customer in the long run, she saw, it could not be dependent on donors. "Market-led solutions that have a social mission, *you* can stand the test of time," she explained. Tala has raised more than $200 million in venture capital funding from twenty-five different institutions, including PayPal's venture capital arm. Raising venture capital, rather than relying on donations, has enabled her to reach more people, much faster. And she's focused on delivering returns for those investors. "I think it's really important to prove that we can be profitable, because that's the only way for others to realize that this customer has purchasing power and potential and that they deserve to be served," Siroya said. She hopes that by demonstrating the success of Tala's model, other businesses will follow and create a world in which Seema and other women like her have even more opportunities.

Driven by Gratitude

Meena Sankaran would have loved to work for a nonprofit in 2004 after she graduated from the University of Texas at Arlington with a masters in electrical engineering. She desperately wanted to make a positive difference in the world. But she just couldn't afford to; her legal and financial situations were too precarious. She needed to earn enough money to send some back to her family in India to help them live comfortably. And she needed to find a job that would sponsor her H-1B visa. Otherwise, she would have to leave the United States.

Sankaran's parents had grown up in the state of Tamil Nadu in southern India; her ancestral town is so small that it isn't even on Google maps. Her father was one of thirteen children, none of whom finished high school; he worked in a chemical factory making about $6 a month. When her parents, who had had an arranged marriage, started a family, they decided that educating their daughters and teaching them to be independent thinkers would be paramount. That was unusual for people of their generation in a patriarchal country like India.[26] "My mother was a rare woman who was interested in sports. She played volleyball while going to college. That was uncommon in India for women ten years after [the country's] independence," Sankaran recalled.

Sankaran spent her early childhood in Hyderabad, in a three-hundred-square-foot home with a shared outdoor bathroom. "We made ends meet, but we couldn't afford a water storage tank or filter system or anything like that, so we generally had one hour of water a day," she said. The family then moved to Mumbai, where they lived in a five-hundred-square-foot apartment. They would boil water three times for cooking and four times for drinking. "It was such a strong family unit, it was nothing but positive energy about how you make the most of what you have, how you always remain grateful for what you have. Not once did I ever think, *Why don't I have a TV? Why aren't we going to the movies?* There was never a thing about 'Why not?' and more like 'I have this.'" What she did have was a family who supported her earning a bachelor's degree in electronics engineering at the University of Mumbai. That support extended even to the crazy notion of applying to graduate school in the United States. "I had an insatiable drive, in terms of wanting to make a better life for my parents. They had sacrificed so much for me and my sister. . . . I thought, *If I'm in India, I don't know how many years it'll take me to make that happen, given the circumstances.* That was 1996, and the tech boom hadn't yet come to India."

Sankaran's father borrowed the money for the application fees to seven schools. She was accepted by all of them but chose UTA because it was the only one that allowed foreign students to be eligible for the much lower in-state tuition. She remembers that some in their community criticized her parents for letting her, an unmarried girl, leave home and travel internationally, but her father defended her. Her family mortgaged their small apartment to buy her a one-way air ticket to Texas—her first time in an airport and the first time anyone in the Sankaran family had traveled overseas.

When she arrived on campus, Sankaran realized that her scholarship didn't cover her living expenses. So she took two part-time jobs and worked as a teaching assistant for physics undergraduate students. She called her parents once a month, and her father went every day to an internet café to send her an email for moral support. She was grateful not only for her family but also for the mentorship and financial support of a UTA professor who, with his wife, became surrogate parents, attending her graduation to take pictures to share with her parents back in India.

It happened that in 2004, when Sankaran graduated, the cap on H1-B visas was dropped to just a third of what it had been the previous two years.[27] Despite her academic success, the only job she could find that would sponsor her H1-B visa was at a telecom company in Los Angeles. She couldn't afford a car and spent more than a month making an hours-long bus commute. When her boss learned about it, he lent her the company's spare truck and another colleague gave her driving lessons. When Sankaran found out that she was earning less than others with the same degree were, she remained stoic. "Every day was an adventure, I just completely went with the flow and just thought to myself, *If you just take it day by day, you just keep moving forward.*" That attitude paid off: after a few years, she was able to settle her family's debts and buy her parents a comfortable home in Mumbai.

As time passed, Sankaran worked at a series of tech companies, including Cisco Systems. In her free time, she helped run a nonprofit that helped refugees culturally integrate into the United States. After a dozen years, "I felt saturated," she recalled, "like I'm working on technology only to improve technology issues and to help tech companies get better." She was always advised to make her money and *then* do philanthropic work. But after stints at two startups, she wondered, *Why can't I do something where my sole purpose is a goal of impact where I can do both—where my work is my purpose? Why can't I put everything I learned about technology and work to solve a societal problem?*

In 2014, she decided to start a company that would help people, so she made a list of the global issues where her expertise could have the most impact. Before she homed in on one area, she went on a backpacking trip in Nepal, her first real break from work since she'd moved to the United States. While she was at the base camp of Mount Everest, a 7.8-magnitude earthquake hit, setting off a deadly avalanche. "They emptied out base camp and put us all in a camp together to monitor the avalanche," she recalled. "For five days or so I was sitting boiling snow for water and eating bars. Some people were scared because the bridges were falling and we didn't know if we could walk through it, but we still decided to walk through; I was really sick, and I was throwing up half the way." When she arrived at a second camp, US helicopters were carrying Americans out. But they wouldn't airlift Sankaran out; she was still an Indian citizen who had been in the United States on a green card. "I had to get Indian forces to actually care, which was very hard because there were so many Indians and Nepalese people who were stranded and needed help before me."

After she made her way home to the United States after that traumatic experience, her mission became even more clear: "I was so grateful, and there was no longer an ounce of doubt about what I wanted to do—technology with an impact." She had spent five days boiling snow to survive; nothing seemed as fundamental to global health as water.

Within ten days of returning to Silicon Valley, Sankaran registered a company called Ketos, which monitors water for safety and minimizes water loss. To start with, she decided, she would first focus not on economically underdeveloped countries but on the United States, where in many places water purity is an issue—often an overlooked one. In 2015, the year she founded Ketos, nearly 21 million people in the United States relied on community water systems that did not meet basic health standards, and 14 percent of all water in the country was lost in leaks.[28] Ketos developed a device to monitor both water quality and water loss: the company would install the system for free at municipal water systems, factories, and farms and charge a fee for those customers to access and use the data. "Let's say you are a city, you could have ten thousand units outside homes. It looks at usage, at your pressure anomalies, to find leaks, and it helps you shut off the leaks, so everything is controlled remotely," Sankaran said. She explained that a farmer or manufacturing company would traditionally pay an employee to drive around to collect water samples and then pay a lab as much as $100,000 annually to measure four key metrics, depending on the frequency of testing. Ketos's devices gave customers the equivalent of constant testing on twenty metrics and access to analysis of the data without their employees having to physically drive to a well. She said her service cuts the cost of EPA-standard water testing by 90 percent.

The second system Sankaran developed helps farmers monitor groundwater for carcinogens. The company has earned patents for its hardware, which detects toxins and models whether a crop is unsafe and whether a certain zip code is likely to be impacted by cancer based on its water quality. "We're detecting water quality data that hasn't existed before on a national level."

Despite the widespread demand Sankaran saw for cost-effective water-monitoring systems, she couldn't convince any investor to write her a check in the first year and a half of operating Ketos. Investors with whom she connected through her software jobs told her they thought water problems were the province of "third-world countries" and should be solved by nonprofits. She may not have been a fit for their portfolios, but she also sensed that they were dismissing her because neither she nor her idea fit the Silicon Valley mold. "One guy straight up asked me if I was going to have a white male cofounder," she recalled. "I realized I have two options: either let this die or put all my money into it to make the prototypes and validate the proof of concept. Then I started going to sustainability-focused investors, and the bar was high even though they were aligned on the mission. You had to derisk the business, prove the hardware, you needed revenue, you needed to show customer demand."

Eventually, though, she was able to win some investors who were looking for startups with an environmental or social purpose, and then she quickly scaled up, deploying her tools across the United States. Once she proved her concept with US farms and municipal water systems, she started introducing it in developing countries. In towns in Mexico, where soda had been a safer drinking option than public water systems, her technology helped address an emerging diabetes crisis. In 2017, the company was selected for a "smart village" project hosted by UC Berkeley and the Bill & Melinda Gates Foundation, which chose Ketos to deploy its solution in twenty-five villages in the southeastern Indian state of Andhra Pradesh.[29] She was finally able to give something back to communities similar to the one that had given so much to her: "These villages, some of them were getting water once in four days; we were able to bring it down to once a day. That was the most fulfilling project." Between 2020 and 2021, Ketos tripled its customer base, had gathered more than 20 million water safety data points, and had expanded to locations in Brazil, Peru, and Israel. As Ketos continues to grow, Sankaran believes, the price of its water-monitoring hardware will decline enough to be deployable everywhere.

What drove Sankaran, from the moment she boarded the flight from Mumbai to Texas to her decision to start a company, was a profound sense of gratitude to her parents and all the other people who had helped her along the way. That gratitude is something I heard echoed by Allen,

Moseley, and Siroya. They all expressed appreciation that they could run a company whose success is measured not just by its return on investment but also by its impact on the environment and the livelihoods of people in need.

In my twenty years as a journalist, I've met hundreds of female entrepreneurs. Indeed, the commonalities that I saw in those women inspired this book. But it was not until I undertook the work of stitching many of their stories together that I saw a connection between gratitude and leadership. After I interviewed Sankaran, I went back and searched my interview transcripts for the words "lucky," "grateful," and "gratitude." In about a hundred interviews I found that women had used those terms more than sixty-five times. More than a half-dozen women had said that something in their life was "a blessing." Cuyana founder Karla Gallardo felt lucky that her parents had given her access to education and enabled her to see the world, which had inspired her to give back to the people in her home country by investing in factories there. Similar feelings were echoed by other women you'll read about in the chapters ahead: Whitney Wolfe Herd said she was grateful for the challenges she had faced at Tinder because they had given her the inspiration to found her company, Bumble. LanzaTech CEO Jennifer Holmgren felt lucky that her family had moved to the United States at a time when the LA public education system was robust and the public imagination was captured by the space race. PagerDuty CEO Jennifer Tejada felt fortunate to have had male mentors and sponsors who had connected her to opportunities while holding her to very high standards.

Gratitude seems to be a force driving entrepreneurs to launch purpose-driven companies. The sensation and practice of gratitude have been the subjects of extensive psychological and academic research. In 2010, UC Davis psychology professor Robert Emmons led a series of studies revealing that people who cultivate gratitude experience a range of physical benefits, including stronger immune systems and lower blood pressure. They also report higher levels of happiness and are more helpful, generous, and compassionate.[30] Academics have also found what they call an "upward spiral" between gratitude and humility, in which the two emotions reinforce each other.[31]

Perhaps it is no surprise, then, that gratitude benefits leaders. Those who show gratitude to their employees see a measurable benefit and are more likely to inspire grateful employees. A University of Pennsylvania study found that grateful leaders of groups of fundraising callers were able to motivate their employees to make 50 percent more successful calls.

Gratitude has a particular effect that explains why it's such a valuable leadership tool: it has been found to foster long-term thinking and reduce the drive for short-term gratification. In 2014, David DeSteno, a psychology professor at Northeastern University, designed a study with a series of twenty-seven questions to test participants' desire for immediate cash versus their willingness to wait for larger rewards in the future. The participants were asked to recall and write about an event that had made them feel grateful, happy, or neutral before being asked to choose between different reward options: $54 now or $80 in thirty days. In other words, they could wait a month and make a nearly 50 percent "return" on the investment. And the study wasn't hypothetical: the participants could either walk away with the cash or wait for a check in the mail.

The researchers found that the participants who wrote about neutral or happy times much preferred the immediate payout. But those who described feeling grateful were significantly more likely to choose the more rational longer-term payout.[32]

But here's what's most interesting: a participant's degree of patience was correlated to the *amount* of gratitude he or she reported feeling. "Positive feelings alone were not enough to enhance patience: Happy participants were just as impatient as those in the neutral condition," DeSteno noted. But the more grateful people were, the more patience they had. "Willpower can and does fail at times. Having an alternative source of patience—one that can come from something as simple as reflecting on an emotional memory—offers an important new tool for long-term success."[33] Patience, of course, is crucial to building a company with long-term value. And the combination of gratitude and patience is a hallmark of purpose-driven leaders.

This is where women, once again, have the advantage. A study by professors at George Mason and Hofstra Universities studied the way women and men react to receiving gifts. They found that women "reported less burden and obligation and greater gratitude," and they evaluated the expression of gratitude to be "less complex, uncertain, [and] conflicting." This tendency to embrace and even enjoy gratitude yields not only personal benefits but professional ones as well. The professors wrote that it "might allow women to initiate, maintain, and strengthen relationships by acknowledging and validating the importance of others in their life." Men, on the other hand, tended "to view gratitude as more challenging, anxiety provoking, and burdensome." The professors posited that that is possibly because men regard the expression of gratitude as evidence of vulnerability and weakness. (These differences, they noted, are not inborn but the results of socially prescribed gender norms.)[34]

Driven by Long-Term Thinking

Zume CEO Julia Collins was raised in a family that prioritized gratitude and service, and she found herself particularly attuned to those ideals in 2018, after her son was born.

Three years earlier, she and her male cofounder had pitched VCs on their startup idea: a robot-enabled pizza production line and special food delivery trucks that would bake pizza on the way to the customer. It was the first step in what they envisioned as a broad food-tech platform. They raised a few million dollars from five male-led funds. In many ways Collins's résumé fit the pattern of startup entrepreneur: she had an undergraduate degree from Harvard, an MBA from Stanford, and a wealth of experience building food businesses. But she was an outlier—not only because she is a woman but also because she is Black. Between 2009 and 2018, companies with a Black woman founder accounted for only *.06 percent* of all venture capital dollars. Between 2018 and 2019, that number increased to .27 percent of all VC investment dollars. To put that into perspective: about one in every sixteen people in the United States is a Black woman, yet Black female founders drew about $1 in every *$370* invested by VCs.[35]

But Collins and her cofounder appealed to investors with their futuristic *Jetsons*-like pizza robots: it was an idea that would make Jeff Bezos's delivery drones blush. And Collins had another, more serious angle: she wanted to use enormous data sets (including the weather and what TV shows or sports games were on that night) to predict customers' pizza demand. Those models could, theoretically, reinvent the supply chain in a more eco-friendly way. Collins had seen firsthand that restaurants' inability to predict orders caused massive amounts of food to be discarded (the food and agriculture industry is responsible for a third of all global greenhouse gas emissions).[36] But data could be used to calculate demand and to source directly from farmers. "You could reduce waste, farmers would have better outcomes," she remembered dreaming. Under her watch, Zume also developed a compostable pizza box made from sugarcane, which won awards for its design (it was engineered to keep pizza crusts crispy).

By 2018, the company had 270 employees. To keep fueling its growth, Collins and her cofounder connected with SoftBank, the fund famous for helping Uber create the trillion-dollar ride-sharing category (and infamous for quixotically pouring billions of dollars into WeWork). SoftBank's legendary CEO, Masayoshi Son, had recently announced a $100 billion "Vision Fund" to pursue his three-hundred-year plan to invest in artificial intelligence and robotics. SoftBank's strategy was by that point clear: inject an enormous amount of capital into a company so it can quickly grow, dominate a market, and cripple its rivals. The Vision Fund invested a whopping $275 million in Zume, at a valuation of $2.25 billion. It was a massive leap from its initial $170 million valuation the prior year. The deal made Collins the first Black woman to found a "unicorn," a startup valued at more than a billion dollars.

But something else happened right after SoftBank flooded Zume with money: Collins became a mother. Her feelings of responsibility about climate change took on a new, more vivid color. "I know it sounds so trite, but it's the truth. I just realized, if we only have a decade to get this done, how in the world can I not devote the full force of my being—and I am a force—to just solving this problem?" she asked. She became what she calls a *climatarian* and took steps to minimize her own family's environmental footprint. She began eating a plant-based diet, bought carbon removal credits to offset the impact of her air travel, tried to eliminate single-use plastics, started growing food at home, and committed to walking or biking anywhere less than a mile away.

In November 2018, she returned from maternity leave as the Soft-Bank investment was closing. "I just did not believe that I could stay in my role at Zume and also fulfill my personal mission to really truly create a sustainable food system and help tackle climate change." So she quit.

But then she had to figure out how to channel her energy into something meaningful. Before her young son, Mosi, woke every morning, she would quietly go into her living room and recite a gratitude prayer. She thought about how grateful she was for her success. She also thought of her grandparents, who had moved as part of the Great Migration from the South to the Bay Area, where her grandfather had built a practice as the first Black dentist in San Francisco. "In the Collins family you grew up understanding that part of your mission on the planet was to be of service to others. So, great that you got into Harvard, you got into Stanford, but what are you doing to be of service? Are you giving back?"

It was during that daily practice of reflection that Collins kept returning to something she had learned: at current rates of erosion, the earth has only about sixty years' worth of farmable topsoil left. In 2019, she identified her next step. In September 2019, a year after leaving Zume and its SoftBank war chest, she launched Planet FWD, a food company with the mission of using consumer products to tackle climate change. The first step was to launch Moonshot Snacks, a snack brand, starting with crackers. The ingredients are grown entirely with regenerative agricultural practices, which aim to increase biodiversity, enrich the soil, store carbon in the ground, and restore groundwater over the long term. The second step was a software platform to help consumer goods companies become more sustainable. As of the end of 2021, more than fifty food, fashion, and beauty brands were paying Planet FWD a recurring fee to use its software to understand their environmental impact. The company works with its customers to reduce their footprint by sourcing lower-emission ingredients from farmers who use climate-friendly practices, improving packaging, and using clean energy. For unavoidable emissions, the company helps brands source carbon offsets.

Collins's intention is to benefit farmers as much as the environment. "The median farm income last year in the US was negative fifteen hundred dollars. There's incredible injustice in land ownership and the diminishing of Black landowners and farmers," she said, citing data about the dramatic decline in Black farm ownership in the past century to just 2 percent of farmland. And the remaining Black farmers struggle to compete with conglomerates.[37] Collins said she wants her platform to enable brands to source ingredients from small farms, "who are doing the right thing in the soil and for their people. Yes, we are talking about creating more equality and more justice."

For that ambitious plan, Collins raised $6.8 million in seed funding—nearly all of it from people of color, women, or both. She intentionally selected investors who would not pressure her to grow too fast or lose sight of her environmental focus. "Why do I want to create more wealth for another generation of white male billionaires who frankly are already okay? That's not as exciting as creating generational wealth for the next generation of women and people of color who are building intergenerational wealth through their funds." (Her conservative fundraising strategy for Planet FWD stands in sharp contrast to the $420 million Zume raised. Soon after Collins left Zume, it reportedly laid off half its staff and shut down its pizza-making and AI software business to focus on producing environmentally friendly food packaging.)[38]

Now Collins says she's driven by gratitude for the opportunity to have an impact over the next century. "It's a privilege to be alive during this very narrow window of time, when it's still possible to take action. Time definitely looks different from the new eyes of being a mom. And if I do my job right, I won't see the full effects of the work that I'm doing at Planet FWD maybe within my lifetime."

She's also grateful for the ability to engineer environmental impact into the company's business model. She warned, "If you don't, things only become more complicated, and the more investors that you have at the table who have these venture expectations, for x return in seven years or bust."[*]

Collins's approach is the real-world equivalent of the Northwestern University study that found that people who practiced gratitude opted to wait a month for $80 rather than taking $54 today. It's Collins's gratitude that is driving her not only to help others but to do so with the longest time horizon possible. In addition to promoting long-term thinking, gratitude—both for a leader's employees and the opportunity to solve a problem—is also a central feature of servant leadership. It's that same approach that drove Mosely, Allen, Siroya, and Sankaran to build sustainable business models rather than nonprofits. In their financial success, these women will set a model for others to prioritize purpose along with profits.

Starting any company requires grit. What the founders in this chapter demonstrate is how women can embark on their entrepreneurial journeys loaded for bear with a surplus of purpose. By focusing beyond a company, on its potential to help humanity, entrepreneurs can find greater sources of inspiration and also determination. That additional fuel to keep working and innovating in the toughest of times is simply good for business.

---

[*]In March 2023 Collins's Planet FWD sold its Moonshot division to Patagonia Provisions, a certified B Corp which sells responsibly sourced food and beverages. Collins continues to run Planet FWD.

Three

Leading with Empathy

Hacking Big-Picture Solutions

When Toyin Ajayi arrived in the small West African nation of Sierra Leone in the summer of 2009, she was one of only fifty doctors in a country of 7 million people. And technically, she was not yet able to practice. With a bachelor's degree in biology from Stanford University, a master's degree in economics and international development from Cambridge University, and a medical degree, with distinction, in clinical practice from King's College London, all that stood between Ajayi and her medical career was the completion of her residency. Loaded with debt and ambition, she had turned down a job as a junior physician in London to build a nonprofit that aimed to improve the health care conditions in Freetown, Sierra Leone's capital. She had partnered with a like-minded friend to work with the country's Ministry of Health and Sanitation and was ready to get started.

It was at Ola During Children's Hospital, the country's only government-run pediatric hospital, that Ajayi had determined that she and her small team could do the most good. She herself had grown up in landlocked Nairobi, Kenya, on the east side of Africa and had seen her share of poverty. She had learned even more about poverty from her physician father, who had worked with international nonprofits to improve maternal health amid the AIDS epidemic. So Ajayi was no stranger to dilapidated public health systems. Yet when she arrived in Freetown, she was shocked by the conditions of the pediatric patients. They suffered from everything from malnourishment to malaria to trauma from motorcycle accidents, which is a leading cause of death in Sierra Leone. But it was water, she recalled, that presented the biggest problem. "You'd turn the taps on, and no water would come out."

Freetown is a port city that juts out like an underbite into the Atlantic Ocean, rimmed with white beaches and two busy harbors. As one of the westernmost port cities of Africa, it became a home for freed North American and British slaves in the 1800s (it was founded ten years before Liberia, its more famous freedom-promising neighbor to the south) and now had a population of 1 million people. Though the country had been mostly peaceful and mostly democratic since 1998, Sierra Leone's economy was hobbled by Ebola outbreaks and the suspicious flight of its natural resources—mostly diamonds—overseas. Despite the country's seven major rivers, considerable reserves of groundwater, and *six-month* rainy season, the government had not been able to organize and finance a reliable method of distributing potable water to Freetown's most impoverished district. Instead, the poor relied largely on private wells that either dried up soon after the rainy season or were contaminated by wastewater.

Ajayi saw all that firsthand on her daily treks through the city: children splashing in untreated water that flowed from sewage pipes and women spending hours walking to fetch safe water for their families to stave off the persistent problems of diarrhea, dehydration, and countless other waterborne diseases. It is hard to overstate the importance of clean water to a hospital. Without the ability to wash hands, infections spread with ease. Doctors also need water to sterilize instruments in order to perform even the most basic procedures safely.

Ajayi knew that the hospital had originally been designed to connect to the big water tank next to it, but in the dozen years since its construction, water had never flowed from the taps. Every bit of water the hospital used was carried into the building from the community pump or from a big tank of water that the hospital would occasionally buy. One day she walked the perimeter of the hospital and noted all the pipes that should have been connection points. Despite the water company's insisting that the hospital was indeed connected to the municipal water supply, she hired a plumber to inspect. Digging revealed a broken water pump and broken pipes. Ajayi raised additional funds to repair what no one had ever realized was broken. "The day we opened the faucet and water came out, I felt like I climbed a mountain," she recalled.

Though Ajayi had not arrived in Freetown equipped to troubleshoot municipal utilities, she was generally equipped to solve problems inexpensively. She had spent her first year after college based in San Francisco, traveling the West Coast of the United States while working for the federal Department of Health and Human Services. Her job was to deploy grants of $5,000 and $10,000 to nonprofits working to prevent HIV. That experience, she explained, was about "How do you take a small amount of money and a bunch of elbow grease, and people who really know what the issues are, to try to intervene and build solutions?"

That question—and Ajayi's natural drive to solve problems with limited resources—became the cornerstone of her work mindset and the key to her success in Freetown. It's also typical of those in similar circumstances. A study at the University of Notre Dame found that people who live in extremely resource-poor environments can be highly innovative in different ways. The professors evaluating the data reported that although Western theories of creativity emphasize the importance of access to resources as key to gaining a competitive advantage, in resource-poor environments, entrepreneurs benefit from *jugaad*, the Hindi word for "hack."[1]

Jugaad means "finding a low-cost, intelligent solution to a problem by thinking constructively and differently about innovation and strategy." In a case study of a dozen problem solvers in rural India, the researchers examined how, because of a lack of resources, those individuals found new, valuable opportunities. One of the key parts of their approach, the researchers noted, was "assertive defiance," or an unwillingness to accept constraints on resources, thinking, or behavior. This is the characteristic that motivates trial-and-error experiential learning to use available resources for new purposes—in other words, hacking.

Necessity-driven *jugaad* can be seen clearly in the growing influence of entrepreneurship by women in low-resource countries around the globe. According to Babson College's Global Entrepreneurship Monitor, countries with lower per capita income and higher unemployment have higher rates of female entrepreneurs.[2] Women are more than 20 percent more likely than men to say that necessity rather than opportunity was their motive for starting a company.[*] In the areas of health, government, education, and social services in which Ajayi was working, women outpace men in their entrepreneurship in countries of all income levels around the world.[3]

Within just a few months, Ajayi's running-water *jugaad* radically changed the conditions at Ola During, but the children who were brought into the hospital continued to be perilously ill. One of the biggest hurdles was a lack of overnight care because doctors refused to work the night shift. The doctors, Ajayi recalled, "were too scared—it was in a really unsafe neighborhood. So how do you create incentives and a structure so doctors can work overnight?" She answered the question by raising even more money to hire and train security guards. She also created a room for doctors to sleep in when they were staying on call.

---

[*]Globally, 27 percent of women entrepreneurs say they started a business out of necessity compared to 21.8 percent of men, according to the *Global Entrepreneurship Monitor 2018/2019 Women's Entrepreneurship Report*.

Even with round-the-clock doctors, she said, there were more crucial issues to address: "We didn't have a supply of blood for blood trans-
fusions." To help, she asked that every admitted child's parents donate
blood even if it didn't match their child's blood type. By making that part
of the treatment process, Ajayi created a self-generating blood bank. It
relieved some pressure, but the hospital still struggled to keep up with
the crush of sick patients. That pushed her to try to discover other roots
of its problems.

Ajayi's instinct to find the underlying, often hidden source of a
problem and to look at the broader context of challenges is not unique
to her. In fact, it is representative of a larger trend studied by Barbara
Annis, the founder and CEO of the consulting firm Gender Intelligence Group and author of five books on how educating employees
about gender differences (which are influenced by a number of factors,
including culture and the environment) can stimulate creativity and
profitability.

In the late 1980s, after a successful career as the first woman in sales
at Sony, Annis ran a consulting company to coach women to achieve success in the male-dominated business world. But as she sat in conference
rooms, she saw more clearly that she was asking women to change and
men to do nothing. What is being lost, she wondered, if women are being
forced to fit a mold created with a male prototype? She studied gender
differences and workplace behavior, and her philosophy evolved: yes,
men and women think and behave differently, but that is not a problem
that needs to be fixed. Those differences should be sources of strength in
an organization, not liabilities.

One key difference Annis identified is that women are more likely
to demonstrate contextualized, or *divergent*, thinking. In other words,
they tend to integrate more information into their approaches to problem
solving. She said that women take this more comprehensive approach because the female prefrontal cortex develops earlier and more completely
than the male's. In contrast, she says, the male brain is more likely to lean

toward more "convergent" thinking: focusing on one topic without straying to look at connected topics.

In a conference room full of executives looking for a solution to a problem, the men are more likely to be pushing toward an answer, while the women are more likely to ask about something tangential to get a better idea of the larger context. Expanding from one point to connected topics enables women to identify a broader assortment of solutions.[4] Put more simply, men may be more focused on handling the narrow priorities of Mars, but women, from their perch on Venus, are more likely to consider the whole solar system.

Ajayi saw that it wasn't enough to try to help one sick patient at a time within the narrow bounds of clinical medicine. In order to really help patients, she needed to fix the systemic problems behind their immediate symptoms. She devoted a lot of time to reviewing data about the families who were bringing in children that were near death—in many cases, far too late for medical intervention. She assumed that they had waited to come in because the hospital was far away and inaccessible. After reviewing hundreds of patient charts, she noticed that many of the addresses listed were close by. In many cases, parents who were right around the corner from the hospital were reluctant to bring their sick children in. But she couldn't figure out why.

The year before, in London, Ajayi had conducted postpartum visits in new mothers' homes, so she started walking around the neighborhood around the hospital to figure out the thought process of local parents. As she did, she encountered families living on dirt floors, with wobbly corrugated walls barely able to keep out the wastewater that flowed through the slums during the rainy season. Ajayi already knew that less than half the population was vaccinated for preventable diseases such as measles. But there, sitting on the dirt floors and talking to the mothers of patients, she saw the self-fulfilling death spiral of Sierra Leoneans' relationship with modern medicine. (Sierra Leone has the lowest average life expectancy in Africa: fifty-six years.) Because they had seen so many from their community die *after* being admitted to the hospital, they didn't trust the system. Sierra Leoneans viewed the hospital not as a refuge or place of healing but as a morgue. They were reluctant to bring in their sick children. Ola During was a last resort.

"I started asking people, 'What happens when your kid is feverish, when they're not eating, what do you do? Where do you go? What does a sickness mean to you?'" she said. The answer was often the same: they went to the woman selling traditional remedies right outside the hospital. "This woman has never been to nursing school, but people trust her because she's part of the community and she's accountable. They know her family. If what we're trying to do is earn trust and earn the right to take care of people, *that's* our competition."

One day, on her way back from talking with mothers who lived in the neighborhood, Ajayi stopped at the woman's stand and bought a bunch of different traditional remedies. For years she carried them around at the bottom of her purse, as "a reminder of how humble I should be as a doctor." There was no quick fix, she realized, to earn trust. To improve the hospital's accountability with patients, she had to make a series of changes.

She started by giving doctors and nurses name tags—"so people could say, 'That person was great to me, they work for me.'" She and her team also instructed everyone at the hospital to try to explain more clearly how they decided on medical treatments. Ajayi learned that families didn't understand the hospital's triage system. They assumed that those who were rushed to the front of the line were not the most urgent cases but in fact were paying bribes (a 2018 survey found that 50 percent of Sierra Leoneans who had contact with key public services during the previous year said they had paid bribes to access health care).[5] "We had to explain what triage means," she said, "and that means when your child comes in and they're sick, they're going to get seen first." She worked with community members to improve outcomes. The fact that their children were healthier improved trust and built a virtuous cycle.

Ajayi was doing more than just practice medicine; she was helping to improve the dynamic between the people who needed help and those who might give it. Once she saw that change, she realized she had even greater ambitions: "I wanted to build systems to figure out an oxygen supply and to train dozens of doctors." But she realized that she couldn't pursue those ambitions without completing her residency.

Anxious to start as quickly as possible, Ajayi looked to the United States, which offered the shortest residency program. She settled on a family medicine specialty, believing that it would provide her with the most varied tool set when she returned to Freetown. She applied to a single program, at Boston Medical Center (her sister was studying in Boston, so at least she would have a free place to stay). "I had only enough money for one plane ticket, which was the plane ticket that would get me out of Sierra Leone if I got in."

Ajayi was accepted, and she used the last thousand dollars of her savings to get from the West Coast of Africa to the East Coast of the United States, not entirely sure what she'd learn in the final chapter of her formal education in medicine.

It's not just in Sierra Leone that mothers make health care decisions for their families. In the United States, female consumers make 80 percent of health care buying and usage decisions.[6] And women are generally more proactive than men in the way they manage their own health and health care. A 2019 Oliver Wyman survey found that women are 76 percent more likely than men to have visited a doctor within the past year, and they pick up three-quarters of household prescriptions.[7]

Women also comprise the vast majority of people delivering the care. More than three-quarters of all hospital employees and people working in doctors' offices are women, as are almost 90 percent of home health care workers. And women now outnumber men in medical schools.[8] Yet despite the fact that women both create and consume so much health care, they lead only 19 percent of hospitals, and make up only 30 percent of the C-suites of health care companies and 13 percent of those companies' CEOs.[9]

But in the health startup arena, women are starting to make gains and are drawing a larger percentage of venture dollars. In 2019, women-led digital health startups drew 14 percent of deals, up from 11 percent in 2017.[10] And of the more than 360 companies that a leading health VC firm, StartUp Health, has backed, 32 percent were founded by women, far more than the 6.5 percent of all VC deals that go to female-led companies.[11]

Many of these women are doing what Toyin Ajayi did: identifying problems, getting to the root of issues within systems, and finding new solutions.

Seeing Forests *and* Trees

When April Koh was a sophomore at Yale, she was so depressed that she couldn't muster the energy to walk the two blocks to her psychiatrist's office. What was particularly painful about trying to manage her depression was how long the processes of trying different psychiatrists and treatments took and how ad hoc and experimental it felt. "I was in an incredibly privileged position," she said. "And ultimately it was still a bad experience."

Though she felt lonely in her mental health struggle, Koh knew she was hardly the only one experiencing it. In fact, one of her closest college friends at the time had a debilitating eating disorder. "I watched her go through four different providers, seven different drugs. I watched her go in and out of the hospital. Ultimately, she left school for her condition. And that was devastating for me," Koh recalled. Her friend missed two and a half years of college and was hospitalized multiple times before doctors finally figured out a treatment that worked.

This is not an uncommon issue. The process of diagnosing mental illness and prescribing effective remedies has long bedeviled the health care industry. The array of afflictions can be so varied as to seem almost unique to each patient. Andrew Solomon, the author of the seminal book *The Noonday Demon: An Atlas of Depression*, explained, "Most depressive disorders are thought to involve a mixture of reactive (so-called neurotic) factors and internal ('endogenous') factors; depression is seldom a simple genetic disease or a simple response to external troubles."[12]

Interventions are no different. The Mayo Clinic lists five major categories of antidepressants—each with a half-dozen brand-name drugs to treat it. Though some patients with depression benefit mightily from psychotherapy and medications, some people, like Koh's friend, struggle to find effective pharmacological treatment. There is no rule book explaining how different treatments will work for different people. And psychiatrists are naturally influenced by their recent success with certain treatments or perceived similarities among their patients.

Koh took a break from Yale to do a stint cofounding an e-commerce startup, then spent her senior spring poring over academic journals. She was looking for opportunities to digitize mental health care beyond just tools to make it easier to, say, schedule appointments. One day, she came across a paper in the *Lancet Psychiatry* that identified the twenty-five variables that were most predictive of whether a particular antidepressant would work to treat a patient's depression.[13] Dr. Adam Chekroud and his team had aggregated data sets on thousands of people from clinical trials, including information on patients' race, education level, state of employment—and how they were feeling. The questions covered varying types of insomnia and lack of appetite and probed patients' behavior, such as whether they avoided certain activities. The data also included whether a particular pharmaceutical—a generic version of Celexa—had worked.

Chekroud used all those data to train a machine learning model to predict whether that treatment would be effective for different disorders—a model that was more accurate than a psychiatrist reviewing the same data. When patients took the algorithm's recommended treatment, they were more than two times as likely to recover as the national average. Chekroud also happened to be at Yale (he was getting his PhD in psychology, having already completed a masters in neuroscience), so Koh emailed him and invited him to coffee. In that very first meeting, Koh pitched him on turning his research into a business, arguing that the more surveys and outcomes that were fed into his algorithm, the more accurate it would become.

Koh was onto something. In the last two decades, algorithms have increasingly been used in every industry to understand trends, predict outcomes, and remove the subjectivity of human analysis. For example, a study conducted by the economist Sendhil Mullainathan and popularized in Malcom Gladwell's book *Talking to Strangers: What We Should Know About the People We Don't Know* found improvement in outcomes in the court system when the subjectivity of a human (i.e., the judge) was replaced by the dispassionate analysis of an algorithm. Out of 554,689 bail hearings conducted by judges in New York City over five years, Mullainathan found that of the 400,000 people judges released on bail, more than 40 percent had showed some recidivism. When the machine learning program looked at the same raw data offered to the judges (minus the in-person assessment), it predicted the outcomes with 25 percent higher accuracy.[14] In other words, the computer, on average, beat the judge. Koh saw a similar, huge opportunity to improve depression treatment outcomes by bringing Chekroud's analysis into the real world; his algorithm wouldn't replace a psychologist but would help accelerate treatment and eliminate some of the wasted time of trial and error.

"What my cofounder was able to prove was that the most successful and the most accurate approach in precision mental health care today involves taking behavioral self-reportable variables to predict the outcome," she explained. ("Self-reported variables" is science speak for "answers to a survey.") In 2016, Koh graduated from Yale and won a spot as a fellow at Yale Entrepreneurial Institute to develop the idea into a startup, Spring Health. She and Chekroud realized that to build comprehensive data-driven mental health care treatment, they would need to expand the scope of their data. So they started off by aggregating data from clinical and pharmaceutical trials along with (anonymized) electronic health record data.

When I spoke to Koh about her partnership with Chekroud, I couldn't help but think about Barbara Annis's findings. The company clearly benefited from the mixed-gender partnership. According to Annis's theory of gender intelligence, in business, collaboration between men and women (and their respective convergent and divergent approaches) actually yields more success than a male-dominated approach or a female-dominated one.[15] Spring Health followed that pattern. Chekroud focused on improving his model, while Koh looked at the broader contextual implications of growing and scaling it. Together, they could draw on their very different skill sets—a psychiatry PhD and startup experience—to distribute the approach to practitioners worldwide. Chekroud's work on a particular tree, and Koh's ability to see the forest around it, were highly complementary. (There are many examples not just of the collaboration of male and female leaders, but of married couples in particular, such as Insurify's Snejina Zacharia, who works with her husband. A number of married couple cofounders have had massive successful outcomes, notably Eventbrite's CEO Julia Harz and Chairman Kevin Hartz, who took the company public in 2018, and VMware cofounders Diane Green and Mendel Rosenblum sold their company to EMC, which later sold to Dell.)

By 2017, Koh and Chekroud had relocated to New York and collected enough data to pitch the company to investors. Later that year they raised $8 million in seed funding, enabling them to build a system that companies can offer to their employees alongside medical and dental health coverage. The more patients they served, the more data they gathered to make the algorithm more accurate. In fact, Spring Health addresses not only treatment possibilities but also relapse, compliance, and behavioral modifications. The algorithm is precise enough to recommend specific providers, which can be booked within a day. In 2020, Spring Health published a study reporting that the company's patients recover eight weeks faster than the national average. Chekroud has continued to conduct research like the study that originally captured Koh's attention (the company has published thirty papers about its findings in various medical journals).

By the end of 2021, Spring Health had more than two hundred corporate clients, giving more than 2 million people access to its services. At the time, the company had raised nearly $300 million in funding at a $2 billion valuation. The pandemic certainly hastened its growth. "In 2021, mental health was fully destigmatized—we started to see board-rooms talk about mental health, and we started to see CEOs talk about their mental health journeys—which led HR leaders to pay much more attention, which led to investments in it," Koh said. "I think mental health is becoming another pillar of employee benefits."

When Ajayi landed in Boston in the summer of 2012, the contrast to Freetown was extreme. Massachusetts is, to put it mildly, a high-resource state. It has the highest density of health care workers in the country. The Boston area alone has more than a quarter-million health care workers in a population of less than 5 million.[16] Boston Medical Center is the largest "safety net" hospital in New England, with three-quarters of its patients coming from low-income populations. The patients Ajayi saw there as a resident were racially, socioeconomically, and culturally diverse. She had access to interpreters who spoke more than thirty languages.[17]

Ajayi, who describes herself as a "striver," soon established a simple but demanding routine in her eighty-hour week: see twenty-five patients a day, write up notes on each of them, and make each of them feel personally taken care of, the way her patients in Freetown had. She focused on building a trusting relationship in just a few minutes. She would always sit down, which she says was unusual in the thrumming environment of Boston Medical. She would never interrupt a patient and would always repeat back what he or she had said to make sure she understood. Then she would explain her treatment plan to help the person understand the process. For Ajayi, that technique was a kind of high-speed interpersonal *jugaad*.

One day, she walked into an examination room to find a woman in her sixties who had come in complaining of a persistent cough that she worried would disrupt her granddaughter's baptism. Ajayi examined her throat and listened to her lungs, then prescribed an inhaler to deliver cough-suppressing steroids. As Ajayi quickly jotted down some notes before moving to the next patient, the woman quietly mentioned that she hadn't been to a doctor in thirty years. Ajayi's hand had already turned the doorknob, but she felt in her gut that something else was wrong.

"The 'spidey sense' that I had been suppressing because I was so busy just trying to get to the next room stopped me while my head was out the door," she said. She had experienced plenty of resistance to medicine in Freetown. But this was *Boston*. "Who doesn't see a doctor in thirty years? Why? And why did you come today, of all days?"

Ajayi turned around, walked back in, sat down across from the patient, looked her in the eye, and asked her if there was anything else that had been bothering her. With that pause, that eye contact, and that moment of connection, the woman opened up—she had noticed "a thing growing out of the side of her chest for months, and she was too scared to find out what it was." It turned out to be cancer. Ajayi figured out what specialists the woman should see to help start her on a course of treatment.

The experience stunned Ajayi. She had thought that her efficient empathy was working. But she now realized that she had prioritized the wrong objective; she had been merely seeing the highest possible number of patients rather than producing the best long-term outcomes for them. Because of that, she had almost missed a breast cancer diagnosis. "I remember being absolutely devastated, leaving her room, and sobbing in the bathroom because I almost majorly fucked up," she recalled. She had almost missed earning the woman's trust—just as the hospital in Freetown had failed to earn the trust of the community.

Ajayi tearfully recounted the near miss to her supervisor. "Where do I turn myself in?" But she wasn't judged or reprimanded. Her supervisor's attitude amounted to "It happens."

That was even more shocking and even more upsetting to Ajayi. She felt like it would have been acceptable to miss such an obvious diagnosis. Soon she understood: there were no repercussions because her mistake wasn't something tangible in the medical system, such as failing to order a test. The thing she had failed to do—talking eye-to-eye with another human being—was something she felt was neither required nor expected. If a patient didn't report a symptom, the doctor wasn't to blame.

"Doctors can get sued for lots of kinds of mistakes. You can *not* get sued for *not* talking to a human and building trust with them," Ajayi pointed out. She decided, "I don't want to be practicing in a system that would reward me for having *not* asked the question and being on time, seeing all my patients that I could—a system that does not reward me for sitting down and taking a minute to understand and intervene. It was just like, 'Oh, shit. Success at the job that has been laid out for me is this thing, and I think success for me as a doctor and as a human is a whole other thing.'"

The desire to connect with patients is an extension of the empathetic, contextual approach that Koh used to identify the opportunity for Spring Health and Ajayi deployed to look at the hospital's broader issues in Freetown. Various studies have found that women are more attuned to others and able to determine what emotions a person is experiencing and to react appropriately.[18] That skill, which is sometimes described as emotional IQ, or EQ, is particularly valuable if, like Ajayi, you need to understand a patient's full circumstances—all the fears and challenges at home—to fully treat a problem.

The "Reading the Mind in the Eyes" test was developed by University of Cambridge professor Simon Baron-Cohen to measure social cognition; it found that men and women infer and respond to nonverbal cues differently. Initially intending to analyze autistic patients, Baron-Cohen asked a control group of men and women to describe the mental state of a person based on a black-and-white photograph of his or her eyes, using one of four words, such as *anxious*, *determined*, *apologetic*, *defiant.* The results were overwhelming: women were consistently better than men at identifying mental states based on a photograph.[19]*

On average, women are also better at feeling others' pain—a valuable skill for a physician. That was found in a 2019 UCLA study of people's brains reacting to images of pain in others: females showed higher emotional responsivity and homed in specifically on the experience of pain.[20] "One way that I understand your pain is that in my own brain, I mimic what would happen to me if I felt the pain myself," one of the professors wrote. According to the study, in females, the area that mimics the pain of others shows a bigger response. "That's an indication that women's response is more empathic; they're feeling other people's pain more than the male participants are."[21]

Another neuroscience study out of Cambridge University found that women scored an average 10 points higher on an 80-point "Empathy Quotient" test than men did. The researchers who conducted the study were looking for a genetic variable that might explain the vast differences between men and women. Interestingly, they found none.[22] In other words, the differences were entirely attributable to societal pressures and acculturation. Nurture, not nature, had created the gender empathy gap.

Female friendship has also been found to foster empathy, according to Deborah Tannen, a linguistics professor at Georgetown University who has written numerous books about gender differences in communication. When male friends are posed with a problem, they're likely to quickly give each other advice, wrote Tannen. But when women hear their friends vent, they'll likely ask for more context or about how a friend feels. "Taking the time to explore a problem, to ask questions and listen to the answers, and then use the answers in formulating further questions—all this sends a metamessage of caring."[23]

For Ajayi, carefully probing follow-ups proved a valuable way to

---

*Anyone can test his or her own social cognition with the online version of the test at http://socialintelligence.labinthewild.org/mite/.

figure out the context of patients' problems. For business leaders making decisions, context and empathy are valuable.[*] What the research shows is that, on average, men see the trees; women see the forest.

Fixing the Water Supply

After Ajayi's diagnostic near miss with the cancer patient, she began to chafe at what she saw as the negative by-products of Boston Medical Center's hyperefficient, not-terribly-empathetic style of care. On one occasion, she says she felt like she was forced to discharge an eighty-two-year-old who didn't speak any English and was paralyzed from the waist down. "We effectively sent him to the street. We said, 'You don't have insurance to go to a nursing home, so we'll wheel you out to the curb and, like, you're done.'" Though Boston Medical had vastly more resources than Ola During, she realized that, as in Freetown, "You've got to fix the water supply. The basics are so broken, and this is a state that has universal health care. There are more hospital beds than we need, and yet people don't actually get better and they're not getting dignified care. They're shuttling in and out of the emergency room over and over again for things that we can take care of."

Ajayi's heightened empathy is a critical contribution to a system that doesn't have empathy ingrained into it. The employer-based US health care system does not care why you have been laid off from your job. It does not care to anticipate your genetic predispositions and risks. The two stakeholders with the most lobbying power, the insurers and the hospitals, have incentives that are at loggerheads: the former to provide the least care; the latter to provide the most care. Neither necessarily has an incentive to provide the *best* care.

---

[*] A 2020 Businessolver report found 83 percent of both men and women said they'd consider leaving their current organization if offered a similar job at a more empathetic one. And about three-quarters of men and women said that greater diversity in leadership makes companies more empathetic.

Driven by empathy, once again Ajayi went on a fact-finding mission to understand her colleagues' perspectives on the system's shortcomings. She started to question doctors at Boston Medical Center about what their discharged patients were going to eat and where they were going to go once they were no longer under their care. "What if he was your grandfather?" she would ask. Often her colleagues did not know how to handle her questions, which she believes was in part because it was a young Black woman who was posing them.

"When coming out of the mouth of a person who looks like me, it can be so triggering and upsetting to people," she explained. To confront the issue, she would ask them, "Tell me back what I said, please, that upset you?" and when people told her that she had sounded "aggressive," she would point out that she hadn't raised her voice or been disrespectful. " 'If my clinical partner in residence, a tall white guy, had said the same thing, would you have given him the same feedback?' There was something very gendered about it, and of course, in retrospect, very microagression-ish."

Having grown up in a country of Black people, Ajayi had always conceived of her identity through the lens of gender, not race. "I grew up in a place where girls and women felt unsafe moving around the world, where people in every position of power were male," she said. Often, she thought back to an experience from her childhood. When she was ten, her mother had taken her to the doctor after a few days of a low-grade fever. The doctor had discovered that the young Ajayi had appendicitis and rushed her into the operating room for an emergency appendectomy. "I came to in an open ward, with the male surgeon yelling at my mother that she was irresponsible for having waited until she was done with work to take me to see the doctor. How dare she prioritize her career over her child?" Ajayi's mother was so affected by the doctor's criticism that she quit her teaching job to become a stay-at-home mom. But Ajayi wondered, "What about my father? He's not even in the country. Who's yelling at him?"

She said, "I never thought of myself as doubly disadvantaged because of my race until I came to America." That awareness of racial inequities made her feel as though her work at Boston Medical Center in the city's South End, with a population that was more than half non-white, was all the more important. After she completed her residency, she decided she saw enough need around her in Boston, particularly among communities of color, that she should delay her return to Sierra Leone.

The best way to ensure that she could really connect with patients, she figured, was to take a job as a generalist who oversaw patients' medical care over the course of their hospital stay. In that role, she could arrange her twelve-hour days to give each patient at least an hour of her time. She also started experimenting with other ideas. She gave patients her cell phone number. She met with patients' whole families to explain a complex problem. "You'd be shocked at how many family members of someone with a chronic condition like cancer have never had uninterrupted time to ask their loved one's doctor what's actually happening," she said.

Ajayi found that form of practicing medicine more rewarding, as it allowed her to listen to her "spidey sense." But she still found the same people returning to the hospital every few weeks. "It was for stuff that is preventable and treatable and rooted in their social needs and rooted in their community."

Then, one day in 2013, she met Robert Master. Since the 1970s, Master had been running a nonprofit to address the way underserved patients with chronic health problems tended to weigh heavily (and expensively) on the public health system. His organization grew into the Commonwealth Care Alliance, which operates as a home-based health care plan for people who qualify for Medicaid and Medicare. Ajayi was interested in Master's approach and took a job at the organization, focusing on patients struggling with substance abuse and homelessness. In her work she started to understand what was preventing many of her patients from making progress. She remembered one patient telling her "Dr. T., I'm not noncompliant, I'm defiant." Ajayi realized that "Her desire to not take her medicine, not follow up, not answering the phone when we called, was her attempt to exercise some agency in a world that gave her no dignity and no control."

To address patients' feeling of a lack of control, Ajayi spearheaded a number of projects, one of which involved getting the Massachusetts Department of Public Health to allow paramedics to give treatment inside patients' homes, rather than requiring them to be brought into the ER. That small innovation afforded a measure of dignity to her patients and avoided the expensive ambulance ride to the hospital, a trip that would often exacerbate the cycle of triage-and-discharge. She was so impressed with her governmental counterpart in the paramedic care negotiation, Iyah Romm, that she eventually hired him to join her at Commonwealth. Romm himself had a personal connection to community-oriented care: his mother had served as a midwife in the Atlanta community where he had grown up. And after suffering a fall down a flight of stairs when he was in medical school, he had become blind. His struggle to get a proper diagnosis and treatment had inspired a mission to make the health care system more navigable.

Then, in late 2016, Romm told Ajayi about a call he had gotten from Google's New York–based incubator, Sidewalk Labs. It was looking to invest in and incubate startups addressing urban infrastructural challenges. Together, he told her, they could create something to tackle the systemic health care problems that had frustrated them both for so long. Romm would be CEO and Ajayi, chief health officer.

"It was very clear to me that this was as close as I was going to get to a seat at the table, and it was a pretty good shot," says Ajayi. She was resigned to not being the company's CEO. "It's not like I felt like I was being robbed of something. But in the context of the structure that we were in, it was not lost on either of us that he got the phone call and this would be my opportunity to build the thing that I wanted to build." In the spring of 2017, Ajayi and Romm quit Commonwealth and moved to New York.

Systems Thinking

Amid a broader boom in "health tech" companies, there has been particular growth in companies focused on women's health. In 2020, funding for women-focused digital health startups more than doubled from the prior year to $418 million across twenty-two companies[24]—after 2019 had seen a 79 percent increase in the number of deals investing in women's health care companies and a 36 percent increase in total funding to them.[25] The category of companies that use technology to specifically improve women's health, "femtech," is projected to grow to $50 billion by 2025.[26]

One of those companies is run by Melissa Hanna. Her mother, Linda, is a lactation consultant in Los Angeles who says she's helped more than 100,000 babies through hospital lactation programs and as the founder of a mobile lactation consulting service, My Nursing Coach. Linda Hanna and a handful of her nurses make house calls in vans outfitted with the best breastfeeding tools, pillows, pumps, and herbal supplements for milk production. They charge as much as $300 for a ninety-minute visit (the visits are sometimes covered by health insurance). It is an impressive endeavor, but Hanna hadn't spent much time thinking about Linda's business until she moved back home in 2013 while she was pursuing her JD/MBA. She noticed that her mom and stepdad, the company's COO, were flooded with calls from anxious moms seven days a week. Demand was a good thing, but none of the anxious moms wanted to see anyone but Linda, which resulted in stress to both the customer and the provider. The younger Hanna wanted to offer what she'd learned from working at startups (and from her MBA classes) to help her parents manage the situation. They weren't particularly excited about her meddling in their small business but agreed to let her tag along to observe their daily operations.

One morning, Melissa and Linda Hanna pulled up to the Hollywood Hills house of a celebrity couple. The wife was crying, her breasts bared, as she tried to nurse her infant on the couch. The husband was pacing. Linda was issuing directions in her loud New York accent: "The nipple shield is like a condom, okay? No one wants to use it long term." She held up a curved piece of plastic designed to protect breasts from the sharp tug of an infant's gums. The husband perked up at the mention of condoms, and Linda called him over, asking him to pay attention as she applied the tool and helped the infant latch. She explained why it was a temporary fix: "Like any other part of your body, when you block the friction, you're going to reduce the response you have, and that's why condoms aren't as fun." As Melissa watched with a combination of mortification and fascination, Linda then explained what the new parents should look for so they could wean the baby off the nipple shield and use the friction response to build the mom's milk supply. The couple was rapt with attention.

Later that day, the mother-daughter duo visited a small house in a low-income neighborhood in South Los Angeles, where a grandmother was taking care of her daughter's five children, including an infant. The mother, they learned, had been readmitted to the hospital for a few days. Linda, who had been sent by Children's Hospital Los Angeles as part of its free health care program, advised the grandmother about formula and a feeding schedule. Hanna was shaken by the sight of roaches scampering across the floor, but Linda was unfazed and cracked jokes with the older woman to relieve her stress.

In those two visits, Hanna saw why her mom was so popular: both the celebrities and the inner-city grandmother would remember Linda's advice because she had given it with attention, wisdom, and humor. Her real value was that she *wanted* to make herself obsolete by empowering parents with tools and confidence—so they wouldn't have to call her back. Though clients raved that Linda was unique and unable to be replicated, Hanna felt that that kind of empathetic communication and context gathering could be not just replicated but also scaled.

The key, Hanna discovered, was that Linda wasn't just a genius lactation consultant, she was actually functioning as a kind of platform to connect all the pieces of a new mom's medical journey. It hit her on her twenty-sixth birthday, when they were out to dinner at a Chinese restaurant. "My mom's phone is just vibrating off the side of the table. I'm like, 'Mom, for one night can you just be here with me and stop texting your patients?'" But Linda wasn't texting patients. She was texting the doctors, who were anxious to receive updates on the patients they had referred to her. Linda was helping the physicians adjust their care plans to facilitate infants' weight gain, while also flagging medical issues in moms and newborns and suggesting referrals to specialists.

"My mom would do a group text, and she'd say, 'So-and-So, meet So-and-So, you're now connected for pelvic floor health treatment!'" said Hanna. It was coordinated care across a network—a supply chain of doctors, medical specialists, and doulas. The problem was that much of the data lived in Linda's head and her contacts lived in her phone. Hanna envisioned creating a software platform where mothers could document problems, connect with providers and one another, and be routed to any needed additional care—without 24/7 administration by Linda Hanna.

After shadowing her mother for two years, in 2014 Melissa Hanna decided to build a company called Mahmee that would scale Linda's magic in the way she gathered information, explained treatments, and empowered new moms to feel in control. Even more important, an app would take information and custom care plans beyond those parents wealthy enough to pay for Linda's visits—or lucky enough to get them through subsidized local services. Linda warned her daughter that she'd be frustrated if she tried to fix a broken industry and urged her to use her graduate degrees to tackle another problem. But Hanna saw that US maternal mortality rates spike not in the first days of life but in the months that follow, when Mahmee could have a dramatic impact.[27] She saw a clear opportunity to deploy technology to bring the United States' maternal mortality rate down to the level of those of similarly wealthy countries.

Mahmee launched the first version of its platform in 2016, and today it sells its digital tools to doctors' offices around the country. Health care providers bring every practitioner they refer onto the platform to access patient data. New parents get regular virtual check-ins that monitor everything from jaundice in a baby to postpartum depression in a mother.

It's a system that works, and there are data to prove it. Mahmee identifies what it calls "escalated health concerns" in 20 percent of its patients every year. That is consistent with national averages for risks during pregnancy and postpartum. In other words, Mahmee users seem to be representative of the larger population *and* the platform catches a broad range of medical issues. For example, one new mother was messaging on the app with her lactation consultant and complained that breastfeeding was difficult because her hand was twitching. After the consultant probed further, she learned that the entire left side of the woman's body was twitching. The lactation consultant urged her to go to urgent care and contacted the woman's obstetrician to alert her to the concern. It turned out that the new mother had an infection in her uterus. "Had we not caught that when we did, her physician said, she likely would have needed a hysterectomy," Hanna said.

To get Linda-level treatment into inner cities, Mahmee is deployed through government-funded programs such as Healthy Start. The company helps local providers tap into grants to offer Mahmee for free. It's all part of Hanna's plan not only to break the silos of treatment but also to get insurance coverage for every step of the process. "One reason nutrition and prenatal classes haven't been covered up until now is that insurance companies say it's out of network because the health professionals who do this work are not connected to them," she explained. "Now they're all connected to each other and they're all in Mahmee, so now there is no excuse for the insurance companies not to fund this care."

New Systems for Those Left Behind

The growth of companies such as Mahmee and the broader femtech market contrasts with a decades-long history of women's health issues being overlooked. It's a problem that began, ironically, with an effort to protect women. In 1977, the FDA took the extraordinary step of excluding women of childbearing age from *all* Phases 1 and 2 drug research—after trials for Thalidomide, which had been prescribed to pregnant women to prevent nausea, caused birth defects.[28] The change was made despite clear findings that cardiovascular disease, sexually transmitted diseases, and many other illnesses tend to present differently in women and often require different treatment. Different hormones, weight, and metabolic enzymes also change the way women process drugs. For decades, the basic testing of appropriate dosage for women was neglected. This neglect had broader implications. "The lack of funding for women's disease in effect maintains women's lower economic status," a 2007 paper in the *Journal of the Royal Society of Medicine* stated.[29]

In response to this injustice, a group of female scientists teamed up in the 1980s to create the Society for Women's Health Research. Thanks to their advocacy, the Public Health Service Task Force on Women's Health warned in 1985 that the lack of research focus on women's health compromised the quality of women's health care. The following year, the National Institutes of Health encouraged—but didn't require—researchers to include women in clinical studies. In 1992, a report found that women were still underrepresented in drug trials. Even when women were included, data were still not analyzed to determine whether their responses were different from those of the men tested. It wasn't until 2014 that the NIH conceded that there was an issue of male bias in preclinical trials. Astonishingly, it didn't mandate that research include female lab animals in trials until 2016.[30]

Christina Jenkins, the lead investor at Portfolia FemTech Fund, has said she hopes that the entire femtech category will become obsolete as the medical establishment integrates women-specific issues into mainstream companies.[31] But for now there is a growing industry focused on women's health issues. The US fertility market is estimated to reach $15.4 billion in 2023, more than double the $7 billion worth of business it generated in 2017, according to the investment bank Piper Sandler. The sector drew nearly $650 million in venture funding in 2018, according to PitchBook, and women are—not surprisingly—far more likely to lead companies in the sector than in any other startup area.[32]

One fast-growing part of the industry is egg freezing, which was declared a clinically viable technique by the American Society for Reproductive Medicine in 2013.[33] It's a crucial tool to address the trend of American women having babies later in life; the birth rate for women aged forty to forty-four increased more than fourfold from 1985 through 2012.[34] About one-fifth of women in the United States have their first child after age thirty-five. And about one-third of those women have some kind of fertility problem.[35] (That's because women's natural peak fertility remains between their late teens and late twenties, before declining significantly beginning at age thirty-two.)[36]

Egg freezing is a physically and financially taxing process. It involves a round of hormone injections to stimulate the ovaries to produce multiple eggs, which are then retrieved under mild anesthesia or sedation. The process, or "cycle," typically costs around $10,000, and, depending on the number of eggs a woman produces, multiple retrieval cycles may be needed. The older a woman is, the more cycles are usually necessary, at an even higher expense. About a quarter of those with impaired fertility go untreated because of prohibitive costs.[37] Egg-freezing clinics generally recommend that women consider egg freezing around age twenty-seven, when they're toward the end of their peak fertility period, because women implanted with eggs retrieved from a younger mother have lower miscarriage rates. In fact, the incidence of miscarriage is correlated not with the age of the mother at the time of implantation but with the age of the mother at the time eggs were frozen.[38]

Preventive Thinking

Tammy Sun was thirty-five years old and living in San Francisco in 2015 when she and the man she had assumed would be her life partner broke up. She wasn't totally sure she wanted to have kids, but after the end of the relationship, she knew for sure that it wasn't going to happen anytime soon. Sun is by nature a planner and at the time was working at Evernote, an online tool for planning, research, and project management. When she heard that thirty-five was the age when her fertility would start to decline steeply, she decided she wanted the option of having more time to think about the possibility of motherhood.

Sun had learned about egg freezing from her friends and from news headlines the year earlier when Apple and Facebook had begun offering coverage of the service to lure top female talent. She figured that trend had trickled down to her smaller tech employer, and she booked an appointment at a fertility clinic to start the process. She submitted the first bill to her insurance company and was surprised when it came back unpaid. She called her company's human resources hotline and learned that it was not a service Evernote covered; only a handful of the biggest tech companies did, and nearly every other employer-based plan considered it elective. Sun ended up paying nearly $40,000 out of pocket for four rounds of egg retrieval.

She became obsessed with the resource and information mismatch: egg freezing is most valuable for women to do when they're young. But this is precisely the period of life when they don't have the resources to pay for it. There was also an imagination gap. Behavioral psychologists say that people frequently suffer from something they call *optimism bias*, the idea that *they* won't be subject to adverse outcomes. The twenty-seven-year-old Tammy Sun would not have imagined that the thirty-five-year-old Tammy Sun would have her relationship fall apart and would wish that she'd frozen her eggs—unless, of course, the twenty-seven-year-old's health care plan treated egg freezing as routine, rather than an elective procedure for yuppie breeders.

Sun began to think of ways to make this kind of reproductive coverage the rule rather than the exception. In 2016, along with a reproductive medicine expert, Dr. Asima Ahmad, she founded Carrot, a fertility benefits company, to make it easy for employers to offer this service. Carrot allows employers to set a dollar value for how much they will cover for each employee—typically around $10,000. As soon as a company signs up, Carrot encourages its female employees, no matter how far they are from wanting to start a family, to educate themselves about fertility and their options, including egg freezing and even surrogacy. Carrot uses its growing scale to negotiate discounts at fertility clinics that lower costs by about 20 percent.

The company's business grew slowly until 2017, when the Uber engineer Susan Fowler published an exposé on the sexism and misogyny rampant in Silicon Valley. The bad press prompted both startups and publicly traded Goliaths to take steps toward refashioning their cultures to be more welcoming to female employees. Companies such as Carrot reaped the benefits. The first-to-market fertility leader, Progyny, which at the time focused largely on in vitro fertilization (IVF), had cornered the business of big companies such as Facebook and Google. But Carrot was able to sign up many of the smaller Silicon Valley companies that Progyny didn't bother with. Many of those smaller companies at the time would soon become giants (Netflix and Stitch Fix were early Carrot clients).

Carrot has grown to more than 250 corporate clients that offer its services to employees in more than sixty countries around the world. Those employers provide Carrot valuable data on what has worked for similar patients and what employees should try *before* the costly IVF procedure, such as an AI-powered bracelet called Ava that advises on optimal timing of sex. Carrot also collects data on the less costly, better outcomes that come from earlier egg freezing with younger eggs. Unlike Progyny, Carrot provides global coverage and positions itself as a solution for people with "social infertility," the term for LGBTQ+ people who want to have kids and women without partners. In 2019, the company's growth tripled, and in 2020, as the covid pandemic swept the globe, Carrot rolled out a number of virtual initiatives, including telehealth for fertility treatment at home and a virtual pharmacy to fill fertility-related prescriptions. In August 2020, the company closed another $24 million in funding at a reported half-billion-dollar valuation.

Sun believes that egg freezing has the potential to be as transformative for female professionals as the birth control pill was in the 1970s. "What I think really matters [about egg freezing]—and what the pill really did—is giving women all of the science that is currently available, all of the infrastructure and support products and services to design your life in the way that allows you to express your highest purpose," she said. "If your highest purpose is to be a mom and to have five kids, if your higher purpose is to have kids in your forties and work for ten years building something, that is really important." As of the end of 2021, Sun was forty-one and hadn't yet tapped into her egg bank.

Corporate America has begun to see things the way Sun does. Nearly 60 percent of US companies with over five hundred employees include at least some fertility treatment coverage, as of 2020, and 11 percent cover egg freezing, up from 5 percent in 2015.[39] In addition, seventeen states mandate that fertility benefits be included in employer coverage.[40] The category is growing but still not yet mainstream in the United States, which has among the highest average cost for IVF—an estimated $12,000. And with less than 2 percent of babies born as a result of IVF, the United States has among the lowest rates of use in the Western world.[41*]

One chain of fertility clinics that provides egg freezing and IVF directly to consumers (and is a rival of Carrot) is Kindbody, which was founded in 2018 by Gina Bartasi. Kindbody says it has aggregated so

---

*In EU countries where IVF isn't subsidized, an average IVF cycle reportedly cost between $2,500 and $5,000 in 2016.

much information about fertility outcomes that it can save insurers about 30 percent. It mines data to recommend the most effective treatments and charges $6,500 for egg freezing, just over half the typical cost. As of late 2021, it was partnered with sixty-three employers to provide treatment to their employees.

But thirteen years earlier, in 2008, Bartasi was thirty-eight years old, newly married, struggling to get pregnant, and part of what she calls Manhattan's "DINKY" (Dual Income, No Kids Yet) affluent population. She had sold a successful publishing company and could pay for the best doctors in the city. But at the time egg freezing was still experimental, and she was past the point of trying to preserve her fertility; she was anxious to get pregnant *now*. Bartasi had been disappointed by the experience of working with a specialist. "I waited more than six months to see the celebrity doctor: The walls were white, the chairs were white. He had on his white coat," she remembered. She had been a CEO with dozens of employees reporting to her, yet as she sat with the fertility expert, she felt "it was very clear, I was the subordinate because I was the patient and he was, you know, the godlike figure because he could give me a baby."

He actually helped Bartasi conceive two babies, which was typical of IVF at the time; doctors would implant two or three embryos to increase the chance of a pregnancy.[*] For Bartasi, that resulted in a high-risk pregnancy and premature delivery, with massive stress and expense. "I had severe preeclampsia, was rushed to an emergency C-section, and my twin boys were in NICU for five weeks, and my husband's employer had to pay that medical bill," she recalled.

The desire to give women an experience more positive than her own sparked a second career. She's since been the CEO of three fertility companies, making her a sort of elder stateswoman of femtech. Her first venture was Fertility Authority, which gave women access to information,

---

[*]In the last ten years, multiple-birth IVF pregnancies have declined; clinicians have tools to screen eggs for potential issues and implant just one.

community, and assistance in finding doctors, and was later acquired by a company that manufactured an early embryo viability test. Bartasi was named CEO of the two combined companies, which was rebranded Progyny (Carrot's goliath competitor). After years of hearing employers ask to purchase services directly from doctors, she decided to move from the fertility insurance business to the fertility doctor business. She founded Kindbody in 2018 and decided that the majority of its practitioners would be female (only a quarter of practicing fertility and ob/gyn physicians are women).

Kindbody's thirty fertility clinics, spread across the country between SoHo and San Francisco, are full of potted plants and blush-colored sofas, and feel more like upscale spas than doctors' offices. The millennial-friendly aesthetics are no accident. Bartasi is trying to reach women when they have maximal fertility *options* rather than intractable infertility *problems*. A $10-a-month subscription gives its clients access to general ob/gyn visits. Kindbody also promotes the proactive, fertility-preserving potential of freezing eggs by providing a complimentary blood test for the anti-Müllerian hormone at its mobile "fertility bus" clinics around the country. The test assesses how many eggs are in a woman's ovarian reserve, a strong indicator of how quickly her biological clock is ticking.

This push by Sun, Bartasi, Hanna, and Ajayi to get ahead of problems is reflected in many studies that have found that women are more likely than men to be proactive when it comes to their medical care. (This proactive approach is echoed in the work of other female founders in the space, such as Anne Wojcicki, who founded 23andMe to give people access to their genetic data and empower them with insights about health risks.) The Oliver Wyman study that tracked the growth of femtech startups attributed women's health care proactivity to the fact that "women are more likely to find the answers they need on their own after not being taken seriously by medical professionals."

This desire to be more proactive is supported by studies of men's and women's brain science. A study published in *Brain Structure and*

Function tested how fast men and women respond to certain tasks. It identified that for more complex tasks, though males are faster, females are more accurate and consistent. The study found "a more proactive and cautious cognitive processing in females and a more reactive and fast cognitive processing in males."[42] With their tendency to be more methodical and detail oriented in perceiving communication cues, women apply that approach to complex situations.

Building on those data, Bonita Banducci, a lecturer at Santa Clara University, teaches a Gender and Engineering class that focuses on how relational thinkers "connect the dots" better than more focused individualistic thinkers do. She cited the example of former Yahoo! and Autodesk CEO Carol Bartz. The veteran Silicon Valley executive described to Banducci, when she was VP of Worldwide Field Operations at Sun Microsystems, how she had seen her male colleagues miss the opportunity to identify systemic issues. "The men would consider what is the [highest priority] problem, choose the highest-priority solution, and apply that solution without looking at all the interrelated factors of the problem or the solution," Banducci wrote. The men "wanted to fight fires as they came up. [Bartz] said she could prevent fires from happening."

Bartz said the men on her team had resisted. In their view, the "fire prevention" gambit amounted to Bartz's "not being a team player: stalling the action, [getting into other people's turf], and getting in the way of 'the play' the CEO wanted to call." Bartz's greatest contribution—seeing the complexity of all the factors that would need to be addressed—was perceived as disruptive and was criticized for delaying solutions.[43]

In June 2017, Toyin Ajayi and Iyah Romm arrived in Manhattan at the gleaming glass tower known as 10 Hudson Yards. They settled into the offices of Sidewalk Labs, which Alphabet, Google's parent company, had launched two years earlier with the grand ambition of improving city life, starting with New York's. In their new workspace, Ajayi and Romm sat next to one team that was using machine learning to redesign public spaces; another was creating an open-source app to help the New York City Department of Parks & Recreation study public life.

Why was health care a priority for an incubator devoted to the parochial concern of improving city life? Because local health care is a more powerful way to improve a city than one would think. A 2016 study by the economist Raj Chetty and his colleagues found that though affluence has a big effect on life expectancy, zip code is an even more important indicator. After controlling for other factors such as race, poor people live much longer, for instance, in San Francisco than they do in Gary, Indiana. Chetty wrote that zip codes with better health outcomes "have public policies that improve health . . . or greater funding for public services, consistent with the higher levels of local government expenditures."[44]

Ajayi and Romm developed their company, which they named Cityblock Health, to serve as a primary care provider to underserved areas. They had noticed that the patchwork system of emergency rooms and ICUs was ineffective at collecting data on the patients who used their services most, those with chronic and mental illnesses and substance abuse problems. Now, with funding from Alphabet, they could do something about it.

Unlike Commonwealth, Google's Sidewalk Labs gave them access to data scientists who could collect and analyze patient outcome information and identify trends among the city's poorest health care customers. Ajayi and Romm took those data to insurers (mostly Medicare and Medicaid) and developed partnerships that would pay Cityblock based only on outcomes, not, as payments typically made, on the volume of care provided.

With those aligned incentives between provider and insurer, Cityblock went through insurers' historical data and claims history to get the names of the most expensive patients, the so-called complex populations. Then its team drove around, asking questions until they found them. "Imagine there's a patient in her forties who's kind of homeless, has some undiagnosed mental health challenges, or some trauma, and has high blood pressure, something like that. They go to the emergency room multiple times a month because they have a place to sleep and someone will give them a sandwich and a blanket," Ajayi explained. Each one of those visits costs between $1,000 and $1,200, and "in the hospital the doctors have got to do *something*, so she's getting labs or X-rays or stuff she doesn't need to justify this whole continuum of care. That's a meaningful expense and it's not atypical." Every time the homeless patient goes to the emergency room, she's told to see her primary care physician. If she does happen to have a GP and does go see him or her, that physician often doesn't have the data about her trip to the emergency room. "Or if they have the data, they don't have the emotional energy or the time or the incentive to ask what's going on." Even if the doctor takes the time to talk eye-to-eye as Ajayi did that day in Boston, "if the patient says she's hungry and cold and has no place to sleep, the doctor says, 'That's beyond medicine, I've got nothing for that.' Then the cycle continues."

So Cityblock built its business to center on developing patient plans that incorporate both medical interventions and assistance with social services, to help preempt expensive emergency room visits. "Think of it as a one-stop shop for your health, your physical health, your mental health, and your social needs for underserved communities," said Ajayi. Patients are given a person to call who's not a doctor or nurse. That "community health partner," who's more like a social worker, spends hours listening to each patient's story, helps fill out housing applications, makes sure the patient sees a primary care doctor. Cityblock hires directly from the communities it serves, as a patient is more likely to speak to someone with a similar background. Ajayi's team also visits patients in their homes, shifting the power dynamic and gaining visibility into the patient's life. And Cityblock practitioners have "an incentive to improve their health outcomes, and then we decrease their cost of care," Ajayi said.

Yet for all of its mission-oriented outlook, Cityblock is still staunchly focused on proving the business case of that better care. Ajayi believes that more stopping and listening and fewer trips to the emergency room will ultimately make more financial sense for insurers. As a VC-funded for-profit company, she and her colleagues want to show their backers that systems that perpetuate high-quality health care can be lucrative when applied in other zip codes. The company aims to serve 10 million people by 2030, with comprehensive care that bridges social services and medical treatment.

In November 2021 Romm took a leave of absence as CEO, followed by a period in which investor Andy Slavitt was interim head of the office of CEO. In March 2022 Ajayi was appointed CEO of Cityblock.

Ajayi remembers the moment she realized that the Cityblock system was working. It wasn't when one staffer found low-cost housing for one of its most chronically ill patients or when another matched a patient with a substance abuse program. It was when she was comparing notes with Elizabeth McCormick, one of Cityblock's most senior physicians, in a clinic hallway. Suddenly, from down the hallway, Ajayi heard a homeless patient yell, "Hey, Lizzie! Lizzie, I need you *now!*" McCormick paused her conversation with Ajayi, turned on her heel, and marched into the patient's exam room. McCormick had earned the trust of her patient by feeling like part of her community—just like the traditional healer selling herbs outside the hospital in Sierra Leone. Like that healer, "Lizzie" was familiar with her patients, knew their names, and would always be there for them. And unlike Ajayi's colleagues in Ola During, at Cityblock the doctors didn't need to introduce themselves with name tags; the patients already knew them.

That call down the hallway demonstrated the impact of what happens when leaders deploy "contextual thinking." It's no coincidence that this approach was found in women such as Ajayi and "Lizzie." In fact, contextual thinking—the instinct to try to understand the world around a particular problem and not just the problem itself—is really another way to describe the concept of empathy. Empathy is putting yourself into someone else's shoes to understand the totality of their experience. Gathering context, what someone is feeling and thinking and perhaps unable to describe, enables leaders such as Ajayi to figure out what their patients need. It also drives them to figure out what tools could empower those patients over the long run, as Linda Hanna did with her new-mother patients and April Koh and her partner did with the broad-based questionnaire to determine Spring Health patients' best course of treatment.

That empathy in action, of Linda and Lizzie, of April and Toyin, aided by the technological tools that extend their reach, is the promise of a system that could meet its customers where they are. It is the promise not just to offer them a Band-Aid but to change their lives. The promise of comprehensive, proactive care is offered not only by Cityblock but also by Tammy Sun and Gina Bartasi's desire to offer affordable fertility tools to women before they even realize they need them. We find that same approach in Hanna's Mahmee, designed to pick up on clues of problems among young mothers and infants before they know they have a problem. When calling out "Lizzie!" is no longer just the odd habit of people in a rebellious Brooklyn-based health care startup, the product of the US health care system will be closer to its promise. Until then, Ajayi and her teams will continue to see their patients and continue to meet them where they are.

Four

Engineering Smart Teams

A Growth Mindset

Nine days after her birth, Deidre Willette's father was killed while serving in the air force. Deidre's mother, widowed at nineteen, raised her along with her four half and stepsiblings in the 1960s and '70s in Stockton, in California's Central Valley. The city was and continues to be surrounded by farmland and offered few opportunities outside of agriculture. But the US military has a policy of paying for the education of all surviving family members of service members killed in action until age twenty-two. And so her father's death became a dual feature of Deidre's life, both casting a tragic pall over it and conferring a valuable opportunity on her. With her mother's and stepfather's encouragement, she explored that opportunity—and, knowing that the clock on the benefits was ticking fast, she did it as efficiently as possible.

"What I most focused on when I was growing up was 'How do I leave?'" she recalled. The only two career possibilities that could help her achieve escape velocity, she believed, were medicine and law. By eighth grade, she had decided on the latter, having figured out that she was good at writing and liked to argue.

Throughout high school, she loaded up her summers with extra classes, earned credits at the local community college, and did ride-alongs with the local judge. By her senior in high school she completed the first two years of her college requirements, so she entered UC Santa Cruz as a junior. She then matriculated at Loyola Law School in Los Angeles with two years left on her late father's free education clock.

That was when she realized that she had a problem: she hated law school. All of a sudden, after years of doggedly pursuing a plan, she was unmoored. She turned her mind back through the high-density years of education—was there anything she had enjoyed or been good at that she could now turn to? She remembered one experience: a course on computer programming she had taken at Santa Cruz. So that summer, while her classmates interned at law firms, she worked at a company that made custom computer chips for aerospace and defense manufacturers.

Despite her novice status—or perhaps *because* of it—Deidre almost immediately identified a potential for increased efficiency at the company. Given how economical and organized she had been at acquiring an education, she was horrified by the low-tech production method of that putatively high-tech company. "They were doing something that I thought was really stupid: they were making these instructions for how to build computer chips *by drawing them on paper*," she said. Not only did the process waste time, but she calculated that its imprecision was costing the company as much as $200,000 a quarter; that was the cost of a single ruined production job.

The protolawyer in Deidre Willette was not shy about making her argument: "I said, 'You guys, if we used a computer and created a digital library we could save a lot of money and a lot of pain.'" Her proposal was compelling enough to convince the company to spend about $15,000 on Mac computers—and to put Deidre, a newcomer, in charge of the team digitizing chip assembly instructions. Sure enough, with the dramatic reduction in errors that they enabled, the computers quickly paid for themselves. The company even altered its customer tour to feature the modern digital approach of Willette's team.

She really enjoyed redesigning a system. "I thought, *This is great—you see something that can be improved with a better process and tools, you make it happen and get rewarded.* It wasn't that I was in love with technology, I was enamored with 'How do we make things better?'—problem solving." And thanks to the burgeoning field of computing, there were plenty of inefficiencies to be eliminated and problems to be solved. She didn't go back to law school. (More on her later in the chapter.)

Around the time Deidre Willette was changing career paths in the 1980s, the researcher Carol Dweck was developing an area of behavioral psychology known as *mindset theory*. The basic concept is that there are two types of mindsets: a "fixed mindset" is the belief that personal qualities such as intelligence and character are innate and immutable and cannot be improved on; a "growth mindset," on the other hand, is the belief that through effort and experience, you can grow and change. Dweck's research, which she began in the 1970s and continues today, led to a wholesale change in educational and parenting approaches: no longer were teachers and parents to praise children's innate abilities ("You're so smart") but rather their effort ("You tried so hard").[1]

Studies have shown that reinforcing a growth mindset has a measurable positive impact on the brain's inner workings. Researchers inspired by Dweck's work found that when students conditioned for growth mindsets made a mistake, they actually experienced more brain activity than did their fixed mindset peers. Students who believed that they *could* improve actually did, and they had a greater awareness of their errors. Their extra brain activity indicated that they were also making connections and using their mistakes to grow.[2]

Back in the 1980s, Dweck also discovered a worrying disparity in mindsets between boys and girls. She observed that the higher achieving a fifth-grade girl was, the more likely she was to give up when facing a really challenging problem. On the other hand, bright boys treated tough material as an exciting challenge. Dweck proposed a theory for this counterintuitive finding: teachers generally needed to work harder to get boys to sit down and focus, so they gave them more feedback that emphasized the importance of putting in effort (those boys had potential if they tried their hardest). Smart girls, who tended to be less unruly, were praised for *already* being "bright," which unintentionally telegraphed to them that their intelligence was fixed. The disparity in mindsets that Dweck identified throughout adolescence wasn't innate but rather conditioned. This became known as the "bright girl effect."

This research may have started in the classroom, but it's no surprise that a growth mindset is valuable for business leaders: it makes them more likely to seek out challenging situations and to be open to feedback, especially negative feedback. Dweck and her colleagues expanded their study to business and found that a growth mindset is extraordinarily valuable in a corporate environment. In one study they asked workers at seven large corporations if they agreed with this statement: "When it comes to being successful, this company seems to believe that people have a certain amount of talent, and they really can't do much to change it." When they compiled the results, they found striking differences between the companies whose employees disagreed with the statement (and had a growth mindset) and those that agreed with it (and didn't). At companies with a growth mindset culture, supervisors rated their employees as more innovative, collaborative, and committed to growing. At those with a fixed mindset culture, they found frustration among employees—they said that just a small handful of stars were highly valued, and they were worried about failing and pursued few innovative projects.[3]

In 2017, Dweck returned to her decades-old research to test whether the fixed mindset that had been conditioned into "bright girls" was still evident in that generation after they had grown up. She studied four hundred participants, giving them an intelligence test and then asking whether they agreed with a range of statements, including this one: "No matter who you are, you can significantly change your level of intelligence." She found no consistent relationships among gender, mindset, and intelligence. Whatever the evidence for the "bright girl effect," for women, a fixed mindset did *not* persist into adulthood.[4] In fact, younger women tend to have more fixed mindsets and older women tend to have more growth mindsets, according to a collection of seven thousand employee self-assessments analyzed by the consultancy firm Zenger Folkman for *Harvard Business Review*. Young women's more fixed mindset was attributed to the fact that their competence is "constantly (and unfairly) questioned" and they're forced to prove themselves—so they are limited from seeing their potential to grow. As women age and understand better their ability to learn and adapt, they tend to shift not just to a growth mindset but one in which they actively seek to better themselves through new opportunities and challenges.[5] According to Dweck's best-selling book *Mindset: The New Psychology of Success*, instead of "proving," those bright older women were oriented toward "improving."[6]

An "Improving" Outlook on Founding and Hiring

One woman who embraced a growth mindset in middle age is Gail Becker. She had been working at the public relations firm Edelman for sixteen years when in 2016, for the first time in her life, she decided to take a huge professional risk. At fifty-two years old, she was exhausted by her corporate job and burdened by working-mom guilt. Her thirteen- and seventeen-year-old sons struggled to manage their celiac disease, which causes a damaging immune response whenever the small intestine encounters the gluten in wheat, oats, rye, and barley. It caused not only a nutritional issue for her kids but a social one as well. "Their friends used to come over on Saturdays, and like a lot of parents, I would stick a bunch of frozen pizzas in the oven and give lunch to everybody," she says. "My boys said to me, 'Don't *ever* serve our friends gluten-free pizza. Always serve them the regular pizza and only serve *us* the gluten-free pizza.'" They were embarrassed by the way the gluten-free pizzas looked, smelled, and tasted.

Becker herself had no special fondness for gluten-free frozen foods, which were often loaded with more preservatives and sugar than their counterparts made with flour. So, after a long day of work, she would experiment with gluten-free recipes. The first time she tried making cauliflower pizza crust from scratch, she was pleasantly surprised that it did not provoke an eye roll from her children; in fact, they asked her to make it again. The problem was that it took ninety minutes. There was no way for her to carry a high-powered corporate PR job and devote that much time to cooking.

Around the same time, Becker's father passed away. A survivor of the Holocaust, Martin Becker had emigrated to the United States and started a small salvage business (Gail Becker had worked the register as a child), which eventually earned him enough money to buy a small house in the heart of San Francisco. By 2016, when Becker inherited the house, thanks to the real estate boom, it was worth a million and a half dollars.

Becker's father had always encouraged her to do something that had meaning for her. So after some soul-searching, she invested the proceeds from the sale of his house into a new business to mass-produce healthy, gluten-free pizza. She called it CAULIPOWER (yes, all caps). Her PR background gave her the tools to get started. The first thing she did was commission market research, which found a significant demand for healthy, gluten-free alternatives to the current staples in supermarkets' frozen-food aisles. With the confidence of those findings and the help of some consultants, she set about figuring out recipe design, manufacturing, and supply chains.

Instead of surrounding herself with food industry veterans to compensate for her inexperience, she applied her own growth mindset to her hiring practices. She judged candidates based on their potential, rather than their résumés, hired a hairdresser as her executive assistant and a former consultant as her COO. In fact, as of 2021, more than a third of the company's fifty-five employees had had no prior food industry experience. She invested in training anyone who needed to fill a knowledge gap.

She sold her first frozen cauliflower pizzas in 2017 in thirty Whole Foods stores. Less than a year after starting the business, she managed to negotiate distribution to hundreds of Walmart stores *before* raising a single dollar of venture financing. Within months, CAULIPOWER was in Walmarts nationwide. In its third year of operations, the company generated $100 million in revenue. Becker attributes this success to her team's scrappiness—their willingness to learn new things and challenge traditional business practices. "When a business like CAULIPOWER demands so much time, so much attention, I think passion and commitment matter as much as expertise and maybe even more," she explained.

Her employees' growth mindset was put to the test when the covid-19 pandemic shut down food trucks and food shows, eliminating the work of more than a dozen employees whose jobs required interacting with customers in person. "We gave all those people different jobs—and stretched their comfort zones in a variety of different roles." Those roles included building a cookbook of quarantine-friendly recipes and working on contactless frozen-food delivery. Becker believed that everyone on her team could adapt, and they did. The company innovated throughout the pandemic and launched new pizza varieties and flavors as well as a low-calorie pasta line.

Collective Intelligence

One afternoon in 2009, 220 fraternity brothers and sorority sisters on the Northwestern University campus were trying to solve a fictional murder. The majority of the students were placed in groups of three, and each trio hailed from the same Greek house. The teammates were not necessarily friends, but all shared the code and culture of their fraternity or sorority.

Each group was given a transcript of a detective's interrogations of various murder suspects and twenty minutes to solve the crime. An intense discussion would ensue. But then, five minutes into the twenty-minute session, a new participant would arrive to help. For some groups, it was a member of the same sorority or fraternity—what the researchers called an "in-group member." Other trios had a more awkward interruption: someone from a different Greek house—an outsider—joined them. After the groups attempted to identify the culprit, the researchers collected each group's answers and tabulated the results.

What they found was surprising. The groups that had been interrupted by someone from the same Greek house solved the mystery correctly 54 percent of the time. But the groups that had been interrupted by a stranger—an "out-group" member—solved the mystery a stunning 75 percent of the time. Furthermore, among the groups where all three original members hadn't already figured out the correct answer, adding an out-group member versus an in-group member more than doubled their chance of arriving at the correct solution, from 29 percent to 60 percent.[7] Whatever the comforts and camaraderie conferred by shared culture, it appeared to adversely affect problem solving.[8]

As the researchers looked more closely at the interactions, they saw that the groups joined by newcomers had not performed better because, as one might think, the newcomers had brought a fresh perspective to the proceedings. Instead, they found that the mere presence of a stranger had caused the original group members to be more thoughtful about how they processed information. When the students had been joined by someone from their own group, they had merely encouraged the newcomer to confirm the theory that the group had already developed in its initial five-minute discussion. When an out-group member had arrived, though—a stranger with less of a shared value system—it had prompted what the researchers called *social sensitivity*. The groups had naturally had to work harder to explain their thinking; they evaluated the evidence much more carefully and arrived at the solution with far more accuracy.[9]

Another study, published in *Science* in 2010, supported this idea by detailing how a group's "collective intelligence"[*] does *not* correlate to the average IQ of the team but rather to three key markers. The first marker was each member's "social sensitivity" score, as measured by the "Reading the Mind in the Eyes" test (referenced in the context of CityBlock Health's Toyin Ajayi in the prior chapter). The second was conversational turn taking: participation in discussions was spread more equally among the team's members.[10] The third marker for collective intelligence was more of a surprise: teams with more women outperformed teams with more men. To be clear: teams didn't perform better if they had *equal numbers* of men and women, they performed better if they had *more women*.[11]

Conversational turn taking is a hallmark not just of smart groups but also of innovative ones. Another study of scientific teams found that the most innovative groups learned from their mistakes, figured out how to avoid repeating actions, and kept iterating their processes.[12] Turn taking was highly correlated to each of these key elements. And because women are more conscientious about turn taking, researchers found that the presence of women in a group is likely to increase the amount of innovation.

This research about conversational turn taking driving innovation is, in fact, connected to the studies about a growth mindset. Groups can be smart and innovative if the people in them push one another to grow. When the people in a group ask one another questions, listen to all the opinions, and challenge assumptions, it means that they are pushing themselves to improve. So it makes sense that groups with more women score higher; the fact that women are more skilled at social sensitivity and conversational turn taking causes them to orient a group toward growth and innovation.

---

[*]"Collective intelligence" was defined as a group's ability to perform a wide variety of cognitive tasks.

The Out-Group Advantage

Jennifer Tejada was raised by her Filipino American businessman father and her mom, who was a full-time parent, to have a growth mindset and stretch her abilities. In high school she was student body president and captain of the golf team. Then she played Division 1 golf at the University of Michigan. But it was after college, when she worked for five years at Procter & Gamble, that she learned to apply that growth mindset to her work. At the consumer products giant, she was told that her individual success would be measured in relation to her team's success. But more important, her boss at P&G established that upon entering a cohort, she and her colleagues should challenge *why* the team was doing something a particular way. That method of working echoed her upbringing and enabled her to rise through the ranks. "You're a fresh set of eyes when you come in, and you're not afraid to ask those questions," she said. "I learned from my mom, there are no dumb questions except the question you don't ask." She went on to run strategy, operations, and marketing at various software companies and served as CEO of one of them.

Then she brought that team-improving focus to PagerDuty when she joined as CEO in 2016. PagerDuty helps about eighteen thousand companies, including Peloton, Slack, and Zoom, keep their digital services running by monitoring systems and diagnosing issues to help prevent outages. PagerDuty had been managed by the male cofounder engineers who had developed its software, and Tejada was the quintessential "out-group" stranger to the startup's culture. She had a liberal arts background and a business management and organizational behavior degree—she was an experienced manager, *not* a coder. Before she joined the company, PagerDuty's management team had been less than 15 percent female, and its employee base was about a quarter female.

Tejada feared that PagerDuty's reputation as a startup run by a group of male software engineers could limit its growth; she'd seen at other companies that more diverse teams were more innovative. "If you look globally at the developer community and more broadly at the employee that builds low-code or no-code apps and solutions, that's a much more diverse community," she explained. (Low-code and no-code software enables people with little technical experience to build apps and websites.) So she told PagerDuty's cofounders—and everyone else she met at the company before taking the job—that she needed to make diversity and inclusion a priority. "Part of that was, I'm old enough to not care what people think of me now, and I have less to prove," she recalled.

Her first order of business was reframing the way the company sold its software. Some buyers, Tejada noted, might not have the technical backgrounds to understand all the jargon in the company's messaging. So she worked with her engineers and salespeople to understand what experience they wanted their customers to have and what problems they were solving for. Then she'd say, "Now walk me back to the technology that *enables* it—but it is not a technology-first proposition." That perspective helped create a number of key customer-facing services and broke the silos between the technical and business sides of PagerDuty: "Historically it was sort of treated like the developers were people in the boiler room writing the code underneath the product that the sales and marketing organization took to market," Tejada said. "I thought there's this opportunity to unleash the creativity in the power of design in bringing developers to the center, as opposed to them hearing secondhand what a business wants."

Meanwhile, she implemented strict hiring strategies, including a mandate that any candidate interviewing to work for one of her direct reports had to interview with her, too. "I can help you close them. And if they end up not going well, you and I made that mistake together," Tejada explained. It's also how she checks that half of the candidates are women or people of color: "The Rooney Rule [an NFL policy requiring teams to interview an ethnic minority candidate for each coaching position] doesn't work. If there's *one* underrepresented person on the slate [of candidates], we know that person is very *unlikely* to get hired statistically," she said. "So I started the change at the very top, and then it's a lot easier to push the change through the organization. There were times when we would wait and lose a good candidate in order to get a balanced slate, and that's when people really understand you mean business."

In about four years, by the end of 2020, Tejada had more than tripled the company in size to seven hundred employees and it boasted a senior leadership team that was half female, a board that was half female and two-thirds non-white, and a global workforce that was 40 percent female and 40 percent non-white.[13] (These numbers dwarf the tech average: for context, at the same time Amazon's management was 27 percent female and just four of its forty-eight top executives were women.)[14] The results of Tejada's focus on breaking corporate silos and diversity proved to be a competitive advantage. Within two years of her arrival, PagerDuty was named by *USA Today* as one of the best small and midsized companies for diversity: "If nobody else is making the effort to hire great women, great people of color, and we double our efforts, *this* is a way for us to outcompete," she said. "I think we attract underrepresented people more effectively than other companies do; when we go to hire diverse people, they look at our company and they know they aren't being picked as the box-checking underrepresented person, because they're joining a team that is *already* diverse."

Diversity has been found to yield financial benefits, too: it is associated with "increased sales revenue, more customers, greater market share, and greater relative profits," according to a 2009 analysis of more than five hundred companies.[15]* As discussed in the first chapter, a 2015

---

*Another study of financial experts found that ethnically diverse groups in both the United States and Southeast Asia were more likely to price stocks accurately than more homogeneous groups, which were more likely to have financial bubbles because traders put undue confidence in the decisions of others like them. Those traders were also more likely to accept offers farther from a stock's true value when working with those from their same ethnic background. As with the fraternity brothers and sorority sisters, the diverse groups' accurate pricing wasn't due to outsiders bringing new ideas but rather the *presence* of diversity, which inspires traders to scrutinize others' behavior and their own decision making.

McKinsey report calculated that the most racially diverse companies[*] were 35 percent more likely to have financial returns above the industry average, while those with the most gender diversity were 15 percent more likely to have returns above the mean.[16][†]

That should benefit female leaders, because they're more likely to have diverse teams.[17] There's also evidence of financial incentives for women to work for women: World Economic Forum reported that female CEOs pay their high-earning female reports more than male CEOs do.[18] Plus, more than half of senior-level women said they consistently take a public stand for gender and racial equity at work, compared to 40 percent of senior men. And two thirds more senior-level women than men said they mentor or sponsor women of color.[19]

Transparency

While Tejada drew on the value of diverse teams at PagerDuty, Deidre Willette continued to work to improve the operations at a series of other companies, from Zinka, a maker of brightly colored zinc oxide sunscreen, to Consilium Software, which made management systems for manufacturing companies. In the meantime, she married a software engineer she had met at work, Daryoush Paknad, who had emigrated from Iran, and started going by his last name.

During that time, Deidre Paknad also had a daughter, which gave her a new perspective. She started to fantasize about her ideal workplace—a place with "absolutely zero sexual harassment and no artificial gender cap, where no one ever confuses *enthusiasm for the product* we're launching with *romantic interest* ever again." When her daughter was two, she teamed up with her husband to create such a

---

[*]Those in the top quartile for racial and ethnic diversity.
[†]McKinsey noted that diversity itself doesn't translate into productivity, but that when companies commit themselves to diverse leadership, they are more successful.

workplace; in 1996, they launched CoVia Technologies, one of the first web publishing technology companies. Among other things, it converted paper articles into digital format. Its first twenty employees managing global, multilingual digital content were women from countries around the world.

Initially, the company thrived, providing portal technology and content for the likes of the United States Olympic Committee and Wells Fargo. Paknad thought a more experienced CEO would be better equipped to accelerate CoVia's growth, so she and the board agreed to hire a new CEO to replace her. But that CEO started just as the dot-com bubble burst, which turned out to be exactly the wrong time. When it came to navigating the dot-com recession, a scrappy founder like Paknad would have been more nimble, in Paknad's opinion, than a CEO who was accustomed to operating with the resources of larger companies. Less than three years later, the company shut down. She watched the implosion of her company with profound regret, feeling she could have saved it, and vowed not to make the same mistake with the next opportunity. That opportunity came in the form of a job leading a nascent software company called PSS Systems.

When Paknad arrived at PSS, it was aiming to help companies secure and encrypt their documents. She quickly shifted the company to focus on addressing new regulatory requirements that compelled large organizations to identify and collect documents for litigation. In just a few years she transformed the software company into the leader in the e-discovery and governance market. And she delivered a successful outcome to the company's investors: in 2010, IBM made an offer to buy the company, and Paknad took over the leadership of IBM's other offerings in the category, along with PSS's products. Two years later, she led the acquisition of another software company, StoredIQ, and she grew the combined business. She says that at the time about half of IBM employees and most of her reports worked from home. Quickly, she realized that in contrast to a small startup environment, where everyone was in constant conversation, her team members, spread out around the world, weren't connected to one another—or to the team's collective mission. "I had line of sight to no one," she said, "and they didn't have line of sight to each other, either."

Instead of resigning herself to the established culture, Paknad approached the challenge with relentless energy, adding to her schedule recurring conference calls, meetings, and weekly reviews to ensure that everyone understood group goals and how they might contribute to them. "I tried to use the same technique and tactics I used at PSS at IBM, except I had so many more layers, so many more countries and time zones, that it was unbelievably labor intensive," she recalled. "To make sure everybody knew the hill to climb and to find out how much oxygen was left in the tank—that was like fifty percent of my time. And it was such manual, repetitive motion without scale."

Paknad soon realized that the effort it took to drive transparency and clarity across the organization was so massive that she would likely get worn down or lose her sense of urgency; she was exhausted but didn't want that to happen. Her primary strategy for combating stress was regular exercise with her husband: they both loved cycling, and he competed with a team. One day in early 2013, she noticed the shared software Daryoush and his teammates used, called Strava. It showed each person's performance, so that each team member could quickly figure out how to optimize his or her own training habits. Daryoush and his teammates were able to use that transparency about their results to train smarter; they started winning more races even though they were training less frequently. In a way the software, by giving each team member visibility to the others and their results, was achieving part of what Paknad was aiming for with all of her disparate teams at IBM.

Together Paknad and her husband realized that the power of transparently sharing results and objectives could be applied to companies. With the right software, any manager would be able to do what Paknad had been spending so many additional hours doing for her teams—but *without* putting in extra hours.[*] In 2013, she and Daryoush founded a new venture called WorkBoard (she as CEO, he as chief technology officer), and in January 2014, she departed IBM. WorkBoard's software helps organizations clarify their intentions and measure their progress. Managers can make sure that a mission is clear and each team's contribution is well understood, just as Paknad did when she was running her first startup. Companies pay an annual subscription for the results management software, which is designed to align teams around transparent objectives and key results, or OKRs, and automate monthly business reviews. The company also created a framework that's designed to enable people on every level of a team to define what they want to achieve and strategize how they'll get there—and not to be hierarchical and expect decisions to come down from the top.

The need to clarify strategy is apparently massive: research findings published in MIT's *Sloan Management Review* in 2018 found that only a quarter of managers could list three of their company's five strategic priorities and a third of leaders could not list one.[20] WorkBoard's approach has drawn the investment of Microsoft and the software giant Workday. They're also customers, as is a range of other companies, including Ford Motor Company, Cisco Systems, 3M, and IBM. The pandemic intensified the demand for WorkBoard's product when knowledge workers around the world started working remotely, just as Paknad's teams at IBM had. The company has more than doubled in size in each of the last four years.

One of WorkBoard's biggest innovations was the way it transparently lays out teams' objectives and key results—including the obstacles to achieving them—for the whole organization. Just as Daryoush could

---

[*]A 2008 study conducted by IDC and sponsored by Cognisco, an employee assessment company, found that US and UK businesses lost $37 billion every year because employees misunderstand company policies, business processes, or their job function; two-thirds of those losses are due to unplanned downtime.

see where his cycling teammates were succeeding and where they were struggling, WorkBoard creates a clear map for a company to understand each team's progress. Because the challenge areas are visible across the organization, the software invites employees from any team to contribute solutions and ideas. The focus on the best outcomes for the collective places a premium on ambition, learning, and progress and aims to remove the fear of failing because an individual has aimed too high. An additional side effect of this standardized system is that it degenders the analysis of results and performance.

Paknad knew from her experience that teams could achieve more, faster if each member of the team could focus on what needed the most attention. (Addressing the hard stuff first runs counter to the way people typically run meetings, starting with what's going well and leaving discussions about struggling projects for the end, when time is running out.) "The platform shows you what needs your attention; you don't have to search for it," Paknad emphasized. "If a team's outcomes are always 'in the green'—it's probably not aiming for the best outcomes. It's shifting away from 'What do you know for sure we can do? What's our minimum bid, to what does awesome look like, and how do we get there?'"

WorkBoard's software is designed to encourage employees to aim high. When teams fall short, leaders are trained to ask what the team can learn instead of what went wrong. Earlier in the chapter I mentioned the study that found that people with a growth mindset had more brain activity following their making a mistake. Paknad's software imbues a company with a growth mindset by inviting people from across the organization to bring ideas and ambition about how to keep the whole organization learning and iterating.

Many other CEOs I spoke to in the course of writing this book, including Jennifer Tejada, along with a number of male CEOs I've interviewed for CNBC, push their teams to experiment with new ideas in order to quickly identify what's not working. Tejada has a weekly review in which she and her team discuss *only* areas that are failing, to figure out why they are doing so and to learn from those mistakes.

This kind of aiming for lofty goals isn't always comfortable. Indeed, that is borne out by the research. In fact, there is a coda to the Northwestern Greek murder mystery study. When the researchers conducted exit interviews with the participants, they found an interesting quirk: the groups that had been interrupted by in-group participants (students with a shared culture and shorthand) expressed a high degree of confidence in their solution to the "crime." To these groups, it *felt* as though they had worked incredibly well together (on average, of course, they had not). The groups that had been interrupted by total strangers judged themselves to be much *less* effective and expressed much *less* confidence in their solution, even if it turned out to be the correct one (which it was, far more often). In the words of the researchers, "The work felt harder but the outcomes were better." Diverse teams produced better outcomes not because the problem *was* any harder but because the experience of incorporation of diverse ideas *felt* harder. This echoes researcher Bonita Banducci's examination of "fire prevention" strategies in the last chapter: female leaders bringing in new perspectives to figure out how to get ahead of problems were seen as disruptive and stalling action. When it came to problem solving and innovating, the experience of discomfort in a group dynamic was a feature, not a flaw.

The Female Participation Effect

When it comes to fostering collaboration, Paknad and Tejada are gender exemplars. Numerous studies have found that companies with higher female representation exhibit better corporate performance. But the underlying reasons for this outcome were not widely understood until 2008, when professors from Columbia University and the University of Maryland's business schools launched an investigation into what they called the "female participation effect."* They asked the top 1,500 companies from 1992 to 2006 a key question: Do female managers improve the performance of their firms, or do better-performing firms do a better job at attracting and developing female managers?

In their research, they found that the answer was "both": female managers improved performance, and better-performing firms were better at identifying, attracting, and developing female managers. The key quality that women tended to exhibit in both these scenarios was something that Paknad and Tejada both noticed about their own management styles: women manage in a less hierarchical, more interactive, and more collaborative way.† The data also revealed that companies with the highest relative R&D budgets—presumably indicating the greatest focus on innovation—tended to benefit the most from the female participation effect.[21]

Since that initial study, other studies have developed more nuance and shape to this idea. A 2017 Korn Ferry study analyzed interviews and conducted psychometric assessments of fifty-seven women who had led Fortune 100–sized companies, asking about each woman's career trajectory, her drivers (e.g., "desire for power, challenge, or work-life balance") and her competencies (e.g., "resourcefulness").[22] They also evaluated the women's personality traits, such as optimism and confidence. The takeaway? The women "highly value the contributions of others, and moreover concede that they can't single-handedly bend the future to their will." In effect, the women understood that even if their whole team worked hard, some amount of failure was inevitable—but it didn't mean that they *expected* to fail. In fact, the psychometric assessments found that the female CEOs' confidence was near the average for CEOs. The one

*This is the term academics use to describe how and why female participation at companies generally improves performance.
†According to various studies, women tend to manage in a less hierarchical and more interactive style than their male counterparts do, leading to more teamwork and better motivation.

area in which they scored higher than their male counterparts did was humility.

In fact, humility is closely tied to all the characteristics highlighted in this chapter: a growth mindset and nonhierarchical leadership—also called "communal" leadership. A growth mindset is enabled when humility is paired with confidence: the idea that, no matter your achievements, you should and you can improve. Humility inspires people to stop and listen, take turns in conversation, and reconsider their assumptions. The humility of a CEO causes her to believe that everyone can learn and grow, and to hire based on potential, not experience. Humility enables smart ideas to surface from every corner of a company.

Paknad engineered humility into WorkBoard's software; it orients employees to focus on their opportunity for improvement and the potential to learn from one another. Tejada enforced a corporate humility at PagerDuty by breaking silos so the engineers could learn from the sales team and vice versa, and she said she works to enforce an open culture. "Nothing will drag the engagement of a team down more than a brilliant asshole. Every now and then one sneaks their way in and starts to wreak havoc in the organization; you've got to get rid of them," she explained. She says her goal is to ensure that everyone in the room participates and knows that "their voice is not only wanted—it's necessary."

What's particularly interesting about humility and all those connected traits is that they are not the exclusive domain of female leaders. Men can—and often do—find opportunity in these approaches. I've seen male leaders from tech giants to nascent startups benefit from deferentially soliciting ideas from across their organizations. There's no reason anyone should be trapped in a set of cultural expectations of "masculine" or "agentic" leadership—the idea of being assertive, independent, and followed by subordinates. A 2015 study of Dutch, Spanish, and American managers examined what happened when men adopted stereotypically female traits. They found that when male leaders acted the way female leaders were expected to act—communal and cooperative—they stimulated more cooperation than if they acted in a "male" way. The same was true of women; communal behavior fostered cooperation, and (stereotypically male) authoritative behavior squashed it. The researchers concluded, "We show that it is the gendered construction of male leadership that is the issue rather than (only) leader sex."[23]

In essence anyone, male or female, can reap the benefits of the stereotypically female way of managing teams. Though a managerial style focused on communal leadership may be associated with women, men and women should both embrace it. And if a challenge to established practices causes a bit of discomfort, well, that means it's working.

Part II

Fixing Problems

Five

Reforming Broken Systems

Rejecting Cultural Numbness—from Inside and Out

Though she had posed for the photograph weeks earlier, thirty-seven-year-old Sallie Krawcheck was still surprised to see her face on the cover of *Fortune* magazine halfway across the airport terminal in her hometown of Charleston, South Carolina. The photo captured her staring stoically ahead, her short blond bob partially obscuring the name of the magazine. The headline read "The Last Honest Analyst."[1] It was the summer of 2002. "I remember catching a glimpse of the magazine cover out of the corner of my eye and walking over to it and picking it up. The picture was actually larger than my own face," she recalled.

"The Last Honest Analyst" referred to her role as the chairman and CEO of Sanford C. Bernstein, an independent research boutique. Since its founding in 1967, Bernstein had built a reputation for in-depth research and analysis of companies' long-term potential, rather than predicting their quarterly results. The firm had largely avoided the conflicts of interest that emerged as Wall Street financial institutions expanded, but in Krawcheck's days as an analyst, it had started to participate in lucrative IPO underwriting. When she was named director of research, she pulled the company out of that work because of potential conflicts, giving up millions of dollars in fees. At the time, analysts at big firms rarely issued negative reports—or "sell" ratings—on big stocks, because their firms were constantly looking for new IPO underwriting clients or protecting their relationships with existing ones. Unfettered by those conflicts, Bernstein approached its work differently. For instance, while other firms' analysts were promoting telecom stocks, Bernstein's predicted that the industry was going to implode. And when General Motors' stock was called a loser by nearly every firm on Wall Street, Bernstein's auto analyst was a rare bull (in both cases, Bernstein was right).

Krawcheck continued to resist the pull of investment banking—which would have brought profits along with its potential conflicts of interest—after Bernstein was acquired in 2000 by the money management firm Alliance Capital Corporation. "I remember the director of research at Goldman Sachs said, 'Sallie, you can't survive if you're not doing investment banking. It is so easy for us to hire [your analyst] because we can pay him double what you can without sneezing.'" And he was right: choosing to play outside the traditional game had created an acute staffing problem for Krawcheck. "We had lost a whole bunch of research analysts because we weren't buying into the bubble. We were saying the bubble was a bubble." Yet despite those challenges, she made a radical decision to triple the size of her research team.

Sticking to her own rules and doing things her own way had earned Krawcheck accolades as a top analyst since her first year in that role.[*] "I didn't see myself as a stock picker . . . it was more of a storytelling picture-painting exercise as opposed to a 'buy here, sell here, trade there.'" And

---

[*] In 1994, *Institutional Investor* voted her the number one analyst, the first time such an inexperienced analyst had topped the list.

she was modest enough to know her weakness: pitching to sales forces of (mostly male) stockbrokers. Those audiences were eager to hear a clear buy-or-sell story. "I was so nervous when I would get up to speak to the sales force that my voice would shake, I would lose all of my saliva, and I would think I was going to pass out," she recalled. "So I had to find sort of a different way to get ahead."

A few months after seeing the *Fortune* cover, the legendary Citigroup CEO Sandy Weill approached Krawcheck to take over one of the company's most embattled divisions, Smith Barney. Citigroup had fared worse than most during the 2000 dot-com bust: in 2002, the firm had been ordered to pay a then-record $215 million fine to settle accusations that it had used deceptive lending practices. And Smith Barney had been levied the biggest fine among its peers, $400 million, for allegedly hiding conflicts and issuing falsely positive appraisals of companies with which it had financial relationships.[2] Weill wanted to reform the company's practices and its image, and Krawcheck's outsider status made her the perfect candidate for the job. For Krawcheck, it was an opportunity to remake Citi's research group.[3] The outsider was now inside the world's largest bank.

Wall Street was then, and continues to be, dominated by men. Between 1983 and 2005, an average of 16 percent of analysts were female.[4] (As of 2019, that number had grown to 34 percent.)[5] And women are in the minority in a range of roles in financial services, making up only 14 percent of fund managers—a statistic that held steady from 2000 to 2019.[6] The higher up the leadership ladder, the greater the gender gap: women comprised 62 percent of accountants and auditors, but just 12.5 percent of CFOs within the Fortune 500, as of November 2018.[7] In her new position, Krawcheck couldn't help but feel like a unique specimen.

Two years after taking over Smith Barney, Krawcheck was elevated to CFO of Citi and then put in charge of the wealth management group, which had recently run into a slew of regulatory issues: in Japan, its private bank had been banned from operating, and the group's financial advisers were fleeing in droves. Within a few months, the 2008 financial crisis hit, and the stock market cratered. Krawcheck says she soon discovered that during her predecessor's tenure, Citi had sold some clients "safe" investments whose worst-case scenario had been presented as an 8 percent drop in value. Instead, their value had dropped to zero. The risk had been inaccurately represented.

The last honest analyst and most powerful woman on Wall Street understood why Sandy Weill had hired her: this was a chance to do the right thing.

Krawcheck approached Citi's new CEO, Vikram Pandit, and advocated for partially reimbursing clients who had been misled by the bank, even though Citi had no legal obligation to do so. She says Pandit refused and told her that there was no reason that the company should take such a large financial hit. Krawcheck felt the issue was important enough to go above the CEO's head to the board of directors, but she knew that doing so would come at a cost. "At that point I've been told to sit down and shut up and asked, 'How much do I love my job?,' because if I continue to push, then I'm *going* to lose my job," she recalled.

In order to make her decision, Krawcheck did what she would've done as a young analyst: she gathered information. Her colleagues were split, with half telling her to think of the good she could continue to do if she held on to her job, the other telling her she should walk away with her moral compass intact. That night, she went home to her family. Her son was fourteen and her daughter eleven—just old enough to understand that kind of ethical decision. She asked herself what she would want her children to see her do. "Once I asked myself that, that's an easy, easy answer. I'm going to try to get these people reimbursed because we made a mistake."

At the next board meeting, attended by former Treasury secretary Robert Rubin, Krawcheck presented her reimbursement plan, positioning it as a long-term solution to prevent lawsuits and build goodwill. "I remember the CEO sort of sitting looking down at his lap, not looking around," she said.

The board did ultimately vote in favor of partial reimbursement, but Krawcheck's victory was a provisional one. "I obviously was going to lose my job, but he couldn't fire me right away," she told me. Gradually, responsibilities were stripped from her, in what she called a "constructive dismissal"; she resigned, and she said the company refused to vest her stock.[8] "The price of my honesty, of my trying to do the right thing, was a lot of money. . . . It made it a pretty financially expensive decision." Since then, three of Citi's then board members have apologized to her about her firing. She laughed. "You know, 'You took a courageous stand, we as a board should have stood up for you.' I remember thinking *That and two dollars gets me a cup of Starbucks coffee.*"

The fact that Krawcheck felt compelled to voice opposition to what she saw as amoral behavior is found in larger patterns of women in the workforce. Various studies have found that women are less inclined than men to rationalize unethical behavior.[9] To explain how businesses can create conditions for unethical behavior to arise, the psychologist Merete Wedell-Wedellsborg coined the term "cultural numbness." She wrote in *Harvard Business Review* that employees can gradually become so accustomed to a company's culture and its practices that "no matter how principled you are . . . the bearings of your moral compass will shift toward the culture of your organization or team." The longer one stays at a company, the more he or she is likely to experience "moral capture" and do more to fit into a culture than stay true to his or her personal beliefs.[10] Perhaps because of their outsider status, women appear to be more resistant to cultural numbness than men are. A meta-analysis of studies of gender differences in perceptions of ethical decision making among twenty thousand respondents found that women are more likely than men to perceive specific hypothetical business practices as unethical.[11]

Krawcheck wasn't the only high-powered woman fired during the

2008 financial crisis. The two other highest-profile women on Wall Street at the time—Lehman Brothers CFO Erin Callan and Zoe Cruz, a copresident at Morgan Stanley—both lost their jobs. Several years earlier, two researchers in the United Kingdom had noticed the public flaying of female CEOs and decided to investigate. They found that women were 63 percent more likely than men to be recruited into leadership roles that were already unstable, a phenomenon known as the "glass cliff" (the authors also found that women were, on average, more likely than men to pull organizations out of the ruts that they had inherited).[12]

Krawcheck had been a victim of a glass cliff and was headed to a quieter life as a member of the Wall Street emeritus class, pursuing passion projects. In 2013, she bought a networking organization that included thirty-five thousand businesswomen, founded by Goldman Sachs alumnae to support women in finance. She renamed it Ellevate Network and hoped it would nurture the next generation of Sallie Krawchecks.

Krawcheck was still the most visible woman on Wall Street, so she was regularly asked if she wanted to start an investing firm for women. She dismissed it as a "junior varsity dumb idea. That's not what I do." She figured, "I run big, complex, global businesses. Women don't need their own thing, and if they do, it's going to be a lipstick-and-mutual-funds idea, and I don't need that."

Then, one morning, as she was standing in her bathroom applying her makeup, she started to think about all the *other* women putting on mascara who weren't served by the very banks she had helped run, who had been left out of Wall Street's wealth creation engine. "I realized, 'Oh, my gosh, we have a retirement savings crisis! Son of a gun, this *is* a woman's issue!'" Women customers hadn't been her focus at the Wall Street brokerages because women were known to save, rather than invest; studies have found that women keep 71 percent of their assets in low-return cash, compared to 60 percent for men.[13] Wall Street banks knew that and so catered their services to men. Given the steady rise of the stock market, that fact had cost women across the country dearly. Maybe, Krawcheck thought, women were putting their money under their mattresses because there wasn't a product available to help them put it into the stock market. Maybe it was a self-fulfilling prophecy.

"We spend so much time telling women to ask for the raise, to know their worth . . . but putting together a diversified investment portfolio, that takes fifteen minutes," she said. "It's by far the highest return on fifteen minutes of anything possible. But yet we've had this emotional barrier, because we've been socialized that we're not good at investing, and then we look at an industry that doesn't reflect back on ourselves." She realized that she had accepted as a fact, rather than recognized as a problem, the massive gender gap in investing.

Now that she was an outsider again, she could see it more clearly.

And so she developed the idea of an investing platform that would focus on women. With her large network of Wall Street contacts, she took the idea to all the big investment banks, explaining that they could adapt their existing infrastructure to this new product. One by one, her old colleagues and competitors dismissed the idea as "niche" and passed.

Realizing that she wasn't going to find another home inside that corporate world, Krawcheck decided to pursue this idea on her own. An opportunity revealed itself with the rise of "fintech," web platforms such as Betterment and SoFi, which make financial tools affordable and more broadly available to regular consumers.

In 2015, she began pitching the company she had named Ellevest to VCs and surveyed hundreds of women about their investing goals. She brought on a male cofounder who had built tools that enabled banks to manage accounts and lend online and she surrounded herself with staff who were more familiar with fintech than she was. Her president brought a long history in the sector, and the chief investment officer, who had a PhD in engineering economic systems, had worked at Charles Schwab and other digital investing companies. Krawcheck drew the financial research firm Morningstar as the lead investor in her first fundraising round. In May 2016, Ellevest launched as a digital platform to help women invest and plan for retirement. Thanks to the availability of inexpensive fintech tools, she and her team built a "robo-adviser" for about $4 million, compared to the more than $1.2 billion she said it cost to build digital wealth management tools during her post-Citi stint at Merrill Lynch.

Ulu Ventures' Miriam Rivera, who invested in Ellevest's second financing round, said that when she was evaluating the project, it was Krawcheck's leadership that showed the most promise. "She had the ability and the skills to operate at the highest levels of global financial markets, which is very hard to come by in a startup founder. She understands scale, too," said Rivera. She and her colleagues were impressed by the way Krawcheck had built a team to complement her weaknesses. "There is a benefit to the humility that women possess because it helps them recognize their own blind spots. They also appreciate that there are things they don't know. Frankly, that sets them up for success because they're better learners."

When Krawcheck was building Ellevest's algorithm, a centerpiece was the idea that retirement planning for women should *not* be based on the average male life span, which is standard at many institutions— because women live an average of four years longer. Krawcheck said that Ellevest's investment algorithm "is the only one that takes into account gender. As we know, women earn less; as we know, women's salaries peak sooner; as we know, women spend more time out of the workforce. If you assume the individual coming through your investing algorithm is an 'average individual,' then you shortchange women substantially."[*] It took an insider who had become an outsider to notice.

In surveying hundreds of potential clients, Krawcheck's team identified something else about female investors: when potential customers were asked about their risk tolerance, women tended to say they needed to think about it—and never came back to the platform. Whereas men tend to have an appetite for risk taking, for women the mere mention of

---

[*] This is similar to the way the FDA eliminating women from medical trials short-changed women's health.

the word raised a red flag. So Krawcheck reframed the question from how much they were willing to lose to what they wanted to gain by investing.

Krawcheck also wanted to make sure that Ellevest didn't serve just affluent white women like her but *all* the women who were being overlooked by the big banks. So she launched Ellevest with low fees and no investing minimum. "We wanted to be as inclusive as we could, and investing minimums are by their nature, let's face it, sexist and racist, because women and people of color don't have as much money as white men," she told me.

Krawcheck kept running surveys and focus groups and meeting with women to ask what *they* wanted. For instance, wealthier women felt they weren't being served at the traditional banks and wanted more options. So Ellevest expanded beyond being a traditional robo-adviser, adding high-touch services including financial planning and the ability to pick individual stocks. In response to women saying that they want to earn more money, the company launched executive coaching. Ellevest's approach continued to pay off throughout the market volatility of the pandemic. During that period of uncertainty, rather than laying off employees, the company transparently reduced salaries—Krawcheck cut her salary to zero—and she granted options on her equity to employees to make up for their financial losses over the period of salary reductions. During the weeks in which mutual funds saw unprecedented net outflows, Ellevest actually saw more investment dollars coming in. In June of that year, the company introduced a tiered membership plan ranging from $1 to $9 a month for access to financial planners and career coaches, educational programs, banking accounts, and a no-fee debit card. In November 2020, the company announced that Allianz Life Ventures had led a $12.3 million funding round. In March 2021, Krawcheck announced that the company had doubled its assets under management in the prior year to reach $1 billion and every week of the year, clients had put more money into their Ellevest accounts than they had pulled out.[14] In April 2022 Ellevest raised a $53 million Series B investment round to deepen its offering and provide personalized coaching.

Tackling Toxicity in Entrenched Systems

The structures of power in business are highly resistant to change: scale, not innovation, has given incumbency its greatest protection. Incumbents in many sectors, from social media to high finance, aren't just too big to fail; they're too big *not* to succeed. Until the rise of digital tools that allowed upstarts such as Chime and SoFi to challenge the Goliaths, the way the big banks tended to change was from the inside—and change was slow and rare. As an agent of change, Krawcheck typifies a certain kind of female reformer: rising through the ranks, defying the odds, and finally earning a role as one of the bank's primary decision makers. Then, when a conflict arises, she tries to do the right thing within the system and stands up for her morals—before suffering a traumatic ejection and rejection.

This cycle is so ingrained that it seems unavoidable. For years after being pushed out of Wall Street, it didn't even occur to Krawcheck that she could execute an idea outside the system. It took years of rejection—and the realization that the only way to pursue her idea was on her own—before she drew on her power as an outsider.

Women at the highest ranks in business can exist in a paradox: even when they are insiders, they're often still outsiders. If they do make it to positions of leadership, they're usually among a small minority. The system they're working in most often was built by, and is being perpetuated by, a largely homogeneous group of white men.

When a successful woman is rare, she is by definition "othered," a status that, for all its awkwardness and discomforts, can actually confer some advantages on an organization. Krawcheck and her ilk, when inside, can push for an outsider's approach. When they step outside the system, they can deploy their experience and perspective powerfully.

As a journalist, I have been lucky to meet many businesswomen in positions of power, and I have found them to be profoundly inspiring. I relate to some of their experiences: Krawcheck's story of coming home after a challenging day to dinner with her kids and Cuyana's Shah telling me about pumping breast milk between business meetings. Over the course of reporting this book, I've come to realize that there's another reason why I seek out female contacts. As a journalist I have to be able to understand new fields such as cryptocurrency and NFTs and dive into unfamiliar ones such as space travel and the auto industry. I find the context and explanation women offer particularly valuable in situations when I'm looking for a broad understanding of a landscape, the tensions underpinning an industry, or where the risks of a bubble are. I think that's because women tend to maintain perspective about how a company or an industry works. That's because they can feel like outsiders even when they're inside; they can be less susceptible to developing cultural numbness—less accepting of the status quo—because they're not really part of the status quo.

This kind of reformer—one who maintains a sensitivity that forestalls "cultural numbness"—is uniquely positioned to identify a business's blind spots. It's a special combination: the expertise and knowledge of an insider and the perspective and insight of an outsider. It's why I believe women leaders have an advantage in scenarios that require the overturning of entrenched ways of doing business. Changing established systems can take years or decades, but countless women are taking independent approaches to creating alternatives—services, products, and content for female consumers.

One reformer who rejected corporate cultural numbness—along with real-world social mores—is Whitney Wolfe Herd. Her success inside a company that followed the industry's rules—in her case online dating—came earlier than Krawcheck's. At age twenty-three, soon after graduating college, Whitney Wolfe was working at the startup incubator that hatched Tinder. One of the dating app's cofounders and its first VP of marketing, she used her familiarity with fraternities and sororities, having been in one herself, to market the dating app and drive its meteoric early growth. But two years later, she found herself in an unexpected position: unemployed and suing her former company for sexual harassment.

She won't discuss the lawsuit or the terms of the settlement, but she's clear that it seemed to her that the culture at Tinder was just as broken and toxic as the world of online dating it aimed to serve. According to her filed complaint, the end of her romantic relationship with one of her cofounders came when he became "verbally controlling and abusive." In the suit she alleged that after the breakup, three of her cofounders variously called her, in front of colleagues, "whore," "slut," and "liar" and said they wanted to strip her of her title because they thought having a female cofounder reflected poorly on the startup. (Tinder settled the lawsuit with no admission of wrongdoing and the cofounder who Wolfe had dated was suspended and eventually resigned.)

Wolfe realized after her expulsion from Tinder that she had developed a numbness, not just to the way she says she had been treated in the professional setting of an internet startup but also to the gendered roles she and her female friends were expected to play in their dating lives. "Dating felt really unfair. For my friends, for myself, watching my mother go through a divorce and get back into the dating world. . . . It felt like women were essentially at the whim of the men," she recalled. "I realized we [at Tinder] were actually just perpetuating the system that I felt was already broken in the real world by setting up a digital ecosystem where it just follows the same rules as society—men were the hunters."

As she had those revelations, she was also enduring a wave of media coverage and harassment unlike anything she could ever have imagined. TechCrunch described what it said was intimate details of her dating life. That sent her into a paralyzing depression. For weeks she lay in the dark, scrolling through belligerent tweets. "What broke my heart—I hated the way social media could come for me, I hated the way the dating system was broken. It was like a perfect storm, because all these different things that broke my heart all kind of formed into one big cloud over my head." Before the internet age, her public and embarrassing ejection from Tinder would have perhaps caused a few harassing or heavy-breathing phone calls. In 2016, the online attacks on her by digital trolls were brutal and constant.

When that cloud started to lift, she began to tinker with a project that might alleviate her own personal challenge: a new social network only for women with a quasi-utopian mission of banning abuse and mandating compliments. About a month into the development of the platform, she got a call from Andrey Andreev, a billionaire entrepreneur behind some of the largest social networking apps in Europe and Latin America, offering her a job at his London-based company. She declined and instead pitched him her girl-power network. Andreev didn't think it would work. Instead, he suggested that she apply that positive approach to a dating platform. He offered her virtually unlimited resources—in exchange for 80 percent of the company (Wolfe would keep the other 20 percent).

Wolfe was reluctant to work for Andreev. His empire included dating sites that bore strong similarities to the one she had recently escaped. But Andreev promised her independence, and after the Tinder lawsuit had given her a sort of Silicon Valley scarlet letter, she knew it would be hard to convince other investors to bet heavily on someone whose prior leadership had been so fraught. "The way I thought about this was, this actually may be a once-in-a-lifetime deal," Wolfe Herd recalled.

So she took the deal and started crafting a dating service that would empower women by using its platform to rewire the social code of dating: only women would be allowed to make the first move. Bumble launched in December 2014, a mere six months after Wolfe left Tinder. Once a match between users is made, the app functions like a digital Sadie Hawkins dance, requiring women to start the conversation. To motivate its users to act (rather than just keep swiping and looking for something better), the app has a Cinderella twist: every message from potential matches turns into a pumpkin within twenty-four hours (though women can pay a subscription fee to extend the spell—or see a list of expired princes). For same-sex couples and nonbinary users, either party can make the first move. With that simple alteration to a dating app's mechanics, Wolfe hoped to change the power dynamic of its user base. She found that the dynamic was also better for its male users: "All of a sudden that rejection has been alleviated. And because the rejection becomes eliminated, there's a lot lower risk for aggressive or abusive reactions."

By 2017, when she married Michael Herd and added his name to hers (they didn't meet on Bumble), Whitney Wolfe Herd's app had been downloaded 22 million times. By 2020, that number had grown to 100 million. The positive psychological effect of the platform that Wolfe Herd reported wasn't just anecdotal; a study published in the peer-reviewed journal *Informing Science* found that women on the "counterheteronormative" Bumble platform felt more positive psychological benefits than did those on traditional platforms where both men and women can make the first move, including "self-efficacy," "perceived competence," and, most tellingly, "psychological empowerment."[15] (The dating app that the researchers used as an experimental control in the study? Tinder.)

Bumble's success proved that there was real value that had been locked up by men's hegemonic control of the online dating industry. "This huge, multibillion-dollar question is: What do women want? This is a huge question that primarily men have been trying to solve for centuries. I have this theory that if you want to know what women want, put a woman in charge and let her build it," said Wolfe Herd. Dana Settle, a cofounder and managing partner at the venture capital firm Greycroft, which invested in Bumble, agreed. "Whitney saw firsthand all of the things that were so terrible that were happening in the underbelly of the dating world," Settle said. "Having a very clear perspective on what's wrong, coming from inside the industry, seeing a problem, helps you know how to fix it." Bumble's success did not go unnoticed by the rest of the industry; in 2018, Tinder enabled a feature that lets women choose to be the ones to start a conversation.[16]

But even with all its success, Bumble still had a problem that was rampant throughout the online dating industry: men were sending women unsolicited lewd photos. And women hated it (they flooded customer support with thousands of angry emails). Wolfe Herd and her team deployed a massive amount of technology to counter the problem: machine learning tools successfully identified lewd material with 98 percent efficiency and blurred it before a user could see it.

But it wasn't enough for Wolfe Herd to address the issue on her own platform and to use her anti–dick pic technology as a feature to compete against her rivals; she saw it as a societal issue. She wondered why, if there's a law prohibiting men from exposing themselves in public, there was no law prohibiting its digital equivalent. So she hired a lobbyist who seeded the idea for a bill that would make sending an unsolicited nude or sexual photograph a misdemeanor. Wolfe Herd herself introduced the bill before the Texas Senate (she was visibly pregnant at the time). It passed unanimously. In March 2022 the UK government announced it would make cyberflashing a criminal offense under the proposed Online Safety Bill, which Bumble supported. The following month Virginia passed a Bumble-backed bill that established a civil penalty for any adult who knowingly digitally sends an unsolicited intimate image. Her plan to get the law passed at a federal level was sidelined by the pandemic, but as of this book's publication, Wolfe Herd's team is working with lawmakers in California and New York.

Wolfe Herd is among a number of female business leaders who have used their position to advocate for legal change. Another example is Beautycounter's Gregg Renfrew, whom I wrote about in the introduction. She could have used her company's commitment to maintaining the highest safety standards as a competitive advantage. But instead, she's been trying to give away that advantage by lobbying for laws to ban toxic ingredients across the industry. She founded a coalition to fight for health-protective laws at the federal level and has personally held more than a hundred meetings on Capitol Hill and testified at a congressional hearing on cosmetics reform. In 2020, she helped pass two landmark California clean beauty laws. Legislating away Beautycounter's competitive advantages did not impact her company's performance or valuation; in 2021, she sold the company to Carlyle for $1 billion.

Meanwhile, Wolfe Herd faced an internal cultural challenge at Bumble when it turned out that her initial hesitation about Andreev had been well founded. In July 2019, *Forbes* published an expose of alleged tax avoidance and misogyny at Andreev's company Badoo. Interviews with thirteen former employees detailed nauseating workplace behavior that ranged from naming software updates after porn stars to company parties with nudity and cocaine.[17] Wolfe Herd found herself in an awkward position, caught between her personal mission and her boss's bad behavior. Though Wolfe Herd told *Forbes* that she had never witnessed that kind of behavior, how could such a visible proponent of female empowerment be aligned with someone accused of enabling all sorts of misogyny, discrimination, and harassment? Badoo's parent company, MagicLab, hired a firm to investigate the allegations. In November 2019, Andreev announced that he was selling his entire stake in MagicLab to the private equity firm Blackstone and stepped away from the company. (He denied wrongdoing himself and denied knowledge of alleged wrongdoing by others.)

Having a different perspective from the status quo paid off for Wolfe Herd: Blackstone named her CEO of Bumble's parent company, including the much larger Badoo; its app had been downloaded 400 million times. The combined company, which had 42 million people using its dating apps monthly in 2020, was renamed Bumble. Wolfe Herd's hesitation may have been founded when Andreev offered to invest in her. But the success of her outsider's plan to reinvent dating culture ultimately put her in charge of a much bigger empire of dating services, giving her much more potential to implement change.[18] Her experience with online bullying and harassment gave her firsthand knowledge of the power of the internet not just to re-create the worst aspects of the public square but also to make that square even more vicious and instantaneous—and global. And she demonstrated that when the creator of a product shares the same perspective and sensibility of the consumer of that product, the potential for value-positive innovation is enormous. Sometimes the difference between the legacy product and the female-authored one can be simple, whether it is the tuning of an investment actuarial table or applying the Sadie Hawkins principle to a dating platform.

Throughout 2020, Bumble continued to grow as it adjusted to the disruption caused by the global pandemic, adding features such as video dates. In February 2021, the company went public; Wolfe Herd rang the opening bell of the Nasdaq with her one-year-old son on her hip. On its opening day, the stock started trading up nearly 77 percent, and Wolfe Herd became the youngest female founder to take a US company public.

Changing Narratives

Though the internet offers the possibility of amplifying the worst impulses in the real world, there is another cultural phenomenon that has been around for a lot longer: Hollywood. It is the United States' most powerful export, not just its billion-dollar superhero franchises and global stars but also its archetypes, which establish Western societal mores—for good and for ill (*Birth of a Nation* revitalized the KKK; *Bambi* hastened the decline of recreational hunting).[19]

Though it's possible to detect the cultural influence of an archetype, it is more challenging to measure the effect of the *absence* of one. But consider this: in the early 1980s, the percentage of computer science students who were women rose steadily, reaching 37 percent in 1983. That June the independent studio MGM, whose only other recent hits featured an agent with the code name 007, released a low-budget thriller starring Matthew Broderick about a teen hacker who unwittingly wades into the Cold War and helps the United States narrowly avoid a nuclear collision with Russia. *WarGames* became a huge hit and a cultural touchstone, both in the United States and abroad (it premiered at the Cannes Film Festival). The movie's formula (brainy white male outcast finds meaning and heroism in science) would be repeated again and again in *The Last Starfighter* (1984), *Real Genius* (1985), *Weird Science* (1985), and *Short Circuit* (1986), among others. By the time *Hackers* came along in 1995, it was seen as radical for even *one* of the six lead roles to be played by a woman (Angelina Jolie). In the meantime, the percentage of college students studying computer science who are women declined steadily and flatlined around 17 percent between 2008 and 2014, slowly increasing to 21 percent by 2019.[20] These movies, of course, are not solely to blame for the 20 percentage point decline in female representation in computer science over two decades. But it's clear that *not* seeing female characters valorized and rooted for in such roles had an impact on our collective consciousness.

A lack of those types of female parts was what Reese Witherspoon grew up with. She began her acting career as a teenager in 1991, captivating audiences with her performances in *Election*, *Cruel Intentions*, and *Pleasantville*. By the early 2000s, she had become a reliable box-office draw, playing likable young women in romantic comedies including *Legally Blonde* and *Sweet Home Alabama*. But in 2012, after a string of box-office disappointments, she grew frustrated with the shallow, patronizing roles being offered to her. She had fought hard to succeed in Hollywood, playing by the rules and even winning an Oscar for her portrayal of June Carter Cash in *Walk the Line*. But now she realized that she didn't like the game and it wasn't getting any better. She wanted new roles—smart, mature, complex leading roles for an actor like herself. So she began to meet with the heads of the major studios, asking what kind of big projects they had in mind for her. One studio chief suggested that they could simply take a male-led screenplay and just change the gender (that strategy was actually used in the development of the hit Angelina Jolie film *Salt*, which was originally set to star Tom Cruise).

Though Witherspoon may have been the latest actress to approach the issue, she wasn't the first to understand that Hollywood had a problem. A measure of whether a film is dominated by the male gaze is called the Bechdel Test: to pass, a creative work must feature at least two women who have a conversation with each other that is not about a man. The test, which was invented in 1985 by the writer and cartoonist Alison Bechdel, rose to prominence in the 2010s, when the Geena Davis Institute on Gender in Media applied it to hundreds of films. The institute, which the actress founded in 2004 to analyze representations of women, found that fewer than a third of speaking roles in film were played by women and fewer than a quarter of films featured a female protagonist.[21] The exception was found in films written or directed by women—in those films women were more likely to be given substantial dialogue and featured as protagonists. Unfortunately, the sample size was comically small; fewer than 9 percent of all widely released studio films made between 2010 and 2015 had been directed by a woman.[22] In 2015, the institute reported that only 17 percent of top-grossing films had a female lead, while male characters had twice the amount of screen time as female characters and spoke twice as often.[23]

Witherspoon was sick of living in that world. When she turned to her husband, a talent agent, to vent her frustration, he responded that if she let studios create the opportunities for her, she was, by definition, going to be at their mercy. One area of cultural output in which women *were* dominant, he noted, was fiction; according to some surveys, they represent 80 percent of the reading audience.[24] Witherspoon had herself always been a voracious reader, so why not start reading a bit more . . . deliberately? She gave her agents instructions to send her manuscripts of soon-to-be-published books with interesting female protagonists. She optioned nearly a dozen, including a twisty thriller about a frosty, implacable wife who vanishes from her seemingly perfect life. The project, *Gone Girl*, picked up momentum when David Fincher, the most successful thriller director in Hollywood, signed on. For Witherspoon's first film project that she wasn't acting in, she and Fincher cast the British actress Rosamund Pike.

As *Gone Girl* progressed, Witherspoon busied herself with another producing opportunity: she had optioned Cheryl Strayed's memoir, *Wild*, before it was released and became a massive best seller. She cast herself as Strayed, the stripped-down drug addict hoping to find peace and redemption on a grueling hike up the Pacific Crest trail. It ended up being a win-win. *Gone Girl* came out in October 2015 and was a huge hit, grossing nearly $370 million worldwide (Witherspoon's share of the producers' profits made her millions), and Pike was nominated for an Oscar for Best Actress. The lower-budget *Wild* hit theaters two months later, grossing more than $50 million, and earned Witherspoon her first Oscar nomination in nearly a decade, along with a Best Supporting Actress nomination for Laura Dern, who played Strayed's mother. The simultaneous success of the two films Witherspoon produced, which yielded three indelible female roles, demonstrated her entrepreneurial abilities. But the biggest benefits of Witherspoon's exerting control over her destiny were still to come.

In 2015, it was rare for global movie stars to act in TV shows. The theory held that if audiences were accustomed to seeing stars on the small screen, they wouldn't make the effort (or spend the money) to seek them out on a bigger one. Witherspoon, however, was noticing a shift. "I started to see a bigger opportunity," she told me in a 2017 interview at the Milken Institute Global Conference. "Seeing numbers going down for women actually going to the box office, I started really thinking, these women aren't *stopping* watching content, they're seeing it in *different* ways, they're seeing it on Netflix, they're seeing it on HBO." That convinced her to apply her literary approach to TV. She turned to a novel by the Australian author Liane Moriarty, *Big Little Lies*, which followed a group of women in an affluent coastal town trying to hide their secrets. She reassembled her *Wild* team, which included director Jean-Marc Vallée and Laura Dern and enlisted another movie star, Nicole Kidman, and one of the most successful TV showrunners of the last thirty years, David E. Kelley. The package incited a bidding war, and the resulting show—the second season of which included the Oscar winner and Hollywood legend Meryl Streep—was a huge hit for HBO. It was such a game changer for the industry that Richard Lovett, the head of the powerful Creative Artists Agency, reportedly told his agents that every one of CAA's clients should consider any and all TV offers as seriously as they would film.

With three massive successes under her belt, Witherspoon decided to start a business that could systemize and scale the creation of content for, by, and about women. She named it Hello Sunshine and teamed up with the digital media company Otter Media, a joint venture between The Chernin Group and AT&T, as her investment partner to build the company and help with its operations. Otter Media's president, Sarah Harden, became an adviser.

Like Witherspoon, Harden had succeeded in the male-dominated entertainment industry. A native Australian with degrees from the University of Melbourne and Harvard Business School, she rose through the ranks at News Corp and Fox, where she ran a division out of Hong Kong. When her News Corp boss, Peter Chernin, left to form the Chernin Group, she joined him. There she focused on companies at the intersection of media and technology, investing in direct-to-consumer media brands through Otter Media. They targeted rabid fan groups called *microaudiences*. These included the anime platform Crunchyroll and Rooster Teeth, which produces male-skewing video game content. Otter Media's strategy was to build content that was delivered directly to fans through a variety of models, including subscriptions, social media, and events.

When Harden first met Witherspoon over brunch at her house one Sunday morning to talk about what kind of content they would create, Harden saw that she could apply that content and community model to a "macroaudience" of over half the population: women. "We just saw this huge white space," Harden recalled. "I knew the content I love to watch and the content global audiences love to watch as well."

Harden knew that building that type of business from scratch was hard—Crunchyroll and Rooster Teeth had built their brands and communities over many years before being acquired and scaled by Otter Media. But Harden knew that in Witherspoon's stardom, they had a unique opportunity. "I remember leaving that meeting and thinking *You know what, I think this is the one example when you can start from scratch—because you're not starting from scratch*," she recalled. "You've got Reese, she had maybe thirteen or fourteen million followers. And she already had these incredible successes as an actress and producer with *Gone Girl* and *Wild*."

In 2016, Hello Sunshine launched with the backing of Otter Media to produce female-driven content for film, TV, and digital platforms. To build its brand and community, the company launched Reese's Book Club; when Witherspoon recommended a book to her millions of @reesesbookclub followers on Instagram, it often became a best seller. A year after the company launched, Harden became interim CEO while continuing to run Otter Media. Then she moved over to be CEO of Hello Sunshine full-time in 2018. Harden knew from her work with anime and video game sites that between major film and TV projects, Hello Sunshine would need to maintain a regular cadence of interactions to grow the brand's audience. Monthly book recommendations and daily posts on social media provided valuable feedback and enabled millions of fans to have a daily relationship with Witherspoon and Hello Sunshine. "We *have* to structure a media and entertainment company for the next fifteen years of media, not the last fifteen; [we aren't tied to any] legacy infrastructure," says Harden. "We have to be in constant conversation with the audience."

Hello Sunshine could talk to its fans from the moment Reese's Book Club recommended a book through its development into a film or series all the way to its release. "Part of the power is building our audiences—we have the ability to talk to them, and leverage that. We pick a book, and it's pretty much guaranteed a best seller, with debut authors, debut women of color authors," says Harden. And unlike traditional media companies, which typically bring in a social media team after the fact (when it's time to market a show), Hello Sunshine's social media content creators are involved throughout production, so they have a library of photos and videos to give fans the feeling of unfettered access to the sets and the stars. "I can look at the analytics on my phone for Facebook and Instagram and tell you exactly who's watching my Insta stories," said Witherspoon in our 2017 interview. "Each frame of it is trackable. Each frame is data." And the data are a powerful tool that can inform marketing and create hits.

Big Little Lies lit up water-cooler conversations just as the streaming content boom was exploding. Witherspoon's nascent studio became hugely in demand. She was among a handful of celebrities Apple featured at the unveiling of its streaming service in September 2019, promoting Hello Sunshine's *The Morning Show*. In spring 2020, Hulu promoted Hello Sunshine's *Little Fires Everywhere* as a flagship exclusive show, and Amazon Prime Video ordered a limited series, *Daisy Jones & the Six*. All three were based on books Witherspoon had promoted in her book club. While Apple, Amazon, HBO, and Hulu were using Witherspoon and Hello Sunshine to draw audiences, Witherspoon and Harden were using those platforms to promote Hello Sunshine and its brand.

Though Harden and Witherspoon's mission began with a focus on female representation, they soon discovered that broadening that scope would lead to bigger commercial outcomes. They wanted to close what they called the "authorship gap" between consumers' interests and the people who were creating content—not just women but also Black, Latinx, and other underrepresented voices. For two white women, that meant making sure the diversity of characters on-screen was reflected in the team behind the camera. On the Hulu series *Little Fires Everywhere*, based on the novel by Celeste Ng, the actor Kerry Washington was a producer and partner. The company made sure that the composition of the writers' room reflected the experiences depicted in the show from race to class to personal experiences with adoption. "It's not just about representation, it's not enough to have reliably good storytelling that reaches audiences. To make anything good, it's going to need to be authentically authored," Harden said. They continued their approach of highlighting diversity both on-screen and behind the camera with two Apple TV+ series, *Truth Be Told*, starring and executive produced by Octavia Spencer, and *Surface*, starring and co–executive produced by Gugu Mbatha-Raw. For Netflix, Hello Sunshine adapted Tembi Locke's *From Scratch*, a selection of Reese's Book Club, into a series starring Zoe Saldaña and directed by Nzingha Stewart.

That ethos also extends to the way Harden runs Hello Sunshine. Whereas most star-driven Hollywood production companies are designed to showcase and enrich the star, Hello Sunshine more resembles a Silicon Valley startup in that its employees hold equity. That meant its sale to a private equity–backed media company for $900 million in August 2021 benefited everyone who worked at the company. "Now we're just doubling down on our mission," Witherspoon told me in an August 2021 interview on CNBC about the deal. "Now we're going to have the ability to tell more stories, to hire more female filmmakers, to promote and lift up even more authors."

Their success, Harden explained, will show that this kind of content is worth making. "You have to drive the results and the excellence, so you're going to get the next shot and the next shot. We talk about the consequence of economic success; it's not because we want to get rich and make money. If we don't have financial power, we don't have the power to determine our own destiny. Otherwise people just say no. It's hard to reform the system from within. You have to step slightly outside of it and do it, and *then* say 'Fucking look over here.' And you have to do it by economic success. Show, not tell."

The value of Hello Sunshine's content is twofold: economic success proves the value of authentically authored content, driving more investment to creators who are women and people of color. And the variety of content about previously overlooked topics that these creators tackle—sexism, race, class—starts powerful conversations with a social impact.

Hello Sunshine's success is a reminder that, whatever the overt side effects of *Birth of a Nation* or the invisible, insidious side effects of *WarGames*, Hollywood can achieve a monumental positive impact on the culture. Movies such as *Black Panther* and *Wonder Woman*, which centered on two audiences that were considered unable to drive a box-office hit, were massive box-office successes. They disproved the idea that "nontraditional" cultural products—those not produced by a white male creator and not centered on white men—are destined to be "niche."

Changing Culture with Content

Some content creators don't want to have cultural impact be just a side effect of their work but rather the centerpiece. And some don't have the privilege and access associated with being prosperous straight white women. One such creator who has demonstrated the universal appeal of an underrepresented story is Lena Waithe.

Waithe spent the mid-2000s working as a production assistant—coordinating schedules, getting coffee—with only occasional opportunities to share creative input. Already at the bottom of the Hollywood food chain, she was further separated from the ranks of rich kids who could afford to take unpaid internships: she was a queer Black woman who had been raised by a single mother on the south side of Chicago. But she managed to find jobs with Black female creators early in their careers; by 2010, she had worked for the showrunner Mara Brock Akil and the directors Gina Prince-Bythewood and Ava DuVernay. (Prince-Bythewood would go on to become the first Black woman to direct a big-budget superhero movie, *The Old Guard*, and DuVernay would be the first Black woman to direct a $100 million movie, *A Wrinkle in Time*.)

"I didn't have any real access. It was just grit and me in the Columbia College semester in LA program," Waithe said. She impressed her bosses with her work ethic, and, she said, "these women just started to root for me." With that support, she landed a job as a writer and actor on Aziz Ansari's Netflix anthology series *Master of None*. For the show's second season, Waithe cowrote an episode inspired both by her family's Thanksgiving traditions and by her coming out to them. In 2017, at thirty-three years old, she became the first Black woman ever to win an Emmy Award for comedy writing. Onstage she declared, "The things that make us different, those are our superpowers" and gave special acknowledgment to her "L.G.B.T.Q.I.A. family."[25]

The next year, the series she had been working on launched on Showtime: *The Chi*, also based on her youth. She also wrote and produced the hit 2019 film *Queen and Slim* (she gave the director job to the Black woman, Melina Matsoukas, who had directed her Emmy Award–winning *Master of None* episode). She made political statements—and magazine headlines—when she wore a rainbow-colored cape to the

Catholic-themed 2018 Met Gala and was named one of *Time*'s 100 Most Influential People in 2020.

Waithe occupies rarefied air in Hollywood as a creative person whose association with a movie or TV show elicits a certain set of expectations from the audience. A Lena Waithe story will be provocative and formally daring and will not shy away from exposing the outmoded racial shibboleths of contemporary American culture. (A headline in the *Los Angeles Times* about her hit show: "Does Amazon Prime's *Them* Take Its Racist Violence Too Far?") She is aware that focusing on inequity both in her art and in her public profile makes some people uncomfortable, and she sees that as necessary.

"I think after the Emmy it was about 'Okay, I have a platform, and I really want to use it,'" she said. "The industry is a little messed up, the world is messed up. We have systems in place that we have to break down or rebuild on both sides. Who knows how many stories we've missed out on because the industry wasn't open-minded enough or forward thinking enough to allow artists to tell their stories when they see fit?"

To make sure more of those stories had a chance of being created and heard, in 2015 she launched a production company, Hillman Grad Productions (its first production was *The Chi*) to focus on content from underrepresented voices. In 2021, she partnered with the record company Def Jam to do the same in music and with the publisher Zando Projects to create a book imprint.

In 2015, she also made a routine of spending Saturdays having coffee with any young Hollywood aspirant who sought her out. Gradually, she collected mentees and helped them by organizing writers' groups and convening them for special screenings of new movies such as *Crazy Rich Asians* and *The Last Black Man in San Francisco*. "I looked at my experience and thought, *I'd like to help people navigate this a little bit better*," she said. She wanted the next generation of diverse creators to understand the unwritten systems of the industry. "The entertainment industry is like this really weird fraternity/sorority, there are these rules that nobody tells you about," she explained. Insight into what to wear for an interview for a writing job (a Kurt Cobain shirt, not a suit) and how to handle micro-aggressions would help anyone who felt like an outsider navigate a culture that Waithe said is "still very sexist, ageist, obviously very racist, and could also be homophobic and transphobic."

In 2020, she formalized her mentorship efforts through a ten-month-long program in which about twenty-five fellows train, network, and apprentice. The goal, she explained, is to create a pipeline of talent to ensure that Hollywood's leaders can't claim that there aren't sufficient diverse executives to choose from. (As of the end of 2021, the program had more than fifty active network mentees and twenty alumni.) In 2021, she partnered with the job site Indeed to launch "Rising Voices," which gives ten Black, Indigenous, and people of color filmmakers $100,000 each to create short films, mentored along the way by Waithe and her frequent collaborators. The resulting work was screened at the 2021 Tribeca Film Festival.

And so what began as a series of Saturday coffees is now a network that includes hundreds of actors, writers, directors, and producers. "My mission as a mentor is to make sure these artists are empowered and that they tell the story the way they see fit, even if it's a way that I wouldn't do it," Waithe said. "Particularly if you're marginalized and you felt invisible and you felt silenced."

It's not just creators who feel overlooked. Nearly half of Black Americans believe that there is a lack of characters on-screen who reflect an authentic experience for their community. According to a 2018 YouGov survey, 71 percent of Blacks and 62 percent of Hispanics said that Hollywood "would do a better job portraying people like them if they hired directors who've had similar life experiences."[26]

In giving a voice to underrepresented talent, Waithe is serving a massive community. But she's actually doing something even more powerful: she's giving more people with highly varied perspectives and experiences an opportunity to relate and connect. "I'd be out in the world, and a straight white dude would say, 'Oh, [your episode about coming out to your family], that's my favorite episode of TV.' I was genuinely surprised, because how could you possibly relate, it's so specific," she said. "I realized that specificity is our friend. The more specific we are, even though it may not be someone's mirrored image of their story, they can relate to the themes that are always universal. All of us are thinking about being accepted with family or trying to balance romance with career. . . . You watch my story, you realize how much we have in common versus the media always telling us how different we are. That's what art does; it connects all of us." And in giving a platform to those who have historically been excluded, Waithe's Hillman Grad Productions is connecting more people to a more varied array of experiences.

Who creates content and services—as Harden puts it, *authorship*—does matter. A desire to better represent the customers you're serving shouldn't simply be a moral one. What the women in this chapter show is that there is a business case for diversity. Indeed, in 2021, McKinsey & Company measured the loss in revenue to Hollywood studios of not making sufficient content for Black audiences: the systemic bias cost Hollywood $10 billion *per year*. (McKinsey has been busy tallying losses; in the first chapter I referenced the firm's 2016 calculation that the United States could add up to $4.3 trillion in annual GDP in 2025 if women were to attain full gender equity.)

The male-dominated investment banks where Krawcheck worked tended to overlook valuable women customers. The male-dominated online dating industry overlooked women's dating preferences. Male-dominated Hollywood has long placed men—white men in particular—in the center of every frame. And it has cost them all a great deal of money. Female leaders are beginning to unlock some of that value.

Research has shown that among female leaders, Krawcheck, Witherspoon, Waithe, and Wolfe Herd look more like the rule than the exception. Whether on Wall Street, in Hollywood, or on the digital dating scene, women can use the knowledge of the systems that never fully accepted them to change those systems and build new, more equitable ones in their place. In fact, their perspective and resistance to cultural numbness gives them a superpower to identify old problems and create new solutions.

Reese Witherspoon has had access to Hollywood's halls of power since she was even younger than Whitney Wolfe Herd was when she co-founded Tinder. Witherspoon achieved the benchmarks set forth by the traditional male standard of power—leading roles, high-profile connections, an Academy Award—but found a higher level of influence working outside those boundaries. Lena Waithe, similarly, saw an opportunity to broaden the spotlight and create a new, more diverse pipeline to change who has access to power in her industry. Wolfe Herd suffered from the worst parts of internet and dating culture and worked to fix those problems, not just for her own customers but for the whole industry. Sallie Krawcheck saw an opportunity to empower women with the financial opportunity of investing—which opens the door to other opportunities as well.

These women attacked cultural numbness not just to try to change the way their own businesses worked but to challenge their industries to do better. And each one of them authentically authored her product or content; it was her perspective that enabled stories and platforms to serve others like her. When such "reformer" businesses succeed, that should inspire more outsiders—and investors—to find new approaches to established industries.

Six

Embracing Change

Reinventing Retail

"Okay, I see. You think this has nothing to do with you. You go to your closet, and you select, I don't know, that lumpy, loose sweater . . . but what you don't know is that that sweater is not just blue. It's not turquoise. It's not lapis. It's actually cerulean."

Thus begins perhaps one of the greatest "dressing-down" monologues in cinematic history, viciously delivered in *The Devil Wears Prada* by Meryl Streep as Miranda Priestly, the megalomaniacal, lightly fictionalized version of *Vogue*'s Anna Wintour. As her dowdy and innocent assistant, Andy, played by Anne Hathaway, stands in terror and humiliation, Priestly continues her devastating assault:

> You're also blithely unaware of the fact that in 2002, Oscar de la Renta did a collection of cerulean gowns . . . then cerulean quickly shot up in the collections of eight different designers. And then it filtered down

through department stores, and then trickled on down into some tragic Casual Corner where you no doubt fished it out of some clearance bin. However, that blue represents millions of dollars and countless jobs, and it's sort of comical how you think you made a choice that exempts you from the fashion industry when, in fact, you're wearing a sweater that was selected for you by the people in this room from a pile of stuff.[1]

It's one of the movie's best and most memorable scenes—and it's also an insightful explanation of the fashion ecosystem. It's an industry that ostensibly serves female consumers, but recently a wave of female entrepreneurs has identified entrenched problems that need to be fixed.

Here's how the system *has* worked: At the top of the industry's hierarchy sits *haute couture*, the official designation of the most exclusive designer houses that meet the criteria of a French organization, Fédération de la Haute Couture et de la Mode. Their one-of-a-kind items, often made by hand, are worn almost exclusively by rail-thin models at fashion shows in Milan, Paris, or New York, after which the same designers typically adapt the styles for *prêt-à-porter*, or ready-to-wear, collections, which are sold at department stores such as Nordstrom and Neiman Marcus.[2] Designers farther downstream at stores such as Banana Republic borrow elements—military epaulets!—for their lower-priced collections. These influences are seized upon by fast-fashion retailers such as H&M that rush to give customers even cheaper, disposable versions of "haute" looks. At the bottom of the food chain are everyday consumers.

Fashion is not alone in its status as a top-down industry; small groups of executives control everything from Hollywood films to the pricing of airline tickets. But fashion does hold a particular kind of sway over consumers, prodding them to purchase new styles at a cadence it determines. And there is little evidence that its pressure is a force for good. Fashion advertising is still largely populated by impossibly idealized versions of its consumer base (the industry's largely unattainable body standards have drawn appropriate backlash). And sizing at many of the most exclusive brands excludes the more than two-thirds of American women who are a size 14 or larger. (Dolce & Gabbana considers a US size 10 to be a "large.") This bias has proliferated among lower-end retailers, even when it runs counter to their financial incentives: only 7 percent of women's clothing at a retailer that sells multiple brands, such as a department store, would fit this size 14–plus supermajority of women.[3] (It is this cultural prejudice that provokes the line by Emily Blunt's character in *The Devil Wears Prada*: "I'm only one stomach flu away from my goal weight.")

The industry also perpetuates a culture of excess in the way it pressures women to update their closets multiple times a year. This is, in fact, an unexpected byproduct of intellectual property (IP) law. Despite lobbying attempts in the mid–twentieth century to earn designers the kind of IP protection afforded to the media and industrial design industries, clothing designs cannot be copyrighted or trademarked. In "The Piracy Paradox: Innovation and Intellectual Property in Fashion Design," two legal scholars argued that the lack of robust IP rules, by forcing designers to constantly invent new looks, inadvertently fueled innovation in the fashion industry. As they explained, "The absence of protection for creative designs and the regime of free design appropriation speeds diffusion and induces more rapid obsolescence of fashion designs."[4]

The constant demand for new styles, coupled with evolving technology, has enabled retailers to bring designs to market more quickly, creating a stream of new looks and fifty-two microseasons per year. Zara gets deliveries twice a week, and Topshop introduces four hundred styles a week on its website.[5] (This is the problem that Cuyana's cofounders, profiled in the first chapter, have attempted to counter by creating a retail line that is seasonless and trendless—and has fewer products.) Environmentalists have raised concerns about the fashion cycle's massive adverse environmental effects. In 2018, shoppers purchased about five times the amount of clothing as they did in 1980, an average of sixty-eight items a year.[6] On average, each piece is worn seven times before it's tossed.[7]

In this fashion ecosystem, department stores traditionally sat squarely in the middle, bridging the haute and the plebeian by introducing accessible versions of runway styles. But the 2008–2009 recession dealt a blow to many department stores, sending consumers to e-commerce behemoths such as Amazon and discount chains such as T.J.Maxx. By 2015, the situation was described as a "retail apocalypse": the number of people employed by US department stores fell by about half between 2011 and 2020, and more than half of mall-based department stores were projected to close between 2021 and 2025.[8, 9] The pandemic only accelerated this trend, causing record shutdowns and bankruptcy filings of a range of retailers, including Neiman Marcus, J.Crew, and Lord & Taylor.

With all of this fashion infrastructure weakened, a new generation of entrepreneurs has asked: What would a retail business look like if it favored the consumer? What if it efficiently and cost-effectively gave her access to fashions that suit her body and style, without the pressure of the fifty-two-season-a-year fashion hamster wheel? What if the fashion industry cared more about serving Andy than it did about serving Miranda?

In the past fifteen years a number of other industries have faced similar reckonings with the disruptive impact of technology: Netflix and other streamers cannibalized TV ratings, Uber decimated taxis, and Warby Parker changed forever the way people fulfill eyeglass prescriptions. But perhaps no industry has seen such massive disruption as clothing retail, not just in what products are sold but in the entire nature of the consumer's relationship with products.

Access, Not Ownership

Over Thanksgiving of 2008, Jennifer Hyman, a student at Harvard Business School, watched in horror as her sister showed off a $2,000 dress she'd bought to wear to a wedding. Thanks to the rise of social media, she hadn't wanted to post photos of herself in the same dress twice, and the purchase had saddled her with credit card debt. *If only she could have rented that dress*, Hyman thought. She started thinking about more than dress rental: What if her sister had a closet that wasn't static but changed with her size and mood and needs? When she returned to HBS, Hyman shared the idea of offering access to a shared designer closet with her friend and classmate Jennifer Fleiss. A natural way to start serving women like her sister would be by renting dresses for special events; immediately, they got to work.

Hyman sent a cold email to the fashion mogul Diane von Fürstenberg, telling her that she and Fleiss had an idea they thought could help her business. Von Fürstenberg agreed to a meeting (Harvard Business School helps open a lot of doors). The next day the young entrepreneurs put on their DVF dresses, drove into Manhattan, and introduced themselves as the cofounders of Rent the Runway. Von Fürstenberg, charmed by their blend of enthusiasm and hubris, didn't think the idea was an entirely terrible one; she could use help reaching younger consumers. With a vote of confidence from one of the industry's most iconic and respected designers, the two friends started dreaming of renting access to wardrobes as deep and fashionable as those in *Clueless* and *Sex in the City*. What Netflix and Spotify had done to DVD and CD collections, they wanted Rent the Runway to do for women's wardrobes.

That is the creation story—and it's a good one—told by Hyman at conferences and on podcasts. But there are two equally crucial elements of the story that get much less attention.

The first was figuring out consumer demand for the new category. Hyman and Fleiss maxed out their credit cards and used Hyman's sister's Bloomingdale's discount to buy more than a hundred dresses in their sizes at the department store. ("Just in case this whole experiment failed, at least we had spent our money on having a great future wardrobe," Hyman said.) The cofounders also used some of their own dresses and borrowed others from friends. They set up a pop-up shop on Harvard's undergraduate campus in April ahead of a flurry of spring events, including formal dances. They invited members of women's social groups, sports teams, and the

Harvard Undergraduate Women in Business club to browse through the 120 dress options; they closely observed which designers the women wanted, how much they'd pay for them, what kind of styles they'd rent, for what occasions, and the condition the dresses would be in when returned. But there was an indelible moment that day that showed them something the data they were collecting couldn't capture. Hyman remembered, "Two women came into this pop-up together and saw from across the room this Tory Burch silver sequined dress that was all over the tabloids at the time— the Kardashians were wearing it. They ran over to it and in the middle of a room with like a hundred people, one of these girls stripped, put on this dress, and everything about her changed. Her body language changed, her demeanor changed, she started tossing her hair, and she turned to her friend and she said, 'I look *so* hot.'"

Hyman understood then that the company was about far more than dress rental; it was selling transformation and empowerment. Though the service at the time was not dissimilar to the decades-old business of tux rentals, Hyman and Fleiss saw that they could make the experience totally different. They wanted customers to feel that they were getting access to a new world of fashion, without making a commitment that would clog their closets and overload their credit card statements. It was that moment that convinced Hyman, saddled with $100,000 of student debt, to give up a lucrative post-MBA job offer and commit herself to an untested entrepreneurial idea.

The other key element in Rent the Runway's founding was when Hyman took the idea to the gatekeepers squarely in the middle of the fashion food chain: department stores. Long before she secured inventory or built a website, she wanted to address potential roadblocks to the business, and at the time, department stores were the biggest purveyors of special-occasion dresses. "I thought, *If we're renting current-season designer clothing at the exact same time as they're selling it, they're going to see us as competition—and hate us*," Hyman recalled.

She knew from her sister's experience at Bloomingdale's and case studies in business school that brands and retailers were interdependent, and as an outsider and potential disruptor, she ran the risk of not just being excluded but being blackballed. Hyman and Fleiss brainstormed which department store CEO was most important to go to first, and they decided they should start with the ones most focused on luxury. That led Hyman to Jim Gold, who was at the time president of Neiman Marcus and CEO of Bergdorf Goodman—plus, he was an alumnus of Harvard Business School, so she could get his email address. Her goal: to convince him that she was respectful and smart so he would give her a chance. She figured that if she tried to launch the company behind the backs of influencers in the industry, they would tell designers not to work with Rent the Runway and to refuse to sell it inventory, which would be crucial for its operations. But if she was transparent about her goals and he understood her plans, she thought he would fear her company less.

While Hyman worked to interest Gold in her HBS-certified perspective on the retail business, she was surprised by something he told her: that women had been effectively "renting" dresses for decades from his stores, without paying for them. In fact, he said that a significant percentage of the time, when women bought a special-event dress from Neiman Marcus, they would wear it with the tags on and return it after the event. (To him, that behavior was the cost of doing business because the same customer was also buying ten pairs of nonreturnable shoes.) Hyman realized at that moment that the opportunity was even bigger than she had imagined. A version of rental behavior already existed: all those purchases and quick returns showed that there was a demand for Rent the Runway's service. And department stores didn't have to see her as competition, because her service would be competing against what was effectively *theft*.

Soon she made the rounds of all the other major dress retailers: Lord & Taylor, Nordstrom, Saks Fifth Avenue, and Macy's (which is the parent company of Bloomingdale's). She discovered that they all struggled with the issue, especially the higher-end stores. "We thought, *The big guys are not going to shut us down because we're going to be doing something that either they're going to be neutral about or they might actually be positive about.*" She also saw the opportunity to participate in a broader consumer shift: Netflix had introduced the idea of paying for access to a movie and TV library rather than owning content in the form of a DVD or digital file, and in the same way that the music world had transitioned from the Napster era of piracy into the iTunes era of legitimate and convenient music consumption, shoppers might embrace an inexpensive and convenient alternative to stealing.

Those meetings were not just an opportunity for Hyman to forestall potential business adversaries; she was intentionally working to win over key allies and contacts within the industry. Learning from the giants that dominated the industry could help her provide an alternative to it, while creating a network for advice and support. "Starting anything of note in your life, let alone a startup, is just the act of constantly asking for things and for people to give you their time, advice, resources, without really knowing what they're going to get in return," she explained. She wanted to make all those people feel good about giving her their time and insight, so she figured that if she could show them the impact of their conversations, they would feel good about investing time in her. So she spent hours on thoughtful, personalized follow-up: first, she would send them a handwritten thank-you note. Then, every few months, she would reach out and explain how their advice had impacted various parts of her business. The relationships she forged while she was building the business have lasted to this day—some turned into partnerships, such as one with Nordstrom. Her end goal was, of course, to grow her business—but in the process, she also became well liked by many in the industry.

For a female CEO, being likable can be essential to success. In a 2019 study, researchers examined how consumers perceived male and female CEOs in audio advertising. They discovered that if people found a female CEO personally likable, they were more receptive to the message she was delivering. This is, of course, intuitive. What was particularly interesting, however, was that people's reception to a female CEO had nothing to do with how authoritative she seemed; the reaction to her message hinged entirely on her likability. For a man, on the other hand, authoritativeness in his messaging was more important than his likability.[10]

That double standard is a frustrating reality for many women in positions of power. It was a reality that Hyman inadvertently dealt with during her department store relationship-building offensive. Through her efforts, she was able to communicate effectively to department stores and brands that her company would introduce consumers to their labels, replace quick costly returns, and mitigate their flight to the cheaper, lower rungs of fast fashion.

But Rent the Runway wasn't just introducing consumers to new brands; it was introducing them to an entirely new alternative to clothing ownership. For consumers, the Rent the Runway experience was novel enough to turn many of them into ad hoc ambassadors. "There could have been a very different version of the Rent the Runway story if when a customer went to that wedding and she received a compliment on the outfit she was wearing, she said, 'Oh, thanks, I'm wearing Tory Burch.' Instead, she said, 'Thank you! I rented the runway, it's an amazing service, and you should do it, too,'" Hyman said. The service grew organically, with 88 percent of customers acquired through word of mouth.

To maximize the impact of customers' excitement about this new kind of experience, Hyman took her belief in personalized follow-up to customers on the platform. Beginning in 2011, women were invited to post a picture of themselves on the Rent the Runway website in the dress they had rented. The feature would capture the range of shapes and sizes that could feel empowered and attractive in rented dresses and disabuse customers of the concern that they might not fit into a dress typically shown on a waifish model. While getting ready to launch the new function, Hyman had a meeting at a powerful fashion magazine. "This editor said we should *never* do this and that it was a terrible idea and that we would ruin any form of aspiration that we had been trying to create," she recalled. "Of course I walked out and I was like, 'We're doing it.'" Once again, she listened to the perspective of the establishment and used it to craft her approach. But rather than following the editor's advice, that disdain reinforced her commitment to launch something that rejected the industry-controlled aesthetic. "We were trying to say to the industry that there's a new way."

The day the feature launched, it was heralded on *The Today Show*, *Good Morning America*, and the cover of the *New York Times* business section. Women across the internet immediately began uploading photos, and to Hyman's and Fleiss's surprise and delight, they also shared their height, weight, and bra size to ensure that others could determine what would fit them. The fashion editor was wrong; items with user photo reviews were rented more frequently than those without them. Customer photos became a defining feature of Rent the Runway; more than 22 million women have shared reviews. A decade later, retailers from Kate Spade to Target have followed Hyman's lead, inviting consumers to upload their photos. The value of soliciting customer stories has been proven in academic research on marketing. In 2017, MIT's *Sloan Management Review* published a five-year study of the automaker BMW and Japan's Suruga Bank that revealed that stories originating from consumers, rather than corporate messaging, had driven an increase in purchase consideration by about a third.[11]

That loyalty and connection helped Hyman and Fleiss decide where to take the company next. Customers told them how they were using the service beyond special events—women were wearing rented cocktail dresses with black blazers to work presentations—and requested accessories to finish their outfits. In response, Rent the Runway built out its closet in the cloud, adding workwear, casual wear, denim, athleisure, outerwear, and everything from purses, jewelry, and sunglasses to skiwear and home decor. In 2016, the company expanded from one-off rentals to add a subscription offering.

Throughout the company's evolution, Hyman has been in constant communication with her designer partners, sharing customer feedback.

"With traditional retailers, designers only know whether an item sold; they don't know how it fit, how it was styled, who wore it, what it was worn to, how many times it was worn, and what quality the garment is," she explained. Those data revealed not only what was working but also where designers' inventory was lacking: larger sizes. For instance, the designer Tanya Taylor learned that just as many women were renting her smaller selection of size 14–plus clothes as her (much larger) collection in sizes 0 to 12. Rent the Runway's feedback convinced Taylor to extend sizing across her styles for retail as well as rental. Hyman said that the company has pushed more than a hundred different designer brands to produce their clothes in inclusive sizing for the first time.

The Circular Economy

Whereas Rent the Runway provided a rental alternative to retail purchases, The RealReal presents a different alternative: temporary ownership of well-made luxury goods, bought from and sold back into a circular resale economy. The dominant platform for high-end consignment shopping, The RealReal has another legendary retail reinvention origin story. But its founder wasn't a young business school student; she was a veteran CEO.

In 2010, fifty-two-year-old Julie Wainwright was shopping in the prosperous Silicon Valley enclave of Menlo Park with her friend and mentor, another successful woman of a certain age, the venture capitalist Ann Winblad. Wainwright noticed that her *very* wealthy friend was browsing the consignment rack at the back of Head Over Heels, a fancy boutique. When Wainwright asked Winblad why she was buying used when she could clearly afford to buy new, Winblad explained that she valued the taste and selection of the store's owner and trusted that the items were authentic. Wainwright was shocked. "Here's someone who's made her own money, loves beautiful things, but also worked hard for her money and wanted a deal," she recalled. That revelation sparked a new e-commerce consignment concept, which Wainwright launched in February 2011: The RealReal. It would mix the lower end of Christie's and Sotheby's fashion sellers with the higher end of eBay.

The inspiration for The RealReal's concept actually stretched further back—all the way to Wainwright's upbringing in the Midwest. Her parents had met at art school; her mother, who had wanted to be a fashion illustrator, had dropped out to marry her father. She had taught young Julie about design—and how to dress to elongate her petite, barely five-foot, three-inch frame. Her father, who ran an advertising art firm, scavenged junkyards in his free time to transform old church pews into seating and discarded wheels into overhead lighting, teaching her the importance of giving items a second life. Those domestic principles were accompanied by an awakening to environmentalism when, in 1969, nearby Lake Erie became so polluted that it caught on fire.[12]

As was expected of women of Wainwright's generation, she was on track to follow the path of her homemaker mother: she got engaged to her college sweetheart, and as he finished grad school she took a semester off college to support him by working on a Monte Carlo rear-bumper assembly line at a GM plant. But when it was time to send out her stack of wedding invitations, she hesitated. "For my dad every day was exciting, and my mother and her friends were worried about laundry, grocery shopping, and school events. I didn't want to live someone else's life—I wanted to live *my* life, which meant being as independent as possible, and that means independent financially." She broke it off with her fiancé.

She graduated from Purdue in 1979 with a degree in general management and a minor in art and entered the corporate world with a job at Clorox. Despite running the successful launch of the Fresh Step cat litter brand, Wainwright saw the lack of female role models in the industry as a sign that her own potential at the company was limited by her gender. So in the 1980s, she took a series of jobs at software companies, which eventually moved her to London. There she met her husband and traveled frequently to Paris, where for the first time she could afford high fashion. She bought a few pieces of Chanel and Yves Saint Laurent costume jewelry and saved up for one dress by the designer Emanuel Ungaro, which fit her perfectly. The experience was thrilling but also stressful. She still remembers the pang she felt when she bought the Ungaro dress: "I kept thinking *I should save this money*, it was so expensive. It seemed absurd—it still does to some degree—that one garment would be the same as your rent." As time went on, she bought mostly department store brands, but she would carefully select a few high-end pieces every year that she felt were worth the investment because she could see that they were made to last.

She continued on to a successful career in the first internet boom as the CEO of Berkeley Systems, a software company she expanded into interactive entertainment, and of the streaming video service Reel.com, both of which she sold. Then she was hired as CEO of Pets.com, which she led through its IPO at the peak of the dot-com bubble. After the stock market crash, the company couldn't raise the money to continue. In November 2001, the very same day Wainwright realized that she would have to shut down Pets.com, her husband asked for a divorce. As she was the far more successful half of the couple, the divorce would cost her dearly. She took a role at her mentor Ann Winblad's venture capital firm, which placed her as CEO in various companies it had backed.

It was a decade after Pets.com's implosion that Wainwright went on that fateful shopping excursion with Winblad; three months later, she incorporated The RealReal. Six weeks after that, she was driving around in a U-Haul, picking up products from wealthy Silicon Valley women who wanted to clean out their closets. She targeted shoppers who had experience with traditional consignment boutiques and marketed to stylists and professional closet organizers who could spread the word to their clients. For her first and most important hire—chief merchant—she approached Rati Levesque, the owner of a high-end boutique that carried a blend of traditional retail and consignment clothing (Levesque would go on to become COO in 2019 and president in 2021). Six months later, the service launched.

The company's primary competition, Wainwright anticipated, would be the auction goliath eBay. But that platform had a few features that alienated shoppers such as Winblad. The first: at the time, eBay had no way of setting a purchase price, which meant that every transaction required an auction. The second was that buyers, at the time, never knew for sure whether they were getting something authentic or a Canal Street knockoff (it has since launched authentication of certain product categories). And finally, because individual sellers had highly varying ways of photographing clothes, eBay felt more like a chaotic bazaar than an orderly boutique.

To serve as a contrast to that chaos, The RealReal developed a system: a sales team (starting with Levesque and Wainwright herself) would go into people's homes to help them decide what to consign and what to keep. Then that team, which started in the Bay Area and expanded to Los Angeles and New York within nine months, would take or ship the items to the company's warehouse so they could be photographed on a mannequin. "I call it 'keeping the romance, the brand alive,'" Wainwright said. Though every piece being resold on The RealReal no doubt had its own story to tell, unlike Rent the Runway, which relied on a customer's unique experience to make a dress appealing, Wainwright didn't want to include items' histories. "It helps people reenvision the item in a way that's current to themselves." To achieve the boutique's curated feel, the company accepted products only from a list of high-end designers and only in new or slightly worn condition. The RealReal authenticates every piece. If customers questioned the authenticity of an item, the company would take it back to reauthenticate it, offering a refund if the customer was unsatisfied with the results. Finally, it was The RealReal, not the seller, that set the price (the company uses data to set the optimal price for consignors, who can earn up to 85 percent of the sale amount).[13]

The company developed tech-driven systems to maintain the streamlined curation of a boutique while operating on the scale of an e-commerce giant. The company uses artificial intelligence and machine learning to set prices on 80 percent of The RealReal's items; experts make the more complicated pricing calls, such as for vintage or rare items. AI also scans and "reads" the photos, generates written descriptions of 84 percent of items (you can't tell which descriptions were written by humans and which by AI), and detects high-risk consignors who might be trying to pass off a fake. Those data and machine learning algorithms enable the company to process millions of products and prepare them for sale, freeing up the majority of the company's roughly three thousand employees to focus on authenticating the most complex and expensive ones.

In her first year, Wainwright raised some seed funding from individuals and brought in $10 million in sales. The following year, she raised a Series A round of more than $10 million. (The consignment model—consignors aren't paid until their items sell—preempted a common VC concern about costly inventory.)* Wainwright saw an opportunity to use physical stores to make it easier for consignors to drop off products and introduce consumers to the brand; in 2017, The RealReal opened pop-up stores in San Francisco and Las Vegas and a permanent space in New York. Between 2018 and 2020, it opened additional permanent locations in Los Angeles, San Francisco, Chicago, and Palo Alto. By the time the company went public in mid-2019, it had raised more than $350 million and had sold 9.4 million items to the 11.4 million people who had registered to shop on the site or downloaded the app.[14]

The RealReal's customers, it turned out, were not just wealthy shoppers such as Ann Winblad but rather a mix ranging from the very wealthy to students; the majority of its customers are now millennials and Gen Z.

---

*Though she did not have to invest in inventory, Wainwright did experience high costs when it came to acquiring new customers as buyers or sellers. Acquiring each new customer cost an average of $139 in advertising in 2018, the year before the IPO, but that investment had a network effect: consignors provided items, which brought more buyers, and the majority of The RealReal's consignors become buyers themselves and spend more on the site.

"Their first experience with a luxury brand is through us," Wainwright said of these younger shoppers. "They buy from us, but they're also saving their money to buy *one* of the [new] originals, because they see the difference is palpable. The quality and design, there's nothing that compares to a luxury product." The RealReal served as a sort of gateway drug to purchasing high-end products. For that reason, Wainwright figured her low-cost alternative to buying new didn't need to be a threat to designers, so she could partner with them. In 2014, she started calling on some of the most popular brands on her platform, making the argument that by encouraging reselling, they could inspire consumer confidence that their items were high quality and resilient. She didn't get much of a response, but in 2017 it became clear that her innovation was no passing fancy: she was nominated to The Business of Fashion's list of the most influential people shaping the industry, and that year, the company sold $500 million worth of products.[15] As her revenues grew, she continued to reach out to luxury brands; instead of just ignoring her, she says she got the clear message that they wanted The RealReal to disappear.

A rare exception was Stella McCartney, a devoted environmentalist who refuses to use leather or fur. She understood the environmental importance of recirculating goods to keep them out of landfills. In 2018, she became The RealReal's first brand partner, giving $100 in store credit to anyone who consigned a Stella McCartney item.[16, 17] Meanwhile, Wainwright continued exploring the environmental advantages of her system. The company's lead Series C investor, a fund called Double Bottom Line Venture Capital, introduced Wainwright to the Ellen MacArthur Foundation, an environmental organization focused on addressing the estimated $500 billion of value lost annually due to clothing not being utilized or recycled.[18] Wainwright started working with environmental scientists to quantify the impact of recirculating each item; The RealReal now lists the estimated liters of water and kilograms of carbon saved by buying consigned, rather than new, items.

By its calculations, The RealReal has had an enormous positive environmental impact. In selling more than 21 million recirculated items as of the end of 2021, it has saved more than a billion liters of water and nearly 22,000 metric tons of carbon emissions—and drawn young consumers looking for an alternative to the fast-fashion machine.[19] The platform has also helped high-end brands embrace more sustainable practices. After a 2018 exposé revealed that Burberry had burned $37 million worth of inventory to preserve its "exclusivity" and prevent resale of its products, Wainwright says The RealReal called the brand's management team and explained the environmental relevance of the circular economy. Burberry enthusiastically signed on to a partnership with The RealReal: to encourage customers to keep Burberry pieces circulating, it gave customers who consigned its pieces access to a personal shopper at its US stores.[20]

Though Burberry and Stella McCartney were excited to collaborate, others viewed The RealReal as a threat. In 2018, Chanel filed a suit alleging that Wainwright's platform was selling counterfeit bags. The claim (hilariously) pointed to a whopping *seven* bags on the TRR website that it said *might* be counterfeit (Chanel claimed millions of dollars in damages).[21, 22] Wainwright disputed the claim: she says that "Discovery materials have come our way," which she believes show that in fact "they were highly threatened by The RealReal and secondhand market." The RealReal filed a counterclaim, and in April 2021 the two companies agreed to participate in private mediation.[23] After a protracted legal battle, in July 2023 the court granted a stay in the case as Chanel and The RealReal agreed to resolve their issues.

As the company grew to sell $1 billion in merchandise in 2019, other retailers, including Gucci and its parent company, Kering, partnered with The RealReal.[24]* Wainwright took the idea of recirculating goods one

---

*The RealReal has an online shop featuring items from Gucci, which shares a parent company with Stella McCartney, Kering; for each purchase, Kering plants a tree. The company won't share the details, but Kering revealed in 2018 that it is "collaborating actively" with the resale platform, which could explain why the platform is listing multiples from its brands, such as Bottega Veneta dresses and Brioni shoes, new with tags in a range of sizes.

step further in 2021 with ReCollection, a partnership with eight design- ers to "upcycle" items that are too damaged to sell—to transform them into one-of-a-kind designs. She is also lobbying the Biden administration to provide a tax incentive for recirculating goods. "They've already col- lected sales tax on it once," Wainwright says. "There could be something that encourages customers to think, *The government wants me to recircu- late goods*."

Before becoming an advocate for changing shopping habits, Wain- wright had for years been defined in the Silicon Valley community by the Pets.com fiasco on her résumé. But as a careful consumer of fashion, she saw an opportunity to apply the innovations of the first internet wave—to digitize and expand an in-person shopping experience while avoiding the pitfalls of costly inventory. To her new enterprise, she brought a unique perspective that had been forged in failure and revealed by experience. Like Hyman's, it was a perspective that was unconstrained by the expec- tations of the status quo and created an entirely new category of customer. Both Rent the Runway and The RealReal provided broader access to pre- viously inaccessible goods.[*]

In a suit against The RealReal, Chanel claimed, with Miranda Priestly–like imperiousness, that only Chanel can sell Chanel and only people who can afford to buy it new should be able to have it. What Wain- wright and Hyman are doing is redefining the relationship between the fashion industry and its customers. Thanks to the new circular business models of Rent the Runway and The RealReal, fashion customers are less captive to the cadences of the fashion industry and better able to minimize their impact on the environment.

---

[*]Julie Wainwright stepped down as CEO, chairperson, and director of The RealReal in June 2022. In June 2023 she launched her new venture capital-backed startup called Ahara. A personalized nutrition company, Ahara uses AI and machine learn- ing to deliver a personalized nutrition plan based on a user's health history and ge- netic and biomarker test results.

Using Data to Deliver Personalization

There is another elite arena of the fashion industry, one that is also provided by Chanel: the experience of luxury shopping. Those who are wealthy enough to sit near the top of Miranda's fashion pyramid enjoy the convenience of personal relationships with in-store stylists who reach out when new products arrive or independent curators who charge a fee to pick new products from top brands. Stylists were largely the dominion of movie stars and the wealthy—that is, until Katrina Lake came along.

Whereas Jennifer Hyman and Julie Wainwright's moments of entrepreneurial inspiration originated with a dress and in a store, Katrina Lake's came in a less dramatic form: an assignment from her boss. It was 2006, and the twenty-three-year-old Lake was working as a junior consultant at the Parthenon Group. A client had ordered up a "blue-sky" project: imagine what the future of retail could look like, using every kind of high-tech innovation on the horizon. The new assignment had the Stanford economics major's mind spinning. Growing up in Minneapolis (her mother, a Japanese immigrant, was a public school teacher, and her father was a physician), she'd had the obligatory high school summer job at her local Banana Republic store. She remembered how frustrated shoppers had been when they couldn't find the right sizes and how much time it had taken her to find correctly sized items in the stockroom.

Lake could relate to frustrations with sizing: she is five feet, two inches tall, and she could never figure out which "petite" options would flatter her. Luckily, her sister was a fashionista who worked at Emilio Pucci and Elie Tahari. "She would look at the new arrivals of everything and she knew how things fit, so she would say, 'Hey, this new designer is great for short people like us.'"

So when given that assignment, she thought back to her own in-store frustrations, studied the rising technology of the second internet wave, and imagined for her boss a new kind of store experience. "It would not be all these racks and everybody finding their own sizes; it would be almost like a museum that you walk through," Lake recalled. "This was before the iPhone, but the idea was you could wave a wand in front of the things you wanted and the wand would be hooked up to your profile, and then you could show up to a fitting room and it would be, like, 'Welcome,' and it would have all the things you wanted in your sizes, but it would also have all the things that were recommended."

Lake's idea never made it to the client. Her boss considered it too technologically ambitious to be feasible. That galvanized Lake. "I was, like, I actually *don't* think those things are crazy. I actually think that these things *are* possible and people would like this better." She decided to spend the next stage of her career making the idea a reality.

Like Hyman, Lake began by approaching the retail establishment. She applied for corporate jobs at Starbucks and The Gap. But the interview process was dispiriting; the types of projects they said she'd be working on made Lake think that these companies were reluctant to change.

Undeterred, she took her passion to a place she considered hospitable to disruption: venture capital. There, she reasoned, she would at least see a range of companies, and maybe she'd find one she would want to work for. In 2007, she took a job at Leader Ventures, a firm that had invested in Google and a range of software and biotech companies, where she searched for a startup that would give her the chance to build her retail technoutopia. But she continued to be disappointed: among the hundreds of companies she saw, there were none that even remotely seemed to fit with her vision. Still, the very process of reviewing so many startups prompted an epiphany: "I met lots of people who were not qualified to be an entrepreneur," she recalled. "I was, like, 'Okay, well, if all these other people can do it, I can probably do it, too.'"

Lake is passionate, but she is also risk averse. So she continued her attempts to pursue a blue-sky retail idea while maintaining an institutional safety net: the hallowed halls of Harvard Business School (she matriculated in the fall of 2009, three months after Hyman graduated). As she studied the growth of e-commerce, she began to realize that it was the internet, not the brick-and-mortar retail experience, that could bring her idea to life. Ultimately, she wanted to replicate what her sister had given her: a service that would know her sizes and preferences, as well as what was cool and new. Lake believed that *that* would be scalable. "It's just crazy to think about all the manual stuff a personal stylist in a store is doing. A computer could very easily look at your purchase history and very easily recommend sizes."

Stitch Fix launched in 2011 as she was finishing her MBA. "It's really just a matchmaking process," she explained about the combination of data algorithms and human stylists to select and send customers clothes. Consumers pay a $20 fee to receive a box with five items curated based on their profile and styles they've selected from a series of photos. They can tell their stylist specifically what they're looking for from that shipment: a dress to wear to a wedding, a swimsuit for a babymoon. If they keep any of them, the fee goes toward the cost of the item. If they keep all five, they get a discount. At the time, Lake subscribed to a Cambridge community agriculture box, a mix of typical produce and more unusual seasonal items such as persimmons. Inspired by how much she loved the surprise of new fruit, she decided that after collecting lots of information from her customers, the stylists would have the authority to surprise shoppers with unexpected items.

The earliest days of Stitch Fix were quite similar to those of Rent the Runway, and not just because they both took place in the heady atmosphere of Harvard Business School. Like Hyman, Lake ran up a $6,000 credit card bill to test-drive her concept on twenty friends. Word spread fast, and dozens of other women signed up. Lake didn't even have a website, but she used a combination of Google Sheets and SurveyMonkey to cull and organize customer data. She stored inventory in her apartment, and customers paid her via PayPal.

But to turn this lemonade stand into a business, she needed venture capital funding. So during her final semester of business school, she flew out to San Francisco every month to pitch Stitch Fix to investors. About twenty of them turned her down; anything that involved holding inventory ran counter to the Silicon Valley preference for technology platforms over physical assets. But in April, she secured a $750,000 investment from the venture capitalist Steve Anderson at Baseline Ventures, which had been Instagram's first investor, among many other prescient bets. After graduation, she made a permanent move to the West Coast to grow Stitch Fix full-time.

Her first priority was to develop the company's approach to data, starting with the simple but crucial step of noting which items tended to work for which type of customer. Back at her job at Parthenon, she had worked on a case for eBay, where she had noticed that the company's massive amount of data seemed, from her perspective, to be largely unorganized. "Even though I didn't know how the algorithms were going to work, I knew that if I asked you what colors you like and what you don't like, and after you tried a pair of jeans, I asked you what part of them fit and what you didn't like about them—I knew that data *was* going to be valuable." She began by "literally just tagging 'This is good for tall people,' 'This is good for short people'—that's such an easy application of data, and that's the simplest one," she explained. "There are so many ways you can personalize, but even just the notion of personalizing by height would be a dramatically better experience, if I can look at not the millions of things out there, but at the ten thousand things that would actually work for someone who's five foot two."

She also quickly established herself as a magnet for talent. Five months after Lake founded Stitch Fix, the COO of Walmart.com joined the company's ranks, and a few months later, she poached the vice president of algorithms from Netflix. Outsiders were stunned by her recruitment prowess. But Lake just shrugged. She knew that Netflix was great at data science, had searched its executives on LinkedIn, and sent a cold email to its VP. "Part of it, I think, is a little bit of naiveté . . . if I already had a bunch of data scientists, the path of least resistance is to go to the people that you know. I think I had a little bit of an advantage in that

I didn't really know that many people with any relevant experience to what I was doing." What had convinced those executives to come work for Stitch Fix, Lake said, was the appeal of taking a fresh approach to a big problem—and also her humility. "Nobody wants to work for a founder that knows everything."

Though the team and customer base were expanding, in 2013, Stitch Fix was still a negative-cash-flow business. Lake needed to raise more money, so she pitched dozens of VCs. Most of them balked, seeing her need for inventory as an albatross that would ultimately prevent the kind of wild growth needed to entice venture capital (other rejections were less reasoned: they told her that the idea itself was terrible and would never work). In February 2013, Lake finally closed a $4.8 million round, followed by another $12 million later that year. But she ran into an unexpected obstacle when a new investor, Lightspeed Venture Partners, put one of its partners, Justin Caldbeck, onto Stitch Fix's board as an observer. Lake alleges that he sexually harassed her. Caldbeck was accused of sending inappropriate text messages to and groping a number of other women. Caldbeck strongly denied the allegations and then apologized to the women he made uncomfortable. The board agreed to remove him. (Lake signed a nondisparagement agreement.)

The alleged sexual harassment of a founder by an investor is not unique to Lake. Jennifer Hyman reported that an investor, whom she can't name, sent her explicit, harassing text messages. When she didn't reply, the investor complained to the company's board that Hyman had been ignoring his input and questioned her fitness as CEO. Hyman explained to the board what had happened and never worked with the investor again. Such situations are, sadly, quite common. A 2020 study of women startup founders reported that 44 percent of them had been sexually harassed, and 40 percent of those women said they had been harassed by an investor—the majority of them saying that they had been explicitly propositioned for sex in exchange for funding.[25]

Lake can't talk about the incident because of the legal agreement she signed—but it's clear that she didn't allow it to sidetrack her business. She set about easing the prevailing concerns from her investors about the high costs of managing inventory by creating an algorithm to use data in service of a kind of retail Darwinism. The company drew on information about what was resonating with consumers to enable a quick "survival of the best fit." Perhaps the most essential data: the products customers returned and why they had rejected them. All that information is particularly valuable because customer preferences reflect real-world interactions with products—*not* the brand associations created by millions of dollars' worth of marketing. Department store layouts are organized by brand, and even e-commerce platforms encourage people to search by designer. But Stitch Fix has no sorting feature by brand, and its results are surprising. "A lot of the national brands that people know and love, surprisingly, don't perform as well in fixes. There's this great democratization: there might be, like, a small indie brand from LA next to a brand that sells a lot to Macy's that everybody's familiar with. If something is always 30 percent off at Macy's, our price will reflect that," Lake said. "And still we see these national brands not performing as well in our channel as they would in these department stores."

The data can also anticipate how preferences will evolve over time: two years after buying torn jeans, a woman might want nonripped jeans, or the algorithm might pick up on the fact that a shopper who moved to New York was gravitating to edgier styles. "We are able to learn from so many people around you who have similar preferences. We can learn from others around you about what are the *right* risks to take if we're trying to break out of the norm." Getting to know the company's users meant figuring out what would be a delightful surprise, like the persimmon in the produce box. It also helped avoid data-driven feedback loops—sending products similar to what already packed shoppers' closets. For that, the company relies on interactions with its 5,600 stylists and an app called Style Shuffle, which turns picking styles to show your style into a game and helps Stitch Fix figure out items that the customer didn't even know she wanted.

By contrast, a department store doesn't know much about its shoppers. "We've historically turned our inventory something like six times a year [nearly twice the average inventory turn of women's apparel retailers in 2020],[26] and that is because we're able to use the data to buy more of the right products to get to the right people."

Like Rent the Runway, Stitch Fix reshaped the traditional fashion hierarchy by prioritizing customer feedback. It has delivered customer requests to more than a thousand brands. For instance, after hearing the chorus of Stitch Fix customer feedback, the denim maker Paige began producing jeans with a shorter inseam. "We learned pretty quickly that there's no downside to sharing this kind of data with our vendors. Our smartest vendors use it to get better, and then they sell better." And Lake has decided to let the data—and, by extension, the people—win, even if their preferences might horrify her fashionista sister. Even outmoded and much-derided cargo shorts made a comeback on Stitch Fix's platform, Lake recalled, laughing. "It's, like, if they want the cargo shorts, they should buy the cargo shorts."

The data can also reveal preferences that brands and designers might never guess. "There are times when brands tell us, 'Oh, our target customer, she's in her twenties, she goes to music festivals, blah blah blah,'" Lake said. "Then we get the data, and we're, like, 'Your average customer is forty-seven years old, she has a couple of kids, and she does *not* live on the coasts.'" For instance, in the 2010s, a number of brands began to sell a shorts-top one-piece called a romper, designed mostly for twentysomethings. But when a Stitch Fix stylist included a romper in a box destined for a fifty-year-old customer, the algorithm picked up on the customer's positive response (the romper was apparently very flattering), and it became a hit among buyers in that demographic.

By 2014, Stitch Fix was profitable. But the company still struggled to serve plus-sized customers. Though department stores offered plus-size private-label brands and there were lower-cost options at Target, few of Stitch Fix's brands offered larger sizes. The company's selection in the category was so weak that Lake decided to stop offering a plus-size selection entirely. "I'm embarrassed just thinking about it—these big taupe sweaters and leopard print dresses," she recalled. "It was just a totally random assortment." But by 2017, the company had millions of customers—it had launched a men's service the prior year—and was a big enough wholesale buyer of clothes to convince more brands that they had to expand beyond size 12. "People used to say that 'Oh, plus size doesn't sell, plus-size models don't sell clothes, or if someone is plus size wearing your brand, it'll be bad for your brand,'" Lake said. "We've actually been able to prove with the data that that's wrong. We can show that inclusive marketing performs better than noninclusive marketing; showing a wider variety of body sizes actually does better." The company even convinced Karl Lagerfeld, a longtime plus-size hold-out, to launch a line with Stitch Fix in 2018.

In the midst of all that expansion, Stitch Fix went public in November 2018; Lake was the only woman to lead an IPO that year and, at the time, the youngest woman to do so before Bumble CEO Whitney Wolfe Herd took that title in 2021.

The company continued to amass data, and the accuracy of the stylists' boxes continued to improve. The purchase rate—the number of items kept by its customers—continued to increase. The company was also seeing great progress from its private-label brand, Hybrid Designs, which had launched the year before the IPO to address product requests that were not being met by Stitch Fix's regular vendors. Though women's clothing needs and requested price points were nearly fully covered by the existing options (the rare exceptions included an all-season cardigan to wear in air-conditioned offices), the house brand is particularly useful in men's and kids' wear. "In men's and kids' [which launched in 2018], there were a bunch of price points and categories where we were having a hard time finding vendors," said Lake. When consumers couldn't find what they wanted, Stitch Fix created it for them.

When the covid-19 pandemic hit the United States in March 2020, the apparel business was one of the first to suffer, as clothing and accessory stores saw their revenue fall by more than half.[27] Between April and June, due to state restrictions, The RealReal was forced to close its four retail stores and six luxury consignment offices, limit the processing capacity at its warehouses, and furlough some of its workers. Though the company had a flood of supply—economic anxiety and an abundance of free time meant that many consumers were cleaning out their closets and reselling—the number of new items sold in the first full quarter of the pandemic fell by nearly a third. In response, the company slashed its ad spending and replaced experts' in-home visits to pick up and assess items with virtual appointments and curbside pickups.

Rent the Runway, which was oriented toward weddings and office attire, suffered even more acute financial pain. Rentals for special events shrank to nearly zero, and more than half the company's customers paused their subscription. In early March 2020, before New York fully shut down, Hyman started restructuring. She accelerated a plan to close the company's four in-person stores and its pop-up location; by the summer, she slashed costs by over half, and she laid off or furloughed nearly half of her employees. "We were going to be in a fight for survival," she recalled. "We were getting real-time insights of subscribers pausing subscriptions, and it looked like I was making quick decisions, but in reality, we had a month of insights that this is going to be a huge problem." A pandemic-induced fall in demand caused Rent the Runway's lenders to calculate a drop in the value of the company's inventory, so Hyman couldn't borrow more under its existing asset-based loan terms. As a result, she moved quickly to refinance the debt and raise new funds. At the same time, she was negotiating with designers to provide Rent the Runway items on consignment, so the company didn't have to purchase all its inventory.

Stitch Fix, meanwhile, was experiencing a pandemic-induced customer acquisition boom as virtually all shoppers went online. The company continued to grow its revenue and profits, sending its stock price up

134 percent over the course of the year. Shoppers, it seemed, looked forward to their "fixes" during the pandemic, even as clothes buying shifted from office wear and party dresses to comfy sweatpants and Zoom-friendly colorful tops.

But for the entire retail industry, even companies with the advantage of not having to rely on physical stores, the uncertainty caused by the pandemic made planning challenging. In the fall of 2020, Rent the Runway accelerated its plans to discontinue an unlimited subscription that enabled women to swap out any four items at a time. Similarly to Stitch Fix, Rent the Runway made the service completely customizable, with the ability to rent more or fewer items each month and pay by the item. Rent the Runway also took a convenience it had offered customers—the ability to buy an item they had rented—and turned it into a new business line, introducing the ability for anyone to buy any product from the rental cycle at any time (previously only members could buy something they already had at home).

As the pandemic dragged on, Wainwright considered more adaptations, and she witnessed a surprising development: in the fourth quarter of 2020, the darkest period of the pandemic, sales were surprisingly robust, driven by a purchasing shift from clothing to jewelry and handbags, items that buyers knew they would still want well after the pandemic was over. Those items tended to be more expensive, so in July 2020 the average price per item sold jumped by 12 percent from a year earlier. And despite the company's spending less on advertising, both the number of active buyers and the amount of web traffic increased.[28] By December 2020, the total value of merchandise sold outstripped the previous year's prepandemic numbers. To increase inventory, the company expanded its B2B vendor program, which allowed brands to sell anonymously on the platform (a more eco-friendly alternative to Burberry's old tactic of burning excess merchandise).

Wainwright also pursued a counterintuitive pandemic strategy: she increased The RealReal's investment in physical retail space, opening two locations in the latter half of 2020, nine in 2021, plus another in February 2022, for a total of nineteen locations by the time this book went to print. She had learned that a third of all new consignors came from retail locations, and customers who interacted with a retail location consigned more than 1.5 times as much retail value as others and spent more than three times as much as online-only buyers. Customers who entered a store were also far more likely to recommend the company than were online-only shoppers.

The pandemic and its months-long disruption to the company's supply chain did slow the company's path to profitability, but the company said it expects to reach full-year profitability by 2024. The RealReal was part of a growing trend that the pandemic accelerated: in 2020, the investment bank Cowen forecast 25 percent compound annual growth for the resale and rental market through 2028, while the traditional retail market, at best, was expected to show percentage growth in the low single digits.[29]

Stitch Fix also identified an opportunity for growth, in expanding to allow customers to shop algorithm-stylist recommendations directly from the website instead of waiting for the surprise of their boxes. Lake also took the pandemic as an opportunity to encourage customers to buy fewer, better-made things (this is similar to Cuyana's "fewer, better" approach described in chapter 1). "The world of five or ten years ago, where you bought things just because they were ninety percent off and on the sale rack but didn't fit you well, that's not a good model for the planet or for the consumer." Now she wants Stitch Fix to sell people two perfect pairs of jeans (with higher margins) rather than convincing them to buy fifteen pairs at 80 percent off. In fact, she retired from the role of CEO in August 2021, stepping into an executive chair position, saying that the move was so she could focus on the service's sustainability efforts.

Hyman insists that her company emerged from the pandemic stronger—when demand was lower, it rolled out improvements to machine learning and RFID technologies to expand the use of automation in its fulfillment centers. Then, in October 2021, she took the company public via an IPO. But she wishes she hadn't had to make so many cuts to her employee base early in the pandemic. "I would have loved to pay all of our employees who we laid off six months of severance. We literally did not have the capital to do that," she said. Like Lake, she said she doesn't have access to as much capital as comparable male founders do. "Airbnb obviously saw a dramatic negative impact from covid but had so much more capital in the bank, they were able to wait a longer period of time before they made layoff or furlough decisions; they were able to be far more generous as it related to severance packages." Hyman said of the long-tail impact of women's limited fundraising, "When women do raise 2 percent of dollars, they're raising lower check sizes, which gives them less opportunities to make mistakes, less opportunities to fail, less opportunities in the height of a global pandemic to have even one week more breathing room."

Lake agrees. It was her struggle to raise money that drove her to achieve profitability just three years after Stitch Fix's launch. "I get credit for making so much with so little, and to be clear it was never my intention to be 'capital light.' It was never my intention to be famous for building a company with not much money. I would have happily built a big company with a lot of money, but that was not a path that was available to me." Though resource constraints can put a company at risk of going out of business faster when crisis strikes—that was the risk Hyman faced during the pandemic—for Lake, capital constraints made her company stronger.

These companies may in fact be stronger for the fact that their leaders would never have been part of the Miranda Priestly establishment. Hyman recalled meeting with a famous designer and his team in 2010; later that day, the brand's president called and told her to get her nails done; the polish was chipped. She remembered him telling her "No one's ever going to work with you, we're not going to work with you, you can't present yourself that way." Hyman was gobsmacked that someone who ran such a big business would be distracted by something as petty as her nails. She saw that she would never fit into his world, and it fueled her determination to create an alternative one. Lake agrees: it was industry insiders who were most convinced that her idea would fail.

The industry may have been condescending and snobby to Hyman, critical of Lake, and dismissive of Wainwright (at least until The RealReal produced half a billion dollars in sales), but the fashion industry still produces beautiful, valuable things that give joy to the wearers. And these three CEOs—and surely others to come—are helping women everywhere access those things, and on their own terms.

Together, Julie Wainwright, Katrina Lake, and Jennifer Hyman have done more to challenge the fashion industry status quo than any other three entrepreneurs, male or female. They're also unique in the broader entrepreneurial landscape; they are three of the less than two dozen female founder-CEOs who have taken their companies public in the history of the public markets. The fact that there's more of an entrepreneurial critical mass of women in retail than in other industries, such as enterprise software or biotech, is not a coincidence. The data (discussed more in chapters 8 and 9) show that VCs are more likely to agree to support women in industries considered more "feminine."

There's also a theory of what happens when the number of underrepresented people hits a certain threshold; it's called *critical mass theory*. It's the idea that when a historically underrepresented group reaches a "considerable minority"—somewhere between 20 and 30 percent—there is the opportunity for social movements to accomplish real change.[30] This concept is frequently cited in the context of political representation—the idea that women can't have a meaningful impact on legislation until they grow from a few token individuals into a considerable minority.[31] For instance, it was only once female representation reached 20 percent of the Senate that women demanded that the Pentagon reform the military's sexual assault protocol. The navy arrived at critical mass when it was required to integrate its ships following a 1978 court decision—after trying various approaches, it now requires all ships to have at least 20 percent women on board.[32] Researchers have found that when there is a critical mass of women—three or more—on a board, they can cause a fundamental change in the boardroom and impact corporate governance.[33]

The critical mass of powerful women in the retail space has had a meaningful impact: it has created value, it has benefited the environment, and, in the eyes of the VC community, it has remade the stock image of the entrepreneur. And when it comes to establishing new patterns, these women defy the norm not just in terms of gender but in terms of age, race, and parenthood. Wainwright was sixty-two years old at the time of The RealReal's IPO, and the Japanese American Lake was thirty-four years old when she and her fourteen-month-old son rang the Nasdaq's opening bell for Stitch Fix's first trade. This variety of role models is part of a wave of female retail entrepreneurs, including the CEOs of Everybody World, which sells recycled cotton, gender-neutral apparel, jewelry startup Mejuri, the bra company ThirdLove, and the size-inclusive brand Universal Standard. It may also inspire the next generation of founders, as well as venture capital investors to look for not just the next Mark Zuckerberg but also the next Katrina Lake.

Imagine if other industries had the same critical mass of female entrepreneurs disrupting the status quo. What else would shift?

Seven

Managing in Crisis

Acting Quickly, Without Ego

On February 25, 2020, Caryn Seidman-Becker, the CEO of Clear, the subscription travel company that uses biometrics to verify travelers' identities, was on an Amtrak train speeding from Manhattan to Washington, DC, when she received a panicked call. A physician friend warned her about the novel coronavirus's growing spread beyond Italy and China: "This is very real, and you guys need to pay attention to it," she remembered him saying. Seidman-Becker's business would be especially vulnerable to the impact of the fast-spreading pathogen, and living and working in high-rise buildings in Manhattan, she and her family would also be at risk. From her phone, she tapped out a grocery order to pack the fridge for her three kids—"I'm a Jewish girl. I needed to stock up on food! My husband thinks I'm nuts because I'm totally neurotic." And she watched the stock market plummet 3 percent.

Then she took the most decisive action of her tenure at Clear:

she canceled the company's entire 2020 media spend—roughly $24 million. "You control what you can control," she said. By the time the train arrived in DC's Union Station, she and her partner had sketched out financial models to manage their costs if air travel stopped entirely and all customers paused their subscriptions. *That* was the worst-case scenario. She disembarked with a plan to keep her employees and travelers safe and to prevent her company, which was backed by venture capital investors and far from profitable, from imploding.

Canceling the media spend was a swift action, but it was not impulsive. In fact, it illustrated a decisiveness that's essential for successful leaders, as revealed in a ten-year study examining what differentiates high-performing CEOs. The key finding in the 2017 CEO Genome Project report: "High-performing CEOs do not necessarily stand out for making great decisions all the time; rather they stand out for being more decisive. They make decisions earlier, faster, and with greater conviction. They do so consistently—even amid ambiguity, with incomplete information, and in unfamiliar domains." People described as decisive were twelve times more likely to be high-performing CEOs. In contrast, smart but slow decision makers could create bottlenecks, causing teams to become frustrated or themselves to be overcautious.[1]

Quick, smart decision making is, of course, particularly essential in times of crisis. Several academic studies, including one from UC Davis cognitive neuroscientist Mara Mather, have found that when subjected to stress, men become more eager to take risks, whereas women take a more practical approach.[2] Three researchers at Utrecht University in the Netherlands found that in stressful situations, when heart rates and cortisol levels run high, men pay less attention to the higher risk of losses and make bigger gambles for rewards than they typically would; women in stressful situations pursue smaller wins that are more attainable and have less downside.[3] This is, to some extent, hormonal, according to studies conducted at Caltech, the Wharton School of the University of

Pennsylvania, Western University, and ZRT Laboratory. Men's high testosterone level makes them less likely to question their impulses, more
likely to rely on intuitive judgment in decision making, and more likely to
think they're right even when they're wrong.[4]

Women, on the other hand, have been found to be more likely to
prepare for the worst because they're typically less overconfident than
men, a behavior closely examined in a study by professors at universities in Vienna and Singapore. Looking at confidence levels in CEOs' first
three years across eight hundred firms, they found that exaggerated self-
confidence often stood in the way of rational decisions. Overconfident
CEOs assessed their financial situations more optimistically than their
colleagues did and reacted less to external and internal feedback. Male
CEOs scored higher on typical measures of CEO confidence, whereas female leaders were found to be more accurate in assessing their own abilities and were much more sensitive to various types of feedback.[5] There's
also evidence that when faced with negative news and in anticipation of
negative outcomes, women respond more decisively than men do.[6]

———————

During the spring of 2020, the shock of the covid-19 pandemic caused
countries around the globe to participate in an entirely new kind of experiment. The stakes were life and death. Events were canceled, stores
and restaurants were closed, and people all around the world were stuck
in their homes, grimly watching and waiting for what might happen next.

Though it had received very little public attention at the time, a
group of experts had tried to anticipate this global catastrophe. In October 2019, mere weeks before a spiky new pathogen would make the leap
to humans in China, the Global Health Security Index, funded by the
Bill & Melinda Gates Foundation, Johns Hopkins University, and others, released an exhaustive and alarming report about the global state of
pandemic preparedness.[7] The group was run by Sam Nunn, the retired
twenty-five-year US senator from Georgia, where the Centers for Disease
Control and Prevention is located. In some ways, the study was eerily

prescient, concluding that given global migration patterns, urbanization, and climate change, most countries were woefully ill prepared to fight a pathogen.

To convey that "wake-up call" more concretely, the report issued a rating for each country's individual vulnerability to a possible pandemic. The rating system assigned particular value to the wealth of each country, figuring (correctly) that countering a pandemic would be resource-intensive. The system also assumed that strong security protocols would be key. A color-coded map accompanied the data, with cheery yellow countries predicted to perform best and ominous red indicating those forecast to perform worst.

With the hindsight of 2022, the map looks like an inverse image of the actual pandemic outcomes. The United States had the best rating. The United Kingdom was number two, as its status as an island gave it a special ability to interrupt migration. Meanwhile, the island nation of New Zealand was assigned a middling orange color (the study's authors fretted over its weak biosecurity measures and the paucity of its health care workforce).

The rest, of course, is history.

As it turned out, all of those indicators were much less predictive than one single indicator that the researchers left out of the study entirely: the gender of each country's leader.

New Zealand, under the leadership of President Jacinda Ardern, lost only *five* people per million in the year following March 11, 2020, when the World Health Organization's director general qualified covid-19 as a pandemic. The United Kingdom, on the other hand, lost 1,845 per million and the United States 1,599 per million. The gender advantage extended beyond those two island countries. As of March 11, 2021, Sweden, with a male leader, had 1,298 covid-related deaths per million, while its neighboring three countries, led by women, had lost just a fraction of that: Denmark had 411 deaths per million, Finland 140, and Norway 117. Germany, with a female leader, had 872 deaths per million, far less than the losses of three nearby countries with male leaders: Spain (1,541 per million), France (1,369 per million), and Italy (1,673 per million).[8]*

For its part, the media took note of the apparent disparities in outcomes between female- and male-led countries.[9] Some posited that the tendency for male leaders to project strength and invulnerability was actually more dangerous when it came to fighting a communicable disease.[10] Others argued that pandemic outcomes actually didn't demonstrate the efficacy of female leadership but rather shined a spotlight on the outsized, terrible negative results achieved by autocratic leaders (in Brazil and Russia) and leaders with autocratic ambitions (in the United States).[11]

The various factors at play invited investigation by two British professors; they studied how 194 countries, with nineteen female leaders among them, had navigated the first three critical months of the pandemic. Controlling for all other factors, such as population and wealth, and those related to national policies, such as the amount of money spent on health care per capita, had the presence of a female leader rather than a male one led to better outcomes? If so, what specific measures had the female leaders adopted that could explain their success?

Ultimately, they found that the female-led nations had performed meaningfully better in terms of the number of covid deaths because their leaders had shut down their countries more quickly (after fewer deaths). It was a result that UC Davis cognitive neuroscientist Mara Mather, who studied how men are more eager to take risks when under stress, likely would have predicted. The female leaders seemed less willing to risk lives, the researchers explained, but had been more willing to risk fallout from locking their economies down. The economic consequences were indeed cataclysmic and immediate—the United States alone lost

---

*These numbers were given to the author by the Kaiser Family Foundation, which provides a global tracker at https://www.kff.org/coronavirus-covid-19/issue-brief/global-covid-19-tracker/ populated with data from the Johns Hopkins University Coronavirus Resource Center, the United Nations World Population Prospects, and other sources.

30 million jobs in a matter of weeks—while the potential death toll at the time was still unknown.* Yet when presented with the choice between saving their economies now and saving lives in the future, female leaders tended to the latter.

These findings are echoed and underscored by separate studies of US states' responses. Because the Trump administration relied on individual states to institute their own policies, academics had a similar natural field of study. Sure enough, in the critical month of April 2020, female governors tended to move more quickly to issue stay-at-home orders than male governors did. The researchers also discovered a remarkable quirk: even female governors who issued the same stay-at-home orders at the same time as their male counterparts had better outcomes. That, they discovered, was the result of the different ways their messages were conveyed. Analysis of 1.2 million words spoken at covid-related briefings found that women governors showed both more empathy and more confidence.[12] Their confidence was expressed by acknowledging all the hard work done by *others*, rather than the power or force of will exhibited by the leader herself. When citizens heard leaders communicating that way, they were much more likely to follow their guidance.[13]

A March 24 Facebook Live stream by New Zealand's Ardern was a master class in this type of empathic confidence: leaning in to a webcam wearing a rumpled sweatshirt (she had just put her toddler to bed), she calmly explained to her citizens how the lockdowns would work. Then she apologized for the startling tone of the emergency alert that had appeared on Kiwis' phones earlier that day.[14] It was an incredible double act: on the one hand, she was a relatable mom struggling with a young child in quarantine; on the other, she was calmly and confidently explaining how her country's citizens could make it through the harrowing trial together.

---

*In the six weeks following the initial pandemic lockdowns, the United States lost a total of 30 million jobs, compared to the 8 million jobs lost in the entire eight years following the 2008 recession.

She was not just yelling through a megaphone; she was serving as a mirror and providing a model.

The relative success of female leaders in crisis extends beyond politics and public health. Jack Zenger and Joseph Folkman, the CEO and president of the leadership development agency Zenger Folkman, wanted to see if women in business demonstrated the same leadership advantage as heads of state do. They had a baseline to compare to pandemic responses, because in 2019, they had conducted a sweeping assessment of more than sixty thousand leaders; women had generally rated more highly. So between March and June 2020, they asked the same survey questions of more than eight hundred leaders, both male and female. Again, women were rated as more effective in thirteen of the nineteen competencies, such as "takes initiative" and "learning agility." But most notably, the gap between men and women widened after the onset of the pandemic. The results also revealed that employees with women bosses had higher levels of engagement. Those employees cited communication, collaboration, and inspiration as the most important traits in their bosses' leadership styles, all categories in which women rated higher.[15]

It wasn't the first time a crisis has revealed the strengths of female leadership. A survey of eight hundred business leaders conducted by McKinsey & Co in the aftermath of the 2008 financial crisis showed that women performed better in three areas that improve organizational performance: people development, role modeling, and participative decision making.[16] A separate study of commercial banks during the crisis found that smaller banks with female CEOs and female board chairs were less likely to fail; they tended to assess risks more conservatively and as a result held more capital reserves.[17] Before the financial crisis there had been few studies about the impact of leaders' gender on a crisis, in large part because there had historically been so few female leaders; the data set had been too small.

Society's view of crisis leadership has generally been colored by the historian Thomas Carlyle's "Great Man" Theory: namely, that the decisions of a small number of *sui generis* powerful male leaders, such as Abraham Lincoln, Winston Churchill, and Franklin D. Roosevelt, have had sweeping historical consequences. The theory has been highly disputed by subsequent historians, but one can understand why it seems valid, especially when the crises are highly delineated (as in one nation versus another nation) and highly dramatic (e.g., the total warfare of the twentieth century).[18] What the above studies show, however, is that when crises are the result of highly distributed social forces—such as a financial crisis that impacted the entire US real estate market or a pathogen that spread globally—Great Women tend to be the more effective leaders.

Michelle Nunn, the president and CEO of CARE USA since 2015, knew what to do when there was an acute crisis such as an earthquake or a flood. The organization's focus on fighting poverty and empowering women and girls had prepared its more than six thousand workers around the world for every possible type of humanitarian response. The largest and founding member of CARE International's fourteen member organizations, CARE USA oversaw projects and teams in sixty-nine different countries and had a playbook for crises that reached across entire continents, such as a famine or an Ebola epidemic.

"We had no playbook for what to do for a global pandemic," said Nunn, who wears small rimless glasses and her curly hair in a short, practical bob. It was the first time the global organization had had every one of its teams around the world fighting an entirely new emergency, each country grappling with unique circumstances. It was impossible to create a unified plan. "It's very different in Burundi than it is in Sri Lanka, with different time zones, different needs, and different governmental approaches and regulations," Nunn explained of the struggle. "All of a sudden we're all in our homes, and not sure where the resources are going to come from to help with this." And because of the exponential nature of the pathogen's spread, CARE needed to respond to every country's crisis immediately.

Nunn's path to the role of CEO of CARE USA originated in a filial commitment to public service. She grew up near the small town in Georgia where her grandfather had been mayor and moved to Washington, DC, when her father, Sam Nunn, started his twenty-five-year career as a well-liked Democratic senator (the same one who coincidentally helped run the 2019 evaluation of pandemic readiness). After college she cofounded an Atlanta-based nonprofit dedicated to engaging people in volunteer activities, built it into a national network, and then merged it with another nonprofit, Points of Light, to create the world's largest organization dedicated to volunteer service. When a Georgia Senate seat opened up, Nunn saw an opportunity to follow in her father's footsteps, and she ran a high-profile campaign. It was a painful experience for the self-described introvert. "I was not hungry for conflict or criticism or public humiliation or public repudiation or public failure," she said. She lost the race.

After the defeat, she spent a few months at home with her two kids before an executive search firm placed her in the role of running CARE USA. The nonprofit was founded in the wake of World War II by a group of American charities seeking to distribute surplus US Army ration packages of food and critical supplies in Europe. CARE expanded to a number of Asian countries, and its mission evolved beyond food distribution to offering more comprehensive help in the developing world. In the 1960s, it expanded to Latin America and then to Africa.

In the early 1980s, an analysis of CARE's impact revealed that investing in women had a multiplier effect on their families and achieved the most dramatic results for a nation's economic and public health outcomes. In response, the organization shifted its resources to focus on improving women's sociopolitical status and encouraging their participation in economic opportunities. CARE runs training programs for everything from how to make money cultivating silkworms and weaving mats to how to get involved in local politics. This strategy has been especially effective at blunting the impact of crises, as women are often the last to eat and subjected to violence, while also expected to be caregivers.

For years, CARE USA had taken the information and used it to its—and women's—advantage. But the 2020 pandemic, Nunn realized, was unlike anything the organization could have prepared to combat. With economic and social opportunities vanishing overnight, women once again were disproportionately impacted: they were nearly twice as likely to lose their jobs and more likely to sacrifice their careers to oversee child care and home education.[19]* That's not all: in April 2020, the United Nations called attention to a "horrifying surge in domestic violence" since the start of the pandemic.[20] As Nunn saw food shortages spreading, she realized that women would likely go hungry first and be responsible for managing the health and well-being of their immediate family and older relatives as well. She was terrified.

Decentralized Decision Making

She wasn't the only nonprofit leader to feel that way. In early March 2020, Claire Babineaux-Fontenot, the CEO of Feeding America, flew from the organization's headquarters in Chicago to her home in Dallas. There, with her husband, grown children, and niece, she watched a TV news report about growing covid-19 fears, which featured a video of shoppers rushing to pull food off supermarket shelves. Anxiously, she changed the channel and changed it again. National and local news all showed the same thing: scared people hoarding food and overrun grocery stores struggling to keep up.

Babineaux-Fontenot was fifty-six at the time and a typically calm and optimistic presence—the kind of person who wears a warm, empathetic smile even when describing her organization's darkest moments. But with

---

*Using data and trends from unemployment surveys in the United States and India, where gender-disaggregated data are available, CARE estimated that female job loss rates due to covid-19 were about 1.8 times as high as male job loss rates globally, at 5.7 percent and 3.1 percent, respectively.

her family pulled tight to her, watching those images, even she lost her easy smile. Immediately, she understood the consequences that panicked behavior would have on her work. Feeding America, which she had led since October 2018, is a nationwide network of two hundred food banks and sixty thousand partner agencies such as soup kitchens and homeless shelters. It's the largest domestic hunger relief nonprofit in the country and the second largest nonprofit overall, behind United Way. "The number one source of food for our network had historically been grocery stores," she said with her long Louisianan vowels. "If retailers don't have enough food to sell to their customers, it follows that they're not going to be able to provide donated food to the charitable food system." When the stock market had plummeted in February, she had already been worried about the slowing of financial donations. But now she saw the source of her physical donations drying up. And she feared that things would only get worse.

So on March 13, Feeding America announced the creation of the COVID-19 Response Fund to help its member banks get the resources and food they needed. Within days, another problem came into focus: the supply chain had broken down nearly completely. Because of the run on grocery stores, the food banks in the organization's network were suddenly competing with retailers—who had previously supplied *them* with excess food. The organization's weekly food purchasing costs went from $50,000 to $500,000, and even when it was able to find donated food, its distribution protocols had to be overhauled to minimize physical contact.[21] Before the pandemic, the organization's food banks had relied on nearly 2 million volunteers per month, but in-person volunteering became a life-or-death proposition, and more than two-thirds of food banks reported needing volunteers. It was a peril that some key volunteers chose to take. "People made the conscious decision, knowing there were risks, that in spite of those risks we were going to find a way because people *needed* so desperately," Babineaux-Fontenot recalled.

As stay-at-home orders were implemented, the images of empty grocery stores perversely contrasted with images of truckers pouring milk away and farmers slaughtering livestock. Farmers had been prepared to sell their food to schools or restaurants, and when those closed, "providing that food to supply the charitable food system was not as easy as it might have seemed to the public," Babineaux-Fontenot explained. "There was a desperate need for protein, for dairy. There *was* dairy out there, but it was not in a form that can be consumed by the people who were turning to us."

Babineaux-Fontenot endeavored to get a special view of the magnitude of the calamity: instead of the organization's typical quarterly survey about the number of pounds of food distributed and inventory trends, it initiated biweekly surveys. It asked how many new "neighbors"—that's what the organization calls people it helps—had never needed food assistance before. And it polled the food banks to learn how long each could operate without running out of food (for some, the food supply dipped perilously close to two weeks' worth). "They *never* close down—part of what was remarkable about our work is that most of our food banks, once they open, they *never* shut down, no matter what happens. During natural disasters, even if the banks are in buildings that get hit, they find a way to get food to people in need.

"Because of my unique family story," Babineaux-Fontenot continued, "I had awareness as young as I can remember anything—I knew there's hunger in America." She grew up in a rural community in Opelousas, in south-central Louisiana; all four of her grandparents were sharecroppers, and neither parent graduated from high school. Her mother was pregnant with Claire in 1963 when she heard of two little kids in a neighboring town who were suffering from neglect and abuse. "My dad wasn't even home, but she heard that those babies needed help, and she just went and got them," Babineaux-Fontenot said. She described her mother as being compulsive about helping people in need: she would see people walking around town who seemed to need food and would take them a sandwich or invite them for a meal. Those two adopted siblings were the first of the

107 brothers and sisters her parents adopted, fostered, or had themselves over the course of four decades. "My little brothers and sisters, I remembered visible signs of malnutrition on the frail bodies of children," she said, remembering the long-term physical and mental health challenges that were the result of early deficits.

At one point, the young Claire Babineaux was living at home with fifteen siblings. "Everyone helped out. We'd go out and pick cotton and dig sweet potatoes," she remembered. The family maintained a garden that everyone would help till and plant, and they raised cattle they grazed around the neighborhood and occasionally a pig they fed on kitchen scraps. No food was wasted. As her parents took on more foster children, they also started helping an organization called America's Second Harvest distribute food in their Louisiana community. Her parents expressed empathy with such consistency, she said, that "It's always been a part of my upbringing, this idea that you don't look past people in need."

Empathy, as a key part of emotional intelligence, has been called "the *sine qua non* of all social effectiveness in working life" by organizational behavior researchers. The need for this leadership characteristic was amplified during the pandemic: six months in, a survey of 3,900 employees and business leaders in eleven nations found that nearly a third of employees said they wished their organizations would act with more empathy.[22] That characteristic is more frequently found in women: they are 45 percent more likely than men to be seen as demonstrating empathy consistently, according to a Korn Ferry study.[23] As discussed in chapter 3, numerous studies have found that women have what professors call an "empathy advantage," outperforming men in a range of behavioral and cognitive measures of empathy, including an ability to respond to others' distress and infer what people might be thinking or intending.[24]

Babineaux-Fontenot was the first in her family to go to college; then came law and master's degrees. She leveraged her study of tax law into work for the state, a tax practice at a major law firm, and then a job at Walmart, where she rose to the position of executive vice president and global treasurer. As she climbed the corporate ladder, she also took on roles at philanthropic organizations, serving on the boards of the Thurgood Marshall College Fund and Court Appointed Special Advocates (CASA). She was living with her attorney husband and their two kids near Walmart's headquarters in Arkansas and managing the finances of the largest company in the world, based on revenue—the embodiment of the American dream. Then in 2015, during her annual physical, the then-fifty-one-year-old was diagnosed with Stage 1 breast cancer. Within days she'd met with a surgeon, and within weeks the cancer was removed. It was caught early enough that her prognosis was good, and she went into remission. But as she returned to work and thought about all the women whose cancer *wasn't* caught so early, she thought, *I don't want an executive job to be my last professional contribution.*

She left Walmart and started working with national cancer nonprofits before taking the top job at Feeding America. After she became CEO, she realized that a decade earlier the organization had been renamed from America's Second Harvest—it was the same Louisiana food bank her parents had worked with to distribute food to their community. "When I first started and would have conversations with people about the work, I would apologize for not starting in this work sooner," she said.

During the pandemic, as she received the results of Feeding America's rapid surveys, her empathy went into overdrive—her make-it-work approach was going to be needed more than ever. Ninety-two percent of food banks reported a spike in demand for food assistance between March 19 and 23. She recalled how one food bank worker "was brought to tears . . . because they were so accustomed to serving *their* community, and they were turning people away that they knew. They knew that this grandmother has never come to them for help before . . . and she now has four grandkids living with her and that she's there out of desperation, that she had to swallow her pride to be there and they can't give her anything." As a woman whose upbringing was a miracle of drive and persistence, whose parents had somehow managed to feed 107 kids, she saw she needed to help her organization do something just as impossible. Feeding America would have to help many more people than the 40 million food insecure it had helped in 2019. The question was: How?

Michelle Nunn was facing a similar crisis in deciding how to deploy CARE's resources. The organization operates directly—deploying aid and running programs—in sixty-nine countries but had never deployed meaningful financial resources in the United States. The pandemic resulted in such acute and enormous needs close to home; at a virtual CARE board meeting, the organization was faced with a big decision: whether to respond to needs in the United States—and directly deploy aid at scale in the country—for the first time in its history. The move was controversial, raising concerns that domestic work could jeopardize CARE's international focus and impact. But faced with data about frontline health care workers being unable to pay their bills and rising levels of hunger and poverty, Nunn and her fellow board members decided that they *had* to act in the United States immediately. "It was the threshold of need within the US," Nunn said. Over the course of a weekend a small group devised a plan to deliver a new version of a CARE package of cash cards for frontline workers and a program to deliver meals to the hungry. They also decided to start running rapid surveys in all the other countries where they operated to better understand the impact of the pandemic on women and girls around the world. As they awaited responses, they moved quickly to follow global guidelines and invest in hygiene, building water stations and handing out kits including soap and sanitizer.

When the surveys came back, they contained a resounding rebuke: "We can't eat soap, we need food." Women in Mali said they had only two days' worth of food and couldn't get to the market. The only way they could earn money to buy food was by selling things, which they couldn't do, either. They were desperately hungry, and they had nowhere to go and no way to make money. One member of a West African savings and loan program said that her migrant-worker husband, isolated at home because of covid, had only two things to do now: beat her and rape her.

Nunn and the CARE team were surprised that their initial efforts had let down the people they were trying to help. They knew they needed to pivot. Nunn had learned during her Senate race how to acknowledge defeat and keep innovating. "Once you've given your concession speech, it's not going to get more public in terms of failure than that, so it equips you to take more risks," she said, remembering how difficult it had been to have people literally throw food at her during a debate at a public fairground. "You learn you can move through failure."

In fact, a 2019 study by researchers at Northwestern University's Kellogg School of Management found that early failure can actually drive later success. They examined the careers of scientists who had narrowly missed winning an important grant from the National Institutes of Health early in their careers and found that those scientists had ended up publishing more successful papers than those who had won the early honor. They investigated whether perhaps failing had weeded out the weaker scientists, leaving only high performers to keep toiling away. Instead, they found that the failure itself had pushed the rejected scientists to work harder—the very same pattern that played out with Nunn at CARE.[25]

As quickly as it could, the organization changed its strategy and gave the women the help they requested. Some asked for patterns to make masks that would meet WHO guidelines. Others asked for ingredients to make soap. Then they quickly ramped up businesses by selling those suddenly in-demand items. In Bangladesh, groups of women set aside money to buy care packages for locals who were destitute and were not allowed to beg during lockdowns. Many savings group members tapped into the funds they had put aside in case of crisis.[26]

That multifaceted approach was possible because CARE is decentralized. Though that seems as though it would be a disadvantage in a pandemic, it turned out to be a valuable tool for Nunn's team to empower people on the ground. "We didn't say, 'Everybody should do these five things.' It was a collection of the organic plans and responses that were led by our country offices, to which we gave the resources they needed to move forward." At the center of much of CARE's work since the early 1990s are Village Savings and Loan Associations—the largest micro-savings program in the world. CARE helps establish self-managed groups of fourteen to twenty-five people, mostly women, who meet regularly to save money for emergencies and provide members with small loans.* Because the savings groups operate independently, they can make changes quickly, without input from CARE or others. Ideas spread across regions, with much communication now via WhatsApp.[27] In 2008, when the Zimbabwean economy tanked and inflation skyrocketed, a few local groups decided to switch from saving money to saving corn and quickly shared that innovation across the country. By early 2020, the groups had 12.5 million members, and another 8 million savings groups were working with other groups that had been inspired by CARE. During the pandemic they served a crucial role in collecting data on what women needed, along with distributing information and resources.

Those efforts were further bolstered by systems to foster innovation that Nunn had invested in early in her tenure. Just before she started working at CARE, the organization had started to gather data centrally, rather than keeping it siloed by region. Instead of just using that data to report to donors, Nunn had pushed to use it to drive decision making and to institute tech tools to amplify the natural "virality" of good ideas. She hired a chief innovation officer and expanded the team to advise social impact programs and connect them with investors, and built an incubator to help projects scale across the world. Now all that investment was paying off: CARE tapped into its network of local savings and community groups to spread messages from local governments about how to avoid infection and where to access resources. And in some countries, savings

---

*Members of savings groups put a fixed amount into a fund, from which they can borrow and repay with interest; at the end of a cycle, the pot is distributed equally, and the group usually starts again. The program started in Niger in 1991, with twenty women, and by early 2020 had grown to more than 15 million members in more than seventy-three countries around the world.

groups started using an app developed in the incubator to adapt the pen-and-paper process to a digital one and keep groups running even when they couldn't meet in person.

Most of all, CARE watched and learned from what women came up with themselves. In Niger, one group asked the local energy company to finance a hand-washing station at the location of their group meetings in exchange for putting up the company's logo. It was a low-level commitment from the energy company and showed the group's entrepreneurial initiative. Other savings groups followed suit. In such stories, and the data gathered about how different groups and regions deployed CARE's resources, the organization saw that the women they were helping seemed best equipped to find solutions.

Now the organization is hopeful that the pandemic could provide an opportunity for women to gain more power. When crises send traditional social structures into flux, it can present a chance to shift power dynamics: CARE found the Syrian civil war brought more women into decision making about family expenses and work, and during World War II, more American women took on jobs outside the home. During the pandemic, CARE found that in the Sahel region in West Africa, women saw a precipitous drop in income. But the organization also saw some hopeful signs: women were taking the lead to organize responses, and men were taking on more child care duties. Women had come together to transform crisis into progress. "Imagine what these women are facing, but one of the mantras from one of the savings groups said, 'Impossible is not for us,'" Nunn said with awe in her voice. "I think that for CARE, this is the moment in which impossible is not for us. There's enormous strength and courage that people are exerting around the world—our opportunity is to just meet that courage with a little bit of support."

Inspiring with an Abundance Mentality

As CARE USA spent the opening months of the pandemic enabling on-the-ground groups to advocate for their own needs, Babineaux-Fontenot and Feeding America also listened to their primary constituents: partner food banks. What they heard was that the food banks needed their parent organization to raise money on a massive scale. In order to do that, Babineaux-Fontenot would have to reeducate a culture in which parents scold their kids to finish their food "because there are hungry kids in Africa or China or India" and couldn't conceive of those problems being close to home. She wanted to make sure that people understood the tangible impact of donating one dollar—which would pay for ten meals—directed to whatever zip code they chose.

With her tax accountant understanding of the numbers and her memory of the hunger in her childhood community, Babineaux-Fontenot led a communications campaign that publicized both horrifying data and personal stories. The organization created a TV public service announcement, and the Walt Disney Company and other pro bono partners drew on celebrity talent to create ads that aired in donated commercial time. Feeding America and its network member food banks also emailed national and local news outlets to report spikes in demand for food assistance and share stories of acute examples of food shortages.[28] "We would say to local media, 'I know there's been footage in Pittsburgh of lines, but I want you to know there was a food distribution in San Antonio where ten thousand cars showed up and we've got video of what happened there.'" Babineaux-Fontenot needed people to understand not only that hunger wasn't limited to distant shores but that *every city* was affected.

Though it had been common for Feeding America to try to enlist celebrity advocates, it had always been hard to schedule time with them or even get their attention. Now they were suddenly available, and thanks to Zoom, the logistical hassle of wrangling time with famous people evaporated. There was also something unique about the pandemic: even the richest and most privileged were on some level impacted, while widening economic disparities were laid bare. "I think people who were in positions of privilege could see their privilege so clearly. They knew they had the luxury of being at home when there were people who, to feed their families, had to leave their houses in the middle of the pandemic, find money for gas, and sit in a line for food," said Babineaux-Fontenot. "We were all in the same storm, but we weren't in the same boat."

Celebrities started to gravitate to the cause, as donating and spreading the word about their donation made them feel productive. Blake Lively and Ryan Reynolds donated half a million dollars on March 17, followed by NFL star quarterback Russell Wilson and his wife, Ciara, who partnered with the private aviation company Wheels Up to donate 10 million meals. They promoted their donations to their tens of millions of social media followers, which broadened awareness of the problem and of Feeding America's solution. At the pandemic's peak, the donor pool was four times its typical size, some young donors sending change from piggy banks. (Babineaux-Fontenot saved handwritten notes in crayon from kids who mailed in coins.)

On April 1, the organization published the culmination of its research: the data showed that the pandemic was on track to result in an additional 17 million Americans suffering from food insecurity in 2020, a 46 percent increase from the previous year. That meant an estimated $1.4 billion in additional resources would be needed in the coming six months.[29] Most shocking was the news that fully two-fifths of the Americans who had turned to Feeding America's network in the first weeks of the pandemic had never before relied on food assistance. "I think this was a jolt to people that said, 'Wait a minute, do you mean this could happen to me?' On the internet, we had this moment that was really ripe for raising that consciousness about how deep and serious those problems were." The day after the report's publication, Jeff Bezos announced a $100 million donation, the largest single gift in Feeding America's history.

While Babineaux-Fontenot succeeded in raising awareness and

securing more funding, demand continued to spike. A solution presented itself on the supply side of the ledger in those images of milk and eggs being trashed by truck drivers on the side of the road. Food waste was a problem all too familiar to Feeding America, which before the pandemic was already the nation's largest food waste recovery organization (it had established the National Produce Program to rescue billions of pounds of excess food from farmers).[*] To quickly ramp up its food recovery efforts, the organization expanded an app called MealConnect, which it had previously piloted in just a handful of cities, to enable any establishment to donate excess food via a volunteer network. DoorDash and Uber served as partners for "last mile" food delivery to vulnerable groups, and the company enlisted Babineaux-Fontenot's old company, Walmart, to expand its donations and to ship to food banks up to five hundred miles away. Just days into the pandemic, the shipping logistics company Convoy created a new tool in its app that truckers used to maximize the efficiency of their routes. If a food and beverage shipment was rejected, a trucker could ping a local food bank and redirect the delivery.[30][†] Those efforts resulted in the organization rescuing 1.8 billion pounds of produce and a total of 4 billion pounds of groceries in 2020, 11 percent more than in 2019 despite the tighter supply.[31][‡]

Every step of the way, Babineaux-Fontenot reassured food bankers and volunteers not to panic: "Guys, this is going to work, people are going to engage, we are going to see the most remarkable outpouring of support." Her displays of optimism not only kept her own spirits up but also seemed to motivate those around her to work even harder. In fact, academics have found that optimism can provide valuable sustenance. One

[*]In chapter 2, I wrote more about food recovery efforts.
[†]The trucker is compensated for the drive—the closest food bank is usually less than forty miles away—and Feeding America provides a receipt for the donation to the shipper to encourage donations.
[‡]In early 2021, Feeding America also began packaging and distributing its own frozen produce recaptured from Wisconsin's farmers and manufacturers.

study conducted at Harvard in the 1950s that demonstrated this earned the nickname "the hope experiment." Professor Curt Richter put rats into a container of water to see how long they could swim; after about fifteen minutes, they would drown. (Experiments in the 1950s were a bit morbid.) So he started to pick the rats out of the water just before that point. He gave them a few minutes to rest and then returned them to the water to see how the hope that they might be saved would impact their survival times. Those rats swam for not another fifteen minutes but *sixty hours*. The hope that help might be coming enabled them to do the physically impossible. Richter concluded, "After elimination of the hopelessness the rats do not die."[32]

Babineaux-Fontenot said that her parents had always tried to instill her with hope, and in the darkest days of the pandemic she tried to do the same with food bankers. She did that by leading with what she calls an attitude of abundance, in a field that too often operates with an attitude of scarcity. "The nonprofit space generally has been relegated to fighting for crumbs," she said. "If you feel like there's a little bitty piece, a sliver of the pie you've got to divide a hundred fifty ways, it changes the way that you relate to each other." But she believed that her abundance mentality— the idea that there are enough resources to share, that more pie can be made—could impact the organization. (The concept of an "abundance mentality" was coined by Stephen Covey in his best seller, *The 7 Habits of Highly Successful People*.) Babineaux-Fontenot reassured member food banks that donations would come through. Over the course of the year, her approach had its intended effect of impacting the way food bankers related to one another. Instead of individual food banks stockpiling excess food because of fear of a shortfall, they volunteered when they had excess to share and turned down financial support when they had sufficient donations from their community.

The instinct to stockpile when fearing a shortage occurs because, as researchers have found, a scarcity mindset impedes decision making. It increases attention toward the scarce resource itself—in Feeding

America's case, food—at the cost of paying attention to unrelated aspects, such as investing in infrastructure or programs to address the causes of hunger.[33] People with a scarcity mindset tend to allocate spending to urgent needs while ignoring other important things that have a future cost. (Similar findings have been used to explain why people in circumstances of poverty often make shortsighted decisions that can cause their situation to deteriorate, such as taking out high-interest-rate loans.)[34]

In contrast, Babineaux-Fontenot's attitude of abundance enabled the food bank network not just to be generous but also to plan for the future. "Start with a premise: 'Let's not fight over this little sliver of a pie, there is a whole other pie coming,'" she said. In the midst of the pandemic, Feeding America expanded its programs to teach job skills and financial literacy and help "neighbors" sign up for federal benefits. In relieving anxiety about near-term problems, she focused her team on long-term, systemic solutions.

Learning from Experience

We left Clear CEO Caryn Seidman-Becker at the train station on that day in late February 2020 when she was making swift decisions to save her business in the face of a looming pandemic. I paused the story of her navigation of an unprecedented crisis to tell the stories of two very different women running nonprofits. Seidman-Becker's venture-backed biometrics startup may seem to have little in common with Feeding America's sprawling national reach and CARE's global challenges. But I chose to break away from her story to tell how those two leaders navigated in crisis to demonstrate the importance of adaptability. Nunn and Babineaux-Fontenot made the best decisions they could, then listened and learned from the people with the most context and then kept on iterating and learning and iterating. Adaptability is applicable to all companies, not just nonprofits, and in all scenarios, not just crises. And Seidman-Becker's approach unlocks more understanding of the value of Nunn's and Babineaux-Fontenot's.

Seidman-Becker said she felt as though she had spent her life preparing to adapt to any possible scenario. Growing up in a Washington, DC, suburb with civil servant parents, she felt most comfortable when she was overprepared and working hard to prove herself. "I grew up in a lower-middle-class kind of environment—you have no safety net, you've got to go out there, and you've got to take risks," she said with a shrug. Her grandfather had survived the Holocaust, and her parents had divorced, which she says set the stage for a lifetime of anticipating disasters. "You plan for the worst, and then, you know, belts and suspenders, what's the backup plan for that?" she explained. "I spend my life looking around corners."

Seidman-Becker developed a mindset of learning and adapting through repeated experience with crises. The dot-com bubble burst in 2000, when she was in her twenties and working at a hedge fund, and she saw how Apple aggressively invested in R&D through those uncertain times, which showed the importance of planning for the long term. "If they didn't do that, there would be no iPods, iPads, the rest is history," she said. A year later, the terrorist attacks of 9/11 took the lives of several of her friends, which seeded a drive to find business solutions to security threats. In the attacks' aftermath she also saw the rebirth of lower Manhattan and the potential for a crisis to spawn growth. When the next crisis—the Great Recession—hit, she was a mother of three children under five years old and running an asset management firm. She panicked and acted quickly to liquidate her company's positions, return capital to her investors, and find her employees new jobs. It was a decisive move, but the wrong one: she pulled everything out of the market at what turned out to be a bottom and lost millions of dollars for her clients. That taught her the importance of staying calm when navigating new challenges.

After that decade of lessons learned, in April 2010, Seidman-Becker and her business partner bought the assets of the biometrics company Clear out of bankruptcy for $6 million after the financial crisis decimated corporate travel budgets.[35] That October, they relaunched the service, which verifies people's identity using patented iris or fingerprint scanning technology. The company charges members a $179 annual fee to verify their identity at Clear kiosks at airports, instead of waiting in line for a TSA agent to do the verification, taking subscribers straight to the head of the security line.

But easing the secure movement of Clear customers through airports was always only the beginning of Seidman-Becker's plan; the more places customers could use the service, the more likely they were to keep paying for it. In 2015, she piloted Clear in three sporting venues, starting with the San Francisco Giants' stadium, Oracle Park, and in 2018 Clear partnered with Major League Baseball to institute biometrics entry and ticketing at all ballparks. (Later some locations added biometrics payments so that users can link a credit card to their Clear account and verify that they are over twenty-one, to buy beer without having to pull out their wallet.) Seidman-Becker also started moving into another area in which customers' identities need to be highly secure: health care. She hired a team to build a health identity business and a HIPAA-compliant back end.

The company took on strategic investments by Delta Air Lines, which offers Clear's service to its frequent fliers, and United Airlines, which expanded Clear's footprint to include all of its hubs. By January 2020, the service had more than 5 million members, was operating in thirty-six airports, and had launched a pilot program with the hospital operator Dignity Health. When the pandemic hit, Clear had just started testing facial recognition technology—the kind that unlocks your iPhone—to enable patients to check into a health clinic and confirm their medical insurance.

As lockdowns began, Seidman-Becker worked to adapt the service to keep subscribers from canceling: she slashed renewal fees and allowed customers to pause their memberships. Whereas Clear members had previously tended to use fingerprint scans (customers were more suspicious of the futuristic-seeming iris scans), after the pandemic hit, the company defaulted to iris identification—which they promoted as "touchless."[36] The company also sent its members branded masks and wipes—a reminder that when air travel did return, moving through the airport quickly and without touching anything would be more important than ever. Remarkably, despite spending on US travel falling by 42 percent from 2019 to 2020, Clear's measure of revenue called "total bookings" declined just 10 percent in the year, as some members paused their subscriptions, and the company's member retention rate dropped just slightly—to 79 percent from 86 percent the year before. In fact, its total enrollments increased 12 percent over the course of 2020.[37]

As Seidman-Becker and her team struggled to keep the core travel part of their business relevant, they saw the opportunity to apply biometrics identification to health care. There was suddenly a massive need for companies to secure and confirm the health and identity of their employees as they moved into and out of corporate spaces. Clear's HIPAA-compliant infrastructure gave it a huge head start, so she invested resources to build a feature called Health Pass to link members' identity to their test results, temperature checks, and health surveys. Employers could buy access to this service for large-scale use. By early April, a full year before a vaccine would be widely available, the company started working to add vaccination status.

With the new health security tool, Seidman-Becker drew on everything she had learned working with airports and local municipalities to connect vaccinators and testing companies to employers who needed to monitor personnel health. In July 2020, the NHL signed up to use Clear's Health Pass app and temperature hardware at its playoff "bubbles": players and staff took a daily survey and had their temperature taken at a Clear temperature-scanning kiosk. The NBA and MGM Resorts International also partnered with the company to screen employees and to get fans and visitors to take health surveys and link to their test results. Corporate office buildings and restaurant owners, including Union Square Hospitality

Group and Founders Table (the owner of a number of chains, including Dos Toros and Chopt), used Health Pass as part of their daily screening process. The Super Bowl piloted Clear's vaccination verification program. "We were a solution looking for a problem," Seidman-Becker said. "And suddenly you have every commissioner of sports and real estate titans and university presidents calling you. We were *born* for a pandemic." All those different use cases were possible because Clear had built a flexible digital identity platform that was prepared to add biometric payments and ticketing. The company, like Seidman-Becker, was prepared to adapt.

In December 2020, ten months after Seidman-Becker's stressful train ride, she faced another, higher-stakes decision about what to do about her workforce. Though covid cases were spiking and there were myriad questions about vaccine deployment, she predicted that travel would return stronger and faster than the headlines indicated. Despite the uncertainty, the data prompted her to take a risk and aggressively rehire the entire team Clear had furloughed—and also add new employees. (This stands in stark contrast to how other industries, such as automakers, pulled back, resulting in shortages when economies reopened.)

It worked: from March 2020 to March 2021, the company expanded to four more airports and launched a new feature to show users precisely how long it would take them to get from their home to the gate. In February 2021, Clear partnered with the state of Hawaii to replace a mandatory ten-day quarantine with proof of a negative covid test result ahead of a Hawaii-bound flight, authenticated through Clear's Health Pass. (It later expanded to add proof of vaccination.) In a vote of confidence for the company's expansion potential, later that month it secured $100 million in investments, largely from strategic partners that wanted to deploy the technology broadly, such as Danny Meyer's Enlightened Hospitality Investments.[38] A year after making those plans on an Amtrak train amid the fear of the upcoming pandemic, Seidman-Becker successfully expanded the company's business with new core technology and an entirely new type of customer.

Seidman-Becker narrowly avoided catastrophe for her startup, just as Babineaux-Fontenot evaded food shortages and Nunn helped women around the world generate income and avoid going hungry. They share the leadership traits of flexibility, empathy, and preparedness. Even before the pandemic, they operated with a sense of intense personal responsibility to get things right. All those characteristics made them particularly well equipped to navigate an unforeseen and unprecedented crisis.

Women's Adaptability Advantage

In chapter 5, I referred to the "glass cliff" phenomenon, in which female executives are more likely to be thrust into precarious leadership scenarios without support and resources. The 2005 study that coined that term analyzed the performance of big, publicly traded British companies. It found that leadership roles were 63 percent more likely to be filled by women during a period of overall stock market decline and illustrated the ways in which women face a disadvantage in the workplace because when they *do* get access to rare positions of leadership, they tend to be positions that have a greater chance of failure.

But the researchers also noticed something about the outcomes of the glass cliff scenarios: in times of general financial downturn, companies that appointed a woman actually experienced a marked *increase* in share price in the months following her appointment. When women were appointed in less volatile times, their appointment was followed by a period of share price stability.[39] That indicates that although female managers are often overlooked or underappreciated, in times of crisis they demonstrate competence and leadership that should earn them more respect.

Other research provides clues about why women might be well equipped to lead companies through crises; they center on the notion of adaptability. Whereas in the 1990s, the business world replaced IQ with a fixation on leaders' "emotional quotient" (EQ), researchers have recently found a more predictive indicator of business success: adaptability quotient, or AQ. In 2011, *Harvard Business Review* deemed adaptability to be "the new competitive advantage. . . . Instead of being really good at doing some particular thing, companies must be really good at learning how to do new things."[40] Adaptable companies are quick to identify, read, and act on signals of change, not just with products and services but also with business models and strategies.[41] They are also good at experimenting, which naturally produces failure. So adaptive companies are tolerant of failure, even celebrating it, to encourage more risk-taking experimentation.

In 2016, Korn Ferry gathered data from fifty-five thousand professionals in ninety countries over five years and found that women outperformed men in eleven out of twelve "emotional intelligence competencies" and scored in the 54th percentile (better than the men's 48th) in inspirational leadership, coaching and mentoring, and adaptability. The resounding result of the study: "If more men acted like women in employing their emotional and social competencies, they would be substantially and distinctly more effective in their work."[42] Claire Babineaux-Fontenot was adaptable when she pivoted her attention to Feeding America's solution to America's hunger problem. Michelle Nunn was adaptable when she let local associations govern the way they would deploy aid from CARE, rather than follow the top-down approach dictated by the Centers for Disease Control and Prevention (CDC). And Caryn Seidman-Becker was adaptable when she used the near-total shutdown of Clear's travel business to pivot to an entirely new business model. That is why, according to research, many people prefer to have women in leadership positions when an organization is in turmoil or a crisis hits.

In 2011, *Harvard Business Review* published a study by two psychology professors examining how college students felt about the gender of a CEO, depending on the state of the company. When asked about a successful company, 67 percent of the respondents chose the male candidate over an equally qualified female one to run the company. But when a company was in crisis, 63 percent of the respondents thought the female candidate should take over.* That was because the students believed that stereotypically female skills, such as communication and the ability to encourage others, are of the utmost importance in challenging times.[43]

This is supported by another study that found that women leaders are trusted more than men in times of turmoil: in February 2019, three professors published "A Female Leadership Trust Advantage in Times of Crisis: Under What Conditions?" to explain why. To start, they created a set of crisis scenarios in which the CEO (sometimes male, sometimes female) either anticipated and managed the emotions of his or her team or did not attend to their emotions at all. Ultimately, the researchers found that people trusted female leaders more than male leaders. That trust, though, was a response not merely to the leaders' gender but to the way the female leaders acted, with a greater focus on interpersonal dynamics and emotions.[44]†

Another explanation for this trust can be found in studies about positivity and reassurance. There's a self-help strategy called *cognitive reappraisal*: the reframing of distressing situations in positive terms to minimize negative emotional impact.[45] Some people call this focusing on the positive; others call it finding a silver lining. Women have been found to be more likely than men to use positive emotions to reframe negative situations as an opportunity for progress. Women might say, "This is hard and horrible, but something good will come out of it," while men are more likely to suppress their emotions and say "This isn't that bad."[46] We can see it clearly in Seidman-Becker, Nunn, and Babineaux-Fontenot's responses to the covid crisis: they paired concern with optimism about the

---

*I discussed this in chapter 5 in the context of the number of female bank executives who were promoted during the financial crisis.

†Another study, published in June 2020 in *Journal of Business and Psychology*, found that the shift from in-person to remote work meant that employees no longer preferred the characteristics of charisma and confidence that are associated with male leadership. Working remotely led to a more meritocratic preference for leaders who excelled at planning and prioritizing.

opportunity to enact lasting change in their organizations and reach more people—the silver lining.[47]

In the past two decades, I have come to know lots of female founders and CEOs. It is their resilience and fortitude that initially inspired me to take on this project. Yet this chapter features two leaders who joined decades-old organizations, along with a woman who reinvented a failed company. One thing these women (and reams of academic research) have shown me is that it's not that female leadership is necessarily better than male leadership; rather, it's that companies whose values and priorities are more evolved and inclusive tend to have female leaders. This presents a chicken-and-egg question: Are women leaders a sign of a good company, or do women leaders cause a company to have the right values?

At the end of 2020, another study conducted by eight professors in the United States and the United Kingdom revisited the question of whether countries with female leaders had achieved better pandemic outcomes.[48] It found that whereas New Zealand had maintained the advantage created by Jacinda Ardern's swift and decisive action, other countries with female leaders, such as Germany, led by Angela Merkel, had not been as successful longer term, particularly during the winter months, when the number of cases spiked. Over the nine months following covid being declared a pandemic, the professors determined, the decision making of female leaders did not directly correlate to lower fatality rates—at least not to a statistically significant degree.

But they did find evidence that countries with a focus on egalitarianism, collectivism, and long-term policy making tended to be more successful in mitigating fatalities. Not only did they find that those cultural values are associated with female leadership styles; the countries that prioritized them were more likely to be run by women.[49]

Female leaders didn't fight covid better; the kinds of countries that elect female leaders did. Women-led countries are more prepared for a disaster not necessarily because they're *led* by women but because the cultures that *elect* women share the values of preparedness, empathy, and adaptability.[50] The study argued that each country's success in fighting the pandemic was less tied to the particular gender of a leader than to the mores of the country; the election of a female leader was an expression of those values. When women lead countries with a culture of egalitarianism and long-term policy making, they have had more success battling the pandemic than men running culturally similar countries have, because they were better able to capitalize on those values.[51]

With each passing month there is more clarity about how various leadership styles and policies impacted covid-19 outcomes, and more findings will certainly emerge. But the study's authors predicted that countries "where core cultural values reward traits often found in women leaders, such as a long-term orientation, a collectivist (rather than individualist) focus, and fewer power disparities in society" will be more likely to emerge stronger from the pandemic.[52]

Eleanor Roosevelt made an apt, now clichéd comparison: "A woman is like a tea bag. You never know how strong it is until it's in hot water." Research shows that more than just revealing how strong women are, crises show that they are in fact stronger than their male counterparts. And their presence may be a sign of a company's resilience.

I believe that the years following the global pandemic will show that women leaders are more likely to capitalize on the opportunities that come during crises. The concept of a glass cliff is typically referenced when women are handed a mantle of responsibility when their chance of failure is high. But times of crisis can also be an opportunity for women to show the enduring value of their adaptability, empathy, and decisiveness. If women succeed in the face of a crisis or when on the edge of a glass cliff, they should have a greater facility to navigate the increasing volatility of our everyday world.

Part III

Creating New Patterns

Eight

Defying CEO Archetypes

The Underestimated Advantage of Nontraditional Leadership Styles

Of the countless sports that are played around the globe, there is only one in which men and women compete directly against each other on an individual basis: horse racing. Women jockeys first started competing against men in the United States in 1969, and the sport was integrated in the United Kingdom five years later. Today female jockeys comprise roughly a tenth of all licensed jockeys in the two countries. Unlike other sports such as tennis mixed doubles and sailing, in which teams include both men and women, in horse racing, men and women (and their horses) compete nose to nose. And consumers bet on thousands of races a year. This confluence of factors provides a giant data set for social scientists to examine beliefs about the abilities of women in a male-dominated oc-cupation.

In the mid-2000s, two of those social scientists, Alasdair Brown and

Fuyu Yang, examined a decade's worth of data from the Tote, the centralized British bookmaking company, to measure the public's perception of gender. What these two professors found was that in general, the British betting markets only slightly overestimated male jockeys and underestimated female ones; women were just 30 basis points (.3 percent) more likely to win a race than the betting markets predicted.[1] That small number indicated that the gambling public was more interested in the data about jockeys and horses' past wins than prejudiced against female jockeys.

So far, so equitable. But the professors also discovered something peculiar in the subset of data about hurdle races. In that particular event, women were far more underestimated and performed considerably better than the betting markets predicted (.54 place better). Why did bettors underestimate women so much more in that particular category?

The only difference between hurdle races and other race categories is that in hurdle races female jockeys were far more rare, comprising just 2.2 percent of all jockeys. The researchers concluded that in fact, low levels of participation in a category *result* in underestimation. When bettors see lower female participation, they assume that a female win is less likely—despite what the data are telling them. So when people bet against women in this category, they're likely to lose. In effect, the impact of seeing much lower representation of one group is powerful enough to outweigh rational financial incentives.

This finding seems naturally portable to the business world, where female CEOs are in a tiny minority (8.8% percent of the Fortune 500 as of May 2022). Researchers at the University of Utah tested the hypothesis that lower participation leads to underestimation by presenting more than two hundred MBA students with two sets of real IPO prospectuses that were identical except for one trait: the gender of the CEO. The respondents were asked to recommend an amount to invest in the IPO and to estimate the IPO price of the stock. Among the cohort who received the "male-run" company prospectus, the recommended investment was almost *four times higher.*[2]

These gender dynamics demonstrate a vicious logical tautology: women don't seem good at hurdle races because they don't often compete at hurdle races and therefore bettors don't back them, and therefore women have less incentive to compete in hurdle races. Women don't seem good at being CEOs because they don't often serve as CEOs; therefore investors and board members don't back them. In fact, female scarcity in the C-suite is so acute that a study found that when a woman is appointed as CEO, there is three times as much media coverage of her as of male appointees.[3]

That attention is not positive—at least not to the investor class. The same study found that when female CEO appointees generated a significant amount of media attention the day of the announcement, their companies' stock price declined an average of 2.5 percent in the immediate aftermath. When minimal or no attention was paid to a woman appointed as CEO, the company's stock price rose an average of about 2 percent. The opposite was true with men: their getting a lot of media attention drove their companies' stock price up, while their getting little attention translated to a minimum impact on the stock price. (It's worth noting that within sixty days the stock prices that had declined after highly covered female CEO appointments tended to rebound and in many cases outperformed those of comparable firms that appointed a man.[4] In chapter 1, I noted that in the first two years after a CEO appointment, female CEOs' companies' stock prices outperformed those of male CEOs by an average of 20 percent.) For female CEOs, the factor driving down the stock price in the near term was not their experience or potential—but rather the media attention to their femaleness.

Just as it would be financially smart to bet on female jockeys in hurdle races, studies indicate it would be smart to invest in companies with a newly installed female CEO on the day that a rush of media attention causes a stock to drop. The punishment inflicted by the betting market after a female CEO is installed is transitory—and the potential rewards are highly durable.

The fact that female CEOs are unexpected, and therefore underestimated, often causes them to find their own ways to prove themselves and to create new archetypes for leadership.

Listening in Order to Be Heard

In 1969, a month after NASA put a man on the moon, Jenny Salem, a nine-year-old who desperately wanted to become an astronaut, moved with her family from the Colombian port town of Barranquilla to Los Angeles, California. Though the move brought her closer to the US space program, it was a difficult transition: young Jenny didn't speak English. She had loved science and math back in Colombia, but in her new American classrooms, surrounded by students and teachers she didn't understand and who couldn't understand her, math became more than just an interest; the universality of the language of math became a life raft. She thrived in science and math classes and fostered a passion she pursued with undergraduate and graduate degrees in chemistry.

Through her studies, she became obsessed with the vast difference between her own educational potential and that of the children in resource-poor countries such as Colombia. "What I could *be*, what I could *achieve* was obviously different being here. And one point three billion people at the time didn't have access to electricity," she remembered learning. "I really cared about the fact that if you didn't have power, your day ended when the sun set. That means you can't read a book, cannot study, cannot do any of those things." As she considered ways to close that opportunity gap, she developed a promethean view of energy: with broad access to electricity, she realized, *anything* is possible.

After her postdoctoral studies in chemistry at University of Illinois Urbana-Champaign in the early 1980s, Jennifer Salem had gotten married and started going by her husband's name, Holmgren. She entered the energy sector at a company called UOP (later acquired by the conglomerate Honeywell), where she focused on oil refinery technology. She worked her way up to oversee a division focused on finding new raw materials to turn into energy—in industry parlance, "feedstocks." Holmgren's predecessors at the division had tested samples' potential for fuel conversion mostly by trial and error. Her first order of business was to institute a more academic approach to testing samples' potential. "What I wanted to do was not only test the sample but also characterize it in a way at a fundamental level, so that we could understand why one sample worked and another didn't," she said. "If you understand something, you don't have to make as many samples; you could go faster once you build your knowledge base."

Putting in the extra work up front proved to be immensely productive. Her team discovered that they could use nontraditional materials to make fuel, including environmentally friendly ingredients such as used cooking oils. Eager to build on that success, Holmgren asked her bosses if she could create a new business line dedicated to commercializing technologies that competed with petroleum or natural gas. The company agreed, and she was a step closer to her goal of expanding cheap access to energy.

But then she faced the dialectical trap of the food-versus-fuel debate. She couldn't justify repurposing farmland for biofuels in developing countries where food shortages were acute. So she started focusing on transforming a far more ubiquitous ingredient: pollution. If she could turn the main ingredient of pollution, carbon dioxide, into fuel, she would achieve the holy grail of environmentally sustainable energy. But her colleagues remained skeptical. Renewable resources were great, but "a lot of people would just laugh at alternative feedstocks—'It's a petroleum company, come on!'" Holmgren said. She told herself, "There's fifty reasons why it's a dumb idea, and you just battle them one by one."

By then Holmgren was fifty. She had built a renewable energy business inside a multinational petrochemical conglomerate, and she was working on the alchemy of converting waste into energy in a cost-effective and environmentally sustainable way. But as time wore on, a solution to that Gordian knot of a problem (and the full support of her fuel-refining parent company) began to seem out of reach. She was considering retiring until one day in 2010 her cell phone rang from an unknown number. It was a headhunter calling on behalf of a New Zealand–based startup called LanzaTech: it was looking for a CEO. LanzaTech was entirely focused on Holmgren's white whale—turning pollution into fuel—but it wasn't using chemistry; it was using biology. Holmgren dismissed the headhunter, explaining that she was no biologist. And she had never even envisioned being a CEO: she wouldn't know how to fundraise in Silicon Valley. But about two months later the recruiter called back, telling her that the renowned technologist Vinod Khosla, a LanzaTech investor, wanted to meet her. Holmgren listened more carefully that time. The conversation eventually led to an introduction to the company's founders, and Holmgren warmed to the idea. "I thought, *Well, gee, if this works it's huge, and it's important and we'll have a real impact on all of the things I care about,*" she said. If it didn't? Well, she was going to retire anyway.

Holmgren's age is relevant to her confidence in taking on a new challenge. Men in their twenties and thirties report having much higher confidence in themselves than women of the same age do (witness the twenty-two-year-old Mark Zuckerberg's famous "I'm CEO, bitch" business cards). In contrast, women tend to gain confidence as they grow older, until the two genders' levels meet at around age forty. Over age sixty, men's confidence declines while women's increases, according to a 2019 report in *Harvard Business Review*. The researchers concluded that young men start off more confident than they should be, while women's confidence tends to grow with their increasing competence. For men, it is not *youth* that is wasted on the young—it is *confidence.*[5][*]

With the confidence of a fifty-year-old industry veteran who understood the value of her expertise and had very little to lose, Holmgren took the CEO role. LanzaTech was using fermentation to turn carbon and other waste gases (pollutants) into ethanol (fuel). Its scientists had found a

---

[*]Men gain 8.5 percentile points in confidence from age twenty-five to sixty, while women gain 29, according to a 2019 study by Zenger Folkman.

naturally occurring bacterium that consumed carbon as an energy source; they used synthetic biology to modify it so that when it digests pollution, it produces chemicals. The organism excretes—or as she put it, "poops out"—chemicals that can be used as fuel or turned into plastic. It's a moon shot technology with the potential to clean the air while simultaneously generating renewable energy. It fulfills Holmgren's alchemical dreams during her time at Honeywell: it could transform something horrible into something valuable. Holmgren would have to bring down the cost of the process while figuring out how to make it work at a massive scale.

What worried her most was the need to convince companies and factories around the world to invest in a technology that was, for now, expensive and fringe. Holmgren is a self-professed introvert; her sentences come out in a quiet, slow cadence with a nearly imperceptible accent. Despite having been awarded about fifty patents and having authored more than thirty scientific articles, she has not shed the shyness of young Jenny from Barranquilla. "My idea of a good time is *not* getting up there and giving a presentation, it is *not* rubbing elbows. These things terrify me," she said. But she told herself that if NASA could put a man on the moon and LanzaTech could turn pollution into fuel, she could overcome her terror of public speaking—or at least figure out how to cope with it. "I had to learn how to do all those things. You have to convince yourself that what you want to accomplish is more important than what scares you and holds you back."

One such coping mechanism was counterintuitive: she always tried to attend business meetings by herself. "If I walked into a meeting with somebody else and they were male, *they* were the people that questions were directed to. I finally realized if I wanted to say something and get my point across, I couldn't be surrounded by a bunch of men." And if she was the only one from her company in the room, she discovered she could use her soft-spokenness to her advantage: "They have to lean in to listen to me, and so they have to pay attention."

Holmgren's preference to listen rather than speak may have been a product of her upbringing and personality, but it's also a common trait in her gender cohort. A number of studies find that men speak significantly more in meetings than women do (one study estimated that it's as much as 75 percent more).[6] And women typically speak less when they're out-numbered, as Holmgren almost always was.

Communication between the genders has been a popular subject of study, especially within the last two decades; Victoria Brescoll, a professor at the Yale School of Management, has made it her area of expertise. One frequently cited study of hers examined the correlation between volubility (the total amount of time spent talking) and power on the floor of the US Senate. As one would intuit, the more powerful senators spoke the most. But when men and women senators were evaluated separately, research-ers found that seniority and power had virtually no effect on how much women talked. All that volubility surplus came from the powerful men.

This can be explained, Brescoll says, by female senators' concern that speaking up "will result in negative consequences."[7] And their concern is valid. Powerful women are usually correct to assume that talking as much as their male counterparts do will provoke a negative reaction. Looking beyond politics, Brescoll found that a female CEO who talked dispropor-tionately more than others in a work setting was rated as significantly less competent and less suitable for leadership than a male CEO who spoke the same amount. Other studies have found that women are interrupted—by both men and other women—more than men are, and "when speaking with a female, participants interrupted more and used more dependent clauses than when speaking with a male."[8] Those dependent clauses often added unnecessary color and were merely tools for "holding the floor."*

---

*A survey of seven thousand evaluations of 1,100 female executives by a consulting firm found that men said their female colleagues weren't loud enough, allowed oth-ers to interrupt them, and apologized often. The survey also found women saying that they felt outnumbered and had difficulty reading the room. One issue cited: some women expressed reluctance to voice an alternate opinion because they felt a decision had effectively already been made.

What is most fascinating about this dynamic is that despite all the studies showing that women speak less than men, women are still perceived to speak more than they actually do. A study of men and women listening to dialogue found that the participants thought that the female voices were talking more than they were.[9]*

There is one scenario in which women actually *do* tend to talk more than men: in more cooperative environments. The study that found men tended to speak 75 percent more than women, found that the disparity disappeared when researchers told group participants that they had to arrive at a decision unanimously, rather than by majority rule. The coauthors found that the consensus-building approach was particularly empowering for women who were outnumbered by men in the group.[10]

One leader who is sensitive to these power dynamics is Shan-Lyn Ma, the founder and CEO of the wedding planning and registry platform Zola, mentioned in the first chapter. Ma said she tends toward introversion, and she has intentionally assembled a leadership team that is a mix of introverts and extroverts. "We found that when we really pushed the introverts to share their opinion, it was very additive and valuable to the discussion," she recalled. "So we thought over time, 'How do we structure conversations in a way that feels like we are getting diverse opinions in order to make the best decisions?' And as our team has more women than the average leadership team, we are acutely aware that the diversity of opinions is what drives better decision making."

To get that equal input, the company created a system: when an issue arises, the senior leadership takes an initial vote to see where people stand. *Then* there is a discussion of the issue in which people defend their

---

*These gender dynamics aren't all disadvantageous for women. A 2016 survey of two thousand employees by Bain & Company found that the top positive characteristic people picked among the top thirty-three leadership traits was "centeredness." Of all the other options—humility, empowerment, openness—the one that dominated was the ability to be mindfully present and "give full attention to others, to make them feel both heard and valued."

vote. "It really helps draw out people's opinion because they were forced to vote before they learned 'Everyone on the team thinks the opposite of me, so I'm just not going to say anything.'"

When I asked Holmgren what she thought of Zola's approach, she told me that it makes a lot of sense if there's a vocal majority and a woman is in the minority. Though she would have welcomed more opportunities to share her perspective, she said that on some occasions the decision not to speak up in a male-dominated room was strategic. By staying quiet, she could digest the conversation and use that information to figure out how to best speak up and win another, more important battle. She also said that being in the minority and feeling alien in new environments offered an advantage: it enabled her to relate to her counterparty's discomfort with adopting a strange new technology. "They're taking a risk, right? So work with them. To me, positioning comes only from listening—'What does he need? What does she need?'—*not* 'What do *you* want?'—it's 'What do *they* want?'" Holmgren said. "If I have to convince the chairman of a refinery to put one of these hundred-million-dollar units in his refinery, it's really important to understand what his motivation is."

As she continued in her role as CEO and forged more deals to implement the company's waste-transforming technology, Holmgren decided that she didn't want LanzaTech to win at that energy race at the expense of other entrants. Instead, she realized that her best shot at slowing global warming and promoting access to energy would come from sharing the company's essential idea (pollution-to-energy conversion) with her competitors. So she did something counterintuitive: she spun off a company, LanzaJet, that would use LanzaTech's proprietary technology to turn pollution into jet fuel. And rather than have LanzaTech remain its sole parent company, the ownership would be shared by partners, including Shell and British Airways. "We wouldn't own 100 percent of it—now, that's a woman thing, right? But we could make it go faster, and we could be smarter." She also structured the investment to avoid the painful process of fundraising twice; anyone who invested in the demo—if it worked—would be committed to investing in a commercial scale facility.

Investors questioned why Holmgren would give up full ownership of LanzaJet, but she had become comfortable with defying convention. "Everybody said, 'You'll never get a gas-eating microbe to be modified to make chemicals,' and we did! That is what the company is—a package of things that people said couldn't be done. Until we showed it was possible, it wasn't." Defying convention has paid off: in her decade-long tenure, she has raised more than $450 million and established partnerships in China, India, the European Union, and Japan to convert waste into jet fuel, bioplastics, and even fabrics.

The fact that she was underestimated in a male-dominated industry, Holmgren said, liberated her to think differently about both the company's technology and how the company should be operated. "I always have to prove that I should be listened to. But then if you are a little bit contrarian—you're *already* contrarian, you don't belong there to begin with—then you can do whatever you want, you can say whatever you want, you can think any way you want." Holmgren exclaimed, "There are no expectations from me, right? If I fail, who cares? Nobody expected me to succeed."

The Two Standards

Indeed, low expectations are not always a bad thing. Psychologists have found that because women are assumed to be less competent in business, those around them are more likely to be impressed when they prove themselves. And when they do perform well, they are more likely than men to be rewarded for their success. This "pleasant surprise" is called the *minimum standard*—the bar that a woman needs to clear for her coworkers and bosses to suspect that she is indeed sufficiently competent. In other words, the "Wow, she's not incompetent!" threshold.

Though this lower minimum standard for women may have helped

Jennifer Holmgren when she was in grad school ("Wow, that female chemist can keep up!"), it has always had an insidious twin on the far-right side of the bell curve: something called the *confirmatory standard*. This is the level that someone must reach in order for those around her to be sure that she possesses a certain positive trait. For a woman to convince people of her competence, the bar is higher than it is for men—she needs to *consistently* display capability to defy the stereotype that women are less competent in business. For a man it's the reverse: it's harder to reach the minimum threshold ("He's not bad at business") but much easier to make people fully confident in his abilities, because his competence is implied by the male stereotype.[11]

For CEOs and leaders, the confirmatory standard (not the minimum standard) is the operative one. For instance, female job candidates are actually more likely than men to be considered for a high-powered job; if a company is putting together a list of candidates, it is likely applying a minimum standard of competence, so a number of women will make it onto the list. But when it comes to actually hiring one of those candidates, it is the confirmatory bar that's applied (they need to be *really* convinced of her competence). And that standard tends to favor men, who benefit from the stereotype of greater leadership expertise.

In general, the more formal and high stakes the scenario, the more likely it is that the higher confirmatory standard will be applied. And of course, the role of CEO is the highest-stakes role in any company. A 2010 study of how minimum and confirmatory standards of competence impact stereotyped groups found that when people were asked to fill out an evaluation—such as a year-end review—the instinct to judge women more harshly was amplified. And for women, the role of CEO—and the path to getting there—brings the highest of confirmatory standards and evaluations. Many studies have also shown that this dynamic is just as harmful toward other underrepresented groups in business, such as people of color.[12] (This is why in chapter 4, PagerDuty CEO Jennifer Tejada says that the Rooney Rule, mandating that just one ethnic minority be interviewed for each position, doesn't work—when it comes to actually hiring, the higher, confirmatory standard is applied. And that's the standard that tends to exclude women and minorities. That's why Tejada requires that half the candidates for jobs be women or people of color.)

So when the soft-spoken Latina immigrant Jennifer Holmgren modestly told us about the low expectations she faced in a room full of men, she was only half right. The world's expectations of a young student from Colombia who barely spoke English were certainly low compared to those of her male peers. But the standards for a female CEO in the energy business were much higher than for a comparable white male.

Radical Vulnerability

Few people have been born with as much advantage—and expectation—as Gwyneth Paltrow. Her parents were a wealthy New York elite power duo: her mother a movie star, her father a successful TV producer and director. Her godfather is Steven Spielberg (she played young Wendy in his 1989 film *Hook*), and she attended the prestigious Spence School on the Upper East Side.

In the early years of her career, Paltrow utilized those advantages—and lived up to the expectations that came with them—to an extraordinary degree. From her first small movie roles, she delivered nuanced performances that seemed effortless and earned critical acclaim. Six years after her first on-screen appearance, in a TV movie, she became a full-fledged movie star with *Emma*, followed by starring roles in *Sliding Doors* and *Seven*. At twenty-six, she won a Best Actress Oscar for *Shakespeare in Love*. During the next decade, she acted in virtually every kind of movie, from raunchy comedies to sweeping epics to musical melodramas. (Proving that she had herself sung in her 2010 film *Country Strong*, she performed a song live at the Oscars.) Through the hits, the bombs, and the stuff in between, she became a fashion icon, credited with making pastel pink trendy when she wore a gown in that shade to the Academy Awards in 1999.

Unlike some of her peers, who had had meteoric ascents and tabloid-driven falls, Paltrow possessed a kind of raw glamour and durable fame. There was, of course, the usual public interest in her relationships with fellow celebrities. But she provoked an even more intense curiosity about her fashion choices, wellness routines, and exercise habits. When she appeared at the 2004 premiere of *Anchorman* with bruise marks on her back, the after effects of the ancient Chinese practice of cupping, it generated dozens of posts and articles.

Paltrow's first foray into business was a 2006 investment in the trainer Tracy Anderson, whom she'd met when she was trying to lose baby weight. During a 2008 interview with Oprah, Paltrow gave Anderson credit for her physique in *Iron Man*, and soon after, Anderson's phone started ringing. Women were suddenly willing to pay a $1,500 initiation fee and $900 monthly dues to access classes and $200 for private training sessions. (Nonmembers can join a group class at one of Anderson's studios for $45.)

By the end of 2008, Paltrow was living in London, having scaled back her acting career to spend more time at home with her kids. As the best traveled and most stylish of her friends, she was constantly being asked where to find the perfect sort-of midcentury bathroom vanity; what was the best low-carb muffin recipe; and where to eat, shop, and stay in cities she had visited around the world. She was turning into a kind of email concierge for her friends. And the more she extolled this London bistro or that Eastern medicine intervention, the more she thought there would be a readership for her expertise.

It just so happened that around the same time, email newsletters with restaurant and shopping recommendations had become the rage in New York and LA. DailyCandy, considered to have produced the original trendy email newsletter, sold to Comcast for $125 million that same year, eight years after its launch. If a cupping mark on Paltrow's scapula could launch a hundred breathless "news" stories, surely an email directly from the source would also find an audience, so she created a simple website asking for email addresses of potential readers. "I was a public figure first. So I had the ability to say, 'Hey, I'm going to start writing about stuff, and if you guys want to check it out, please do.' I think there was already this idea of, you know, people might like my taste in clothes or whatever," she said.

She named her newsletter *goop*—her initials hugging two *o*'s because the branding expert Peter Arnell joked to her that all successful internet companies had a double *o* in their name—and emailed more than ten thousand readers in September 2008. The first missive included recipes for turkey ragù and banana muffins; the second focused on travel tips for London, with a guarantee that she (or one of her discriminating and well-heeled besties) had tried every restaurant and hotel listed. Like the red-carpet photos of cupping marks, the newsletter got immediate attention.

At the time, the internet was still getting used to hearing directly from Famous People. Twitter was only eighteen months old. Paltrow wasn't a cooking expert with products to hawk, as Martha Stewart was (at least not yet). Nor did she occupy a daily place in consumers' living rooms, as Oprah did. So the media were nonplussed by the notion that this famous person, this object of fascination, had the temerity to interact directly with the public. Here was this incandescent talent, so good at portraying other people, deciding instead that she'd rather just be *herself*—and she would decide how to share that self with the world, detoxes, vibrators, meditations, and all.

The newsletter eventually became a media company with a thriving web presence. It was, at the time, based on a brand-new business model known as "contextual commerce." Alongside articles penned by her or an assortment of equally chic women, in 2012 Goop launched an online shop to sell a curated assortment of her favorite products, starting with a $90 white T-shirt. The company earned referral fees and drew payments from brands for sponsored content. The shop went on to partner with Stella McCartney on a Goop collection in 2013 and then did a pricey capsule collection with Valentino in 2015. The products aren't all so exclusive; the company consistently sells an assortment of products that cost less than $50, such as cosmetics, sports bras, and books. But its annual curation of "Ridiculous (and Awesome) Gifts"—including a $5,800 leather toiletries bag one year—despite itself poking fun at its price tags, regularly sparked . . . ridicule.

The media and the public have encountered deviations from the celebrity social contract before: Matt Damon avoided the paparazzi by marrying someone outside the entertainment industry and living far from Hollywood, in Florida; Joaquin Phoenix staged a fake rap-career bildungsroman documentary; David Bowie was hailed as an avant-garde financial genius when he raised $55 million from the sale of "Bowie bonds" collateralized by royalties from his earnings. But famous people rarely exert such active authorial control over their own personas as Paltrow did.

The backlash to Paltrow's authorship was severe. One headline in response to a Goop piece on the value of sleep, snarkily declared, "Gwyneth Paltrow Has Just Discovered Sleep. Neat!"[13] above an image of Paltrow with "I am the worst" printed next to her. In an otherwise glowing column in the *New York Times* in 2019, Wesley Morris summarized the reactions and possible motives of the Paltrow Hater:

> The tearful, gushing (utterly sincere) Oscar speech from 1999 would have set this person off. . . . And the fact that she famously dated Pitt and Ben Affleck, that she married the guy from Coldplay and named their first child after orchard fruit. Maybe that kind of person dislikes the permanent pout of [Paltrow's] mouth or her mild patrician drawl, the private-school privilege of it all.[14]

Rather than flinch, Paltrow made herself even more vulnerable. In 2010, she wrote on GOOP about her struggle with postpartum depression, which she described as "one of the darkest and most painfully debilitating chapters of my life." Anyone reading Paltrow's experience after the birth of her second child could not overlook the fact that she had been born into extraordinary luck, wealth, and privilege. But despite the fact that things seemed to come easy to her, with her luminous skin (maintained with face oils) and postbaby physique (Tracy Anderson), she, too, had struggled. And that struggle had led her on a journey to find nontraditional solutions; she hadn't wanted to take antidepressants and had been thrilled to find a doctor who recommended meditation and exercise. "I thought, *This sounds really interesting, I don't know that much about it*," Paltrow remembered. It worked for her, and she was eager to share all of it.

That act of vulnerability sent her readership soaring.

The academic at the forefront of the study of vulnerability is the best-selling author and researcher Brené Brown, who has conducted thousands of interviews on the subject. Brown, who has appeared with Paltrow on her podcast, cautions against performing vulnerability in an attempt to "hot-wire" connection; oversharing about a personal problem to build camaraderie can backfire. But if vulnerability feels real, it carries huge power. Inspired by Brown's work, three professors at the University of Mannheim in Germany conducted seven studies with hundreds of participants and found consistent evidence that the expression of vulnerability, however uncomfortable it may be, humanizes a person. When participants imagined themselves in vulnerable situations, such as admitting a mistake to work colleagues or being the first to apologize after an argument, they felt weak or inadequate. But when they imagined someone else in those situations, they were more likely to describe that show of vulnerability as desirable and good.[15] The researchers called it the "beautiful mess effect."

For Paltrow, the beautiful mess of struggling with postpartum depression stood in sharp contrast to her otherwise glamorous persona. That humanized her and attracted more readers to Goop's frank reviews of experimental solutions for everything from depression to eczema. Paltrow remembered thinking, *"How come everybody's so scared to talk about, you know, postpartum stuff like sex after childbirth and, you know, libido and weight loss. It all seems so taboo."*

Paltrow continued to make the obligatory fame deposits, including a supporting role in the not-yet-ascendant *Marvel Cinematic Universe*. And the woman who was named by *Star* magazine as the "World's Most Hated Celebrity" in the same year that *People* named her the "World's Most Beautiful Woman" stayed the course. What dramatically amplified Paltrow's vulnerability (not to mention the media spotlight) was her separation from her husband, Chris Martin, in 2014. Famous people are particularly vulnerable when it comes to the intimate topic of divorce, especially when that separation is from a well-liked fellow famous person. Rather than issuing the usual celebrity bromide request about privacy, Paltrow approached the situation the same way she would explore a new wellness technique: she talked to experts, found a new way to come to terms with the (not uncommon) rite of passage, and reported back to her readers, hoping that the approach might give others the same comfort and meaning it gave her.

The key concept she presented, "conscious uncoupling," became an internet schadenfreude vortex, sending so much traffic to Goop's website that it crashed. Headlines called it "utterly obnoxious" (Salon) and "nutty" (*New York Post*). No less a cultural figure than Martha Stewart mocked it, that year referring to her Thanksgiving recipes as "conscious coupling" of ingredients to "honor marital partnerships." (When pressed about that act of shade, Stewart said that Paltrow "just needs to be quiet. She's a movie star. If she were confident in her acting, she wouldn't be trying to be Martha Stewart.")

What resulted was a sine curve of criticism from the media and admiration from customers: the women who bought Goop products and those who read and shared her newsletters. Another *Times* profile of Paltrow describing the company's growth between 2015 and 2017 pointed out, "Every time there was a negative story about her or her company, all that did was bring more people to the site."[16] And as she brought more people to the site, she sold them more and different types of products, some selected from her favorite brands, others designed by herself and produced by Goop.

Paltrow's move to monetize her identity stood out within her generation but echoed bold moves made decades earlier by the pop icon David Bowie. Unlike Paltrow, who presented to the world a version of *herself*, Bowie had constructed alien alter egos such as Ziggy Stardust. Bowie, like Paltrow, understood the value of owning one's image: in the 1970s, he and his manager, Tony Defries, had forgone upfront payment on his first record deal in exchange for retaining control over the master recordings. That decision had kept Bowie earning enormous passive income for decades. But by 1997, he was failing to sell as many albums as he had in his Ziggy Stardust heyday and had shifted his focus to licensing music for the likes of Tina Turner Pepsi commercials. Yet every time he wanted to do so, he had to ask permission of Defries, who still owned half of the masters. To break free of that cycle, Bowie did something unconventional: with the help of an investment banker, he securitized the revenue from his past catalog *and* any earnings from music he would make for the next decade. He turned his artistry into a financial instrument. It was nicknamed "Bowie bonds" and was a success, raising $55 million, which Bowie used to buy out Defries's 50 percent stake. The media responded to Bowie's innovation as if it were another act of avant-garde Warholian performance art. Bloomberg called it "Bowie's latest hit" (implying, incorrectly, that Bowie had recently released something resembling a hit).

The media's varying treatment of Bowie and Paltrow is a study in contrasts. Whereas her highly emotional Oscar speech and vulnerable newsletters rubbed the media the wrong way, his highly performed, highly constructed identities provoked awe. Bowie could suddenly kneel before seventy-two thousand bewildered fans, as he did during a 1992 performance at Wembley Stadium, and recite the Lord's Prayer with unexpected earnestness—and receive no backlash. But Paltrow weeping as she thanked her parents on the biggest night of her professional life was suspected to be a cynical performance of fake emotion. Paltrow was trying to reflect an authentic self in an enterprise; Goop was designed to be as close to Who She Is as an e-commerce platform can be, even if who she is sometimes seemed a little wacky and fringe. She was mocked. Bowie had spent decades constructing identities other than his authentic self—and used those identities as sales tools for his own products and others (he even licensed his song "Heroes" to the 1990s box-office bomb *Godzilla*). Yet he continued to be lionized.

Still, the woman who was named the world's most hated celebrity persisted, and the media's intense criticism was matched by equally potent consumer demand. Paltrow and the executives who ran Goop's finances and operations assembled a team of expert curators and content creators from media, fashion, and retail to expand the company's reach. At the center of Goop's business were the links to products that Paltrow and her team of experts endorsed from her favorite high-end designers and skin care lines. From those sales and data about what readers were drawn to, Goop learned what its consumers wanted, prompting the company to launch its own fashion label and skin care line in 2016. Paltrow explained that "contextual commerce" media-retail hybrid to the National Retail Federation's annual conference in early 2020: "We talk about things we love, we make things we love, and you can buy them on Goop or from other places."[17] The appeal of the products is amplified not just by Paltrow's endorsement but by her (and her fellow experts') narratives about how they're used in their own lives.

Goop as an enterprise has continued to thrive. By 2016, the company had raised $26.5 million from venture capital on a $65 million valuation—and, unlike Bowie, Paltrow had accomplished it without mortgaging a single asset—without giving up a single piece of herself.

Despite Paltrow's ownership of her image and her personal embodiment of Goop, for the first nine years of its operation, she didn't hold the title of CEO. In many ways she functioned as CEO, leading strategic decisions about what business lines to launch, selecting key hires, working with buyers on the assortment of products the website would feature. But the company had a succession of two "professional" executives who one after the other held the top role (one was actually a veteran of Martha Stewart's Omni Media Group). In 2016, after the second CEO left, Goop's board of directors began to set up interviews for Paltrow to meet with leading contenders for the job.

After one such interview, the candidate said to her, "Wow, you really understand this business! You know what your unit economics are, what your marketing metrics are, what your supply chain looks like—you know all this stuff!" Paltrow was sitting across from the applicant in Goop's airy Santa Monica offices, wearing a blazer she had designed for her G. Label brand, her cheeks flushed under the Goop face oil she'd introduced a year before. "The girl in me was like, 'Yay! I'm being validated!'" she recalled. "And the woman in me, or the burgeoning CEO, she was like, 'This is incredibly disrespectful. This is a really patronizing comment.'"

Here was a world-famous, successful entrepreneur, and not even she was immune to the condescending head pat of the minimum standard. Even Gwyneth Paltrow couldn't avoid the oh-she's-not-incompetent! reaction.

"I was sort of trying to reconcile those two halves within myself, the girl that had been socialized to please and be smart," said Paltrow. "And the woman in me that *deserved* what my shrink would call 'the healthy entitlement' that so many women don't have. I thought, basically this person was saying 'Your instincts about your business are right.' I thought, *This is coming out of this strange series of patronizing statements, but I think what they're saying is that I'm the person who should run my business.*"

Paltrow's disquiet in that moment can also be attributed to something called *stereotype threat*—the anxiety that you're going to live up to a negative expectation of your identity group. Dozens of academic studies have examined the way that stereotype threat can impact performance and spark anxiety: when female chess players were made aware of the stereotype that women perform worse at chess than men, they performed worse in their chess matches.[18] And when entrepreneurship is presented as a traditionally male profession, it reduces women's interest in becoming entrepreneurs.[19] Paltrow wanted to defy the image of being a dilettante actress, even though she had already proven that that stereotype did not apply to her. And so she took her most vulnerable step yet.

"The day that I asked my board for the CEO title, it was one of the most exposed feelings I've ever had in my life, because I didn't know if they were going to take my side," she remembered. "Part of my inner voice was like, 'What the fuck are you doing? You can't do this.' The other inner voice was like, 'I am absolutely the only person who can do this.'" (As it turned out, the study on late-arriving female confidence also applies to the then-forty-five-year-old Paltrow.) The board agreed. In the summer of 2016, she finally, officially became the chief executive officer of the company that she had built from her kitchen. "I'm glad that it wasn't their idea, and I'm glad that I was put in the incredibly uncomfortable position of having to ask for it, because I had to force myself," she explained. "I had to force myself to step into it just psychologically, and then I had to force myself into that place of absolute exposure to ask for it, which I think was a really important piece of the puzzle."

As the newly installed CEO, Paltrow found herself navigating similar conflicting demands. She was pushing herself to be willful and authoritative but was constantly aware of the social pressure to exude a kind of feminine, communal warmth. Her persona embodied that paradox; she felt remote because of her wealth and privilege but approachable because of her failures and personal struggles.

This pressure to reconcile two parts of oneself is actually quite typical of the double bind that female leaders often face in professional arenas. In 2018, three University of Wisconsin professors published a report on interviews with sixty women executives from various industries; they found among them a pervasive feeling that they were expected to simultaneously embody a characteristic *and* its polar opposite. The article,

"Dancing on the Razor's Edge: How Top-Level Women Leaders Manage the Paradoxical Tensions Between Agency and Communion," identified key conflicts: women were expected to be both demanding *and* caring, authoritative *and* participative, self-advocating *and* other-serving, distant *and* approachable.[20]

Yet Paltrow seemed to make it all work. In 2017, the year after she was named CEO, she oversaw an expansion of Goop's empire. The company hosted its first-ever wellness symposium and introduced vitamin supplements, selling $100,000 worth of product on launch day. Soon after, she debuted a podcast (Oprah was her first guest) and Goop launched a line of furniture and homewares with CB2.

During that time, Goop drew the ire not just of the media but also of the watchdog group Truth in Advertising. At issue was a $66 jade egg designed to be inserted into the vagina. The beauty guru Shiva Rose claimed that the egg could "help cultivate sexual energy" and "help clear chi pathways into the body," among other things. Truth in Advertising published a report pointing to fifty additional instances when Goop had allegedly made unsubstantiated health claims about products on the site. More headlines came the following year, when the California Food, Drug, and Medical Device Task Force filed a consumer protection complaint and the Santa Clara County DA's office filed suit over false advertising of three products, including the jade egg.[21]

Goop did not admit wrongdoing and eventually settled the case with the California task force and the lawsuit with the district attorney's office, agreeing to pay a $145,000 fine and refund buyers of the egg. (Presumably it took no jade egg returns.) The company also agreed to be clearer about which of its recommendations were experimental treatments and which were backed by science. But Paltrow didn't take that set of legal attacks as a sign that she should focus on fashion and food as opposed to fringe wellness treatments. The board had been confident enough in her to give her the reins of the company, so she was going to trust her instincts. She decided, as CEO, to continue her exploration of wellness.

"I felt like people can beat me up," she said. "I actually don't really give a fuck. Whether celery juice works or doesn't work, there is something here about women wanting alternative ways to feel better and to explore things and—even more importantly—to say, 'And I'm *entitled* to search for an answer.' I knew that despite what the patriarchy had to say about it, this was happening, and I wasn't willing to back down." She could see that there was a movement to pursue a new kind of holistic wellness, and she wanted Goop to be at the center of it. So Goop invested in the validation of products and treatments, creating a science and research division and called on doctors to explain experimental protocols on the site. It started to link to clinical research and admits when evidence is lacking. "Of course we had to grow up," Paltrow said. The investment not only prevented further lawsuits, it also meant that the company could be taken more seriously. Sales of the products mentioned in its articles kept growing.

That general attitude of inquiry also corresponded with Paltrow's evolving leadership style. "I was learning very tactical operational things as I went, and I decided that I would start asking questions," she said. "Instead of being afraid to look stupid and googling acronyms under the desk, I'd just say, 'No, I don't know what that means.' It was deciding 'I don't know if I'm going to be good at this. But I know that I have to try and that I'm going to have to do it in my own way.'" As she asked for more explanation, she was surprised to find that her colleagues seemed to benefit from the clarification as well. Transparency not only proved valuable to Paltrow's staff but, broadly, has been shown to have positive effects on a company's culture: 96 percent of professional women say that they can learn more from a leader who shows vulnerability than one who doesn't, according to a study conducted by Ellevate Network and Berlin Cameron.[22]

While the kind of vulnerability Paltrow demonstrates invites trust and collaboration, its opposite—an attitude of invincibility—has been found to prevent leaders from receiving vital feedback and leads to what academics call "opinion conformity." A study found that high levels of flattery increase CEOs' overconfidence in their judgment and leadership capability. No surprise, overconfidence is found to result in biased decision making—and that drives underperformance.[23]

Ultimately, Paltrow's willingness to ask questions yielded more opportunities. She admitted her inexperience with Excel and, after asking a slew of questions, learned how to analyze the company's sales trends to strategize about what products to make next. Asking questions—onstage—became the centerpiece of Goop's next expansion. The year after she became CEO, the company focused on building out a live-events business with "In Goop Health" summits that featured expert interviews and panel discussions alongside yoga classes, sound baths, and raw, vegan, gluten-free doughnuts. Though Goop was mocked for high prices—$1,000 for a day and $4,500 for the 2019 Los Angeles weekend—the tickets sold out nearly instantly.

In 2018, the company's many revenue streams drew the attention of venture capital firms, and Paltrow ended up raising an additional $50 million from three blue-chip funds, at a $250 million valuation. In early 2019, the company drew additional investment from Greycroft, which wanted to invest in Goop because, according to founding partner Dana Settle, "What we look for in the best entrepreneurs—in the consumer space—is backing the original. The copycats are always fast following. The original—assuming they're excellent at execution, which Gwyneth is—they're always going to win." Before making the investment, Greycroft had commissioned research that found that Paltrow's dedicated fans bought products from all of Goop's categories. Settle was surprised to learn that in addition to Goop's original audience of affluent white women, its fan base had expanded to a far more diverse audience, including younger women and women of color. She attributed that range to Paltrow's "willingness to take risks on things and be wrong, and take being wrong in stride. . . . That made us believe that Goop could be a really broad platform: she could expand into every category and many markets internationally."

The year 2020 marked Goop's big TV debut with the launch of its first Netflix show exploring fringe wellness practices. It premiered just before the covid-19 pandemic started to challenge many parts of the business; pricey live events were turned into free digital ones, retail spaces were shuttered, and many advertisers retrenched. Still, Paltrow was ready to make the necessary adjustments. "She started the year in high-growth mode; then she pulled back, cut a percentage of her workforce, made tough decisions early, and got the business to a profitable level," said Settle in late 2020. "She's had two quarters of profitability after cutting expenses. I'm now more confident she can really build a giant business based on how she's handled things this year. She's continued to do the hard things and do them well." Through the rest of 2020, the company pivoted to focus more on content rather than events and shifted its products to wellness and casual fashion; it also launched a new skin care line and a libido supplement.

In February 2021, the company launched sexual wellness products that showed massive growth: its Double-Sided Wand Vibrator became the company's second-highest revenue-generating Goop-branded item. In March 2021, the company moved into the food business by launching goop Kitchen, a delivery-only "clean" restaurant, featuring Paltrow's favorite healthy recipes, in Los Angeles. By a year after launch, over half the sales from the two locations were from frequent customers who order between once and twice a week. As this book went to press the company was readying the launch of "clean" pizza and rotisserie delivery-only restaurants in the Los Angeles area, with additional locations planned across the country. In early 2022, Goop announced plans to expand its presence in Japan. As of April 2022 when the book went to press, the company said it had raised a total of $135 million at a $400 million valuation.

Imposter Syndrome

It is notable that even women such as Gwyneth Paltrow tend to underestimate their own leadership potential—and can be underestimated by others. A study published in *Harvard Business Review* in 2018 found that self-confidence is distributed evenly between genders; there is no consistent difference between how men and women describe their self-confidence. What *is* gendered is how that confidence is *perceived*. The level of self-confidence women *felt* did not correlate with how self-confident they *seemed* to others. Furthermore, appearing self-confident helped men, enabling them to exert influence in their organization. In contrast, high-performing women did not benefit simply from displaying self-confidence; their influence benefited from that trait only if it was paired with appearing warm and caring.[24]

Academics have sought to understand this self-confidence disconnect by comparing how executives rate themselves with how they are rated by others. When judged by others, women leaders are rated as significantly more effective, but when asked to rate themselves, male leaders described themselves as significantly more effective than women described themselves. In effect, the confidence of female leaders is much lower than it should be, based on how others see them.[25] Another study found that 30 percent of women rate themselves in the top tenth of leaders, compared to 37 percent of men. The more senior the executive, the greater the differential between how women are seen and how they see themselves. At the highest level, 63 percent of men rate themselves as highly effective leaders compared to 49 percent of women at the same level.[26]

Women are also more likely than men to suffer from imposter syndrome. A study of three hundred senior executives from a range of organizations found that more than double the percentage of women (54 percent) as men (24 percent) feel imposter syndrome, or a feeling of unworthiness for their position.[27] (To be clear: this is not a fault of women but rather the result of being faced with bias and chronically underestimated at work.) A number of books have been published on this topic, including *The Confidence Code: The Science and Art of Self-Assurance—What Women Should Know* by Claire Shipman and Katty Kay.

In some situations, however, the self-doubt women too frequently feel can be a valuable tool in decision making. In her book *How Women Decide:*

What's True, What's Not, and What Strategies Spark the Best Choices, the cognitive psychologist Therese Huston wrote that people should dial their confidence down so that they can consider other perspectives when making a decision. Then, when they're executing that decision and communicating about it, they should dial their confidence back up.[28] This is an approach that Holmgren and Paltrow each seems to have mastered in her own way. Holmgren took an academic approach to testing feedstocks, double-checking hypotheses before confidently pushing her company to embrace a new approach. Paltrow questioned acronyms and business practices before launching new products and events.

Though these two women are different in so many ways, one thing they share is ambition and the fact that they have pursued their ambition differently from the expectations of traditional male leaders. Holmgren doesn't match the patterns of male scientist or gregarious tech salesman; Paltrow, as she points out, didn't go to business school (she didn't graduate from college). But they both figured out how to leverage characteristics that have traditionally been seen as weaknesses—introversion, vulnerability, and inexperience—to be effective, iconoclastic leaders. Both were fiercely ambitious while looking nothing like the archetype of an authoritative, unquestioning male leader.

Pundits and academics have examined the narrow archetype of male ambition, questioning whether women are simply less driven or whether they aspire to more things beyond just professional success. As patterns of self-confidence and ambition can be tightly related, it makes sense that just as with self-confidence, nothing has been found to suggest that ambition is inherently gendered. One of the most comprehensive studies of ambition, in which BCG surveyed two hundred thousand employees around the world, found that ambition is not an inherently male or female trait. Women were found to be just as ambitious as men at the outset of their careers, and any decline in women's ambition was found to be due to corporate environments that didn't support diversity. At companies where employees felt that gender diversity was improving, there was no meaningful ambition gap between women and men aged thirty to fifty; they sought promotion at basically the same rate. At companies where employees saw the least progress on diversity—"where women see an uphill battle to reach an unattractive summit," as the study put it—the ambition gap widened.[29] Interestingly, both men and women were found to become less ambitious as they age—perhaps because they began to see that certain goals were out of reach.

Just as important as the fact that ambition is not a gendered trait is the fact that it is not a fixed one, but rather can be nurtured or smothered by corporate environments. Though historically companies may have done more of the latter, that fact opens the possibility for businesses to work to foster ambition. That fact also means that there is potential for both men and women to learn to exploit the overlapping traits of ambition and self-confidence. Everyone can gain value from turning their self-confidence down—asking questions and listening—when it's appropriate and turning it up when it's time to execute. People can turn those dials in their own ways: Paltrow with her vulnerability, Holmgren with her reticence. Those two tools can be just as effective as the bluster that stereotypically attends male expressions of self-confidence, especially if the goal is to invite collaboration.

Holmgren's and Paltrow's leadership styles both defy archetypes, but in other ways, of course, they could not be more different. From a young age, Paltrow loved getting up onstage in front of thousands of people, while thirty-year-old Holmgren preferred not to present to a conference room. Even their voices are opposites: Holmgren has a quiet lilt, and Paltrow projects a strong alto across rooms. What does a Colombian immigrant who rose through the ranks at a petroleum company share with an Oscar-winning celebrity whose dating life has been a tabloid obsession?

After I interviewed the two of them, I was surprised that I kept coming back to their stories and—oddly enough—comparing them to each other. What I realized is that each found her own way to being a powerful force at her company. And neither of them had thought of herself as a CEO.

What this commonality shows me is that the instinct toward pattern matching that I wrote about in the first chapter doesn't happen just with venture capitalists but also inside the egos of entrepreneurs and executives. Inside all of us. By any measure, either of these women was more than qualified to be CEO; Holmgren had spent her career exploring alternative fuel sources, and Paltrow had built a company from her kitchen that was created in her own image. Both women needed to be convinced that they were equipped to wear that mantle. If someone as powerful and connected as Paltrow can feel hesitancy, there are surely women all over the world who feel constrained by the dominant male archetypes of leadership. Pattern matching can be insidious and internal. And it should no longer hold people back.

There is a scene early in the 2010 movie *Iron Man 2* in which Paltrow's character, Pepper Potts, tries to get her playboy boss, Tony Stark, to focus on running Stark Industries. Tony tries to wave her off, but when Pepper continues to press Tony, he reveals that he's making *her* CEO. Pepper is so stunned that she sits down. The movie's tinkling piano score indicates that it is surprising for a woman to be made CEO of a giant company—even though she already seems to be running it. When I first saw the film in 2010, I didn't think twice about the scene, which shows how effective Hollywood is at hiding values in plain sight. When I watched it with my kids in 2021, I couldn't help but think about the cultural forces at play that made Paltrow's path to becoming CEO of her own Stark Industries such a long one. (In chapter 5, I noted that the release of the movie *WarGames* correlated with a decline in women majoring in computer science.)

In 2018, when Paltrow was meeting with investors to secure her company's Series C round of funding, she says she was asked questions such as "Who's the secret guy who's running Goop?" "I was like, 'Wow.'

Again, it was, like, that same thing of being really flattered and really patronized at the same time," she said. Like the female jockeys before her, she was being underestimated—and before she took the CEO role, she had underestimated herself. But she proved the skeptical investors and media critics wrong and broke the betting cycle in her own way. That doesn't mean that now she's waiting for anyone to roll out the red carpet. "It doesn't bother me," she said. "If anything, you know, sometimes I think I feel galvanized by being dismissed."

⊃ Nine

Discovering Resilience

How Female Leaders Navigate Obstacles and Draw on Inner Strength

On January 31, 2000, the St. Louis Rams and the Tennessee Titans met on the playing field for Super Bowl XXXIV. What made the event notable wasn't the game itself but the fact that for the first time, more than a quarter of the game's sixty-one very valuable commercial spots (a thirty-second spot cost around $2 million) touted internet companies (up from two the prior year). Two of those companies were pioneers in e-commerce: Webvan and Pets.com. Both promised customers fast, inexpensive shipping, and both had expanded quickly and expensively. Each had hired an experienced CEO to take it public. Neither company, however, would go on to buy a commercial in the following year's Super Bowl: one liquidated, the other filed for bankruptcy. Both earned the ignominy of being among the worst flops in dot-com history.

The companies' leaders, however, did not face the same consequences. George Shaheen, who had become Webvan's CEO in September 1999, resigned in April 2001, reportedly with a retirement package that included $375,000 a year for the rest of his life.[1] In 2005, he was appointed CEO of Siebel Systems, which five months later merged with Oracle. Webvan's COO and CFO, Bob Swan, who became CEO after Shaheen resigned, became CFO of a publicly traded auto parts conglomerate a mere month after Webvan shuttered (the hire was justified in the press by the company's assertion that the failure had been a "valuable experience").[2] He moved on to greener pastures as CFO of Hewlett-Packard and eBay, eventually ascending the throne as CEO of the Silicon Valley powerhouse Intel.

The CEO of Pets.com, meanwhile, faced the company's collapse under the withering glare of the media and was dubbed by TechCrunch's Michael Arrington "the dumbest person in the Valley." Though she went on to consult for venture capital investors and to run a number of small software companies, media mentions of her would inevitably refer back to her notorious dot-com disaster. Her name is Julie Wainwright, and more than a decade after the Pets.com bankruptcy, a powerful Silicon Valley recruiter told her that she was, in fact, unhirable. The albatross of her brief and long-past failure was an indelible part of Wainwright's identity, whereas George Shaheen and Bob Swan's fiasco had been a chapter that hadn't prevented them from being appointed to other senior positions.

Gender Incongruity

When I started telling investors, executives, and founders that I was writing a book about female entrepreneurship, I heard the same refrain over and over again:

> You have to write about how women are judged more harshly.
>
> You have to talk about how women are held to a higher standard.

> You have to address the crazy hell women have to go through, how
>
> unfair it is, how hard it is to be a female leader.

I didn't hear that just from women; more than a dozen men I spoke to said the same thing.

Many studies have shown that women CEOs are treated much more harshly—and are much more likely to be fired—than their male counterparts. One by University of Alabama professor Vishal Gupta and his colleagues, published in 2020, found that when male CEOs are fired, it's typically a reflection of their poor performance. In contrast, female leaders are vulnerable to being fired regardless of whether a company is doing poorly or well.* In an examination of about 650 CEO dismissals, the researchers saw that women overwhelmingly faced higher risks to their leadership positions than men did. Even when their company's performance is above the median, they are more likely to be dismissed than their male counterparts are—45 percent more likely, to be exact.[3]

There are many theories to explain this trend, but one of the most prominent is called *token theory*. The theory goes that numerical minorities draw enhanced attention, exaggerated stereotypes, and heightened scrutiny. And there's no doubt that in business, particularly its highest ranks, women are a tiny numerical minority. As discussed elsewhere in this book, women hold just 6 percent of the CEO roles of the three thousand largest publicly traded companies in the United States, and within that group, the number of women of color is far smaller.[4]

In a 2012 study called "Failure Is Not an Option for Black Women," researchers asked study participants to read one of eight versions of an article that described a company's performance, leader gender, and leader

---

*The researchers examined the stock and financial performances of 2,390 companies between 2000 and 2014 and excluded CEOs in office for less than a year. About 3 percent of the companies had female CEOs, and the percentage of females fired was 5 percent versus 3 percent of male CEOs fired. They found that women were 45 percent more likely to be dismissed than male CEOs were.

race. Then the participants completed a questionnaire about the leader's effectiveness and typicality. White men were perceived as the more typical and effective leaders. Both women and Black individuals were perceived as less typical leaders. Because of this perceived unusualness, the Black women were judged as "ineffective" when the organization performed poorly. The professors call this *double jeopardy*: there is even greater discrimination against those with multiple marginalized identities than those with just one marginalized identity.[5]

In focusing on a leader's marginalized identity, media attention tends to further exacerbate and reinforce gender bias.[*] In 2016, the Rockefeller Foundation analyzed media coverage of twenty CEOs—eleven women and nine men—during a transition or time of crisis. The media stories about female-led companies mentioned gender about half the time, while only 4 percent of stories about male-led companies did. Of the pieces about female CEOs, 78 percent referred to the CEO's family. Not a single piece about male CEOs mentioned the word. Common topics in the stories about men were their plans for retirement, their postcareer ambitions, and their social lives.[6]

When journalists focus on a CEO's missteps, the gender bias can be even more glaring. In an eighteen-month period from mid-2019 through 2020, when the national reckoning with systemic racism was burning hottest, many leaders were torched for their tin-eared public statements or problematic leadership styles. But the media seemed to take special delight in pillorying the women. During that time a number of female CEOs and founders stepped down or were forced out amid public criticism. Among them were Outdoor Voices founder Tyler Haney, Away cofounder Steph Korey, Refinery29's Christene Barberich, Reformation founder Yael Aflalo, Ban.do founder Jen Gotch, and Cleo founder Shannon Spanhake.

Many of those leaders seem to have genuinely made mistakes. Haney,

---

[*]Yes, even in these pages I am giving more "media attention" to the rareness of female leaders.

for example, was skewered for having created a "mean girls" culture—for allegedly appointing friends to senior roles and creating a hostile work environment.[7] Korey, meanwhile, allegedly sent harsh Slack messages to her employees about a business malfunction. Those messages were highlighted in an exposé on The Verge about the company's "toxic work environment." The then thirty-one-year-old Away cofounder apologized and immediately stepped down as CEO. But then, a month later, she returned to the role, saying her lawyers had identified "deliberate lies and distortions" in the Verge report.[8]

I'm not the only one who noticed this pattern. As those events unfolded, media watchers and tech insiders raised valid questions about whether female founders were being held to a different, higher standard because they were women. In early 2020, The Information noted that volatile male leaders, such as Steve Jobs, were frequently described as passionate, while women were being canceled for similar or even less dramatic behavior.[9] In December 2020, Fortune magazine identified common traits among the women most likely to be targeted: they ran fast-growing, VC-backed startups that emphasized feminist or socially driven missions and had become the celebrity faces of their business.[10] (Such attacks have continued: in late 2021, Spring Health's April Koh was the subject of a critical article by Insider reporting that her hard-driving approach had led dozens of employees to quit. She responded by speaking about her growth as a leader and the company's changes.)[11]

An investor closely watching this pattern is Kirsten Green, a founding partner at the VC firm Forerunner Ventures. The firm has a successful track record of making big investments in a number of female-led, consumer-facing startups, including Outdoor Voices, Glossier, Ritual, Zola, and Away, plus others with male founders. Green said, "Some of those articles, the lens at which they approached women was very unfair." She sees the scrutiny as fascination with outliers and curiosity about the new breed of leader. "It's like, 'Oh, she's a bitch? Not everyone is perfectly happy working there? Oh, that's a good story.'" Green sees that approach as unconstructive and click-baity. "Never mind that those founders had visibility *because* they built businesses that customers loved, that were growing at impressive rates, and that plenty of people *did* want to work at. Somehow that got lost in the story."

After being the subject of many, many negative articles, Julie Wainwright could have accepted that the Pets.com fiasco was going to define the rest of her career. But she didn't. She spent a decade advising, founding, and serving as CEO of various startups before founding The Real-Real, the world's largest authenticated luxury resale platform. When the company went public on June 28, 2019, nearly every media story mentioned her past. Wainwright, remarkably, doesn't take that mistreatment personally. "I've got amazing people I work with every day. I love what I do. What I'm doing is good for the planet. I've made millionaires out of a lot of people at the company, who are mostly women. Every day I'm thankful I took that first step," she said. "There is a double standard, but that doesn't mean you shouldn't do it."

Many women say they've come to terms with the constant additional challenge of a double standard. Rent the Runway's Jenn Hyman faced a similar harsh glare when, at the onset of the coronavirus pandemic, she was forced to lay off all the workers at the company's five retail stores—and she had to do it over Zoom. It was a move that drew headlines and criticism for her being abrupt and heartless, though of course there was no way to meet safely with employees in person. And with nonessential businesses mandated to close their doors, layoffs were the only measure she could have taken to save the company.[12] Then, weeks later, she faced another round of media excoriations because Rent the Runway's warehouse employees continued to work. It was a brutal heads-I-lose-tails-you-win situation: it's heartless to let go of employees, and it's heartless to keep employees on the job during a pandemic, when they might fall ill. In June 2020, Hyman addressed her management decisions in a detailed explanation posted on Rent the Runway's website. She wrote, "The Leadership Team and I were also forced to make previously unthinkable people decisions with incomplete information about how much or for how long this crisis would impact our business." Of course, thousands of other business owners also had to furlough or lay off employees to remain solvent. Yet very few had to endure such a public flogging.[13]

This double standard—the unfair application of higher expectations on different groups—isn't just a quirk of the media. In the business world, it's found in the behavior of "activist investors," firms that accrue more than 5 percent of a company's stock in order to pressure management to make specific changes. An eighteen-year study found that female-led firms were about twice as likely to face an activist threat as comparable male-led firms and that female-led companies are 60 percent more likely to draw simultaneous attacks from multiple activists. Even when the researchers controlled for the fact that women are more likely to be placed in leadership positions when a company is struggling (the "glass cliff" phenomenon discussed in chapter 3), women still had a greater likelihood of being targeted. The researchers running the data concluded that women "face more public display of dissatisfaction and (unwanted) direction, at least from activist shareholders, regardless of the firm's performance."[14, 15]

This harsher judgment is not reserved exclusively for CEOs and founders. A study conducted by *Fortune* of about 250 employee performance reviews found that 71 percent of women and 2 percent of men had received negative feedback. (That is not a typo: 71 percent of women and 2 percent of men.) And women didn't draw just more negative feedback but also a different *quality* of feedback: whereas 81 percent of men received constructive feedback, only 23 percent of women did. The majority of feedback for women centered on "personality traits" rather than "workplace performance." And women tended to be criticized for traits that are valorized in male leadership, such as aggression. So not only are women being criticized for the same approaches men take, but because the focus is on their style, they're deprived of valuable feedback about their professional performance.[16]

This double standard doesn't come into play only when women are receiving feedback, but when they're delivering it as well. Martin Abel, a Middlebury College economics professor, has found that both male and female employees react more negatively to criticism if it comes from a female manager. Employees also report a larger reduction in job satisfaction following a critique by a female boss. That wasn't because people thought their supervisors were incompetent; in fact, workers who said their female supervisor was highly effective were just as likely to bristle at criticism from her.[17]

These findings are supported by other research showing that workers are three times as likely to associate receiving praise with female managers and twice as likely to associate receiving criticism with male managers. In effect, criticism by a woman stings more because gendered stereotypes make it feel so unexpected.[18]

Kimberly Taylor, the CEO of Cluster, a hiring platform for engineers, was inspired by that research to utilize a simple hack: when she wants to give critical feedback, she writes it down and deputizes a male executive to deliver it. She is also very careful not to act angry, because she has read studies about how professional women suffer negative consequences for any displays of emotion.

Yale professor Victoria Brescoll and INSEAD associate professor Eric Luis Uhlmann outlined evidence for this in a 2008 report that revealed that women's expressions of anger can decrease their status and perceived competence and even result in lower wages. (Brescoll also conducted the study about power and volubility in the US Senate featured in chapter 6.) For women, emotions, including anger, are seen as a fixed, internal trait. Women are described as being "out of control" or "an angry person," while men's expressions of anger are seen as a temporary response to external circumstances.[19]

To examine this perception, the researchers conducted an experiment in which they hired actors to express anger, sadness, or no emotion while being interviewed for a job. Study participants assigned the highest status to angry men, but angry women—whether a CEO or an assistant trainee—were accorded a lower status. The researchers found that women have to provide an external explanation for an emotional reaction to avoid suffering from a perceived loss of status or competence, whereas men have to give no reason at all. As they put it, "To the extent that an angry female professional can provide an objective, external reason for being angry, she should evoke less negative reactions."

We've seen this play out in professional sports, notably in the dramatically different treatment of tennis stars John McEnroe and Serena Williams. His on-court tantrums—arguing about calls and intimidating opponents—won him a reputation as a "bad boy," and he was later paid ten times as much as a sports commentator as his female contemporary, Martina Navratilova, despite her better playing record.[20] Serena Williams, at the 2018 Open, was penalized for behavior (haranguing a line judge) that in my view would not have drawn the same punishment had she been a man.[21]

The ways in which women are judged more harshly for workplace behavior even extends to something as seemingly innocuous as cracking jokes. University of Arizona and University of Colorado at Boulder researchers found that when women used humor in a mock presentation, participants were more likely to view it as disruptive, distracting, or masking their incapability, while men's humor was seen as helpful.[22]

The reason women leaders face extra scrutiny for raising their voice or cracking a joke comes down to the fact that such behavior simply is not expected of women. When they are in roles that don't fit stereotypes, women leaders suffer from what psychologists call *gender incongruity*. In 2010, Victoria Brescoll and her colleagues published research in *Psychological Science* showing that leaders in industries that are strongly associated with the opposite sex—say, a female police chief or the male president of a women's college—are more strongly penalized for making mistakes than are those in positions more closely associated with their own gender. When leaders made mistakes, women in traditionally male jobs were judged more harshly and seen as less competent than their "gender-congruent" counterparts.[23] (This has negative implications for men as well, though Brescoll says she couldn't properly measure the reaction to male leaders in powerful, traditionally female roles, because the only one she could find was the male president of a women's college.) Frustratingly, women can also be penalized for achieving success in roles perceived as "male"—because, no matter how they lead, their success is seen as the result of their failure to act in "female" ways, such as being nurturing or empathetic.[24]

Women are expected to be not only more nurturing but also more ethical. In 2020, a study published by the American Psychological Association examined how more than five hundred participants responded to male-led and female-led car companies after either an ethical failure (i.e., failing to disclose a critical fuel sensor issue) or a competence failure (i.e., being unaware of the issue in the first place). When the issue was an ethical failure, the participants were less likely to want to buy a car from the company when the CEO was a woman than when the CEO was a man. But when it was a failure of competence, the participants actually judged women less harshly. If members of either gender failed in their particular arena of gendered expectations—competence and ethics—they were penalized disproportionately for that failure. Though women were judged less harshly than men for competence failures at an auto company, they were not given the same leeway at a company that was viewed as more female-focused; they were judged more harshly for a competence failure at a baby products company.[25] The same study found that the expectation of gender stereotypes can hurt male leaders, too: when a male CEO was described as using traits inconsistent with gender stereotypes, such as being "communal," participants said that they were less likely to buy from his company.[26]

All of this research points to more than just a double standard—it's a double bind. Women are punished for demonstrating traits that have been historically identified as "male" and that are necessary for successful entrepreneurs: ambition and confidence. They're also punished for simply being successful in traditionally male roles. "You cannot be viewed as good in this business if you're not operating with all of the ambitions and tactics that have been attributed as male traits," Forerunner's Green said. "But if you're a woman, people expect you to cultivate a better culture, be a more empathetic leader, more understanding, to have a lighter-touch way of doing things. Males have been getting away with being male leaders, and females are expected to be female *and* male leaders at once." The bar is simply higher.

Hyman said that it's been difficult to be judged more harshly than her male counterparts are, but she pointed out another frustrating element of her experience: being a rare female CEO, she is constantly forced to answer questions about what it's like to be a rare female CEO. The pressure to respond to my interview requests for this book was yet another example of that type of imposition. Her agreement to participate speaks to the value she sees in sharing her story, but she said it comes at a cost. "I probably have to spend twenty-five percent of my time not only with the media but with investors and with external partners, just answering 'What's it like to be a female founder? What's it like to be a female CEO?' What that twenty-five percent of my time has meant is that I haven't gotten to spend that time talking about my business, my unit economics, the new partnership we want to launch," she said. "It's like a double whammy. Yes, it's harder to be a woman, it's harder to raise money, it's harder to get respect from your employees or investors. And then in addition to that, I have to spend time talking about it, which takes away from my capabilities of doing my job."

This creates a paradox: Hyman won't be treated equally until being a woman CEO is normalized. That won't be normalized unless she's out there showing how normal it is for a woman to be a CEO. It's a chicken-and-egg obstacle. And it's not lost on me that the positive aspects of female leadership that this book extolls could theoretically contribute to the "othering" of female leaders. I've discussed this challenge with many women whose stories are included in this book. None of us wants to tokenize female leaders, but until there are more women running businesses, the women who are in that position will attract additional scrutiny because they are rare.

Knowledge Is Power

All of these challenges are part of the double standards that are steeped in societal forces: centuries of misogyny and racism woven directly into business and political structures. Plus there's the natural human instinct toward pattern matching and confirmation bias. Those structures and stereotypes are so entrenched that it would be understandable to become discouraged and give up. So how do these female leaders not only survive but thrive?

A number of women have told me that the secret of not being discouraged by bias or discrimination is simply by recognizing it as such. "If you go in knowing the world is unjust, you don't need to learn the lesson every time you are faced with it," said Ayah Bdeir, who founded the educational technology company littleBits. "So when there are these cases of misogyny or sexism and you interface with them, you just categorize it as that." An engineer who immigrated to the United States from Lebanon and earned a master's degree at MIT, Bdeir has faced both anti-Arab discrimination and sexism, particularly when she was fundraising. "Because I was a woman, I would always get asked, 'Do you have a cofounder who, you know, is the technical person?' And I'd say, 'I'm the engineer. I invented the product from scratch. I have multiple degrees in engineering.' Being an immigrant, you are used to having to deal with that anyways, so I kind of put them in the same bucket," she told me.

Though knowing that bias existed did not fully immunize Bdeir from its impact, it did help her manage her response to it. Identifying a critical comment as reflecting bias enabled her to set it aside without allowing it to deplete her self-confidence. She thinks of it like remembering to wear a jacket in cold weather: "You have to notice it because you have to know what you are dealing with, so you look at it straight in the eye instead of being afraid of it and are like, 'This is what is happening right now, and I am going to just park it here and keep doing my thing.'"

Other female founders employ similar tactics. In chapter 1, I discussed a 2019 study by All Raise that found that when entrepreneurs are fundraising, investors are more likely to ask women questions about downside issues such as employee retention, whereas men tend to be asked about upside promise and growth potential. A number of women, including Bdeir and Cluster CEO Kimberly Taylor, told me that seeing the data laid bare enabled them to prepare strategies. Thanks to those insights, they were poised to flip questions about their business's minimum potential into responses about its maximum opportunity. Women who recognize these patterns and obstacles can design routes around them.

Joan Williams, a law professor and author and the director of the Center for WorkLife Law at the University of California Hastings College of the Law, calls awareness and mastery of double standards "gender judo." "Women in leadership need to display these 'masculine' qualities, but when they do, they risk being seen as bad women, and also as bad people," she wrote. "So savvy women learn that they must often do a masculine thing (which establishes their competence) in a feminine way (to defuse backlash)." To achieve that balance, Williams has found, female leaders adopt communal leadership strategies and signal empathy not because it is intrinsic to their natures but because they sense, accurately, that it works. Some female leaders have found success using metaphors to recode behavior that is commonly associated with men. For instance, some women leaders began referring to customer acquisition work as "gardening" instead of "hunting." Another approach is to reject the impulse to look like the archetypal male CEO, instead dressing in feminine styles.[27]

In many conversations I had during the reporting of this book, the topic of style naturally emerged whenever I complimented a woman on her blazer or inquired about a pair of striking earrings. That prompted a number of women to share the satisfaction they've found in embracing their own style, even if they knew it would draw more attention to them. Underneath the trading of fashion flattery I found something much more complex: to some, dressing in flamboyantly feminine styles felt like an act of rebellion. Many of them admitted that it had taken years of dressing in boxy dark suits to blend in with the guys before they built up the courage to dress in a feminine way that could throw off those familiar with the typical look of VCs or entrepreneurs. Forerunner's Kirsten Green wears fashion-forward designer dresses and jackets, often in bright colors and prints, knowing that she'll stand out in the sea of men wearing Patagonia vests. "I do that for myself—look good, feel good—I appreciate style as fun." She added, "If people want to discredit me because I've come in dressed up, thinking I somehow care more about fashion than I do about the business, that's ridiculous." Cluster CEO Kim Taylor wears bright red dresses and her long, straight black hair down past her shoulders. "I'm not going to show up at an event and dress like men in black, boxy suits. I'd rather be really feminine and stand out," she told me.

In the late 2000s, I was adapting to my new job as a TV reporter on CNBC and generally wore boxy blazers in muted tones—as much camouflage as clothing. Then I met Mindy Grossman. At the time she was the CEO of the Home Shopping Network (it was a gender-congruous job), and she was sitting in a swanky Beverly Hills hotel lobby, where her pink blazer and long pink nails seemed to pop out of the taupe upholstery. To me, she embodied a new image of hyperfeminine power with her long blond hair, dramatic eye makeup, oversized jewelry, and glamorous designer clothes. She was one of several female executives, along with NBCUniversal's chairman of global advertising and partnerships Linda Yaccarino and longtime media veteran-turned-Spotify executive Dawn Ostroff, who inspired me to shed my muted suits in favor of the fitted, bright dresses and stylish leather jackets that pop both on TV and in real life. Thanks to Grossman et al., I've come to understand that fashion can be like armor; it makes me feel stronger and, indeed, more like myself.

Grossman's sartorial choices aren't a tactic but rather an authentic expression of her lifelong love of fashion. It is that passion that drove her to abandon her plan to go to law school, break up with her fiancé, and move to New York to work in the clothing industry. (After HSN, in

2017, she became the CEO of WW, formerly Weight Watchers). Grossman says that bringing her personal style to the office has empowered her employees to do the same. And it's made her a better CEO. "As a woman I never tried to lead two lives. There wasn't the personal Mindy and the public Mindy. It was one. And I never had an issue melding the two and giving people visibility to who I was as a person and how that informed who I was in business." That was particularly unusual in the 1990s, she noted, when she was rising through the ranks at the Warnaco Group and Ralph Lauren and it was more common for women to hide the details of their personal lives from work colleagues. Grossman was open about her commute between Nike's headquarters in Oregon and her family in New York, which had the unintentional effect of "gender judo," reminding her employees that she was a nurturing mother while she was also a tough boss.[28]

Rising Above

The United States Air Force Academy in Colorado Springs is an elite institution that trains fighter pilots, astronauts, and missile maintenance officers. One in five cadets doesn't make it through the four years to graduation. It's one of the most respected and prestigious military training facilities in the world. It also proclaims to have a commitment to "creating a culture and climate where diversity strengthens all personnel."[29] Yet in the early 2000s, you'd have been hard pressed to find a less hospitable environment for a young woman. Roughly a quarter of women regularly dropped out.[*] When Kimberly Shenk began her freshman year at the academy in 2004, her class was 17 percent female. In her specialty, operations research, only 10 percent of her classmates were women. The year

---

*Twenty-five percent of women dropped out in 2016, compared to 23 percent of men.

before she matriculated, an investigation had found that 12 percent of the women who had graduated from the USAFA had reported either rape or attempted rape and 70 percent of women had reported being sexually harassed. Worse, the investigation found that the academy's leadership had largely dismissed the complaints.[30] (The report prompted the institution to implement changes.)

Shenk felt equipped to handle that inhospitable environment because her parents had raised her to believe that she could do anything she wanted—including flying a jet in the air force. She had grown up in a small town on the California-Nevada border, where her father had worked as a rescue pilot for the California Highway Patrol. She had been obsessed with flying from the time she was five, and by age seventeen, she had earned her pilot's license. She had led her school's varsity volleyball team and been recruited to play at several schools, including the Air Force Academy.

The USAFA proclaims its institutional mission to treat men and women the same: they carry the same M16s and packs when they're thrown into the woods for the same basic training. Shenk considered that a draw. But once she arrived at the campus in the Colorado Rockies, she discovered that regardless of the orthodoxy of the institution, individual men often treated her differently in day-to-day interactions, using especially offensive language around her or ignoring her completely. During survival training, members of her squadron were thrown into a van with a bag over their heads to re-create being abducted by terrorists. When the bags were pulled off and it was clear that she was the sole woman in the group, she says she was beaten far more than her male classmates were. "They're creating that environment: this is what you would go through. But why was I put in the center of the room? Why was I always getting beat up as the single female? It was like they were trying to evoke something."

She also felt that she was more deliberately targeted for punishment by superiors, especially for minor infractions and especially in public. When she made a mistake, such as walking with her hands in her pockets, she was yelled at, and she drew additional punishment if she broke from "military bearing" by showing any emotional response. She tried to focus on how to rise above her colleagues' and superiors' targeting her by telling herself "No, I am *not* one of you, I *am* better than this. I can do this better than you, and I want to show you that and I want to get respect." She said she was eventually able to achieve total mastery of her emotions, in part by recognizing that she was being targeted simply because she was a woman. She also learned to tune out the harassment by focusing on her own strength; she had as much a right to be there as the men that surrounded her.

Despite all of Shenk's challenges, she was named Academic All-American at the academy all four years and matriculated into MIT's graduate programs in data science while simultaneously serving as a second lieutenant in the air force. She went on to work as a data scientist for a number of companies, including the ticketing service Eventbrite, before in 2019 founding Novi, a platform for consumer products companies to source and purchase chemicals and ingredients. The company digitizes transactions that were previously handled with phone calls and adds a new level of transparency to the sourcing and pricing of materials.

But it wasn't at the Air Force Academy (10 percent women) that she felt the most gender discrimination. Nor was it at MIT (18 percent).[31] Nor even in the bro-heavy world of tech startups. She felt the most discomfort while pitching venture capitalists to raise money for her new company. Given that Novi and similar no-inventory platforms are all the rage in Silicon Valley (she described it as "Uber for chemicals"), she found it surprising that it took so long to raise funding compared to male founders she knew at the same stage, with similar metrics. In retrospect, one of the reasons she thinks her pitch was rejected dozens of times was that she pitched only to male investing partners. "I love to work hard," she says. "But when you have to go out and be judged seventy-two times over, you have to keep telling yourself, 'No, this is worthwhile.'" As she had done at the Air Force Academy, Schenk stuck it out, and by September 2021, she had raised $11.5 million.[32]

Self-Competition

I have always been curious about how women like Shenk manage to flourish in such hostile environments. How do they not let all the hurdles discourage them? How do they manage to persist and find a path to success, in the face of painful double standards? What do they draw on to find the strength to persevere? As I heard these women's stories and reviewed the data, a surprising (and somewhat counterintuitive) shared trait emerged: they tend to possess strong and secure identities *outside of work*.

In fact, Stanford University psychology professors found that subjects were more resilient in the face of stressors when they were able to reflect on other, unrelated parts of their life, such as family, cultural identity, or even allegiance to a sports team. "When self-affirmed in this manner, people realize that their self-worth does not hinge on the evaluative implications of the immediate situation. As a result, they . . . can respond to the threatening information in a more open and evenhanded manner," they wrote.[33]

I have also noticed that entrepreneurs often feel bolstered by their heritage. Their personal history helps them gain perspective on challenges and access the strength to overcome them. When Kimberly Shenk felt discouraged at the academy or by the challenges of launching a business, she reflected on how her German grandfather had refused to fight for the Nazis. To avoid conscription, he had hidden with her grandmother in a forest in Poland before escaping to Canada with two young children; her grandmother had given birth to Shenk's father during the boat voyage. "They came over with nothing and they didn't know English, and my oma, she's the strongest person you could ever meet and would do any job for the three kids—to make money, to make it work,"

Shenk said. "She cleaned bathrooms and was running around scrubbing floors—they just pointed for her to do things, and she did that for months on end." This strength Shenk found in her heritage is also borne out by academic studies: Emory University professors found that the more children know about their family's history—good and bad—the higher their self-esteem.[34] In moments of hardship, Shenk thought of that legacy of resilient refugees. Her identity wasn't just that of a female cadet facing bias or a frustrated entrepreneur; her heritage was grit and strength, and she could carry that mantle forward.

littleBits founder Ayah Bdeir similarly drew on her family's experiences and her cultural identity as a Lebanese immigrant to rise above gendered expectations both as a grad student at MIT and as an entrepreneur. "What Lebanese people had to do all their life is to be entrepreneurs and to be resourceful and to be resilient because the country has been through a dozen—if not more—wars, civil wars, invasions," she explained. That vivid and separate identity that celebrated adaptation provided comfort and motivation in the face of withering VC rejections.

There is one particular nonprofessional identity I've noticed that many of the women in this book share: athlete. Kimberly Shenk played Division I volleyball and The RealReal's Julie Wainwright and Capway's Sheena Allen played basketball in high school. Cluster CEO Kimberly Taylor was a serious gymnast. PagerDuty CEO Jennifer Tejada played Division I golf. WorkBoard's Deidre Paknad is a competitive cyclist. (There are other examples in this book, including some in the next two chapters.) Those women told me that playing sports had boosted their confidence and taught them the value of pushing themselves.

The self-discipline and teamwork required by competitive athletics have been found to correlate with a range of benefits, including better grades, enhanced leadership skills, and higher self-esteem. Research by the economist and professor Betsey Stevenson found that sports participation drives an increase in female college attendance and labor force participation. Greater opportunities for women to play sports have led to their greater participation in previously male-dominated, high-paid occupations.[35]* Ninety-four percent of women in the study who held the top, C-suite positions were former athletes and 52 percent had played sports at the collegiate level, compared to 39 percent of women at other managerial levels.[36] Another study identified that participating in sports when young enables women to earn more later in life: former college athletes earn about 7 percent more annually than do nonathletes, when controlling for other factors.[37] Perhaps most important is that playing sports encourages self-evaluation and the understanding that one's individual performance can be adjusted and affected by one's own work, not just external influence. Serious athletes, studies found, more often develop the ability to take failure as feedback to make them stronger.[38]

"I didn't ever look at wanting to win as a male thing, it was an athlete thing, and I wanted to win—I am *extremely* competitive," said Christine Hunsicker, who played three varsity sports all four years of high school. In fact, it was her field hockey ability that took her from a small town in rural Pennsylvania to Princeton University. There she found not just a group of teammates but a community of two dozen women who worked together to be tough and win. "It didn't dawn on me until I was in my mid twenties that this was a thing that people did not celebrate in women. Someone who worked for me said, 'You're the most competitive person I've ever met, and I don't mean that as a good thing.'" Hunsicker didn't want to apologize for her drive. She was president and COO of two startups acquired by Yahoo! and Facebook, respectively, and is the CEO and founder of CaaStle, a technology company that owns the size-inclusive clothing rental company Gwynnie Bee and enables retail brands to provide subscription and rental services.

*In the six years after Title IX was enacted in 1972, the percentage of girls playing a team sport jumped from 4 to 25 percent. For every 10 percentage point rise in state-level female sports participation, there was a 1 percentage point increase in female college attendance and a 1 to 2 percentage point rise in female labor force participation.

When she first launched Gwynnie Bee's rental offering, she was surprised that consumers didn't bite; her research had indicated that there was plenty of demand. Instead of starting to tinker with the product, she and her team did the equivalent of reviewing the tape of a losing game: they commissioned focus groups to understand which features didn't resonate and why. Then she returned to the field with a better product. "You have to learn how to lose a game and come back stronger; sports are all about trying and competing at a certain level, getting to the next level and probably failing, continuing to go and figure it out. Using those defeats as motivation is absolutely critical, because every day in business is a series of mistakes and learning how to correct for it." Just as her team had had postgame sessions, she brings her employees together for "retrospectives" to analyze their performance systematically (Hunsicker intentionally does not call them postmortems—after all, nobody died).

Academics have another name for what Hunsicker was doing: "after-event reviews." The process starts with explaining what a team did and how that contributed to the outcome. Then the group is prompted to consider other possible explanations for how their actions led to the outcome. Finally, team members are asked what behavior changes could lead to enhanced performance in the future. In 2012, a group of management professors published the results of a study of the impact of after-event reviews in *Journal of Applied Psychology*. They noted that ambiguous leadership experiences can prompt fear and anxiety, which can limit how well people analyze data. But when reviews are systematic, they "help regulate emotions that might interfere with learning and development . . . and specify clear behavior changes that can improve leadership performance going forward."[39]

Though on the surface it may seem as though sports are about competing with other people, in many ways, they are far more about competing with oneself. Athletes are taught to work with coaches and integrate feedback, but a crucial part of all athletes' progress is assessing performance and measuring gains against one's own benchmarks. These crucial lessons of sport are also applicable to the nonathlete. And the practice of understanding one's strengths and weaknesses ties into fascinating data about where it is that women compete the best.

A study by psychology and economics professors about competitiveness found that although women are somewhat less willing than men to compete against others, they are equally willing to compete against themselves and their own past achievements. They also found that self-competition is just as valuable as competition with others in boosting performance. The professors who conducted the study found that if workplaces can be restructured to be about self-competition—or outperforming one's past results—rather than competing against others, it would reduce gender inequities. [40]

There is hardly an arena more focused on self-competition than dance. Katherine Power began performing with a professional dance company when she was twelve. By sixteen, she had taken the California high school proficiency exam, dropped out of school, and moved to LA to join the dance company of the award-winning choreographer Marguerite Derricks. "She was very aggressive, demanding," Power said. Power performed onstage, in commercials, and in films and remembered, "Everybody was competing for the same spots and performances. You would learn how to go to auditions and get cut right away and know that's not a big deal. I certainly had some hard times where I had to process rejection quite a bit. I think it helped me develop this tough skin, this thing where I literally don't care what people think about me. I will just go out and take a risk."

For Power, constant improvement through practice taught her to focus on working hard and on monitoring her own progress—and to not get distracted by her peers. Constantly auditioning and performing helped her develop the ability to ignore what people thought of her. After she stopped dancing at seventeen, she decided to skip college and instead took an internship with a filmmaker. That led to a full-time job in events promotion. She later joined *Elle* magazine, where she booked talent for its covers and eventually rose to West Coast fashion editor. In 2006, she and her journalist friend Hillary Kerr launched Who What Wear, a newsletter and website that sought to make fashion more accessible through online editorial content and direct shopping links. When the 2008 recession hit, the company cut back but still managed to operate profitably. In 2012, Kerr and Power expanded Who What Wear into Clique Media Group (now Clique Brands) to include more divisions and to offer marketing tools for advertisers; unlike most internet-based companies, it didn't raise venture capital in its first six years.

In 2015, while rival fashion media platforms such as Refinery29 were chasing growth by expanding into news and politics, Power once again defied expectations and pivoted away from content. Instead, she and Kerr used the insights gathered from Who What Wear's readership to do something radical: produce and sell clothes. The cofounders had always admired the partnerships Target did with fashion designers, but no media brand had ever launched a clothing label. When they had a chance to present a retail collaboration to Target, they proposed something that seemed totally counter to the retailer's typically secretive design process: bringing consumers into it. They were surprised when Target agreed.[41] Power and Kerr even shared designs on Instagram, drawing thousands of votes and getting their followers invested in items before they were mass-produced. Target's CEO told them the line exceeded all expectations.

Power continued to follow her instincts about female consumers and the data the company collected about their preferences. She wasn't constrained by the limits of what people with her background had done before, and she pushed quickly into unfamiliar businesses. In May 2019, she launched Versed, a clean skin care line, followed the following year by Avaline, a wine brand she cofounded with Cameron Diaz. In early 2021, she introduced a makeup line, Merit Beauty, and cocreated a special-purpose acquisition company (SPAC) called Powered Brands to invest in beauty and wellness brands.[*] When I noted in our conversation that it's rare for any entrepreneur, male or female, to be involved in so many different businesses simultaneously, Power shrugged and said she has created a system for incubating ideas that works. She knows her strength in being able to identify consumer demand and assemble strong teams. Her confidence, no doubt, was honed by her experience as a competitive dancer, where stereotypically male characteristics such as aggression and ambition were expected of women—and rewarded when displayed.

The success of Power's independent approach speaks to the advantages of self-competition. If you're competing with others, you're following rules someone else has set and letting others define your performance indicators, rather than creating your own. I am acutely aware that I cannot encourage people to get into a time machine and go back to high school to join the basketball team. (I myself did not play competitive sports but did dance seriously through high school and college.) But the lessons of "self-competition" in sports can be found in other experiences. Any experience that provokes self-reflection and provides a strong identity is a powerful tool for women to combat bias and find inner strength.

These external and internal ways I have seen women find resilience—identifying institutional challenges to better navigate them and understanding their own strengths to push themselves to compete—can seem unrelated. In fact, it turns out that they are not.

In 2004, researchers gathered several hundred college students to participate in a series of studies involving a difficult math test. Before beginning their work, one cohort of women was reminded that poor performance would reinforce the negative stereotype that women are worse than men at math. As one might guess, that cohort performed worse than the cohort that received no prompt. Then the researchers made a tweak: the women

---

*In June 2022 Clique Brands sold Clique Media, including Who What Wear, to UK publishing group Future, which owns titles including *Marie Claire*, for $127 million.

who had received the dispiriting stereotype reminder were asked to complete a self-affirmation exercise before taking the test. In that exercise, the women wrote about an important value that was unrelated to the task at hand (and also unrelated to math or to their gender). For that group, the disadvantage disappeared: the women performed as well as the no-prompt cohort did. (For the record, those women also performed as well as the male students did.)[42] Connecting with different parts of their identity strengthened the women's immune system and helped immunize them against the negative pathogen of stereotype. It makes sense that if people feel strong in their sense of self, they can learn not to take criticism personally; they can separate criticisms that are irrelevant or unfair from good-faith critiques that provide an opportunity for self-improvement.

Identity is at the center both of the ways in which women are judged more harshly and also the ways in which they defy or ignore scrutiny. Double standards center on the imposition of identity on women. It is bias that drives people to decide that just because someone looks or sounds a certain way or doesn't fit into a certain group, he or she must be a certain thing. The media imposed the identity of Pets.com's failure on Julie Wainwright, even long after she had proven her success. The investors Bdeir pitched to made assumptions about her because she is a woman and Lebanese. The men in Shenk's squadron picked on her to test the stereotype that women are supposed to be weak and emotional.

An identity as a woman—together with all the expectations imposed upon women—can be an albatross, but it can also be an advantage. It is when women decide how to define their own identities that they liberate themselves from expectations. There are filial identities that we can draw on as a reminder of a legacy of strength. Most important, there are characteristics that can be cultivated. Being a fierce athlete, like Christine Hunsicker, or a creative artist, like Julie Wainwright—those aren't things that are inborn; they are traits that are practiced and developed.

When women measure their own growth in such areas—sports,

dance, art, cooking, or anything else—they are focusing on their own progress. And when women cultivate and define their key characteristics, their identity can be a renewable resource. In strengthening their sense of self, it empowers them to identify the double standard—and all the assumptions and judgments they face—as unrelated to who they really are.

This was the one chapter I was reluctant to write; I actually wrote it last. I thought it would be a self-evident slog through more evidence that it's tough to be a woman in business. The mere act of talking about bias and stereotypes can be dispiriting and make one feel hopeless. I was anxious about wallowing in this depressing reality. Yet having reported and written it, I'm actually tremendously optimistic. That's because I see real strategies for women to identify and mitigate inequities and to push themselves to thrive, such as systematically reviewing their own performance to better understand themselves and drive improvement. Like me, you may not have grown up playing organized sports, but we can all learn the playing field and compete with ourselves in a new kind of martial art. And as with any sport, we can get better at it.

Ten

Creating New Communities

Building Communities to Help One Another Thrive

In my travels as a business news reporter I talk to a lot of people: in January, I go to the Consumer Electronics Show in Las Vegas, in June to the advertising festival in Cannes, France, and throughout the rest of the year to an assortment of conferences and cocktail parties hosted by CNBC and others. At those events I meet, mingle with, and interview CEOs and executives who typically range in age from early thirties to early sixties. Mostly they are men, and mostly they know one another. Occasionally a newbie shows up, usually the CEO of a recently launched company. As the first-timer approaches the table where I'm sitting or the circle where I'm chatting with others, I often act as the "tour guide," introducing the newcomer to the group. I have found more often than not that he (it is almost always a he) already has multiple connections with attendees at the conference, even in far-flung fields. *They've known each other for years!* When I ask how they know each other, the guy typically answers that they were in the same business school class or are in YPO together.

YPO, formally known as Young Presidents' Organization, is an organization of leaders; acceptance to the group brings close relationships with power players across industries, and those relationships naturally yield access to investments and deal opportunities. There are exclusive educational opportunities: a real estate conference featuring the secretary of housing and urban development; private tours of classified aerospace companies. And the group has a key unwritten rule: no matter how busy they are, members are expected to return personal phone calls from each other within twenty-four hours. With access to a Rolodex of industry leaders, members have the promise of a lifetime of success and support.

Founded in 1950, YPO requires that applicants be under forty-five years old and the business leader of a company with more than $13 million in annual revenue or a valuation over $20 million. Members are attracted to the prestige, but also to the professional and personal support of the community. One member, a CEO in his early forties, described the growth he had gained through his "forum," the monthly meetings with his local chapter. Under the reassuring cloak of confidentiality, these get-togethers function like a self-help group, where discussions range from how to fire a CFO to how to negotiate with a board for more compensation to what to do if you suspect your spouse is having an affair. Members interact with those in other forums during outings to studios of world-famous artists, Major League Baseball ballparks, and wine tastings. The idea is for members to enrich themselves culturally while building friendships and trust.

In 2015, the nonprofit, which is member run, started to market the brand to draw more diverse executives, and the push has continued. In the year ending November 2021, the organization recruited 40 percent more new female members than in the previous year and 18 percent of all new YPO membership applicants were female. "YPO is striving to be the most diverse and inclusive chief executive leadership organization in the world," the CEO of the organization, Xavier Mufraggi, said. "We believe that creating this type of environment for our members will have positive ripple effects in their businesses, local communities, and 142 countries in which they reside." YPO has pursued a range of initiatives to support its female members and encourage more women to join, partnering with leading organizations such as The Female Quotient's Equality Lounge at the World Economic Forum Annual Meeting in Davos, Switzerland, and with the United Nations' HeForShe campaign. Yet for all its efforts, a YPO associate confirmed its membership ranks were just 12 percent female as of the end of June 2021, up from 8 percent when it started its diversity push six years earlier. But even at only 12 percent female, the organization believes it is the largest aggregation of female chief executive officers in the world.

That's because women form a tiny minority of presidents and CEOs of large companies. That makes YPO's heavily male makeup the result less of a gender bias than of selection bias: it is a reflection of the corridors of power.

In the course of reporting this book, I spoke to many women members of YPO, including several of the CEOs in this book. I also spoke to many women who *did* qualify for membership and yet had not applied. Some hadn't joined because it was overwhelmingly male—it just didn't feel as though it was for them (no one would say anything on the record). Many of them said they hadn't applied for reasons that had nothing to do with discrimination or bias; they simply didn't have the time. YPO requires its members to attend ten meetings of their "forum" per year. A number of women CEOs in their thirties and forties told me they felt that spending time with their spouses, keeping up with their close friendships, and being home for their kids' bedtime felt more important than attending YPO forums or any other networking events.

This feeling is supported by hard data. Studies have shown that women in the prime years of their careers spend less time networking than their male counterparts do even though they know that it's crucial for career advancement. (A 2014 survey found that 87 percent of women and 84 percent of men over age thirty-five said they consider networking to be important to their careers.) Men and women actually begin at the same pace; they network at the same frequency between the ages of twenty-five and thirty-four. The gender gap grows in the midcareer phase, a period, not coincidentally, during which women are most often starting families. Only a quarter of women over thirty-five said they network at least once a week, compared to 46 percent of their male counterparts.[1] But that gulf cannot be blamed solely on family obligations; women *without* children had a nearly identical drop-off in networking at age thirty-five.[*] That drop-off leaves women—with children or without—at a stark career disadvantage. Sixty-seven percent of men say they have a strategic network of coaches, mentors, and sponsors, but just 41 percent of women say the same.[2]

It's not just at the Consumer Electronics Show and the Cannes Lions advertising conference that I've seen this male dominance of business networking in action. Until recently, panels at business and tech conferences were so predominantly male that they were referred to in the press as "manels." On one occasion, I was invited to moderate a dinner conversation on the topic of e-sports. When I arrived at the tony Hollywood restaurant Pizzeria Mozza, a series of three long tables was set up, seating more than thirty people; I was the only woman in the private room. To turn the awkward tokenism into a joke, I raised a glass to toast International Women's Day (it happened to be March 8). Many in the group were nonplussed; they didn't seem to have noticed that there were no other women there. It was nothing out of the ordinary.

There is something about traditional networking that simply has not worked for women. And women are trying to do something about it.

---

*Just over half of fathers say they network once a week or more, compared to just under a quarter of mothers.

Carolyn Childers and Lindsay Kaplan met each other in 2018 at a Manhattan networking event hosted by a venture capital firm. After cocktail hour they sat down for dinner with about twenty other guests in a private room. They expected to listen to the featured speaker and then meet their tablemates and socialize. But one of the guests asked the speaker a question—and then the two of them didn't stop talking. What had been meant to be an interactive group conversation became a theatrical public dialogue—between two men. By the end of the meal, the guests hadn't even been able to introduce themselves. It was a networking nightmare. Childers and Kaplan didn't actually talk with each other until they were walking out. They realized that they had heard of each other through mutual connections. They shared a moment of dismay at the frustrating networking experience they had just shared and decided to keep in touch.

Childers was the senior vice president of operations of Handy, a platform for finding and booking home services, and Kaplan was vice president of communications and brand at the direct-to-consumer mattress company Casper. Both women believed the prevailing orthodoxy that professional advancement comes from a network. They were in their thirties and reluctant patrons of the New York professional networking scene, a patchwork of tech conferences and cocktail hours. All the positioning oneself for invitations and agitating for access to conferences felt like . . . more work. For every worthwhile encounter like the one they had had with each other, there were too many meaningless two-minute conversations with people whose names they didn't remember. It was a massive investment of time and effort for very little reward. Childers and Kaplan both wanted the same thing: a simple, structured solution to their networking challenges that would give them access to useful, like-minded professionals.

What they wanted, essentially, was an experience like the one YPO provided. But neither woman qualified. Despite all of her success, Childers didn't have a president title. She had graduated in a forty-person high school class in a small town outside Ithaca, New York, and made it all the way to Harvard Business School. Then she had led Soap.com through its sale to Amazon, worked for the e-commerce giant Coupang in South Korea, and become head of operations for Handy, which had been sold to ANGI Homeservices. She was a sought-after executive on New York's tech scene. Yet when it came to mentorship and networking, she felt marooned.

"I was experiencing this thing where, as I got more and more senior in my career, I actually had fewer resources around me. *I* was the resource for other people, *I* was the mentor. There was nothing for me to continue to grow and progress as a leader," she recalled. She asked friends about programs that could help her professional development. But she realized quickly that in order to achieve the YPO criteria, she would need a network like YPO's to get her there. Her frustration was exacerbated by all the ways in which she saw other women also struggling to advance: "There was a moment when a senior executive on my team made this comment that in order to get into the room, women couldn't just be an *average* man, they had to be an *exceptional* woman. Throughout my career I had never felt my gender; it wasn't until I actually hit levels of senior leadership that I started to see that in a much more profound way."

About a year after their first networking event encounter, Childers asked Kaplan to coffee and proposed that they work together to create an alternative to the groups that were just out of their reach. "The idea was, there are five million people who are VP level and above," she remembered. "How do you just focus on *that* demographic and get more of them into true positions of leadership and influence?" In January 2019, they launched Chief, a company providing education and community to women executives at that level.

They hoped to start with about seventy-five people, culled mainly from their own networks and LinkedIn connections. But the demand at launch outstripped their expectations. They debuted the service with close to two hundred inaugural members and quickly built a wait list of over two thousand. By 2020, they had drawn nearly three thousand members and a wait list of eight thousand. They reached nearly eight thousand members in seven cities by the end of 2021, with a wait list of more than three times that many women. Membership is not cheap—$5,800 annually for VP-level executives (approximately 60 percent of members) and $7,900 for C-level executives. But they say it costs less than YPO, which has pricing that varies by region, and a lot less than individual executive coaching, which can run more than $500 per hour for senior executives.[3]* The majority of memberships are paid for not by the members themselves but by their employers (the company also offers financial aid and grants). More than a third of Chief's membership is women of color, compared to the 18 percent of female VPs in corporate America who are women of color.

Though Chief doesn't rely on YPO's model of members getting to know one another while going on enriching outings, there are many similar features. Chief's version of "forums" is called "core groups"; groups of ten women meet every month with an executive coach to work through professional and personal challenges and build stronger connections. The groups are designed to be varied across backgrounds and industries; no single industry makes up more than 10 percent of Chief's membership. This has the twin effects of minimizing potential competition between members and maximizing the learning from diverse experiences. Members can tap into the broader Chief community through digital groups or meet virtually on the company's mobile app and website. Or they can meet in person for panels and events at Chief's locations in New York, Chicago, and Los Angeles, which are furnished in mossy greens, dark woods, and leathers.

Six months after its launch, Chief drew $22 million in Series A funding, led by Kenneth Chenault, a former CEO of American Express and the

---

*According to a Conference Board survey, more than 60 percent of coaches for a CEO and his or her direct reports cost $500 or more per hour.

chairman of the venture capital firm General Catalyst.[*] And it's working: thanks to connections forged by Chief, cofounders of multiple new start-ups have met and women have landed their first board seats. Women have also been hired into a number of leadership roles—including as the CEO of an ad agency.

Redefining Work Relationships

While Childers and Kaplan were looking for the kind of mentorship that would help women like them rise to the C-suite, another woman found herself in the opposite position: Tiffany Dufu was a serial mentor. She was well known for having written a best-selling book on work-life balance, *Drop the Ball: Achieving More by Doing Less*. She had also been a launch team member of Sheryl Sandberg's Lean In organization and before that had run the White House Project, which trains women to run for public office. She had then worked for five years at Levo, a social network for millennial women, where she had run both its partnerships business and a mentorship initiative. As a result of Dufu's book (and the many events where she spoke), women often reached out to her for advice. In her own ascent, she had relied on a deep network of professional contacts to advise her on making career transitions from Seattle to Boston to New York. She felt a responsibility to pay it forward, so when those women asked for guidance, she always said yes.

Dufu was born in the 1970s at Fort Lewis Army Base in Tacoma, Washington. Her parents had grown up in the Watts neighborhood of Los Angeles; when her mother found out she was pregnant at nineteen, she gave up a scholarship to UCLA and urged Tiffany's father to overcome an addiction and join the military. She wanted them to move away from the rough environment she felt would limit her child's potential.

---

[*]Another investor is Alexa von Tobel, a managing partner at Inspired Capital and the founder and CEO of LearnVest, which she sold to Northwestern Mutual.

That led her father, after serving in the military, to earn a PhD in theology. By the 1980s, thanks to her father's military career and his degree, Dufu's parents had moved to a suburban house in the Pacific Northwest (it had, quite literally, a white picket fence). "It showed me the power of mindset; if you want something you've never had before, do something you've never done before in order to get it," she said. While Dufu's father demonstrated the power of acting with agency, Dufu's mother raised her with constant affirmations of love and support.

But then, when Dufu was sixteen, her parents divorced, and all of her family's social and economic capital walked out the door with her father. "My mother unfortunately spun back into that vicious cycle of poverty, addiction, and violence," Dufu said. But she was appreciative of the support her mother had given her in her formative years. "I truly get up every morning feeling a deep sense of gratitude for what she did for *me* in intervening and breaking that cycle," she said. "I'm just trying to get to as many women as I can, in whatever way I need to, to whisper in their ear, 'You're smart, you're loved.'"

Dufu wanted to pay forward the support she had been given, so for years she consecrated every Tuesday and Thursday morning to mentorship. Every woman who reached out to her got a slot. She would give them all variations on the same advice: to find their "crew." "I have a group of people that I call my 'crew,' a group of peers that have really informed my leadership trajectory—they know my ambitions, they helped me create a plan. They mostly hold me accountable and hold my feet to the fire for what I said I was going to do." She would urge the young mentees sitting across the table to follow her lead and assemble a similar group. And they would dutifully note the advice.

But then one Tuesday morning in January 2018, Dufu's 10:00 a.m. mentorship chat seemed to be falling flat. She stopped and asked the woman sipping tea across from her if everything was okay. "No, things are not okay," the woman replied. What she was really anxious about was the fact that she had had to beg her boss to let her skip work that day to meet

Dufu. She already understood the value of having a group of peers and mentors but didn't have a path to get to them. The method that Dufu had been advocating for, the mentee explained, was a highly labor-intensive process. "She walked me through the whole thing," she recalled. "'First, I would have to get access to the cocktail party, the conference, or the event—you were *speaking* at them! Then you want me to awkwardly introduce myself to a bunch of strangers, collect all the business cards. You want me to schedule coffees and teas and lunches? Then you want me to take the time to meet with everyone, find out who I'm compatible with, then you want me to curate a group of seven or eight of us and to coordinate regular gatherings where we're going to put our ambitions together and create plans?'" She was already overwhelmed by a full-time job, three kids, a sick mom, a commute, and a dog.

"It just hit me like a ton of bricks," Dufu said. Suddenly she she says she understood, "*If your life's work really is advancing women and girls, you will immediately stop preaching to women about how they need to find their crew and you will find the damn crew!*"

In May 2018, several months after her fateful Tuesday-morning encounter with that mentee, Dufu launched The Cru for midcareer women. Members pay $499 annually to join a group of ten women from different industries; together they're trained to coach one another and track one another's progress toward personal and professional goals.* The company also facilitates introductions—what it calls "Cross Cru Connections"—with other members who have similar interests. Dufu's approach to networking is designed to give women the structure to build trust with new professional contacts and the permission to be vulnerable and ask one another for help. Unlike YPO and Chief, she decided not to include any experience or seniority threshold for applicants. That broader aperture—plus the fact that the organization has a Black founder—has drawn a

---

*Three-quarters of its members are employees, and a quarter are entrepreneurs.

diverse membership: 60 percent of the community are women of color.[*] Within a year, it had raised $1 million in funding.[†‡]

Cru and Chief have different approaches in the way they gather and coach women, and they are among a broad range of different types of organizations all around the world that serve professional women. These organizations don't always succeed as hoped. One high-profile example is the women-focused coworking space and community The Wing. The company's reputation was damaged in 2019 by reports of an alleged racist incident at the company's West Hollywood location. Over the following year there was a series of reports, including in the *New York Times* and *New York* magazine, in which employees detailed racism they had experienced and the ways in which they had been mistreated and paid poorly. The organization was criticized by the media as an example of the failures of white feminism to be inclusive and acknowledge privilege. Though the company had raised $118 million from blue-chip venture capital investors and celebrities including the soccer star Megan Rapinoe, soon after the pandemic hit, it shuttered its eleven locations, suspended membership dues, and canceled plans to open nine more locations. In the wake of reports of toxic behavior during the Black Lives Matter movement in June 2020, CEO and cofounder Audrey Gelman stepped down. The company restructured to focus on diversity, equity, and inclusion among its employees and members and in February 2021 sold a majority stake to flexible workspace firm IWG.

*Women of color are in a far greater minority than white women in business leadership positions; there are only two Black female CEOs running Fortune 500 companies at the time of publishing this book, and as mentioned elsewhere in the book, about one-third of 1 percent of VC funding in the first half of 2021 went to Black women, according to Crunchbase.

†The Cru was funded in part by Bumble Fund, part of Whitney Wolfe Herd's Bumble, which was included in chapter 3.

‡In September 2023, the Cru was acquired by Luminary, an education and networking platform focused on women and their allies, and the Cru was rebranded as "The Cru empowered by Luminary."

Though The Wing suffered a high-profile fall from grace, there are hundreds of different types of companies and nonprofits around the world that have worked successfully to help women navigate professional challenges. Sheryl Sandberg's Lean In organization has inspired sixty-seven thousand women around the world to start "Lean In Circles." Shelley Zalis's The Female Quotient, which calls itself an "equality services company," offers programs to support women and services to help companies close gender gaps, expanded its global reach during the pandemic. In early 2022 it hosted one hundred dinners across six regions, building up to a global gala in March, when as many as 150,000 women around the world organized their own tables to discuss strategies for closing equality gaps. Some organizations are focused just on inspiring and helping female entrepreneurs, such as Create & Cultivate, Ladies Who Launch, and Million Dollar Women. AnitaB.org, which supports women in technical fields, helps them find jobs and advance at tech companies. But these organizations face a persistent question: How much of an impact do they really have?

Every year a nonprofit organization called Conferences for Women hosts annual events in four states across the country. One speaker at its Philadelphia conference in 2016, the author Shawn Achor, was flying home and telling the stranger sitting next to him about the conference. His seatmate was skeptical about the event. What evidence did Achor have that such events made any tangible impact on the fortunes of its attendees? Wasn't it all just corporate snake oil with a splash of gender thrown in? His seatmate's cynicism provoked something in Achor. As a best-selling author and researcher in the field of positive psychology, he wondered if he could prove his seatmate wrong. So he partnered with his wife, Michelle Gielan, also a researcher on happiness, to take on the challenge, to see whether the value of the conference could be proved one way or another.[4]

Achor's ability to measure the event's impact could have been complicated by the fact that the women who attended were already more likely to be high achievers than a comparable group of female professionals. But luckily, the conference could provide him with a randomized control group: the hundreds of women who had signed up for an upcoming conference but had not yet attended.

And so Achor set about surveying a sampling of the conference group and the control group. What he discovered would have been startling to his cynical seatmate. Of the women who had attended the conferences in Pennsylvania, Massachusetts, and Texas, Achor and his team found that within a year, 42 percent of them had received a promotion. Those who hadn't yet attended—the control group—had just an 18 percent promotion rate. And the findings of what had started as a kind of Delta Air Lines bar bet didn't stop there: three times as many women who had attended the event had earned a raise.[*]

That study showed an impact but still didn't answer the question of *why* Conferences for Women had had such an outsized effect on the careers of its attendees. That answer can be found in data about a characteristic of female professionals: they tend to be reluctant to mix business and pleasure. Though women generally have more close friends than men do, research indicates that they are less likely to use their wider-ranging personal connections for professional advancement. In the 2010 report *The Sponsor Effect: Breaking Through the Last Glass Ceiling*, the economist and professor Sylvia Ann Hewlett and her colleagues wrote that although women are happy to do favors for business contacts, they have an aversion to asking for such favors. Men, on the other hand, are much more comfortable engaging in the negotiating and horse trading of offering and asking for things.[5] The reason something like Conferences for Women can have such a huge impact on women's careers is that it enables them to do something that they haven't been socialized to do.

---

[*]They also found intangible benefits from attending a large gathering of women: 71 percent of the attendees said that they feel "more connected to others" afterward, and 78 percent reported that they feel "more optimistic about the future." Though that doesn't necessarily translate to deals or promotions, this isn't just a side or minor benefit. Achor's research has found a "happiness advantage," which drives improvement in nearly every business and educational outcome.

The greater discomfort women feel about asking for help is also reflected in how they approach asking for recognition. They are less likely to use their network and more likely to rely on their credentials and track record when it comes to advancing their careers. When asked how they had gotten their most recent promotion, 57 percent of men cited personal connections, compared to 48 percent of women. Women and men seem to disagree fundamentally about what matters most to succeed in business; the vast majority of men, a staggering 83 percent, said that who you know counts for a lot, at least as much as how well you do your job. In contrast, 77 percent of women said they believe that promotion is a result of hard work, long hours, and education credentials.

Interestingly, these differences seem to parallel the ways each gender views the functions of personal friendships. A survey given to thousands of employees and reported in *The Sponsor Effect* found that men are twice as likely as women to say they look for friends at work who can help them get ahead. Women say that they look for someone to confide in or lean on—but *not* to use for specific professional gain. When it comes to landing a job or closing an important deal, about two-thirds of men say they wouldn't hesitate to ask a friend for help, but nearly half of women admit to feeling reluctant to do so.[6] The report noted, "Women aren't just convinced their good-girl behavior will pay off. Rather, they're certain that getting ahead by any other means is *dirty*."[7]

All of this well-documented discomfort explains why the conferences—and organizations such as Chief and The Cru—can have such a meaningful impact. These organizations create a structure that makes it okay—makes it *not* "dirty"—to foster relationships explicitly for professional advancement. The founders of Chief and The Cru shaped their services to address that discomfort. If women found discomfort in asking friends for help, the solution, Dufu reasoned, was to redefine the relationship away from "friendship" and create a supportive professional network. "We let our members know that their relationship with their Cru members is going to be different from friendship; it is going to feel more intimate than the relationship you might have with your coworkers, but it should be more objective than friendship. And we tell them that their relationships with their crew members are rooted in intentionality and accountability and commitment," Dufu explained. "If they become friends with one or more members of their Cru, that's beautiful. But friendship is *not* required in order for a Cru to thrive. In fact, it is healthy for some Cru members to maintain enough distance to provide more objective coaching." Chief took a similar approach by deviating from the YPO formula of social (and occasionally overnight) outings. Instead, its format is focused on purposeful meetings of Core Groups, workshops, and speaker series. And on Chief's internal job board, members are encouraged to list themselves or other candidates and offer open positions to members. Online groups on Chief's platform also function as industry-specific marketplaces for the easy exchange of career advice.

During the covid pandemic, this distinction between the personal and professional was cemented further. When the possibility of in-person interactions evaporated, it forced a focus on the professional nature of the support women could offer and ask of one another. And it enabled both companies to vastly expand their reach. Chief, which moved to virtual events and offered recordings of its speaker series, saw attendance grow by three times within months. In May 2020, it raised an additional $15 million and announced its expansion to additional cities without the addition of (expensive) physical clubhouses. The Cru discovered that it could reach women in Tulsa, Cincinnati, and Baton Rouge and dropped geographic restrictions for membership.

The virtual approach also had an advantage that was especially attractive to professional women: it was less time consuming. "Everybody's on time, no one has to worry about the commute. A woman can nurse her baby during her gathering, and another can cornrow her daughter's hair," Dufu said. "One of the key values for us at Chief is the concept of time travel," Childers echoed. "It's not only about the mission of trying to get more women into positions of leadership and getting to a place of equal representation faster than the current pace—that will take two hundred years. It's also in the way in which we provide services and community. We don't have the luxury of spending hours on a golf course and building relationships that way."

In the years since the launches of Chief and The Cru, more research has been done that supports their approaches. A 2019 study by researchers at Notre Dame and Northwestern Universities examined the social networks of successful men and women: for a man, the larger his network, the more likely he was to ascend to a high-ranking position. But for a woman, her network size did not necessarily lead to professional advancement. In fact, women with a large network tended to stay in low-ranking positions, while successful women tended to maintain an inner circle of strong ties to two or three women with whom they communicated frequently.[8] What helped women the most was the combination of being central in their networks *and* having an inner circle of one to three women. Women with those types of connections landed in leadership positions that were 2.5 times higher in authority (and pay) as those of their female peers who lacked that combination. Their inner circles enabled women to understand things such as organizations' attitude toward women, how to navigate job searches, and negotiation strategies.[9]

This study supports Dufu's insight that a valuable network has nothing to do with friendship. For women, the most valuable types of inner circles were those in which the women had minimal contacts in common. The authors of the paper translated the findings into advice for women looking to advance: embrace randomness and diversify your network and inner circle. They also warned against circles that were too interconnected because a group that feels too socially secure may fail to generate key insights and opportunities.[10] This emphasis on the value of diverse perspectives echoes not only the support system created by Chief and The Cru but also the Northwestern University study of fraternity and sorority members' problem solving cited in chapter 4. The Greek house members joined by an outsider didn't just benefit from a fresh perspective; the mere presence of an outsider prompted them to examine their own assumptions and thought processes to a more effective end. The lesson learned from that study—that diverse groups solve problems better—is applicable to networks of women helping one another solve work challenges.

There's one more thing about the power of networks: they build resilience. During the pandemic, the Innovation Resource Center for Human Resources wanted to understand what enabled leaders to be resilient during the toughest of times. It sent experts to conduct in-depth interviews with the five men and women who were considered the most successful leaders at fifteen different organizations. What they found seems almost obvious in its simplicity: "A well-developed network of relationships can help us rebound from setbacks." And resilience is not found in just having that network of supporters, the authors reported in *Harvard Business Review*, "but in truly connecting with them when you need them most."[11]

Targeting Tech's Power Structures

Whereas female-focused networking organizations work to equip their members with the same tools that have long been available to their male counterparts, in some sectors, such as Silicon Valley tech firms, the male dominance has felt particularly impenetrable. But there is a growing movement to remedy that. A range of groups is taking a multipronged approach: they're providing transparency into key data, supporting new female-led ecosystems, and connecting those networks to the male-dominated establishment.

A nexus of Silicon Valley power is in the ownership of startups, which is laid out in a private company's capitalization table, or "cap table," the document that explains how its ownership is apportioned among its founders, investors, and employees. More than mundane corporate charters, cap tables represent a kind of map of the power structures within the tech community. The greater one's ownership of a company, the more one stands to profit from the lucrative liquidity events that happen en route from startup to unicorn to publicly traded behemoth.

Jessica Verrilli was the resident cap table expert at one such behemoth. In 2009, just two years out of Stanford, she joined Twitter as its thirty-fourth employee. By 2015, she was running Corporate Development and Strategy, where she identified products (such as Vine) and businesses (such as MoPub), that could be a good fit for Twitter. When an acquisition made sense, her team would pursue it and negotiate, among other things, the price of the deal. Day after day, Verrilli sat in the company's headquarters in a skyscraper on San Francisco's Market Street, poring over companies' financial data reports. Those reports laid bare each company's revenue, losses, and forecasts; a central document, the cap table, listed all of its shareholders and the amounts of their holdings. It was the best view in tech.

When the company then known as Twitter negotiated a purchase price with a company, Verrilli would look at what's referred to as a "waterfall document," which is built from the cap table to show how the money spent to purchase a company would flow to shareholders. Many of those shareholders stood to make a fortune, and they would take those fortunes and become investors in, or founders of, the next generation of startups. Verrilli recognized the same names (including those of some of her colleagues at Twitter) appearing repeatedly as "angel," or early-stage, investors. That wasn't the only pattern: the vast majority of the names were male. Verrilli's then-colleague Jana Messerschmidt, an engineer who ran Twitter's partnerships, said that the cap tables started to look like a "predictable founder mafia"—a predictable, *predominantly male* founder mafia. The documents revealed that men did not just control the deployment of the vast majority of venture dollars and run a much larger percentage of highly valued private companies; they actually *owned* most of the shares of each startup.

In 2015, flush with their own windfalls from the Twitter IPO, Verrilli and Messerschmidt, along with four other female colleagues who were all quite senior at the company—April Underwood, Chloe Sladden, Vijaya Gadde, and Katie Stanton—went out to celebrate a birthday. By the second round of drinks, they had decided to team up and invest in early-stage startups themselves. Their mission was to colonize the cap tables of valuable startups as successfully as the male mafia had.[12] Pooling their contacts in the industry, they launched a collective called #ANGELS to collaborate on deal flow and information (the eventual investments each would make individually). They figured that teaming up would also be useful to founders by giving them access to their collective expertise. They started writing checks for tens of thousands of dollars, buying small stakes that sometimes ballooned in value. Over dinners and in text and email chains, the friends supported one another during life milestones—marriages, babies, divorces—as well as investing opportunities. They have been pursuing their strategy and investing early in companies ranging from Instacart to Color Health, from Cameo to Coinbase.

Though the #ANGELS were successful at finding opportunity in individual startups, the prevailing systems of power continued to dominate the venture capital industry. While those women were making small angel investments, the firms that were writing the big checks were, as discussed in the first chapter, almost entirely male. In fact, in 2016, less than 6 percent of decision makers at venture capital firms were female.[13] And until the late 2010s, the decision makers at venture capital firms were at least 90 percent male.[14] That started to change only toward the end of the decade, when the rare female leaders in the male-dominated world banded together to create new networks.

One of those leaders is Aileen Lee; she was a partner at the legendary VC firm Kleiner Perkins from 1999 to 2012 before founding her own firm, Cowboy Ventures. For years she worked in an environment in which she felt she could never express her discomfort with being the only woman in the room. She said the tacit message in most of her meetings in those days was clear: "If things happen that make you uncomfortable and you make *us* uncomfortable, that will make *us* not want to work with *you* anymore." In those years, she and a small group of women, most of them the sole female investing partners at top firms, established a routine of regular get-togethers in San Francisco or Palo Alto. The feeling of being stuck in an emotional trap in her workplace made Lee appreciate the community she found among other female VCs.

Then, in February 2017, those conversations changed forever. One night when the group of women convened in Lee's backyard for evening drinks, the conversation immediately turned to the vivid and disturbing blog post Susan Fowler had written alleging that sexual harassment and misogyny was rampant at one of Silicon Valley's most highly valued start-ups, Uber. (Then-CEO Travis Kalanick said it was the first he'd heard of the allegations and hired former U.S. Attorney General Eric Holder to investigate. The findings led to firings and to Kalanick stepping down.) Lee said it felt as though the floodgates opened, and for the first time, the women in her cohort felt comfortable sharing their own feelings of marginalization—and the details of more serious incidents. When six women accused the venture capitalist Justin Caldbeck of sexual harassment in June 2017, Lee and others in her group came together to figure out how to support the victims. In the article that first reported the allegations, Lee was quoted calling on leaders in the industry to be more inclusive and imploring them to protect the women from trolling and retaliation.[15] (Caldbeck was the VC who was accused of harassing Stitch Fix CEO Katrina Lake.)

Then Lee decided to take action. "People could no longer ignore that this was actually happening, so I wrote an email to my women friends in venture and said, 'Let's talk about what we could do together to solve these problems,'" she said. Her inbox was instantly flooded with messages of support. The prevailing idea was that if they could make the culture more diverse—particularly in terms of gender—it would be less conducive to bias and harassment, and women and minorities would have a better shot at success in tech.

In 2018, they formed the nonprofit All Raise to accelerate access to opportunity for women working both as investors and entrepreneurs. The goal was to create a new kind of ecosystem with less bias and more diversity, spanning both startups and venture firms. "The VC industry is so relationship driven; it's so much about information sharing and faith. When you're in a business that's run by ninety percent men, it's probably ninety-eight percent white men who have inherent trust with each other and faith in each other. It's hard for women and minorities to be successful in that eco-system," said Lee. The idea was to create a community and a network that could connect women to key contacts—both male and female. "We were *not* trying to create a separate girls' network. The vast majority of our industry has been men, so we *need* them to change." As of early 2022 the organiza-tion included some 1,100 VCs, both male and female, from more than two hundred firms with a total of $306 billion in assets under management, plus more than 1,700 founders, most of whom are female or nonbinary, who have participated in a bootcamp or pitched to All Raise's network of potential investors. The broader community that had attended an All Raise event by then—virtual or in person—was more than 22,000 strong.

This female-led ecosystem doesn't just sit alongside the establish-ment but rather nests inside it. Pam Kostka, All Raise's CEO from 2019 through 2021, said, "The idea was always to have our hands on both dials [founders and funders] because by moving both simultaneously, that's when you get the exponential ratchet effect." All Raise invites people to post about open jobs at venture capital firms, offering rare transpar-ency into a usually opaque, relationship-driven hiring process. All Raise also highlights the power that founders have in promoting diversity; its Founders for Change initiative asks both male and female entrepreneurs to make a public commitment to build diverse teams, boards, and, when possible, cap tables.[16] During the pandemic what had been a mostly in-person community expanded to a stream of continuous support on Slack as people asked for help with everything from how to shut down a com-pany to where to find a marketing firm to launch a new product.

The organization also works with aspiring entrepreneurs to help them determine if they should raise venture funding in the first place. In some cases it might not be necessary—and the demand for growth imposed by VCs may not create the best conditions for nurturing a new company.

"We try to err on the side of being more open than less open; then we act as a broker, and introduce an entrepreneur to a group of people," Kostka explained. All Raise works with a wide range of companies from Binti, which created software to improve the foster care system, to Tot Squad, a platform that makes it easy for parents to find and book vetted experts and services for kids, to Pluto, a custom pillow company. It connects founders and mentors, coaches them through bootcamps, and then introduces them to potential investors. If investors pass on the opportunity, All Raise shares feedback about why the pitch did not resonate—the kind of feedback that comfortably networked male founders tend to get informally from VCs. In 2019, a quarter of All Raise's introductions resulted in a company securing an investment. (There are no official data on the ratio of pitches to investments, but Silicon Valley folklore says that 99 percent of all pitches are rejected. There's no doubt that a quarter of introductions leading to investments is high.)

Using Transparency to Drive Change

In 2018, the same year All Raise launched, Verrilli, Messerschmidt, and the four others were three years into their #ANGELS investing collective, backing a range of early-stage companies that went on to be valued at many billions of dollars. (The previous year, two of the six women had invested in cryptocurrency platform Coinbase at a $1.8 billion valuation, which ballooned to over $100 billion in 2021 on its first day as a public company.) From the beginning they had hosted dinners with VCs and other women interested in investing, but as they continued to review cap tables, they saw that very little was changing in terms of startup ownership. At the same time, they did see the tech giants such as Google and Facebook publish annual diversity data and that their transparency drove pressure to change. So the #ANGELS published a blog post declaring that the industry should start measuring cap table diversity. Carta, a software platform that enables private venture capital–backed companies to manage their ownership stakes, reached out and offered to help. Carta is used so ubiquitously—by six thousand startups at the time—that it can anonymize and analyze comprehensive data without revealing anything about its customers. It is a cap table panopticon.

The #ANGELS had known that Carta would find a sharp gender disparity in startup ownership, and the numbers were just as bad as they'd feared. Whereas women held about a third of the positions at Silicon Valley startups, they owned just 9 percent of those companies' equity value. (In Silicon Valley, employment at startups is generally accompanied by equity ownership.) They didn't have race and ethnicity data to examine the disparity through an intersectional lens, but they hypothesized that white women owned the vast majority of that 9 percent. In 2018, they published a post on Medium publicizing their findings, calling on the Silicon Valley tech community to close the gender gap in ownership of tech companies.[17] They named the initiative #TheGapTable. They aimed to show that although women's salaries have famously lagged men's (women earned 82 cents for every dollar men earned in 2021),[18] the imbalance in startup ownership is far worse.

One reason for the ownership imbalance is the arcane and asymmetric information involved in negotiating the ownership of startup shares. Silicon Valley insiders quickly develop a reliable sense of how much a product manager or first-year engineer can expect to earn in cash compensation. But the number of shares in a private company that person should demand is far less clear. Much depends on how early in the company's life cycle employment begins and how much demand the company has for a particular skill set. Still, the Carta data indicated that female employees accepted far less ownership than male employees did—they made up 35 percent of employees who hold equity but captured just 20 percent of equity value—likely because they are hired into roles that are rewarded with less stock. Effectively, female employees in Carta's system held just 47 cents for every dollar of equity male employees did. This gap—chasm, actually—doesn't extend just to employees and investors but even to founders. In its first report for the #ANGELS in 2018, Carta noted that 13 percent of the founders in its system were women, and they owned 6 percent of all startups' equity pools. That meant the average female founder owned just 39 cents in equity for every $1 the average male founder owned.[19] (Carta issued updated data for 2020 that showed "no substantive increase in overall representation in ownership for women.")[20]

During one of our conversations, Messerschmidt noted that the cap table gap is "basically back in the 1950s in terms of where the gap was on the salary side," but I discovered that that was a dramatic understatement. The equity gap in 2018—female employees held 47 percent of men's equity in companies—was far worse than the gender pay gap in the 1950s, when women were paid about 60 cents for every dollar a man earned (the pay gap for Black women was and is much wider than for white women).[21]

The #ANGELS published their findings and hosted more and larger events. They ranged from gatherings to educate women on how to angel invest to events to connect and inspire founders, such as one with Gloria Steinem and Annie Leibovitz, as well as ones to provide expert advice on topics such as negotiation, cryptocurrencies, and parental leave. They developed a network to share deal information and recruit women to work at promising early-stage startups, when ownership can be most valuable. "Historically, those networks have been very homogenous, very male and very white. What we're trying to do is create a space where a group of people like ourselves, who weren't historically in those rooms, felt invited and had a chance," said Verrilli. This access to data gives women a road map for what is reasonable to demand, whether it's a female founder trying to figure out how much ownership to give an investor in exchange for a $1 million investment or a female engineer asking to forgo some upfront salary in exchange for a tranche of equity.

The group also brought together the founders of the companies they'd backed—about half were men—to educate them on the importance of diverse cap table representation. They explained that having a diverse investor base does far more than prevent a public flogging (useful) or help attract employees (important). Messerschmidt noted that the women in her group were all just as qualified as, and in some cases more senior than, many of the men who kept showing up on cap tables. Diverse investors do not just add expertise, they also add fresh perspectives, which can be essential for companies looking to serve more than a white male audience. Plus they're able to help draw additional diverse employees—a top female engineer, for example, would likely prefer not to be the sole woman in the bullpen.

The #ANGELS campaign has been successful in encouraging the male leaders at a range of Silicon Valley startups to hire more underrepresented workers. One of them, Rousseau Kazi, the CEO of the workplace discussion management platform Threads, credits the #ANGELS with helping him hire more women at a company that started with four male cofounders. He says those hires have contributed to some of the company's most valuable features. Kazi is among dozens of male founders in #ANGELS' network. And nearly all the group's events have been paid for by venture capital funds run by men. In exchange for their advice and access to their networks, #ANGELS are invited to invest in early-stage startups such as Kazi's and given a spot on those companies' cap tables.

In its work with male founders, female engineers, and aspiring investors, the group focuses on transparency. Its leaders want everyone to understand the current disparities and benchmarks of typical or fair transactions. The #ANGELS have continued to broadcast what's captured by Carta's #thegaptable watchtower.

A 2005 study published in *Journal of Personality and Social Psychology* by Harvard and Carnegie Mellon professors holds a key to why a broad view of the landscape is so valuable for women in particular. Three professors evaluated data from more than five hundred graduating MBA students who entered the workforce. They measured the degree of salary ambiguity in each student's industry of interest and uncovered an unmistakable divide: in job negotiations with clear industry standards, there were no differences in salaries negotiated by men and women. But when industry standards were opaque, female MBAs accepted salaries that were, on average, 10 percent lower than their male counterparts'. The researchers calculated that this gender gap in a thirty-year-old MBA's starting salary would amount to a $1.5 million wealth gap by the time she was sixty-five, when accounting for 5 percent annual interest (but not accounting for inflation).[22]

To further understand the impact of ambiguity, the professors called in more than two hundred adults to participate in mock negotiations. Some of the negotiations were designed to be highly murky and ambiguous: How much would you pay for these motorcycle headlights? Others were designed with clear price comparison information. In the ambiguous negotiations, men expected to pay 10 percent less than women expected to pay and began the negotiation by offering 19 percent less than female buyers. Then the men walked out, paying an average of 27 percent less than their female counterparts. However, when all the participants had access to clear price comparison information, there were no significant sex differences in the target prices, first offers, or negotiated outcomes. The professors concluded that the causes of women's underperformance in negotiating in ambiguous situations were complex and likely in part reflected the stereotype that women are less aggressive negotiators. (One opportunity to study negotiation in the wild is in the real estate industry, where there is a large body of data on how agents negotiate on behalf of clients as well as themselves. Meta-analyses of real estate data published in both 2014 and 2018 found that when controlling for other factors, there was no gender difference in the outcomes male and female agents achieve.)[23]

We certainly don't live in a world where there will always be transparency in negotiations. But educating women to eliminate ambiguity in startup valuations and fundraising is a key way for them to learn to negotiate on a more level playing field. Education is also a crucial way for other underrepresented groups—groups that suffer an even greater opportunity gap—to achieve a better chance of success.

In 2016, digitalundivided, a nonprofit focused on driving economic growth for Black and Latinx women that gathers data and hosts programs, issued a report finding that, at the time, in the history of Silicon Valley, only eleven startups led by Black women had raised more than $1 million. To put this into context: in that same year, the average failed startup raised around $1.3 million.[24] Oh, and that year there were 294 failed startups recorded by Crunchbase.[25]

Stephanie VanPutten (formerly Lampkin) is one of the Black women founders who has raised more than $1 million. In 2015, she founded a diversity, equality, and inclusion (DEI) ratings and analytics company called Blendoor, which later rebranded as BlendScore. When digitalundivided reported that data it prompted her to want to create a network of other women like herself—whom she calls "undervalued overachievers"—to support one another and change the public narrative around Black women executives. "Having been in Silicon Valley for three years at that point, I had been invited to so many female founder things. Being the only Black person in the room, I experienced that bias," she said. "Then, on the other side, I was invited to groups focused on Black founders, and oftentimes I was the only woman in the room. It's very white female, Black male heavy when you get into diversity conversations." So in 2017, she started to invite Black women who had raised *any* amount of venture capital to join an email listserv to share resources and leverage their relationships, creating a group she called Visible Figures, which she gathered for dinners and speaker events with female leaders in business. "The intention was to form a coalition that allowed for leveraging our own political, social, financial capital, instead of relying on external philanthropists. I felt like the narrative was too focused on our challenges and not on our wins."

The group members also benefited from the network and the constant dialog on the email listserv, as they helped one another with "warm introductions" to investors and other business contacts. The community has grown, but its numbers are still tiny: Black women drew only .27 percent of venture capital funding between 2018 and 2019 (up from just .06 percent raised between 2009 and 2017), while Latina women raised .37 percent of VC investment during those two years, according to digitalundivided's 2020 ProjectDiane report.

digitalundivided had been working to help close diversity gaps for years before All Raise and the #ANGELS got started. Lauren Maillian, the organization's CEO, said, "When I first met this organization [as a judge at a 2011 pitch competition], there was a need for more women of color in tech and innovation. Then it was about inspiring them to want to take risks, to innovate, and to have confidence in their ideas. Now that has changed substantially because the fear of taking the risks has decreased but the hurdles have not. So now as an organization, our job is to make sure that those hurdles are not insurmountable."

Ultimately, Maillian is focused on giving women the tools they need to pitch and negotiate in the typically white, male-dominated tech ecosystem. "They think they're prepared," she said of the women who apply to digitalundivided's programs. "But then you're in a VC meeting and you don't understand how a capitalization table works; you have to understand the fundamentals to maintain control of your business." Maillian said that she'd seen too often that women of color had missed an opportunity to grow their business because they were trying to learn the structures of financing while also operating. "I want to make sure that women of color who have big, bold, wonderful ideas and businesses set up solid foundations to have a launchpad for their success."

To build that foundation, the organization runs a series of programs that meet women of color where they are—at all stages of their entrepreneurial journeys. Each program provides advice and a curriculum within the nurturing environment of a small cohort of women. START coaches women on how to turn an idea into a business plan, from which they can graduate to the BIG pre-accelerator program. That program helps fast-growing startups that haven't yet started to generate revenue to improve their business plans, operations, customer engagement, and the like. At the end of the program, participants pitch to investors. Another program provides a grant and coaching to revenue-generating businesses led by Black and Latinx women. For even more experienced entrepreneurs, there's a yearlong Do You Fellowship Program, which culminates in meetings the organization schedules with VCs. Maillian said that it's all designed to create a community and a cycle of mentorship: "We call on the Do You Fellows to inspire, empower, and share their learned lessons and stories with the burgeoning entrepreneurs who come up through our programs and community."

Thanks in part to programs such as digitalundivided, there is slow but measurable progress. By 2018, thirty-four Black women founders and forty-five Latinx women founders had secured more than $1 million from investors. By the end of 2020, that number had grown to ninety-three Black women founders and ninety Latinx women founders.[26] But consider that in 2020, there were more than three hundred investments of more than $100 million *each* in startups—and yes, those startups were mostly run by white men.[27]

The approach digitalundivided takes in fostering the ambition and potential in a group of women is a proven strategy to help women thrive in male-dominated fields such as tech. Female-dominated groups, which academics call "microenvironments," keep women engaged and striving in places where the stereotypes might otherwise tell them they don't belong. This pattern was discovered by three psychology and behavioral science professors during a number of studies. They recruited female undergraduates from engineering courses and randomly assigned them to groups that were either 75 percent women, 50 percent women, or 25 percent women and asked each to solve engineering problems. Regardless of their academic seniority, women in female-majority groups participated more actively than did women in the other two groups. The small groups were also found to boost women's verbal participation in group work, which promoted their learning and mastery.

Perhaps most important, female-dominated microenvironments were particularly powerful in the face of the stereotype that engineering is a masculine field. In the groups in which women were in the minority and reminded of the stereotype, they expressed lower confidence and career aspirations. When the women in the female-majority groups were reminded of masculine engineering stereotypes, they were easily able to deflect them; they expressed high confidence and ambitious career aspirations. "The presence of female peers," the researchers concluded, acts "as 'social vaccines' to decrease women's feelings of threat, decrease the feeling of being under a spotlight, and increase their comfort speaking up."[28] (This is similar to the way women can draw upon their other identities to immunize themselves against stereotypes, discussed in the prior chapter.)

All Raise, #ANGELS, and digitalundivided use the tools of transparency and community to help arm women with information and prepare them to overcome double standards and flatten an uneven playing field. They have also given women valuable bridges into macroenvironments and a more equitable future. The more the broader environment is populated with women immunized against stereotypes, the faster it can achieve a sort of herd immunity against bias.

Unlocking Negotiating Power

Earlier in this chapter, I shared a study that, when I read it, made me feel a little queasy. The study showed that women need transparency in order to negotiate as effectively as men do. Another way of looking at it is this: when a situation is obscure, women are not as good at negotiating as men are. But there's another aspect of the research by those Harvard and Carnegie Mellon professors that is encouraging.

A series of experiments revealed that when women were acting on behalf of someone else, they were able to negotiate compensation agreements that were 18 percent higher than when they were representing themselves. (The shift to negotiating for someone else had no impact on male negotiators' performance.) In fact, women negotiating on behalf of others secured a much higher salary than men did either for themselves or for others—over 16 percent higher than the average negotiated salary.

Bottom line: the most effective negotiators are women negotiating on behalf of someone other than themselves.

The professors explained this with a couple of theories: women may be resisted more strongly by their counterparty when negotiating for themselves because self-promotion seems incongruous with the stereotype of female behavior. And women may be more altruistic (there are numerous studies that show this)[29]* and so would be particularly energized in negotiations in which they felt a personal obligation to represent the interests of another person. Whatever the cause, it's crucial to acknowledge that women do in fact have negotiation skills that can be just as powerful as men's, if not more so. And if women can be acculturated to think of themselves as worthy of applying that negotiating power to themselves—rather than anxious about seeming self-promotional—the potential is significant.

In 2016, a decade after this study was first published, one of its authors, Carnegie Mellon University professor Linda Babcock, tried to design a study to find a solution to this gender-based quirk of negotiating disparity. First, she ran the study again (how much would a subject pay for a motorcycle headlight and so on). Then she asked some female subjects to write about three life events in which they had embodied assertiveness, defended their own interest, or been forceful. After that exercise, all the women, some of whom had done the writing exercise and some of whom had not, once again negotiated over the price of the motorcycle headlights. The women who recalled their past forceful behavior ended up with 42 percent more surplus than those in the control group did. They far outstripped the men.

The researchers also measured the impact of women changing their

---

*In a meta-analysis of twenty-two studies, women were found to be innately more altruistic than men.

perspective on the negotiation. Though the women in the control group performed about half as well as the men did, those who were told to imagine that they were helping a friend before negotiating on behalf of themselves performed right in line with men. When men were asked to change their perception of themselves or the negotiation, it had no impact on the outcome. But for women, a mindset shift yielded dramatic results.[30]

The ability of women to outperform when negotiating on behalf of others ties to the value of microenvironments to shield women from the negative impact of stereotypes. The communities created by companies such as Chief and The Cru and nonprofits such as digitalundivided and All Raise foster the conditions in which women can reframe their perceptions of themselves. They position women to advise one another about how to handle different situations. They help women to give one another the most powerful negotiator—a woman working on behalf of others—while conditioning them to internalize that approach themselves. And they enable women to tap into one another's power.

Eleven

Defeating Bias with Data

Data Reveal the Financial Advantages of Diversity

Among the stories of female entrepreneurship told in this book, I have found a few consistent themes: When leaders are free to be themselves, they can tap into their strengths. When they understand themselves, they can push themselves to stretch and improve. And perhaps most important, diversity, in all its forms, is valuable in business.

These aren't just hypotheses; the data prove them. Startups with diverse founders and companies with diverse leaders and boards perform better. And as I've detailed throughout this book, diverse teams are smarter at problem solving. Historically, the contributions of underrepresented groups, both women and people of color, have been discounted. But that doesn't make sense.

There are signs of change. In some corners of tech, the value of diversity is finally being captured, not just by women supporting one another but also by men. Some among the male Silicon Valley elite are seeing real value not only in connecting with networks of women but also in building, from the ground up, new communities that have a more equitable distribution of women and people from historically underrepresented groups. Because many of these men already have power and influence, they have the potential to quickly and effectively implement change.

Take Ali Partovi, who in many ways is a quintessential Silicon Valley success story. His father taught him and his twin brother, Hadi, coding when they were kids. They graduated from Harvard and as twentysomethings each cofounded a startup, both of which, coincidentally, they sold to Microsoft for hundreds of millions of dollars. They went on to become early investors in Facebook, along with Airbnb, Dropbox, Zappos, and other unicorns, before cofounding the educational nonprofit Code.org, which Hadi runs as CEO. The twins have an evident advantage as part of what *Fortune* magazine called "the world's most techie family," including their cousin, Uber CEO Dara Khosrowshahi.[1]

But the brothers are also immigrants who were only eleven years old when their family fled Iran in 1984 after the revolution and the invasion by Iraq. A year after arriving, they were deported. Though they soon returned, twelve-year-old Ali remained terrified that he would be sent back to Iran and wouldn't be able to finish seventh grade.[2] Though his parents had been successful back in Iran—his father had started a technology university—they struggled after they arrived in the United States.[3] Four of them shared a single room in his grandparents' house in Tarrytown, New York, while his dad commuted to Boston and his mother worked as a secretary by day and a department store salesperson by night.

Being a teenager can be difficult for anyone, especially for a high-achieving nerd like Ali, but his and his twin brother's penchant for technology and hard work resulted in acceptance to Harvard, where they matriculated in 1990. Ali arrived in Cambridge assuming it to be a place where social status would be conferred on the brainiest students. But instead he found a social hierarchy in the exclusive (and largely white) final clubs. "I've definitely felt what it's like to be excluded based on things that are outside your control, like how you were born," he says. But he knows that he had an extraordinary privilege thanks to his family, especially in the head start on coding that his father had given him as a child. He is also aware that whatever his socioeconomic background, he had an advantage in that he could assimilate and wouldn't be instantly categorized based on his gender or ethnicity. "I don't have to overcome a daily level of catching up just because of what I look like. It's hard to imagine what that would be like: no matter how accomplished you are, you have to reset when you walk into a room."

Throughout college Ali took computer science courses but, with the idea of keeping multiple doors open, made the "safe" choice of completing premed requirements. Then, in his junior year, his vision of his life changed when a fellow student launched a consulting company and hired computer science majors to help local tech companies test their software. "When he told me he started a company, I was instantly filled with envy and curiosity and felt like my world was being widened. That option [of entrepreneurship] wasn't even in our vocabulary." Ali joined his friend and ended up helping run the business. With his eyes opened to the potential of entrepreneurship, he switched his major to computer science, and spent more time on the business than on his studies in his senior year. (He managed to graduate summa cum laude and squeeze in a master's degree.)

Soon after graduating, Ali Partovi found a foothold in Silicon Valley, first as an engineer, then as a successful entrepreneur, and eventually as an investor. Enmeshed in the tech community, he and his twin, Hadi, saw that they shared a couple key things in common with many other tech executives, many of whom had learned to code at a young age and had role models to inspire them. So in 2013, they cofounded and funded Code.org to give all children free access to computer science as part of a K–12 curriculum, which Hadi runs. As Ali invested more in startups, he saw that many of the best engineering graduates didn't go the entrepreneurial route but rather followed the safe, well-trod path to Google, Apple, or Microsoft. Having experience with student loans and immigration issues, he could relate to the impulse to take a safe path, but he saw how students, without role models and support to make them comfortable with the risk of entrepreneurship, could miss the opportunity to have a greater impact at a startup. He didn't want the next generation of startups to be founded only by the kinds of well-heeled kids who had created the last generation.

With that perspective on the startup ecosystem, in 2017 Ali Partovi created Neo, a company to support and invest in a diverse group of talented undergraduate engineers and computer science majors. He and a team recruit top students to apply to become "Neo scholars"—to join a network and attend events such as dinners and retreats with leading executives at tech companies. Partovi and his colleagues have given personalized introductions that lead to summer internships and postcollege jobs at promising startups. Neo also recently launched a startup accelerator, giving both funding and hands-on mentorship to recent college graduates who start companies. The firm is selective; about 125 scholars have been accepted in its first four years, and only a few dozen more are accepted each year.[*] Neo works to avoid bias in its evaluation process; whereas most engineering job interviews in Silicon Valley involve a stressful, timed coding challenge, Neo applicants can opt for other formats.

It's not just the scholars who are diverse but also the mentors. "The easy route for me would have been to call up the other balding white men who've been successful," Partovi said. This serves more than just a bleeding-heart desire for representation. He wants to show the students that there is no single archetype for successful entrepreneurs. "From the beginning I felt like it would not be nearly as valuable or interesting for anyone if it's a bunch of people who look like each other. It's more valuable for everyone if it's breaking down barriers." He has brought in speakers such

---

[*]Neo is also designed to be inclusive: the company recruits from groups on college campuses that support engineers who are women and people of color.

as Nick Caldwell, one of the most senior Black engineers in Silicon Valley; he was the chief product officer of Looker, a startup that sold to Microsoft for $2.5 billion, and went on to become General Manager for core technologies at the company then known as Twitter. A computer science major who created the largest network of schools in Africa, Jay Kimmelman, presented to the Neo scholars and urged them to be entrepreneurial outside traditional industry. "It really contrasts with a job offer from Instagram and Microsoft and raises this question of 'What do I really want to do with my life and how can I choose a path that will matter?'" Partovi said.

These efforts are more than just noblesse oblige gestures. They have practical implications for Partovi because Neo isn't a diversity initiative; it's a fund. Partovi tells his scholars that if at any point they decide to start a company (they have no obligation to do so), he is committed to investing in it. "We think about it as incubating people and relationships and giving young people role models and inspiration to consider more adventurous career options." Just as a college buddy's startup opened Partovi's eyes to the possibilities of entrepreneurship, he wants to do the same for the next generation. He sees massive possibilities in what this young, diverse group will accomplish—in both contributing to society and making money. "The core thesis for me is that if you have someone who has overcome a lot of adversity to get to where they are, it's an attractive investment opportunity. That's often true with women in computer science or Black or Latino/Latina computer scientists—they have to work harder or be more resilient, and so on. I think it makes them more likely to be successful founders as well." Neo's success, Partovi believes, could help change the narrative about the value of investing in diversity. The firm is intentionally transparent about its portfolio's diversity. As of February 2022, 49 percent of its capital had been deployed in companies led by female or underrepresented minority CEOs.[4]

He is already seeing results. Though Neo's investments are illiquid, like any VC fund at its stage, in just four years it delivered a 43 percent net internal rate of return, based on private market valuations (that is after management fees). Partovi has created a business model that enables him to expand his own network, expand opportunity to a more diverse generation of entrepreneurs—and make a ton of money.

Changing Hiring Practices

I began this book by exploring the gale-force headwinds that women entrepreneurs face when trying to launch a business in Silicon Valley. I did so because those statistics (women founders drew only 2 percent of investment dollars and 6.5 percent of deals in 2021) were so vividly appalling and, conversely, my own encounters with women entrepreneurs had been so inspiring. The challenging odds faced by women who wanted to start companies was, for me, a natural way into the project of this book. I am ending the book by describing the even bigger roadblocks to equity—at the very earliest part of the funnel.

When I joined a dinner with a dozen of Partovi's Neo scholars, it reminded me that for most young people—women and people of color in particular—there is often no "way in" to the world of Silicon Valley at all. That is why Partovi is working not only to introduce bright young computer scientists to the world of tech giants but, more important, to empower them with the potential to innovate as entrepreneurs.

There's the image of a brilliant founder as a figure who emerges fully formed like Athena from the head of Zeus: Mark Zuckerberg and Bill Gates as Harvard dropouts, Google founders Larry Page and Sergey Brin from a Palo Alto garage. The reality is that entrepreneurship arises from an accumulation of experiences with teachers, colleagues, and patient bosses. The problems of inequity and underrepresentation can't be solved simply by distributing capital to young geniuses who come from all walks of life. They will be solved only when the hiring pipeline into tech giants—and all companies—looks a lot more like the world at large.

It makes me optimistic that someone with Partovi's success has found that there's more value in disrupting the status quo than in protecting it. I see even more reasons to be hopeful about change because of the cadre of female founders who are tackling the corporate side of the bias problem. These women are building tech-enabled tools to enable businesses to hire more equitably—and more effectively. The goal is to reshape the talent base not just for tech companies but for all businesses looking for a competitive edge.

Perhaps the biggest factor in regressive hiring practices is the most familiar one: the résumé. Much ink has been spilled on the ways in which a résumé can be a tool for reinforcing bias: a meta-analysis of thirty years of research showed that if researchers took identical résumés and switch the applicant name from John Williams to Jamal Washington, John landed ten interviews for every one Jamal did.[5] Silicon Valley has provided the world with incredible tools that enable us to process more information than at any other point in human history. Yet hiring has continued to rely on the warm introduction or the standardized coding test (the latter of which has been shown to encode bias into the hiring system). Despite all its technological innovations, the industry has failed to adequately tackle the pattern matching that narrows companies' hiring aperture. That was why the neuroscientist Frida Polli founded a company to replace the entrenched standby of the résumé.

Over the course of a decade at Harvard and MIT, Polli had been studying AI and behavioral science to understand people better. But she wanted to transfer the tools she'd developed out of the laboratory environment and into the world of business. As a single parent, she also wanted to make more money (MIT paid a postdoctoral fellow $40,000 per year). She started by getting an MBA from Harvard Business School.

Ahead of her business school graduation in 2012, Polli watched her classmates go through the recruiting process and take internships and then jobs at banks, consulting firms, and tech companies. What she found was shocking. "The tools we use today to measure people's likelihood of success in a job are both very inaccurate—not very predictive—and they're extremely biased. It's the worst of both worlds. And that's if you're using a tool at all. If you're just using a simple résumé review, the bias is just as bad," she said. "It was particularly salient to me because as a single-parent breadwinner I realized there are a lot of single women out there, single moms particularly in communities of color, that are going to suffer disproportionately from this really antiquated, old, and biased way of hiring."

Thanks to her academic work, Polli knew how to evaluate people for all the things that companies value in potential employees—from learning style to decision-making approach to risk tolerance. And she knew how to calculate how those features could influence their success in the workplace. Together, she figured, those data points could help her craft a better way to hire. So in 2013, she took the risk of starting Pymetrics, an AI-driven system to predict someone's fit for a particular job. In twenty-five minutes, applicants complete a set of twelve games, each of which captures thousands of behavioral data points. The games reveal, among other things, if someone prefers to focus on one task at a time or thrives in a multitasking environment; has a consistent or adaptive learning style; cares more about the amount of time spent on a project or about its outcome. "The company says, 'Okay, this person is empathetic and cognitively flexible and a little bit of an asshole,'" Polli explained. All of this without looking at a résumé or conducting an interview. The AI-based system can also evaluate if an applicant is a good fit for any open position across the organization (she says JPMorgan Chase uses Pymetrics to review applicants for jobs in seventeen different programs). The program also supplies the applicant with the report, "so you learn about yourself, like Myers-Briggs, but very updated for the twenty-first century."

The risk that Polli took has paid off. Pymetrics now works with about a hundred clients and has placed hundreds of thousands of employees, from package handlers to private equity analysts. It reportedly generated as much as $20 million in revenue in 2020, with a broad client base including financial institutions such as Morgan Stanley, consulting firms such as Bain & Company, and big consumer products companies such as Colgate-Palmolive.[6] As the company has grown, Polli has also used the software to analyze companies' personnel: current employees take questionnaires to create a vivid data set about corporate culture. That enables Pymetrics to customize its hiring algorithms to fit a particular company. In August 2022, Pymetrics sold to hiring software company Harver to augment its talent assessment tools and expand Pymetrics' reach. After the sale Polli became Harver's chief data science officer.

Polli says her tools are best equipped for candidates in the first five or ten years of their professional lives—just after the period when Partovi is helping young engineering students with Neo. "You can learn whatever hard skills you need for a job like that, and if you have the soft skills, you can learn them way more easily than if you don't. We've been asking 'Do you have the experience?' when actually we should have been asking 'Do you have the potential?' " (This echoes the way Gail Becker, in chapter 4, looked to hire for CAULIPOWER.)

This focus on "soft skills" is key to diversity, Polli says, because the experiences listed on résumés (and the opportunities that those experiences reveal) are not evenly distributed across race and gender. (My own White House internship was as much a product of my socioeconomic privilege as of my academic prowess.) But Pymetrics has found in the data that there are intrinsic qualities that *are* evenly distributed across gender and race. "It's a great equalizer, and that's the benefit of soft-skill profiling; it's much more accurate than résumés," Polli said. That's why, she said, the company's tools have been able to show not only a massive improvement in diversity among its clients but also significant improvements in corporate performance. Those results include a 28 to 48 percent decrease in recruiting costs and as much as a 48 percent decrease in time spent recruiting.[7] Based on the software results, Polli said, one multinational financial services firm reported a 33 percent increase in sales, and an international cruise line reported a 28 percent reduction in costs. "This whole idea that if you look for diversity, you lower standards is actually totally the opposite of what's true; if you're not looking for diversity, you're actually lowering your standards. That's why Pymetrix is not a diversity creation tool, it's a performance-improving tool that also benefits diversity."

Whereas Polli is working to push companies to hire candidates based on their skills, not the opportunities they've had, Blendoor founder Stephanie VanPutten (formerly Lampkin) is focusing on shedding light on the diversity and inclusion practices of various companies. (She also founded Visible Figures, mentioned in chapter 10, to support Black women entrepreneurs.) Blendoor started off focused on helping companies battle unconscious bias in their hiring, but after the murder of George Floyd, it pivoted to be a ratings and analytics company, providing a sort of FICO score for corporate diversity.

A coder since she was thirteen years old growing up in Washington, DC, a young Stephanie Lampkin spent her summers training in programming languages through a program run by Black Data Processing Associates (BDPA) and competing in programming competitions. After graduating from Stanford with an engineering degree, she worked on software development for Lockheed Martin and Northrop Grumman and in product at Tripadvisor. She also spent five years at Microsoft in various technical roles. That was followed by an MBA from MIT, where she focused on entrepreneurship and innovation. In 2014, she made it far into the interview process for a job at Google as an "analytical lead" and felt confident that her decade of experience made her a great fit. But in the final round, she says a recruiter called to tell her the company thought "she wasn't technical enough" and was going to hire someone else. Then, she says, the recruiter assured her that the company would hold on to her résumé in case a position in sales or marketing opened up.

Sales or marketing? VanPutten is a four-foot-eleven gay Black woman who didn't fit the dominant stereotype of an engineer with high-level technical expertise. She said she had seen in her time at Microsoft that tech companies tended to put technical women into sales and marketing roles. "I knew the code words they were using, and I saw that's how a lot of technical women ended up in roles that were very underpaid with very limited career trajectory," she said. "So I politely declined."

Within a few months of that rejection, Google released its 2014 diversity report, which revealed that 2 percent of its US workforce was Black and 30 percent of its global workforce was female. Google explained its struggle to recruit and retain women and minorities by saying that "Blacks and Hispanics each make up under 10 percent of U.S. college grads and each collect fewer than 10 percent of degrees in CS majors."[8] But ever since VanPutten could remember, she had known Black coders, so the excuse that there weren't enough in the pipeline didn't make sense. "I knew that I had experiences with women and people of color all throughout my career," she said. "It was an inefficiency in the marketplace. Business school teaches you that the ventures that succeed are those that fill a gap, an arbitrage opportunity. It seemed to me that my exposure gave me a competitive advantage to help Google find and attract this talent that they claim doesn't exist."

VanPutten took the opportunity to repair the glitch: in 2015, she founded Blendoor, which at the time focused on offering hiring tools to eliminate potential bias. Blendoor can analyze recruiting data to see how far qualified candidates of different demographics typically make it through a company's recruitment funnel. VanPutten discovered that large companies were focused on talent acquisition but not on talent retention, culture, or mitigating bias, so their overall diversity numbers weren't budging. To give Blendoor's customers a standard way of measuring themselves against other companies, VanPutten developed a way to synthesize all of a company's employee data (public filings, diversity sites, and social responsibility reports) into a "BlendScore," which she launched in 2017, to rank them based on their diversity. The score serves as a way for companies to measure their progress and as a guide for potential employees, who can compare a company not just with its competitors but also with the demographic breakdown of the local population. (Mailchimp, for example, is headquartered in Atlanta, which has a high concentration of Black professionals, yet for years it had no Black executives on its board or leadership team.)

VanPutten found the BlendScore a particularly useful tool in 2020, after the Black Lives Matter movement prompted companies to pledge more than $4.5 billion in solidarity (though a small fraction of the pledged amount went toward criminal justice reform).[9] VanPutten wanted potential applicants to know if the companies that had made donations were actually committed to diversity. When she compared the dollar and workplace numbers, she found the opposite to be true: the companies that had made grand statements in support of Black Lives Matter had an average of 20 percent *fewer* Black employees than those that didn't. It was the kind of data analysis that could help job applicants get to the truth about whether they would want to work for an employer or not.

After publishing that report, VanPutten renamed the company BlendScore and pivoted to focus on data transparency and standardization around diversity, equity, and inclusion (DEI). "The murder of George Floyd was a particularly significant event," she said. "People were awoken to the realities of long, deep-seated institutional challenges for different demographics. That awakening enabled us to be more forward thinking in creating a product that companies would find value in benchmarking and assessing their progress." The company starts with a quantitative analysis of a company's current DEI status, provides targeted recommendations for it to improve its score, and provides access to a pipeline of diverse talent at the VP level and above. "The war for talent will become far more competitive," VanPutten said, "so the biggest value that we provide for companies is this growing area around employer branding. Glassdoor has created good value from a high-level perspective about what it's like to work at a company, but we're taking an even more granular approach by giving people insights based on their identities, which companies they're most likely to succeed in belonging in."*

---

*VanPutten says she sold BlendScore in 2023 and is now consulting and investing in startups.

Expanding Tech's Borders

In addition to tools that improve hiring, there is another crucial initiative that is broadening the gateway to the tech economy: the geographic expansion of what constitutes "Silicon Valley." Until the transition to remote work during the pandemic, that geography had limited hiring by the giants at the epicenter of the tech world to those in a commutable (two-hour) radius from high-priced San Francisco and its tony suburbs.

Irma Olguin, Jr., and her company, Bitwise Industries, are located well outside the Silicon Valley radius, in her hometown of Fresno, California. The city is a high-crime, high-unemployment agricultural center halfway between San Francisco and Los Angeles, although it has little in common with either. Olguin grew up in the small town of Caruthers, population 2,497, fifteen miles to the south of Fresno. In the 1930s, her grandparents had immigrated to the area from Mexico, following work harvesting crops. Her parents and aunts and uncles, everyone she was related to, worked in the fields. "That's what the family does. It's not a question of individuals. It's 'What does the family need?' When we were very young, we got a taste of what it was like to work under the Central Valley sun, and it was everything that Steinbeck says."

Most American teenagers measure their after-school job compensation by the hour. Olguin and her family were paid by the pound or by the row. Starting when she was six, she joined her parents in the fields, participating in a process called "rolling raisins." She helped bundle the grapes that her aunts and uncles had harvested into giant paper cones, the inside of which could reach 140 degrees F. Within weeks, the grapes would turn into raisins. It was one of the easier tasks associated with grape harvesting—nothing compared to the dusty, hot conditions her family endured to make ends meet

One day in 1996, when she was in tenth grade, Olguin heard her school principal announce over the loudspeaker that students could skip afternoon classes to take an exam. So she headed to the cafeteria to take what she didn't realize at the time was the Preliminary Scholastic Aptitude Test (PSAT). She didn't have any ambition of going to college; she assumed that after high school she would avoid the sweltering farm work by getting a job at the local Texaco station or Ace Hardware. "I didn't know what the PSAT meant. I didn't know I would do well. I didn't realize that I had marked a box that said 'Please send me college material,' because I'm sure if I had read that question correctly, I would have marked 'No,' because what does college material mean for a kid like me?"

But Olguin did do well, her results were sent to colleges, and stacks of letters and glossy pamphlets soon arrived. One letter from the University of Toledo contained an offer of a full scholarship. It seemed too good to be true, and in a way it was; the family couldn't afford the $78 it would cost to buy a bus ticket to Ohio.

"We're really proud of you," Olguin said her parents told her. It was the kind of lucky break that they had worked so hard to make possible for their children. "But that's way the hell over there, and there's no way you're going to get there." Seeing that the only thing standing between Olguin and a different kind of life was the price of a bus ticket, her father and her siblings joined her to harvest a different kind of crop from Fresno's sunbaked fields. "My dad would take us out in an old pickup truck, and we would ride on the tailgate, and he would go very, very slow, a few miles an hour, down these country roads. We'd hop off the end of the tailgate and collect sticky cans and bottles from the fields," Olguin told me. The cans and bottles were worth $1.25 a pound. It took them more than three months, but by August they had earned enough for her bus ride.

When Olguin arrived on campus in the fall of 1998, she felt like an alien. Her family had no experience that could help her. She was given an orientation packet, which included a mystifying slip of paper containing a string of letters and numbers; it was, she would later learn, her first email address. She also didn't understand what it meant when a woman asked her to choose the subschool for her major but "thought it would be really neat to take classes in the new glass building in the catalog." That building, as it turned out, was the home of the College of Engineering. Though there were only five other women in the engineering school's class of five hundred, "gender was at the bottom of things that made me different," Olguin said. "It was my ethnicity, then it was being from California, and then it was being Queer." The University of Toledo was predominantly white; the demographic questions on the application didn't include "Hispanic" or "Latino/a" as an option. "It just says 'Other' right there in the category, and I absolutely felt that, from day one."

The school warned repeatedly that the engineering program was so time consuming that students shouldn't expect to work at any outside job. But Olguin's scholarship covered only tuition, housing, and lab fees; if she wanted to buy textbooks—or eat—she would need to work. She spent every semester hustling between the glass engineering building and her jobs at the local Circuit City and Fazoli's Italian restaurant, where she washed dishes. She was motivated by the fear that if her grades dipped, she would lose her scholarship and have to return home without a degree to justify the time she had spent away, not contributing to her family.

But even during that anxious cycle of school and work, she felt the thrill of new opportunities. To complete her degree, she and her classmates had to participate in a work-study program for three semesters. In her final year of the five-year program, she was apprenticed as an engineer, developing a municipal water runoff system. One night, while working late, she ordered pizza, paid twenty dollars to the delivery guy, and surprised herself when she told him he could keep the change. "It was this moment—the world stopped spinning and I couldn't hear anything—but you just know everything's different," she remembered. "Holy shit, I didn't count the change, I didn't need to, in that moment, ask myself if I needed those three bucks for a gallon of gas." She realized how far she had come from the days when she had needed to collect bottles and cans to pay for a $78 bus ticket. This wasn't just success; it was empowerment. And she wanted to find a way to give that feeling to other people.

But Olguin never got to test out what kind of job her engineering degree could earn her, because before she graduated, life changed again when her father passed away. Right after she got her diploma, she moved back home to help support her mother and the rest of the family after the loss of their patriarch. At first she made money by helping people clear out garages, selling Crock-Pots and the like at local flea markets. She soon found work helping local Fresno businesses such as pet stores and hair salons set up websites and design inventory spreadsheets—easy work for a trained engineer.

She was shocked by the demand for such remedial tech intervention—and what a difference it could make to the fortunes of those small-business owners. Inspired by the potential, she started a competition to mobilize the small tech community in Fresno. Then she opened a coworking space, for which she charged a $29 monthly fee. The workspace turned into a sort of clubhouse. As the companies nurtured there began to grow and wanted to hire, Olguin realized that the biggest thing holding back progress in Fresno's small businesses was actually a lack of technical workers.

What Olguin saw was an ecosystem developing, with a virtuous cycle that caused different types of businesses to support one another. She started teaching web development and entry-level coding to fuel small businesses' growth. She also started looking at real estate for those businesses to rent. And in 2013, she partnered with Jake Soberal, an attorney of Mexican American heritage, who Olguin says had grown up on the right side of the tracks in Fresno, to launch Bitwise Industries.

The first phase of the business was a coding and tech skills bootcamp to transition workers out of menial jobs into higher-wage coding gigs. One of Bitwise's first clients was a local technology company, Decipher, that wanted to train local talent so it wouldn't have to move its headquarters away from Fresno. A key to the model was making the majority of Bitwise's students' classes free, paid for by businesses and job-training programs. (If not funded, classes to learn to build web applications cost students $250 with free access to a computer.) The classes can be as transformative to Bitwise's students as Olguin's unexpected PSAT result and bus ticket were to her. "We don't have to wait for accidents to happen to have that kind of story," Olguin said.

The second part of the business was a software development division, staffed by alumni and apprentices from Bitwise's training program. Companies could commission an app, website, or custom software with lower fees than an expert in a major tech hub would charge. The third and final piece of the plan: investing in downtown Fresno real estate, to transform abandoned buildings into offices. Olguin and Soberal rented the spaces to small businesses, many of which employed Bitwise trainees; some were founded by Bitwise alumni.

Four years after launching, the cofounders were ready to raise a Series A round to fund their expansion to nearby cities. It did not go well. Olguin says they pitched more than a thousand potential investors over an eighteen-month period. But she didn't match any patterns of a typical CEO, and the business model didn't match the trend of "platforms" and enterprise software. Olguin was pitching urban revitalization, but investors kept asking "Yes, yes, but are you *doubling* year over year? It almost doesn't even matter doubling *what*," she said. Olguin found that investors would look at her—a tattooed Latina whose purple hair is shaved around the sides—and not even believe that she was the CEO. Instead, they would direct questions to Soberal. The two cofounders eventually worked out a plan: Soberal would make the investors comfortable by opening the pitch; then Olguin would take over to tell her personal story (bottle collecting and all) before showing the data that supported the company's business model. Then it would be back to Soberal to field questions. They figured out a rhythm, but they weren't making much progress with investors—until one day they happened to hear a venture capitalist speak at a local tech conference.

An investor for more than two decades, Freada Kapor Klein, along with her husband, Mitch Kapor, uses a particular metric to weigh potential investments. It's not education level, entrepreneurial experience, or even the core business idea. They focus on "distance traveled"—how many obstacles entrepreneurs have had to overcome, how far they've gotten, and how hard they have had to work to get there. "Genius is evenly distributed throughout society, regardless of race, gender or zip code—but opportunity is not," Kapor Klein said, echoing Frida Polli's research about soft skills.

Kapor Klein started formulating the approach in the late 1990s when she was serving on the board of UC Berkeley's College of Letters and Science. She had created a fund to assist underrepresented students in response to the banning of affirmative action. Over ten years of supporting first-generation collegegoers, she found remarkable results. Not only did they graduate faster than the typical Berkeley student, but 75 percent went on to some sort of graduate school, including med school, law school, and PhD programs. "I learned from meeting these scholars and understanding their stories how that, in some ways, was a better predictor of their ability to succeed than pedigrees," Kapor Klein recalled. "When people with pedigrees hit rough times, they're looking for a solution to put on their credit cards."[10]

In 1999, she and Mitch Kapor, the founder of the software company Lotus, started making angel investments. In the meantime, their philanthropic efforts focused on promoting diversity in tech. They founded the Level Playing Field Institute in 2001 to foster interest in science, technology, engineering, and mathematics (STEM) courses among underrepresented groups, and in 2002 they launched a program called SMASH, a STEM-focused college prep program for students from underrepresented groups.

In 2011, they decided to bring their investment strategy into line with their nonprofit work: they committed their VC fund, Kapor Capital, to investing exclusively in startups that close gaps of access or opportunity for low-income communities and communities of color. (Two gap-closing investments they made were in Thrive Market, which makes healthy food accessible at lower prices and with food stamps, and Pigeonly, which enables people to communicate inexpensively with prison inmates via phone calls and letters.) In 2016, they began requiring companies in their portfolio to commit to new diversity and inclusion measures. As of 2021, 60 of their 102 investments had a founder who identified as a woman and/or was an underrepresented person of color.

In addition to "distance traveled," there is another factor that Kapor Capital looks for: startup concepts that originate from founders' lived experience. The perspectives of underrepresented entrepreneurs, they believe, provide a competitive edge in identifying otherwise overlooked problems. "The closer to home, the more it matches their lived experience, the more determined they are," Kapor Klein said. So far, their thesis has panned out: in 2019, the fund reported that its investments in the previous eight years had far outperformed 75 percent of the investments of similar funds in terms of both internal rate of return and a ratio called total value to paid in (TVPI), which measures a fund's gain.[11]

The day Olguin and Soberal heard Kapor Klein speak at that conference, Olguin turned to her partner and said, "These are our people." She and a few other Bitwise executives didn't feel comfortable joining the crowd that surrounded Kapor Klein as she left the stage, so they found a contact who knew Mitch Kapor and sent him their pitch. The investors eventually went down to Fresno to meet Olguin and Soberal and see their business in action. "It checks every one of our investment criteria, and if we gave it numbers, it would get a perfect score," Kapor Klein said. Her fund rarely leads VC investment rounds, but it made an exception for Bitwise, coleading the $27 million Series A round in 2019, one of the highest ever for a Latina founder.

Bitwise spent the next year growing to the other agriculture-focused cities of Bakersfield and Merced and then to Oakland. By 2020, it had trained about five thousand people, and more than 80 percent of them had found full-time jobs in tech, many increasing their earning potential from less than $21,000 a year to $60,000.[12] Together, Olguin and Soberal also developed and leased about half a million square feet of coworking spaces, restaurants, and other retail spaces in previously impoverished downtown areas.

By the end of 2020, Olguin realized that she needed more capital to meet the needs of businesses and address the supply of young talent, so she and her partner started another round of investor meetings. This time, at the height of the pandemic, she found it easier to connect with venture capitalists who saw value in the company's unusual approach of creating tech ecosystems outside typical hubs. "We didn't change that many things about business; we just invited a different set of people through the front door and paid them to learn like it was their job," she told me. "The results you get are a diverse, inclusive technology workforce."

By early 2021, Bitwise's employee base was representative of the region—more than 50 percent Black, Brown and Native people, 20 percent first-generation immigrants, and just over half female. About 40 percent of the people who went through its Workforce Development Program, as well as Bitwise employees, identified as LGBTQ+. Those workers generated $40 million of revenue in 2020, according to a *Forbes* report on the company. With that proof of concept, the company raised an additional $50 million in February 2021, bringing the total investment raised to $100 million at a $200 million valuation.[13] Along with that funding, the company announced that it would be expanding to five more cities. Olguin also forged a partnership with the state of California to pay for apprenticeships to equip its graduates to work on public-sector tech-related projects. Olguin committed to building a technology workforce that represented each city's community to benefit the diversity of potential customers in the area.[*]

Looking at the results of Kapor Capital's investments, Kapor Klein is surprised that more investors still aren't following their strategy. "Data about diverse companies, diverse funds outperforming the others, that's old news by now. Mainstream VCs . . . say they're objective about their

---

[*]In June 2023 the Bitwise Industries board became aware of a cash deficit, which led to the decision to furlough employees, suspend operations, and terminate co-CEOs Olguin and Soberal. The board also launched an investigation into what led to these events.

processes, but you have to have a warm intro and all of these things where bias just replicates itself." Kapor Klein believes that what will ultimately tilt Silicon Valley to embrace diversity will be a couple of massively valuable IPOs or company sales. Their financial success should inspire other investors to bet on the "distance traveled" of entrepreneurs such as Olguin. The first city Bitwise expanded to outside California was the college town of Toledo, Ohio, where Olguin had been given her very first email address more than twenty years before.

Intersectionality

Olguin's story is a reminder that the challenges for poor women of color are much more intense than they are for the kinds of prosperous white women who populate much of this book. My hope is that the stories and studies of this book can be just as applicable to other underrepresented entrepreneurs, whose disadvantages are most acute. It should not go unremarked upon that as Olguin navigated institutional structures of business, she had in her cofounder, Jake Soberal, what statistically seems to be an advantage: someone who presents as a white guy. Coed founding teams, as I've discussed, draw more than three times the percentage of VC dollars that all-female teams do. But the total that coed teams draw, less than 19 percent of the total funds invested, is still paltry.[14]

It's even more essential to note that Olguin doesn't have just one underrepresented identity but multiple ones, which overlap and intersect. When she felt alien and othered in Toledo, that was not just because she was a rare woman in a male-dominated engineering program but also because, unlike her peers, she was Latinx, Queer, and poor.

The intersection of all those identities matters. Recent studies have found that focusing on the systemic disadvantages of a single identity—such as gender—can have the unintended side effect of creating an even larger representation gap between white women and women of color.[15] It's well documented that women of color suffer from a much larger pay gap with men than white women do.[16]* And the percentage of women of color declines dramatically from entry-level positions into management and executive roles. One study showed that white women benefited significantly from networking programs, whereas Black women tended not to. Networking programs drove a nearly 7 percent difference in the number of white women in management positions but made zero difference in the number of Black women in management.[17]

That's why the venture capital investor Ellen Pao is focused on addressing intersectional diversity in the tech world. She cofounded the nonprofit Project Include to encourage companies to acknowledge and welcome the entire range of identities and to understand the way they overlap. "You're not going to solve the [diversity] problem if you're only thinking about women, because [that focus] is still exclusive," she explained. "If your focus is 'women,' that ends up being just binary white women. Maybe you're opening the door to them a little bit, but your attitude and your mentality [are] still oriented around exclusion."

Pao's commitment to improve workplace dynamics dates back to 2012, when she sued her employer, the legendary VC firm Kleiner Perkins, alleging gender discrimination. She lost the case three years later, but it opened the floodgates to a conversation about bias in Silicon Valley.† The public discourse was so intense that the lawsuit inspired seven female leaders in tech, including investors and market research experts, to come together to examine the scope of the problem. They polled more than two hundred women with at least ten years of experience in large companies, startups, and venture capital firms. In 2016, they reported shocking statistics: 90 percent of the women had witnessed sexist behavior at conferences and company meetings, and two-thirds had felt

---

*Black women earn 62 cents for every dollar earned by white men, compared to the 82 cents that the average of all woman earn as of 2020 data from the U.S. Bureau of Labor Statistics.

†After losing her lawsuit, she spent two years as CEO of Reddit, where she worked to tamp down harassment on the platform.

excluded from key networking opportunities because of their gender. A full 60 percent reported unwanted sexual advances, and of those women, more than half said the advances had been by a superior and one-third said they had feared for their physical safety.[18]

If data could reveal the problem, Pao believes, it can also help reverse it. In 2016, she teamed up with Erica Joy Baker, a former Google employee who had made waves when she circulated a spreadsheet for employees to share their salary data (it revealed stark pay inequities). Along with five other women, they launched Project Include, a nonprofit dedicated to giving companies effective ways to hold themselves accountable for their diversity. The first step, they decided, was addressing what they saw as hollow and performative commitments to address sexism and racism (similar to the billions later committed to Black Lives Matter–related philanthropy).

It is common for tech companies to tout the meritocratic purity of their operations: the best product wins, the best employee wins, the algorithm fine tuned to maximize user engagement wins. A 2010 study, however, revealed the risk of the meritocracy myth. Organizations that presented themselves as meritocratic still favored men over equally well-performing women.[19] The professors saw that it was almost as if the avowal of meritocracy gave people a false sense of security about their lack of bias. To address that often false belief, Project Include presented companies with ninety-seven detailed recommendations, many of which focused on metrics such as measuring their current diversity, tracking their promotions and pay gaps, and numerically charting their progress.

Project Include also invited startup CEOs to join a paid course with a group of peers, called Startup Include, to regularly discuss their organization's challenges and progress regarding diversity. The wide scope, Pao explained, was purposeful: "It has to be comprehensive, so it's across every interaction you have in your organization, not just hiring; it's promoting and paying and laying people off. You have to make sure you're fair, and you need to use metrics and hold people accountable to them." (Among the three dozen high-profile startups that have participated, most of them run by white men, are high-profile Silicon Valley and San Francisco–based companies such as Coinbase and Patreon.)

After nine months, the Project Include team followed up with nearly 350 employees in five companies. The program, they discovered, had had a measurable impact. The companies that had participated had seen an increase in the racial and ethnic diversity of employees hired, and more women had been hired than the industry average.[20] They had also measured an increase in employee satisfaction with communication, as well as perceived opportunities for growth and advancement. In a postpandemic world where competition for talent is fierce and employee retention can make or break a business, those data are valuable.

A Competitive Advantage

Increasingly, white male Silicon Valley incumbents are investing in intersectional diversity. And they're not making financial commitments just because it's the ethical thing to do but because they know it's the best approach for their businesses. Time and time again, data have shown that diversity at companies yields better results.

One of the companies in Project Include's first course was Asana, a software platform designed to improve team collaboration and work management, founded by Facebook cofounder Dustin Moskovitz. Moskovitz has written about why he was drawn to the mission of increasing inclusivity: not just for social justice purposes but to attract the best talent. "The only thing harder than D&I in the tech industry is recruiting, so at some level we can't afford to not be inclusive," he wrote in a blog post. "Research also clearly demonstrates that companies with more diverse teams are more innovative, make better decisions, and are more effective at achieving their financial goals. It's a better way to work."[21]

That same interest in efficiency motivated Josh Kopelman to, after a decade as a venture capitalist, investigate the impact of diversity in his own investments. In 2005, after successfully selling a startup, he started First Round Capital to invest in early-stage companies. His team took the typical approach of evaluating companies' market potential, competition, and business plan. Because they invested before the companies had much of a track record, they also relied in part on their gut evaluation of a founder's potential. Their instincts tended to be right: First Round invested a mere half-million dollars in 2010 in Uber, which was worth $2.5 billion by the time of the company's IPO in 2019. It also made prescient bets on the eyeglass retailer Warby Parker, the AI lending platform Upstart, and the online gaming platform Roblox, all of which went on to have IPOs that were very profitable for the firm.[22] By 2015, the firm had backed dozens of unicorns and was a leader in early-stage investing. But the partners wanted to understand what specifically contributed to the firm's hit rate, so they brought in a data scientist to measure thirty different factors at the three hundred–plus startups the firm had backed over ten years. They wanted to know which factors were most predictive of success.

Some interesting trends emerged: solo founders far underperformed founding teams and founding a startup outside a big tech hub such as northern California or New York tended to yield better results. But that paled in comparison to the most dramatic finding: companies with a female founder performed 63 percent better than those with all-male founding teams. And of First Round's top ten investments in its decade of operations, three of them had at least one female founder. That success rate for female founders outpaced First Round's overall ratio of companies with a female cofounder—20 percent—and vastly outpaced the percentage of VC dollars that goes to a company with all-female and coed teams, which was at the time and continues to be less than 3 percent.[23]

"When we saw the data, we thought it was important to share it,"

Kopelman explained.[*] "We should have had a portfolio full of female founders. But I'd say the finding really helped shape and change the percentage of our companies [since then]." In 2016, First Round hired Hayley Barna, a cofounder of Birchbox, one of First Round's successful female-led startups. Kopelman said that once she joined, he saw how broad and diverse her range of contacts was. "She was getting—by far—a ton more female founders pitching her than all of my partners and I were. We could no longer use the argument that 'Hey, we have good relationships, [female entrepreneurs] can find us,' because we realized that we could do better and we should be doing more."

That prompted Kopelman to rethink the firm's pattern of hiring former First Round founders as investment partners. Though the practice had ensured that the firm intimately knew the people who were helping them deploy tens of millions of dollars of capital, "it wasn't a diverse network. . . . One of my biggest regrets was not realizing that sooner." To remedy the issue, Kopelman expanded the varieties of experience his firm was looking for. Then, in 2020, he read a polemic drafted by a young partner at Kapor Capital, asserting that if a firm doesn't publicly declare that it is hiring—it's deliberately excluding people from underrepresented groups who may have less access to the whisper network of tech jobs.[24] Now when First Round is looking to bring on a new partner, it does something that is still radical for the VC industry: it publishes a job description.

In the four years after Kopelman and his colleagues learned that First Round's female-led companies performed better, the percentage of the firm's investments led by a woman or underrepresented minority grew

---

[*]In 2015 First Round also conducted a "State of Startups" survey of five hundred venture capital–backed founders, three-quarters of whom hadn't been backed by his fund, which revealed striking statistics about the lack of gender diversity in tech. It was stunningly clear that women-led companies were more focused on their own diversity: 44 percent of women-led companies had a 50/50 gender ratio compared to a quarter of men-led companies, and nearly 90 percent of women-led companies had initiatives in place to increase diversity, compared to 62 percent of men-led companies.

from 20 percent to 35 percent. First Round hasn't released numbers since then, but says the percentage has continued to increase. And the firm's day-to-day operations have changed. At pitch meetings, senior partners used to lead the conversations, but now the fund has its investors do a pre-vote *before* the discussion begins. (This is the same approach I wrote about in chapter 6 that was adopted by Zola CEO Shan-Lyn Ma to avoid groupthink and ensure that quieter employees' ideas are heard.) Then First Round brings in a third-party moderator. This has led to more selectivity in its investments; no longer can a "point partner" with a special affinity for a founder steamroll his or her colleagues into investing. The firm's term sheet also now contains a "diversity rider," which stipulates that the startup must commit to bringing on diverse investors (alongside the still largely white male First Round crew). Kopelman believes that doing so has also helped the firm secure more deals—even with white male founders. Those founders tell Kopelman that they are glad to have the support and guidance to diversify their cap tables. "I can say that we believe in our hearts there are meaningful economic reasons to be doing it, more than just a sense of fairness and equity," he said.

Profit-Motivated Change

All of these stories have a common thread: there are not just moral reasons for embracing diversity but also compelling economic ones. This, to me, is the number one reason to be optimistic that we have finally arrived at a moment for change. The research presented in every chapter of this book makes a multipronged case for diversity. Investors will always chase profits; Silicon Valley shouldn't ignore the creation of value that comes from hiring and investing equitably. And I'm hopeful that all sorts of businesses will start to understand the measurable value of giving women and other underrepresented groups an opportunity to thrive.

There is perhaps no more vivid avatar of capitalism than Wall Street's most elite bank, Goldman Sachs. It is closely watched by the media and often emulated by companies in the financial sector and beyond. In 2018, it introduced Launch With GS, a commitment to invest $500 million in startups with diverse founders and in funds with diverse managers. "We understood that diverse and inclusive teams outperformed, but they weren't getting the capital," said Stephanie Cohen, the former global co-head of consumer and wealth management, who oversaw the initiative for four years. Of that half-billion dollars, the majority was invested in startups with founders who are women or people of color, including Billie, a razor-maker startup; Burst Oral Care; and BentoBox, a company that designs software for restaurants. The rest was invested in funds run by diverse managers.

"The world is awash in capital, it's really hard to find good investments, and yet this whole area, where inclusive and diverse teams should produce outsized returns, is underinvested. We said we want to put money behind that," said Cohen. In 2020, the company also started hosting an annual cohort of Black and Latinx entrepreneurs to coach them over the course of eight weeks about fundraising and growth strategies. The program culminated in a presentation to two hundred outside investors. The response was positive, and Goldman decided to make it an annual program.

"We didn't make this a separate thing inside of Goldman; it's embedded directly in our growth equity business on purpose because ultimately what we want to do is change the way we're managing, thinking, and sourcing across the entire business," Cohen explained. "It wasn't a philanthropic endeavor. It was totally for profit. We believe they're going to deliver outsized returns. It was really important to us that we were making it part of the business because we think that's more sustainable." And in its sustainability, it would be vivid and visible to the whole industry, not just some siloed DEI initiative.

At the time of this book's writing, it's still too early to calculate any hard measure of the program's impact, especially because all the investments are less than three years old; venture capital investments often take a decade to yield a return. But every indication so far is that Goldman's investments are having a meaningful impact: the fourteen early-stage companies with both female and male Black and Latinx founders that participated in Goldman's 2020 cohort raised more than $200 million in the eighteen months after the end of the program—all from investors other than Goldman Sachs. Another measure of the impact of Goldman's strategy to invest in female-led VC firms: the first five that received Goldman's backing have since raised an additional $1.5 billion in capital for subsequent funds. And those following funds were 60 percent larger than those Goldman had invested in. That indicates Goldman's ability to support the firms it backs and help them drive growth. In 2021, Goldman doubled its commitment, planning an additional $500 million investment, because it saw a greater untapped opportunity. One of the companies in Launch with GS' 2021 cohort was Mahmee, the maternity and pediatrics telehealth platform I wrote about in chapter 3. In May 2022 Goldman Sachs Asset Management led a $9.2 million series A investment round into the company. This speaks to the opportunity and could inspire others to follow.

The women profiled in this book are, by definition, exceptions. They are the winners in a brutal and unfair game with rules that have been etched deep into the playbook of our society. It would take a much longer book to examine all the women who have tried and failed to navigate a capital raise and whose dreams have died on the rocky shoals of systemic inequities. Imagine what a different world we might live in if those "unknown soldiers" of entrepreneurship had been given a fair chance. What's been lost is not just individuals' livelihood but actual value—to the economy, to investors, to the world. (According to McKinsey's calculation, gender equity could add trillions of dollars to the annual US GDP.)[25]

Goldman Sachs didn't invest in diversity just because it was the right thing to do; its executives knew it could make them money. The hundred corporations around the world that use Haver's Pymetrics software to hire based on data-predicted potential, rather than pedigree, have improved their hiring results, and saved time and money. Tech giants don't use tools such as Blendoor because they feel bad about bias in the recruiting process; they do it so they can hire and retain the best employees. When companies eliminate traditional barriers to entry for the tech industry, tech workers become diverse. And cities such as Fresno, where no tech opportunities were thought to exist, suddenly flourish.

The good news I found in reporting this book is that solving the issue of diversity in tech requires no special sense of mission or highly developed conscience. Indeed, when companies focus on data—dispassionate, unbiased, stereotype-free data—encouraging diversity naturally becomes a priority. Diversity shouldn't only be the goal of do-gooders; it also is a side effect of paying attention to data.

It is worth noting that, of course, not all women leaders will succeed, nor will they be without fault or flaw in their approach to management and leadership. But in light of the heightened attention to women because of their rareness in leadership roles, and the human instinct to pattern matching, it's essential to identify the rare failures and frauds among flameouts of high-profile female leaders as just that—rare. Characterizing rare failures as the norm would be a mistake, perpetuating a false stereotype that could lead to the oversight of another generation of female leaders. I'm optimistic, because I see signs that investors and tech giants are increasingly waking up to this reality. I'm hopeful that people and companies will ultimately follow the data and understand their relationship to it. If we do, the world will be a better, more equitable place, and the individuals in it will have a better chance to achieve their full potential.

Learning Lessons

Like many kids, my two sons have always loved superheroes. Our toy box has always been populated by plastic figurines of the mainstays: Superman, Batman, Iron Man. One day in 2014, I looked at the pile of muscled plastic men strewn across the rug and decided it was time I added some female heroes to the mix. There weren't many options, even in Amazon's seemingly infinite scroll, but finally a Supergirl action figure arrived at the house. Upon opening the box, my older son, Henry, who was then three years old, asked, "Where's the rest of her shirt?" Supergirl was indeed wearing a crop top, along with a low-slung miniskirt and high-heeled boots. What bothered me then, and has stuck with me since, was that she also had giant, buoyant breasts, a tiny waist, and perfectly toned abs—not the kind of feminine ideal I wanted seared into my son's mind. What bothered Henry, I realized, was that, to him, superhero attire should be designed for speed and protection during violent altercations. Her exposed midriff and bare thighs were weird and, most important, highly impractical.

In the intervening years, the culture has started to reflect the demands of consumers like me who wanted more inclusive images of women and their capabilities. In 2015, Marvel was called out for what many saw as consumer product sexism when it failed to produce a Black Widow action figure upon the release of the second Avengers film. That same year, Target eliminated signs that labeled toys as for boys or for girls, in what was described as a "desegregation of children's products." In 2016, Mattel introduced three new Barbie body types along with a line of more ethnically diverse dolls. The following year, Wonder Woman made her big theatrical debut, followed by Captain Marvel and Black Widow. I was particularly exhilarated by the women of 2018's *Black Panther*, many of whom eventually got their own action figures. I preordered one of Shuri, Black Panther's sister, who begins the film as his techy, spunky inventor sidekick and over the course of the film evolves into a potent hero herself. Once Shuri and Wonder Woman were in the toy mix, I quietly pulled the old Supergirl from my boys' Ikea bin and put her into a drawer in our home office where, in early 2020, I began to report and write this book.

Soon after, two things happened: there was a global pandemic, and, just before its onset, my younger son learned to read. In the absence of playdates and in-person school we indulged his and his brother's superhero obsession. Our home became a sort of Library of Alexandria for Marvel and DC comics; our sons studied each page as though they were analyzing ancient texts. Their monkish devotion not only gave me time to work but also yielded intense dinner table debate about the advantages of various abilities (time travel trumps flying) and the risks of certain weaknesses (Aquaman's loss of power in the desert is preferable to Batman's general mortality).

My boys became most interested, though, in origin stories. They told me they preferred the heroes who created their own powers, such as Iron Man and Batman, to those whose powers were magically bestowed upon them, like Thor, or those who were alien, such as Superman. I, too, gravitated to the characters with agency, though I did worry that my sons would think that the clearest examples of self-creation were an arrogant boss like

Tony Stark or a mopey scion like Bruce Wayne. The iconography and allegory of superheroes became part of our family discourse. That was why, as I got deeper into the writing of this book, I took Supergirl out of the drawer and placed her next to Shuri on a shelf by my computer. For months they stood watch over me, a reminder of the patronizing stereotypes women face and the potential to create new representations of female power.

Whenever I found a particularly vivid study about pattern matching or implicit bias or when I completed a surprising interview, I would look up at Supergirl, with her wasp waist and buxom chest, and Shuri, with her practical action suit and weapons of her own design. So many founders had told me stories that illustrated how they were expected to present like a sort of Supergirl—a demure cousin of Super*man*, with exactly the same powers bestowed upon her thanks to the luck of her Kryptonian heritage. But in fact, the women I was writing about had so much more in common with Shuri, the figure who had created all that technology herself.

I set about writing this book because I had a strong sense, from years of accumulated encounters with female entrepreneurs, that there was something special about them. At the outset, I expected to find at least a few innate traits—superpowers—shared by these impressive women, and I did indeed find a number of powerful commonalities. Women tend to have an attention to context and an instinct to search for structural solutions rather than quicker but more temporary fixes. They are more likely to seek out diverse perspectives and incorporate them into their decision making, and they tend to pursue purpose-driven companies and show vulnerability. All of these things are conducive to successful leadership, yet are less often recognized as essential traits for a successful leader.

What was most surprising to me about those characteristics, though, was that they were *not* innate. I found that women had, over the course of their careers, *created* their powers by practicing and honing a series of strategies and approaches.

In the introduction, I wrote about how I felt empowered to address sexist recrimination because I'd read a study that found that women were more likely to be criticized for their style than their substance. That was one of several key insights I have been drawing upon myself, and believe can be deployed by anyone, at any point in a career:

1. Superpowers don't always look like powers.

In reporting this book, it has become clear to me that there is no one type of leadership that always works, nor is there a singular trick to navigating challenges. What's been most striking to me is that there is a vast gulf between the traditional idea of good leadership and the traits that actually contribute to good leadership.

For two years I spent my nights and weekends chronicling the stories of women who were often wildly different from one another, whose successes were due to their complex and nuanced approaches to leadership. Their varied approaches looked nothing like those of the strident founder-visionary, a monomyth that reigned in the business world where I spent my days reporting. (Indeed, those who had tried to mimic stereotypical male leadership styles often foundered: Elizabeth Holmes cast herself in Steve Jobs's image—an aspiring Supergirl copying Superman.) In that mainstream business world, there have traditionally been a handful of qualities associated with innovative leaders, especially those in tech: vision, exactitude, and unwavering confidence. Think of Jeff Bezos and Elon Musk inventing entirely new business categories and then shooting rocket ships into space or Mark Zuckerberg and his "I'm CEO, bitch" business cards early in his career. Another high-powered, high-paid CEO once told a frustrated employee who warned him that his expectations for a product launch were not "living in reality," "That's your problem. *You're* living in reality. You need to be with me, in *my* reality."

The images put forth by CEOs and their marketing machines create a dangerously narrow image of powerful leadership. In fact, research shows that there is a more varied and counterintuitive set of leadership qualities that yield better results—for both women and men.

There are some women in this book who have qualities that would not look out of place on a stereotypical male tech leader: Julie Wainwright is independent and persistent, Christine Hunsicker is incredibly competitive, and Katherine Power doesn't care what people think about her. And there are plenty of male leaders who demonstrate, and benefit from, the more stereotypical female approaches I describe in this book.

But superpowers, I've found, often don't have anything to do with power itself. Caryn Seidman-Becker's neurotic anxiety about planning ahead for worst-case scenarios doesn't exactly scream confident and unflappable leadership, nor does Jennifer Holmgren's preference to listen rather than to speak or Gwyneth Paltrow's requests for explanations of business acronyms.

Lots of different characteristics, particularly those traditionally thought to betray weakness, can in fact belie counterintuitive strengths. Toyin Ajayi slowed down and shifted the power dynamic to put her patients in charge. Gwyneth Paltrow admitted that she didn't understand jargon, which gave her team permission to ask questions. Stitch Fix's Katrina Lake's willingness to be forthright about her lack of expertise made her an executive talent magnet. Many of the women in the book, from Sallie Krawcheck to Jennifer Tejada, drew upon the advantage of their outsider perspective to serve a larger consumer base. These are indeed superpowers. But they may be hard to identify because they don't fit the commonly held leadership rubric.

These superpowers did have one crucial thing in common: not a single one of them is innate, bestowed at birth. Though Christine Hunsicker may have been born more competitive than the average person, she deployed her competitiveness not just against rival teams but also to improve herself: she used after-event reviews to systematically analyze her performance both on the field and in her business. Jennifer Holmgren had a tendency to listen rather than talk, but it was only after years of negotiating deals that she figured out how to use her reticence to learn what her counterparties really wanted. Anyone can develop a strength. The women in this book, and all of us, are more likely to acquire powers the way Shuri does, through invention and tinkering, than to have them bestowed upon us like Supergirl.

2. We all get scared, and that's actually a good thing.

When I was a young reporter at *Fortune* magazine interviewing much older men, I was often struck by their apparently unwavering confidence. But the more people I interview, the more I realize that no one is ever entirely sure of him- or herself. I keep returning to a study I mentioned in chapter 8 showing that confidence alone is not necessarily a good thing: If leaders don't have even a tiny inkling of doubt in their decision making, then they're not considering all scenarios—or they're not being honest. They're all just making the best decisions they can with all the data they have in a particular moment.

What's just as important as having self-confidence is knowing when to dial it down to absorb information and consider a range of opinions. Being honest about your lack of certainty—signaling vulnerability—can invite trust and encourage people to share honest feedback. Then what's important is finding the right moment to dial self-confidence back up again, to execute. It's actually the balance of self-confidence and humility that enables a growth mindset, which seems valuable for anyone.

The idea that self-confidence not only can be on a dial, but that it should be, is reassuring. It means that when I feel intimidated or anxious, it's not a permanent state, and I have the power to adjust it. There's a time and place for anxiety: for me, that's when I'm preparing for a high-stakes exclusive TV interview. I try to be grateful for that feeling of nervousness because it drives me to overprepare, so that if something doesn't go as planned, I can handle it. It was a similar anxiety about not wanting to let people down that inspired Michelle Nunn and her team at CARE to listen to people on the ground and respond to them, rather than imposing a top-down strategy. It was fear about environmental catastrophe that inspired Julia Collins to formulate her company to have the biggest long-term impact. It was concern about missing a diagnosis that inspired Ajayi to create systems to treat the whole patient.

But there's a time when we can all benefit from letting go of fear and embracing self-confidence, even if it doesn't feel entirely earned in that moment. It's that same self-confidence that Claire Babineaux-Fontenot demonstrated when she counseled food bank workers to adopt an attitude of abundance, whatever their fears might be. It's all going to work out, she told them. She couldn't, of course, know that for sure—except she knew that by believing it, she could make it so.

3. Understand your obstacles.

From the start, I wanted this book to be oriented around solutions women leaders have found, instead of fixated on the problems women routinely face. In the process of reporting, though, I discovered that the two are inextricably linked. The fact that female founders have never drawn more than 3 percent of all venture capital dollars and women of color draw a tiny fraction of that is important to understand—along with all the structural biases that perpetuate those facts. I saw that understanding these forces, no matter how grim they seem, can be a valuable tool to help circumnavigate them. It's much harder to achieve equity when we don't realize just how far from it we currently are. And it's much harder to manage and neutralize double standards if you don't see them.

Acknowledging a challenging situation is not admitting weakness or defeat. In fact, it's another form of preparation and a key step toward accomplishing meaningful change. If women who are fundraising know that the questions posed to them will likely focus on their business's downside risks, they can anticipate how to reframe the conversation into a discussion about their company's potential. If they know that their team will doubt and question them if they show anger, they'll find different modes of expression. Those like Cluster's Kim Taylor, who was wary about backlash for delivering negative feedback, can develop a strategy to selectively delegate those notes to male managers to deliver.

With my intense career and busy family life, I used to think a lot about the Serenity Prayer: knowing which things I could control and which I couldn't and figuring out how to avoid spending time on the latter. But my perspective on that has started to change. Yes, I should focus on the things I can control—my attitude, my ability to persist in the face of discouragement—but I should also spend time trying to understand the things that I can't, such as someone's reaction to me, and larger systems, such as entrenched sexism. If I were a jockey competing in a race category with particularly few women in it, I'd want to know that the betting odds were dramatically against me *because* I happened to be in a tiny minority. Those odds are *not*, as outlined in chapter 8, based on my ability. I may not be able to change those structural forces, but in delineating their contours, I'll be better positioned to get around them.

4. It takes a village.

In fact-checking this book, I followed up with my sources and subjects to make sure I had gotten all the details and contexts of their stories right. In addition to providing some corrections, a number of women noted that although everything I said was accurate, they felt that I hadn't adequately featured the contributions other people had made to their success. Toyin Ajayi wanted to make sure it was clear that in Sierra Leone she had partnered with a team to transform the Ola During Children's Hospital system. Claire Babineaux-Fontenot and Michelle Nunn reminded me that they wouldn't have been able to accomplish anything without their colleagues and, most important, the people on the ground. Certainly no one in this book became successful alone. The most successful leaders are those who are able to draw the most out of their teams. Study after study has found that the smartest teams are diverse, not just in terms of gender and race but also in their range of backgrounds and viewpoints.

The advantage of communal leadership is a theme woven throughout this book. Perhaps that's no surprise—it's a style associated with women—but the real revelation might be how strategic collaboration has nothing to do with a stereotypically feminine, warm and fuzzy welcoming of ideas. Instead, it has everything to do with embracing the discomfort that can come when outsiders stimulate new perspectives. I often think about the study in chapter 4 about the sorority and fraternity members who performed far better when they were joined by an outsider; it was not because the newcomer provided better ideas but because his or her presence forced the original group members to reconsider their own perspective. And the teams that performed the best reported that reconsidering their approach had felt far harder than accepting the unchallenged assumptions of the original group.

Communal leadership isn't simply a kumbaya welcoming of all ideas but rather the strategic work of drawing out opposing views and figuring out how to make the clash of perspectives result in a productive outcome. I remind myself of this when I'm working with my colleagues to figure out a fresh take on a complicated news story: if we arrive at a consensus too easily, it means we're not pushing one another hard enough. We saw this in action with WorkBoard's Deidre Paknad, who devised systems to solicit the best ideas from anywhere in a company, and PagerDuty's Jennifer Tejada, who broke silos and got salespeople and engineers to collaborate. Other leaders in this book found success only when they drew upon ideas from outside their organization's headquarters and power centers. Tala's Shivani Siroya struggled to launch her service in the Philippines until she sent a member of her team to live there for six months to understand the unique needs of the market.

As founders told me about all the places they had drawn ideas and solutions from, I learned a lot about just how big a village is needed to grow a startup: investors and mentors, peers and partners. Stitch Fix's Katrina Lake was grateful for the guidance of her first investor, Steve Anderson. Julie Wainwright benefited from The RealReal's partnership with the designer Stella McCartney, which served as a gateway to partnerships with other brands. Even before she'd established her business, Rent the Runway's Jennifer Hyman benefited from preemptively forging relationships with CEOs from the retail establishment.

How those villages are composed is crucial; they reach across gender lines. Though this book is focused on women, I have learned that partnership with men is not optional—it's essential. Once when my husband and I were in an argument, he tried to make the case that we were just different: "Men are from Mars—" I interrupted him and exclaimed, "And women are from Earth!" Whatever the relative advantages and disadvantages of gender (both innate and socialized), in fact, collaboration between men and women has been found to be the most valuable pairing of perspectives. I saw this in the partnerships between Spring Health's April Koh and Dr. Adam Chekroud and Cityblock Health's Toyin Ajayi and Iyah Romm.

These sprawling, complex villages reminded me to look for ideas everywhere. I was struck by Hyman's routine of following up months later to let someone know how much she'd benefited from his or her advice or insight. It's a practice I've started to adopt. Words are free, yet there's massive goodwill to be gained from reminding people how much they've helped you, seeding the potential for more guidance down the road.

5. Nothing is more powerful than women helping one another.

When I feel most overwhelmed with life and work, I think about the data in chapter 10 that explain the power of female-dominated microenvironments, and I make a point to organize dinner with a group of friends. I may feel as though I don't have time, but being with a group of women who aren't necessarily in one's industry yields real, measurable value in helping navigate challenges. I still get chills when I remember the study that found that small groups of women could eliminate the feeling of discouragement they had gotten from learning about the stereotype that engineering is a masculine field and the other experiment that found the strongest negotiators are women who are negotiating on behalf of someone else. That fierceness can be unleashed and adapted so women can apply it on their *own* behalf. I'm hopeful that women will begin to feel liberated from the socially imposed discomfort about asking other women for professional help. The likes of Chief and The Cru are gathering women to do just that and empowering the next generation of female leaders by coaching them to offer one another support.

There is an old canard about the generation of women who entered business in the 1980s and '90s: because they were often the only woman in the room, they had little incentive to help one another and the next generation of women. That perception of a zero-sum game, in many cases, fostered the wrong kind of competition, and both women and corporate America lost out. Now I feel that the opposite is true: it seems that women understand that they'll do better if they have other women around them. And I'm glad to say that in many situations—boardrooms and executive suites—the number of women is nearing the point of critical mass that I discussed in chapter 6. Once women in leadership hit the 30 percent that's key for a minority group to effect real change, the power dynamic can shift.

I wish I had space to write about all the ways I've seen women come together to lift one another up. I could fill books about organizations that are not specifically designed to be about women's empowerment but are indeed doing just that. The US women's soccer team started a conversation about equal pay and has created a new generation of strong athlete role models for girls *and* boys. Now the expansion of the National Women's Soccer League through new teams such as Angel City in my hometown of Los Angeles is creating high-profile images of female strength in sports and beyond. Women are using organizations such as WW to support one another and celebrate NSVs—non-scale victories—to focus on all the varied things they are proud of in their work and home lives. Ethel's Club, a wellness platform for people of color, helped its members navigate issues such as seasonal depression and cultivate their creative passions. Seeing these examples of varied groups supporting women in their personal and professional journeys reminds me that we can find—and offer—help everywhere.

My hope was for this book to help change the narrative of what it means to be an effective business leader and to expand that definition to feature women and their leadership styles. So in the course of my reporting, there were plenty of times I felt anxious that some of the companies would be wiped out by the time the book went to print. I was concerned that such defeats might work against the new narrative I was articulating and could undermine the data about the underestimated advantages of female leaders. There is, of course, a high failure rate for all startups, regardless of the gender of the founder, plus a heightened risk due to the pandemic's changes to consumer demand and business models. The fact that women raise less money means that their companies have less of a financial cushion in tough times. Women leaders are also typically judged more harshly than their male peers, becoming the subject of cringey click-bait headlines for things such as being too "aggressive" or "demanding" (as detailed in chapter nine). Several of the CEOs and founders in this book have faced near cancellation—Jennifer Hyman for her handling of layoffs and Spring Health's April Koh for creating a demanding culture—behavior equal to or pale in comparison to that of their male counterparts. Others have made mistakes that have had serious consequences on the trajectory of their companies. But just because female founders are rare (and their failures rare among their group) does not mean that they should draw added scrutiny, or that they should become a symbol for their group. If male leaders who misstep are considered simply a bad apple, female leaders should be afforded the same.

The reality is that the vast majority of the companies profiled in this book survived one of the most turbulent chapters in recent economic history and remain in business. Most of them thrived, and many accomplished major milestones while I wrote this book. Three went public: Bumble in February 2021, Clear in June 2021, and Rent the Runway in September 2021. Two of them had major sales to high-profile firms: Gregg Renfrew's Beautycounter to Carlyle and Reese Witherspoon's Hello Sunshine to a Blackstone-backed company, Candle Media. Others grew and raised money at high valuations; in September 2021, Toyin Ajayi's Cityblock Health was valued at a reported $5.7 billion *and* April Koh's Spring Health raised money at a $2 billion valuation. There is still plenty of time for any number of the companies included here to fail or their status to change after publication—but even so, what their founders accomplished during the time I was writing this book is meaningful.

In fact, over the course of the two-year project of researching and writing this book, the new vision of leadership I have profiled here started to colonize the old one, as women introduced images of new types of founder-visionaries. I watched as the exceptional group that had drawn less than 3 percent of VC dollars began to have an outsized impact. When Bumble went public, Whitney Wolfe Herd rang the opening bell of the Nasdaq with her toddler on her hip. Rent the Runway's all-female C-suite celebrated its IPO at the Nasdaq with their kids. And Spanx founder Sara Blakely showed a new emotional image of leadership, tearfully handing out first-class plane tickets to employees after selling her company—more like Oprah than Jack Welch.

As I examined the effectiveness of these women leaders, they validated and demonstrated to the world my hypothesis. That's why the goal of my book shifted from simply telling stories of the power of female leaders to demystifying the internal dynamics of women's exemplary approaches.

The more these women's leadership models—communal, empathetic, vulnerable, and purpose driven—become part of the established canon, the more *all* companies will gain. The sooner we recognize how characteristics that have nothing to do with "power" can be effective tools, the more businesses will profit from different perspectives and approaches. None of the strategies in this book are the exclusive domain of women; there's plenty of evidence that everyone could benefit from adopting the unexpected superpowers of women leaders.

➲ Acknowledgments

I want to thank the publishers, who took a risk on a first-time author. Ju-lianna Haubner, thank you for believing in this book from the beginning, and for guiding—and editing—me through this process. Ben Loehnen, it's a dream to get to finally work with you. Jofie Ferrari-Adler, Meredith Vilarello, Alexandra Primiani, and everyone at Avid Reader and Simon & Schuster, I'm so lucky to get to work with such a phenomenal team. I want to thank my agent, Eve Atterman at WME, for encouraging me and helping me turn this crazy idea into a proposal, and then into something I could share with the world. My TV agent, Henry Reisch, thank you for being my coach, therapist, and cheerleader. Thank you to my amazing publicity team at Fortier PR, Mark Fortier and Jessica, for finding mean-ingful and creative ways to amplify the message of this book.

This book exists because of the many women and men who shared their time, stories, and insights with me—not just in the past two years of this project, but over my entire career in journalism. The access you gave me to your feelings, fears, and homes (via Zoom) was invaluable. You educated me and pushed me to consider my own biases and assumptions.

You were patient with my dumb questions and more patient with my repeated fact-checking. You inspire me and make me hopeful for the future. I am so grateful to all the people who appear in these pages.

I want to express my deepest thanks to the many more women and men who offered their time and insights and who helped me test my ideas—and who were *not* featured in these pages. Your generous introductions to founders and your trenchant insights into the startup landscape and leadership traits were essential to this project.

I want to particularly thank the venture investors who brought me into their work, explained their investment theses, and generously introduced me to so many phenomenal entrepreneurs: Aileen Lee, Ann Miura-Ko, Heidi Patel, Theresia Gouw, Lynne Chou O'Keefe, Maha Ibrahim, Sonja Perkins, and Juliet de Baubigny. Dana Settle, thank you for sharing your perspective and pushing me to move past outmoded terminology and thinking around female leadership. Elisa Schreiber, your eagerness to help and share your contacts yielded so many valuable introductions and brought so many of these stories to life. Desiree Gruber, thank you for the unending generosity of your ideas and relationships, and for bringing me into your phenomenal network of Force Multipliers. SaraJane Simon, thank you for being a phenomenal resource. Lori Wachs, I'm so lucky to have entered your orbit of connections. Kara Nortman, thank you for always being a force for change, and for brainstorming and pushing me to think counterintuitively. Anu Duggal, thank you for your honesty about the challenges women face and your passion to close gender gaps. Sarah Kunst, thank you for pushing me to be comprehensive in my definition of diversity. Arlan Hamilton, thank you for inspiring me and talking through undervalued opportunities and overlooked advantages. Sydney Thomas, thank you for prompting me to think about the value of embracing disparate perspectives. Tina Wells, you were the first female entrepreneur to inspire me when you were just a teen. Shelley Zalis, thank you for being so encouraging and generous and for creating welcoming spaces for women around the world with the

Female Quotient. Dana Kanze, thank you for helping me understand the data about the double standards women face.

I am grateful to all the entrepreneurs who graciously talked to me about their journeys but whose stories this particular project couldn't accommodate: I could write a book about each of you. I want to thank: Everybody World cofounders Iris Alonzo and Carolina Crespo, HopSkipDrive CEO Joanna McFarland, Tot Squad CEO Jennifer Beall Saxton, MD Ally CEO Shanel Fields, Partake Foods CEO Denise Woodard, Maven CEO Kate Ryder, SOLV Health CEO Heather Fernandez, Modern Health CEO Alyson Watson, Ethel's Club CEO Naj Austin, The Mom Project CEO Allison Robinson, Justice for Migrant Women founder Monica Ramirez, Binti CEO Felicia Curcuru, Tequitable CEO Lisa Gelobter, Care Academy CEO Helen Adeosun, Lola cofounder Jordana Kier, DreamBox Learning CEO Jessie Woolley-Wilson, Guild Education CEO Rachel Carlson, Cloudflare COO Michelle Zatlyn, ShearShare cofounder and COO Courtney Caldwell, Blavity CEO Morgan De Baun, Magic Leap CEO Peggy Johnson, Mighty Networks CEO Gina Bianchini, Databento CEO Christina Qi, Anastasia CEO Anastasia Soare, Hint CEO Kara Goldin, and so many more.

I want to thank my writer friends, Chris Cox, Julie Schlosser, and David Spiegel, who shared their time, ideas, and constructive criticism: you made this book so much better. I want to thank my fellow writers who offered encouragement, practical advice, and guidance through this new and daunting process—Eve Rodsky and Jessica Yellin, I don't know how I got so lucky to have your support. Elise Loehnen, Reza Aslan, and Jessica Jackley, thank you for your encouragement and example. I want to thank my friend Keleigh Morgan and her team at Sunshine Sachs Morgan & Lylis who generously connected me to their clients, and Sarah Rothman and her colleagues at the Lede Company who helped me with theirs. Thank you to Meaghan Curcio, Emily Janoch, Jemma Wolfe, and Noora Raj Brown, who were patient partners in fact-checking. Brooke Hammerling, thank you for helping me spread the word. Sarina Sanandaji, thank you for your introductions and encouragement. Thank you Mandana Dayani for your amazing ideas and connections.

I want to thank my friends who provided inspiration, support, guidance, and much-needed laughter through long writing slogs: Jade Chatham, Ann Parker McKeehan, Bettina Korek, Jamie Kantrowitz, Kathleen McCarthy, Ashley Martabano, Emily Aviad, Caroline Chiles, Scarlett Lacy, Annie Armstrong, Jessica Weinstock, Sara Kippur, Alexa Chopivsky, Ashley Jacobs, Ellie Knaus, and Marshall Heyman.

I want to thank my bosses and colleagues at CNBC who inspire me to be entrepreneurial in the way I pursue stories and direct in the way I tell them. Lacy O'Toole, you have been my North Star for so many years. Katie Slaman, you make me a better reporter. Stephen Desaulniers, I'm so lucky to have you as my proactive producing partner. Harriet Taylor and Sally Shin, I'm so lucky to have gotten to work with you on elevating women's voices and telling stories of the people who are closing gender gaps.

Above all I want to thank my family. This book wouldn't have been possible without my parents, Paul and Sharon, who took my kids overnight every Saturday so I could write. They inspired me to report and write this book with their own example, and convinced me that my feeling of nervousness was actually that of excitement. This book wouldn't have been good if it were not for my husband, who tolerated all my ill-timed brainstorming sessions and editing demands. Thank you, Couper, for letting the study of female leadership dominate our family's past two years. I'm grateful to Adam, my always-supportive brother and friend. To my mother-in-law, Susan Samuelson, thank you for sharing ideas and academic research. I'm grateful to my extended Boorstin, Silver/Horowitz, and Samuelson families for your love and the model you've set of persistence and creativity.

And I'm thankful for my sons, Henry and Ben, for questioning everything and reminding me to do the same. I hope some day you look back on this book as a relic of an outdated age in which men and women didn't have equal access to entrepreneurial opportunities to change the world. My hope is that you inherit a better world that the women in this book have helped to create.

→ Notes

Introduction

1. *In fact, female founders*: Joanna Glasner, "Something Ventured: Despite Blockbuster Venture Investment, Female Founders' Share of VC Funding Falls," Crunchbase, September 21, 2021, https://news.crunchbase.com /news/something-ventured-blockbuster-venture-investment-female-found ers-funding-falls/.
2. *(This is part of a broader lack*: Catalyst, "Women in Management (Quick Take)," Catalyst, August 11, 2020, https://www.catalyst.org/research/women -in-management/.
3. *The following two weeks*: Jeff Cox, "US Payrolls Plunge 701,000 in March amid the Start of a Job Market Collapse," CNBC, April 3, 2020, https:// www.cnbc.com/2020/04/03/jobs-report-march-2020.html; Christopher J. Goodman and Steven M. Mance, "Employment Loss and the 2007–09 Recession: An Overview," US Bureau of Labor Statistics, April 2011, https:// www.bls.gov/opub/mlr/2011/04/art1full.pdf.
4. *At that moment, one study*: Kieran Snyder, "The Abrasiveness Trap: High-Achieving Men and Women Are Described Differently in Reviews," *Fortune*, August 26, 2014, https://fortune.com/2014/08/26/performance-review -gender-bias/.

One: Overcoming the Odds

1. *The $330 billion*: PitchBook and NVCA, "Q4 2021 Pitchbook/NVCA Venture Monitor," NVCA, January 14, 2022, https://nvca.org/wp-content/uploads/2022/01/Q4_2021_PitchBook_NVCA_Venture_Monitor.pdf.

2. *We hear a lot about*: "America's Women and the Wage Gap," National Partnership for Women & Families, March 2021, https://www.nationalpartnership.org/our-work/resources/economic-justice/fair-pay/americas-women-and-the-wage-gap.pdf.

3. *Between 2011 and 2020, startups*: Gené Teare, "Global VC Funding to Female Founders Dropped Dramatically This Year," Crunchbase, December 21, 2020, https://news.crunchbase.com/news/global-vc-funding-to-female-founders/; "The US Female Founders Dashboard," PitchBook, January 4, 2022, https://pitchbook.com/news/articles/the-vc-female-founders-dashboard; Jordan Rubio & Priyamvada Mathur, "An Exceptional Year for Female Founders Still Means a Sliver of VC Funding," PitchBook, January 10, 2022. https://pitchbook.com/news/articles/female-founders-dashboard-2021-vc-funding-wrap-up.

4. *Just 1.2 percent of venture capital dollars*: Marlize van Romburgh and Gené Teare, "Funding to Black Startup Founders Quadrupled in Past Year, but Remains Elusive," Crunchbase, July 13, 2021, https://news.crunchbase.com/news/something-ventured-funding-to-black-startup-founders-quadrupled-in-past-year-but-remains-elusive/; "BLCK VC's Mission Is to Connect, Engage, Empower, and Advance Black Venture Investors," BLCK VC, https://www.blckvc.com.

5. *A 2020 study found that businesses*: "Still Building: Project Diane 2021 Update," Digital Undivided, Project Diane, April 2021, https://www.digitalundivided.com/reports/still-building-project-diane-2021-update.

6. *Of the more than two thousand companies*: "Only a Fraction of U.S. IPOs Have Female Founders," Visual Capitalist Datastream, 2020, https://www.visualcapitalist.com/female-founders-in-us-ipos/.

7. *The numbers are particularly shocking*: "Annual Report 2020," National Women's Business Council, 2020, https://cdn.www.nwbc.gov/wp-content/uploads/2020/12/21113833/2020-NWBC-Annual-Report.html.

8. *Though women make up*: "Behind the Numbers: The State of Women-Owned Businesses in 2018," Women's Business Enterprise National Council, October 10, 2018, https://www.wbenc.org/news/behind-the-numbers-the-state-of-women-owned-businesses-in-2018; Rieva Lesonsky, "The State of Women Entrepreneurs," SCORE, March 24, 2020, https://www.score.org/blog/state-women-entrepreneurs.

9. *In 2019, Silicon Valley Bank*: "Women in Technology Leadership 2019,"

Silicon Valley Bank, 2019, https://www.svb.com/globalassets/library/up loadedfiles/content/trends_and_insights/reports/women_in_technology _leadership/svb-suo-women-in-tech-report-2019.pdf.

10. *As a woman, she was*: Michael Patrick Rutter, "Mapping Gender Diversity at MIT," MIT News, October 25, 2017, http://news.mit.edu/2017/mapping -gender-diversity-at-mit-1025.

11. *Insurify, in its success, is an outlier*: Nicolás Cerdeira and Kyril Kotashev, "Startup Failure Rate: Ultimate Report + Infographic," Failory, March 25, 2021, https://www.failory.com/blog/startup-failure-rate; Patrick Ward, "Is it True That 90% of Startups Fail?", NanoGlobals, June 29, 2021, https:// nanoglobals.com/startup-failure-rate-myths-origin/.

12. *"I can be tricked"*: Nathaniel Rich, "Silicon Valley's Start-up Machine," *New York Times Magazine*, May 2, 2013, https://www.nytimes.com/2013/05/05 magazine/y-combinator-silicon-valleys-start-up-machine.html.

13. *A 2021 survey*: Paul Gompers et al., "How Venture Capitalists Make Decisions," *Harvard Business Review*, March–April 2021, https://hbr.org/2021 /03/how-venture-capitalists-make-decisions.

14. *(An estimated $51 billion*: "Wedding Services Industry in the US—Market Research Report," IBISWorld, April 29, 2021, https://www.ibisworld.com /united-states/market-research-reports/wedding-services-industry/.

15. *Cuyana's success illustrates*: Collin West and Gopinath Sundaramurthy, "Women VCs Invest in Up to 2x More Female Founders," Kauffman Fellows, March 25, 2020, https://www.kauffmanfellows.org/journal_posts/women -vcs-invest-in-up-to-2x-more-female-founders.

16. *Women represent a mere 13 percent*: Pam Kostka, "More Women Became VC Partners than Ever Before in 2019 but 65% of Venture Firms Still Have Zero Female Partners," All Raise, February 7, 2020, https://medium .com/allraise/more-women-became-vc-partners-than-ever-before-in-2019 -39cc6cb86955.

17. *In addition to the fact*: Richard Kerby, "Where Did You Go to School?," Medium.com/@Kerby, July 30, 2018, https://blog.usejournal.com/where -did-you-go-to-school-bde54d846188.

18. *There's another factor*: Nathan Heller, "Is Venture Capital Worth the Risk?," *New Yorker*, January 20, 2020, https://www.newyorker.com/magazine/2020 /01/27/is-venture-capital-worth-the-risk.

19. *VC firms with diverse representation*: All Raise and PitchBook, "All In: Women in the VC Ecosystem," All Raise, 2019, https://files.pitchbook.com /website/files/pdf/PitchBook_All_Raise_2019_All_In_Women_in_the_VC _Ecosystem.pdf.

20. *Another study found that VC firms*: Paul Gompers and Silpa Kovvali, "The Other Diversity Dividend," *Harvard Business Review*, July–August 2018, https://hbr.org/2018/07/the-other-diversity-dividend; "The Power of Diversity: Why Homogeneous Teams in Venture Capital Are Bad for Business," West River Group, September 21, 2021, https://www.wrg.vc/diversity.

21. *The second factor lies*: All Raise and PitchBook, "All In: Women in the VC Ecosystem."

22. *One woman cited*: Ibid.

23. *Women own just 23 percent*: "2020: A Study Analyzing Equity Distribution by Gender, Race & Ethnicity, & Geography," Carta Equity Summit, December 8, 2021, https://www.cartaequitysummit.com/2020-a-study-ana lyzing-equity-distribution-by-gender-race-ethnicity-geography-carta-equity -summit/.

24. *Investment rounds of this size*: Gené Teare, "The Most Recent Startup Invest- ments over $250 Million in 2019," Crunchbase, June 17, 2019, https://news .crunchbase.com/news/the-most-recent-startup-investments-over-250-mil lion-in-2019/.

25. *Companies with only male*: Data culled and analyzed for the author by Crunchbase.

26. *But companies with at least one*: Gené Teare, "EoY 2019 Diversity Report: 20 Percent of Newly Funded Startups in 2019 Have a Female Founder," CrunchBase News, January 21, 2020, https://news.crunchbase.com/news /eoy-2019-diversity-report-20-percent-of-newly-funded-startups-in-2019 -have-a-female-founder/.

27. *According to a 2020 PitchBook survey*: "All In: Female Founders and CEOs in the US VC Ecosystem," PitchBook, 2020, https://files.pitchbook.com/web site/files/pdf/2020_All_In_Female_Founders_and_CEOs_in_the_US_VC _Ecosystem.pdf.

28. *The first landmark study*: "Women Matter: Gender Diversity, a Corporate Performance Driver," McKinsey & Company, 2007, https://www.mckinsey .com/business-functions/people-and-organizational-performance/our -insights/gender-diversity-a-corporate-performance-driver.

29. *In the two years following*: Daniel J. Sandberg, "When Women Lead, Firms Win," S&P Global, October 16, 2019, https://www.spglobal.com/en /research-insights/featured/when-women-lead-firms-win.

30. *According to a* Harvard Business Review: Jie Chen et al., "Research: When Women Are on Boards, Male CEOs Are Less Overconfident," *Harvard*

Business Review, September 12, 2019, https://hbr.org/2019/09/research
-when-women-are-on-boards-male-ceos-are-less-overconfident.

31. *In 2015, the venture capital firm First Round*: "First Round 10 Year Project," First Round, 2015, http://10years.firstround.com.

32. *In 2018, Boston Consulting Group*: Katie Abouzahr et al., "Why Women-Owned Startups Are a Better Bet," Boston Consulting Group, June 6, 2018, https://www.bcg.com/publications/2018/why-women-owned-startups-are
-better-bet.

33. *Similarly, racially diverse founding teams*: Collin West, Gopinath Sundaramurthy, and Marlon Nichols, "Deconstructing the Pipeline Myth and the Case for More Diverse Fund Managers," Kauffman Fellows, February 4, 2020, https://www.kauffmanfellows.org/journal_posts/the-pipeline-myth
-ethnicity-fund-managers.

34. *McKinsey quantified that*: Kweilin Ellingrud et al., "The power of parity: Advancing women's equality in the United States," McKinsey & Company, April 7, 2016, https://www.mckinsey.com/featured-insights/employment
-and-growth/the-power-of-parity-advancing-womens-equality-in-the-united
-states#.

35. *The number of female-led unicorns*: Janna Glasner, "Here Are the New 2021 Unicorn Startups Founded by Women," Crunchbase, August 18, 2021, https://news.crunchbase.com/news/here-are-the-new-2021-unicorn-startups-founded-by-women/.

36. *The number of companies*: Data compiled for the author by Crunchbase, January 2022.

37. *As of 2020, women accounted for*: Cydney Posner, "New Survey: Diversity on Fortune 100 and Fortune 500 Boards," Cooley PubCo, June 9, 2021, https://cooleypubco.com/2021/06/09/board-diversity-fortune-500/; "Women on Corporate Boards (Quick Take)," Catalyst, November 5, 2021, https://www
.catalyst.org/research/women-on-corporate-boards/.

Two: Building with Purpose

1. *Silicon Valley's poor showing*: "Annual Report 2020," National Women's Business Council, https://cdn.www.nwbc.gov/wp-content/uploads/2020/12
/21143334/NWBC-2020-Annual-Report-Final.pdf.

2. *Among businesses dedicated*: Niels Bosma et al., "Global Entrepreneurship Monitor: Special Topic Report: Social Entrepreneurship," Global Entrepreneurship Research Association, 2016, https://www.gemconsortium.org/file
/open?fileId=49542; University of Cincinnati, "Men Start Businesses for the

Money: Women for the Social Value," ScienceDaily, April 3, 2012, https://
www.sciencedaily.com/releases/2012/04/120403124404.htm.

3. *When asked what drives*: "2021 Small Business Trends: A Look at the State
of Small Business in 2021," Guidant Financial, 2021, https://www.guidant
financial.com/small-business-trends/.

4. *Men, on the other hand*: Francesca Gino, Caroline Ashley Wilmuth, and
Alison Wood Brooks, "Compared to Men, Women View Professional Advancement as Equally Attainable, but Less Desirable," *Proceedings of the National Academy of Sciences of the United States of America* 112, no. 40 (2015):
12354–59, https://doi.org/10.1073/pnas.1502567112.

5. *In 2017, 80 percent*: Siri Terjesen, "Social Entrepreneurship Amongst
Women and Men in the United States," National Women's Business Coun-
cil, February 2017, https://cdn.www.nwbc.gov/wp-content/uploads/2017
/02/13134000/Social-entrepreneurship-amongst-women-and-men-in-the
-United-States_021617.pdf; Niels Bosma et al., "Global Entrepreneurship
Monitor, 2019/2020 Global Report," Global Entrepreneurship Monitor,
2020, https://www.gemconsortium.org/report/gem-2019-2020-global-report;
Geri Stengel, "Women Entrepreneurs Fuel Social Change and Economic
Growth," *Forbes*, February 3, 2016, https://www.forbes.com/sites/geristen
gel/2016/02/03/women-entrepreneurs-fuel-social-change-and-economic
-growth/?sh=36a346182c59; Diana M. Hechavarria et al., "Are Women
More Likely to Pursue Social and Environmental Entrepreneurship?," in
*Global Women's Entrepreneurship Research: Diverse Settings, Questions and
Approaches*, edited by Karen D. Hughes and Jennifer E. Jennings (Northamp-
ton, MA: Edward Elgar Publishing, 2012), 135–51, https://www.elgaronline
.com/view/edcoll/9781849804622/9781849804622.00016.xml; Diana M.
Hechavarria et al., "Taking Care of Business: The Impact of Culture and
Gender on Entrepreneurs' Blended Value Creation Goals," *Small Business
Economics* 48 (2017): 225–57, https://link.springer.com/article/10.1007
/s11187-016-9747-4.

6. *Most often, women are pursuing*: Kyle W. Knight, "Explaining Cross-national
Variation in the Climate Change Concern Gender Gap: A Research Note,"
Social Science Journal 56, no. 4 (2019): 627–32, https://doi.org/10.1016
/j.soscij.2018.08.013.

7. *In 2016, Harvard Business School professor*: Matthew Lee and Laura Huang,
"Women Entrepreneurs Are More Likely to Get Funding if They Emphasize
Their Social Mission," *Harvard Business Review*, March 7, 2018, https://hbr
.org/2018/03/women-entrepreneurs-are-more-likely-to-get-funding-if-they
-emphasize-their-social-mission.

8. *Much has been written*: Matthew Lee and Laura Huang, "Gender Bias, Social Impact Framing, and Evaluation of Entrepreneurial Ventures," *Organization Science* 29, no. 1 (2018): 1–16, https://doi.org/10.1287/orsc.2017.1172; Gené Teare, "EoY 2019 Diversity Report: 20 Percent of Newly Funded Startups in 2019 Have a Female Founder," Crunchbase, January 21, 2020, https://news.crunchbase.com/news/eoy-2019-diversity-report-20-percent -of-newly-funded-startups-in-2019-have-a-female-founder/.

9. *One group of students*: Lee and Huang, "Women Entrepreneurs Are More Likely to Get Funding if They Emphasize Their Social Mission."

10. *Data show that women*: Pablo Brañas-Garza, Valerio Capraro, and Ericka Rascón-Ramírez, "Gender Differences in Altruism: Expectations, Actual Behavior and Accuracy of Beliefs," *SSRN Academic Journal*, 2016, https:// arxiv.org/pdf/1606.04900.pdf.

11. *When it comes to helping*: David P. Schmitt, "Are Men More Helpful, Altruistic, or Chivalrous Than Women?," *Psychology Today*, March 10, 2016, https://www.psychologytoday.com/us/blog/sexual-personalities/201603 /are-men-more-helpful-altruistic-or-chivalrous-women.

12. *All those data lead*: Lee and Huang, "Women Entrepreneurs Are More Likely to Get Funding if They Emphasize Their Social Mission."

13. *billions of pounds of edible produce*: Dana Gunders, "Wasted: How America Is Losing Up to 40 Percent of Its Food from Farm to Fork to Landfill," National Resources Defense Council, August 16, 2017, https://www.nrdc .org/resources/wasted-how-america-losing-40-percent-its-food-farm-fork -landfill.

14. *There was also the environmental*: "Over 1 Billion Tonnes More Food Being Wasted than Previously Estimated, Contributing 10% of All Greenhouse Gas Emissions," World Wildlife Fund, July 21, 2021, https://www.worldwildlife .org/press-releases/over-1-billion-tonnes-more-food-being-wasted-than -previously-estimated-contributing-10-of-all-greenhouse-gas-emissions.

15. *Indeed, in 2020, funds*: Paul Sullivan, "Investing in Social Good Is Finally Becoming Profitable," *New York Times*, August 28, 2020, https://www.ny times.com/2020/08/28/your-money/impact-investing-coronavirus.html.

16. *A focus on social impact*: Diana O'Brien et al., "Purpose Is Everything: How Brands That Authentically Lead with Purpose Are Changing the Nature of Business Today," Deloitte, October 16, 2019, https://www2.deloitte.com/us /en/insights/topics/marketing-and-sales-operations/global-marketing-trends /2020/purpose-driven-companies.html.

17. *And social impact can*: Afdhel Aziz, "Global Study Reveals Consumers Are Four to Six Times More Likely to Purchase, Protect and Champion

Purpose-Driven Companies," *Forbes*, June 17, 2020, https://www.forbes.com/sites/afdhelaziz/2020/06/17/global-study-reveals-consumers-are-four-to-six-times-more-likely-to-purchase-protect-and-champion-purpose-driven-companies/?sh=2e0c4ead435f; "Better Business, Better World," Business & Sustainable Development Commission, January 16, 2017, http://businesscommission.org/news/release-sustainable-business-can-unlock-at-least-us-12-trillion-in-new-market-value-and-repair-economic-system; Ben Schiller, "4 of Our Biggest Global Problems Are Big Business Opportunities," *Fast Company*, February 8, 2018, https://www.fastcompany.com/40526823/4-of-our-biggest-global-problems-are-big-business-opportunities.

18. *Academic studies have found*: Jennifer Mencl and Douglas R. May, "The Effects of Proximity and Empathy on Ethical Decision-Making: An Exploratory Investigation," *Journal of Business Ethics* 85, no. 2 (2009): 201–29, https://philpapers.org/rec/MENTEO-5.

19. *Deborah Small*: Deborah A. Small and Uri Simonsohn, "Friends of Victims: Personal Experience and Prosocial Behavior," *Journal of Consumer Research* 35, no. 3 (2008): 532–42, https://repository.upenn.edu/cgi/viewcontent.cgi?article=1200&context=oid_papers.

20. *In 2018, she founded CapWay*: Mark Kutzbach et al., "How America Banks: Household Use of Banking and Financial Services, 2019 FDIC Survey," Federal Deposit Insurance Corporation, 2019, https://www.fdic.gov/analysis/household-survey/2019execsum.pdf; Lending Club Corporation, "Nearly 40 Percent of Americans with Annual Incomes over $100,000 Live Paycheck-to-Paycheck," Cision, https://www.prnewswire.com/news-releases/nearly-40-percent-of-americans-with-annual-incomes-over-100-000-live-paycheck-to-paycheck-301312281.html.

21. *Women are typically*: Clare O'Connor, "Woman-Led Tala Raises $30 Million Series B for Micro-loans via Smartphone," *Forbes*, February 22, 2017, https://www.forbes.com/sites/clareoconnor/2017/02/22/woman-led-tala-raises-30-million-series-b-for-micro-loans-via-smartphone/?sh=6722a40359bb.

22. *That mutual trust works*: Kevin Voigt and Caren Weiner Campbell, "1 in 6 Small Business Administration Loans Fail, Study Finds," NerdWallet, October 3, 2017, https://www.nerdwallet.com/article/small-business/study-1-in-6-sba-small-business-administration-loans-fail.

23. *What's good for Tala's customer base*: Susan Fowler, "What Maslow's Hierarchy Won't Tell You About Motivation," *Harvard Business Review*, November 26, 2014, https://hbr.org/2014/11/what-maslows-hierarchy-wont-tell-you-about-motivation.

24. *This management theory centers*: Errol E. Joseph and Bruce E. Winston, "A Correlation of Servant Leadership, Leader Trust, and Organizational Trust," *Leadership & Organization Development Journal* 26, no. 1 (2005): 6–22, https://doi.org/10.1108/01437730510575552.

25. *Though men also employ*: G. James Lemoine and Terry C. Blum, "Servant Leadership, Leader Gender, and Team Gender Role: Testing a Female Advantage in a Cascading Model of Performance," *Personnel Psychology* 74, no. 1 (2019): 3–28, https://doi.org/10.1111/peps.12379.

26. *That was unusual for people*: Abhishek Singh et al., "Development of the India Patriarchy Index: Validation and Testing of Temporal and Spatial Patterning," *Social Indicators Research* 159 (2021): 351–77, https://doi.org/10.1007/s11205-021-02752-1.

27. *It happened that*: Kumar, "H1B Visa Total Cap Stats from FY 1990 to 2023," RedBus2US.com, February 1, 2022, https://redbus2us.com/h1b-visa-total-cap-history-from-1990-to-current-year/.

28. *In 2015, the year she founded*: Maura Allaire, Haowei Wu, and Upmanu Lall, "National Trends in Drinking Water Quality Violations," *Proceedings of the National Academy of Sciences of the United States of America* 115, no. 9 (2018): 2078–83, https://doi.org/10.1073/pnas.1719805115.

29. *In 2017, the company*: Solomon Darwin and Henry Chesbrough, "Smart Farming in Andhra Pradesh, India: An Open Innovation Approach," Berkeley Haas, November 10, 2017, https://kogylqkcui2fs1p14cln7p16-wpengine.netdna-ssl.com/wp-content/uploads/2019/04/Smart-Villages_White Paper-Nov.-27-2017-Final.pdf.

30. *In 2010, UC Davis psychology professor*: Robert Emmons, "Why Gratitude Is Good," *Greater Good Magazine*, November 16, 2010, https://greatergood.berkeley.edu/article/item/why_gratitude_is_good.

31. *Academics have also found*: Elliott Kruse et al., "The Upward Spiral Between Gratitude and Humility," *Social Psychological and Personality Science* 5, no. 7 (2014): 805–14, https://escholarship.org/content/qt77v6z086/qt77v6z086.pdf.

32. *Gratitude has a particular effect*: David DeSteno et al., "Gratitude: A Tool for Reducing Economic Impatience," *Psychological Science* 25, no. 6 (2014): 1262–67, https://doi.org/10.1177%2F0956797614529979.

33. *But here's what's most interesting*: David DeSteno, "Gratitude Is the New Willpower," *Harvard Business Review*, April 9, 2014, https://hbr.org/2014/04/gratitude-is-the-new-willpower.

34. *A study by professors*: Todd B. Kashdan et al., "Gender Differences in Gratitude: Examining Appraisals, Narratives, the Willingness to Express

Emotions, and Changes in Psychological Needs," *Journal of Personality* 77, no. 3 (2009): 691–730, https://mason.gmu.edu/~tkashdan/publications/gratitude_genderdiff_JP.pdf.

35. *Between 2009 and 2018*: "Where Are the Black & Latinx Female Founders?," Digital Undivided, 2020, https://www.projectdiane.com/.

36. *she wanted to use*: Judith Goldstein, "Food Tech's Environmental Effect," Modern Restaurant Management, September 7, 2016, https://modernrestaurantmanagement.com/food-techs-environmental-effect/.

37. *"The median farm income"*: Nadra Nittle, "Black-Owned Farms Are Holding On by a Thread," Eater, February 23, 2021, https://www.eater.com/22291510/black-farmers-fighting-for-farmland-discrimination-in-agriculture.

38. *Soon after Collins left Zume*: Deirdre Bosa, "SoftBank-Backed Zume Is Laying Off Half Its Staff and Shuttering Its Pizza Delivery Business," CNBC, January 8, 2020, https://www.cnbc.com/2020/01/08/softbank-backed-zume-cuts-360-jobs-closes-pizza-delivery-business.html.

Three: Leading with Empathy

1. *A study at the University of Notre Dame*: Dean A. Shepherd, Vinit Parida, and Joakim Wincent, "The Surprising Duality of Jugaad: Low Firm Growth and High Inclusive Growth," *Journal of Management Studies* 57, no. 1 (2017): 87–128, https://doi.org/10.1111/joms.12309.

2. *According to Babson College's*: Julian E. Lange et al., "2018/2019 United States Report," Global Entrepreneurship Monitor, 2019, https://www.babson.edu/media/babson/assets/blank-center/GEM_USA_2018-2019.pdf.

3. *Women are more than 20 percent*: Amanda B. Elam et al., "2018/2019 Women's Entrepreneurship Report," Global Entrepreneurship Monitor, 2019, https://www.gemconsortium.org/file/open?fileId=50405.

4. *One key difference*: Barbara Annis and Keith Merron, *Gender Intelligence: Breakthrough Strategies for Increasing Diversity and Improving Your Bottom Line* (New York: Harper Business, 2014), 33.

5. *They assumed that those*: Josephine Appiah-Nyamekye Sanny, "Sierra Leoneans Say Health Care Hard to Access, Beset by Corruption—Especially for the Poor," Afrobarometer, February 28, 2020, https://afrobarometer.org/publications/ad346-sierra-leoneans-say-health-care-hard-access-beset-corruption-especially-poor.

6. *It's not just in Sierra Leone*: Jackie Davalos, "Women's Digital Health Startups Reap Record VC Funding on Covid Surge," Bloomberg, April 19, 2021, https://www.bloomberg.com/news/articles/2021-04-19/women-s-digital-health-startups-reap-record-vc-funding-on-covid-surge.

7. *And women are generally*: John Rudoy and Helen Leis, "Females Are Discontent but Darn Proactive About Their Health and Healthcare," Oliver Wyman, March 7, 2019, https://health.oliverwyman.com/2019/03/females -are-unhappy-but-darn-proactive-about-their-health-and-he.html.

8. *Women also comprise*: Linda Searing, "The Big Number: Women Now Outnumber Men in Medical Schools," *Washington Post*, December 23, 2019, https://www.washingtonpost.com/health/the-big-number-women-now-out number-men-in-medical-schools/2019/12/20/8b9eddea-2277-11ea-bed5 -880264cc91a9_story.html.

9. *Yet despite the fact*: Terry Stone et al., "Women in Healthcare Leadership 2019," Oliver Wyman, 2019, https://www.oliverwyman.com/our-expertise /insights/2019/jan/women-in-healthcare-leadership.html; "Women CEOs: The Path Forward for Healthcare," Korn Ferry, 2018, https://www.kornferry .com/content/dam/kornferry/docs/article-migration/WomenLeadershipIn Healthcare.Jan2019.pdf.

10. *In 2019, women-led*: Claire Liu, Megan Zweig, and Natalie Yu, "The State of Gender Equity at Healthcare Startups and VCs in 2019," Rock Health, December 2, 2019, https://rockhealth.com/reports/the-state-of-gender-equity -at-healthcare-startups-and-vcs-in-2019/.

11. *And of the more than*: "Meet the Top Health DisruptHERS of 2020," StartUp Health, March 2, 2020, https://healthtransformer.co/meet-the-top-health -disrupthers-of-2020-3c8c32bbe57c.

12. *"Most depressive disorders"*: Andrew Solomon, "Anatomy of Melancholy," *New Yorker*, January 4, 1998, https://www.newyorker.com/magazine/1998 /01/12/anatomy-of-melancholy.

13. *One day, she came across*: Adam Mourad Chekroud et al., "Cross-trial Prediction of Treatment Outcome in Depression: A Machine Learning Approach," *Lancet Psychiatry 3* (2016): 243–50, https://memlab.yale.edu/sites/default /files/files/2016_Chekroud_etal_Lancet(1).pdf.

14. *For example, a study*: Malcolm Gladwell, *Talking to Strangers: What We Should Know About the People We Don't Know* (New York: Little, Brown, 2019).

15. *When I spoke to Koh*: Kate Everson, "Development and Gender Brain Wiring," Gender Intelligence, July 22, 2015, https://www.genderintelligence .com/development-and-gender-brain-wiring/.

16. *It has the highest*: Jeff Smith, "Cities with the Most Healthcare Workers," *Self*, April 2, 2020, https://www.self.inc/blog/healthcare-workers-by-city.

17. *Boston Medical Center*: "Family Medicine Residency," Boston Medical Center, https://www.bmc.org/family-medicine/education/residency.

18. *Various studies have found*: Simon Baron-Cohen et al., "The 'Reading the Mind in the Eyes' Test Revised Version: A Study with Normal Adults, and Adults with Asperger Syndrome or High-Functioning Autism," *Journal of Child Psychology and Psychiatry* 42, no. 2 (2001): 241–51, https://docs.autismresearchcentre.com/papers/2001_BCetal_adulteyes.pdf.

19. *"The 'Reading the Mind'"*: Simon Baron-Cohen et al., "The 'Reading the Mind in the Eyes' Test: Complete Absence of Typical Sex Difference in 400 Men and Women with Autism," PLOS ONE 10, no. 8 (2015), https://doi.org/10.1371/journal.pone.0136521.

20. *On average, women are*: David Olmos, "When Watching Others in Pain, Women's Brains Show More Empathy," UCLA, February 27, 2019, https://newsroom.ucla.edu/stories/womens-brains-show-more-empathy.

21. *According to the study*: Leonardo Christov-Moore et al., "Empathy: Gender Effects in Brain and Behavior," *Neuroscience & Biobehavioral Reviews* 46, no. 4 (2014): 604–27, https://doi.org/10.1016/j.neubiorev.2014.09.001.

22. *The researchers who conducted*: Varun Warrier et al., "Genome-wide Analyses of Self-reported Empathy: Correlations with Autism, Schizophrenia, and Anorexia Nervosa," *Translational Psychiatry* 8 (2018): article 35, https://doi.org/10.1038/s41398-017-0082-6.

23. *Female friendship has also been*: Deborah Tannen, "Why Men and Women Talk Past Each Other About Their Problems," Thrive Global, August 24, 2017, https://thriveglobal.com/stories/why-men-and-women-talk-past-each-other/.

24. *Amid a broader boom*: Jackie Davalos, "Women's Digital Health Startups Reap Record VC Funding on Covid Surge," Bloomberg, April 19, 2021, https://www.bloomberg.com/news/articles/2021-04-19/women-s-digital-health-startups-reap-record-vc-funding-on-covid-surge.

25. *after 2019 had seen*: "StartUp Health Insights Report: 2019 Year End," StartUp Health, 2019, https://www.startuphealth.com/2019-q4-insights-report.

26. *The category of companies*: Frost & Sullivan, "Femtech—Time for a Digital Revolution in the Women's Health Market," Frost Perspectives: Transformational Health, January 31, 2018, https://ww2.frost.com/frost-perspectives/femtechtime-digital-revolution-womens-health-market/; Kitty Knowles, "After Years of Neglect, Femtech Is Getting Substantial Investment," *Financial Times*, March 22, 2020, https://www.ft.com/content/125cffea-69c9-11ea-a6ac-9122541af204.

27. *But Hanna saw*: Christopher Ingraham, "Our Infant Mortality Rate Is a National Embarrassment," *Washington Post*, September 29, 2014, https://

www.washingtonpost.com/news/wonk/wp/2014/09/29/our-infant-mortality-rate-is-a-national-embarrassment/; Elizabeth C. W. Gregory, Claudia P. Valenzuela, and Donna L. Hoyert, "Fetal Mortality: United States, 2019," *National Vital Statistics Reports* 70, no. 11 (2019): 1–20, https://www.cdc.gov/nchs/nvss/index.htm.

28. *In 1977, the FDA*: Katherine A. Liu and Natalie A. Dipietro Mager, "Women's Involvement in Clinical Trials: Historical Perspective and Future Implications," *Pharmacy Practice* 14, no. 1 (2016): 708, https://www.ncbi.nlm.nih.gov/pmc/articles/PMC4800017/.

29. *For decades the basic testing*: Anita Holdcroft, "Gender Bias in Research: How Does It Affect Evidence Based Medicine?," *Journal of the Royal Society of Medicine* 100, no. 1 (2007): 2–3, https://dx.doi.org/10.1258%2Fjrsm.100.1.2.

30. *In response to this injustice*: Gabrielle Jackson, "The Female Problem: How Male Bias in Medical Trials Ruined Women's Health," *Guardian*, November 13, 2019, https://www.theguardian.com/lifeandstyle/2019/nov/13/the-female-problem-male-bias-in-medical-trials.

31. *Christina Jenkins*: Estrella Jaramillo, "Femtech in 2020: Investors Share Trends and Opportunities in Women's Health Technology," *Forbes*, January 8, 2020, https://www.forbes.com/sites/estrellajaramillo/2020/01/08/femtech-2020-investors-trends-and-opportunities-in-womens-health-technology/#7ce5d0567d54.

32. *The US fertility market*: Beth Kowitt, "Fertility Inc.: Inside the Big Business of Babymaking," *Fortune*, January 21, 2020, https://fortune.com/longform/fertility-business-femtech-investing-ivf/.

33. *One fast-growing part*: Committee on Gynecologic Practice, "Oocyte Cryopreservation," American College of Obstetricians and Gynecologists, January 2014, https://www.acog.org/clinical/clinical-guidance/committee-opinion/articles/2014/01/oocyte-cryopreservation.

34. *It's a crucial tool*: Quoctrung Bui and Claire Cain Miller, "The Age That Women Have Babies: How a Gap Divides America," *New York Times*, August 4, 2018, https://www.nytimes.com/interactive/2018/08/04/upshot/up-birth-age-gap.html; T. J. Mathews and Brady E. Hamilton, "First Births to Older Women Continue to Rise," NCHS Data Brief No. 152, May 2014, https://www.cdc.gov/nchs/products/databriefs/db152.htm.

35. *About one-fifth of women*: "Infertility," Office on Women's Health, https://www.womenshealth.gov/a-z-topics/infertility.

36. *That's because women's natural*: "Having a Baby After Age 35: How Aging Affects Fertility and Pregnancy," American College of Obstetricians and Gynecologists, October 2020, https://www.acog.org/womens-health/faqs

/having-a-baby-after-age-35-how-aging-affects-fertility-and-pregnancy; "Female Age-Related Fertility Decline," American College of Obstetricians and Gynecologists, August 2008, https://www.acog.org/clinical/clinical-guidance/committee-opinion/articles/2014/03/female-age-related-fertility-decline.

37. *Egg freezing is a physically*: The Ethics Committee of the American Society for Reproductive Medicine, "Disparities in Access to Effective Treatment for Infertility in the United States: An Ethics Committee Opinion," *Fertility and Sterility* 116, no. 1 (2021): 54–63, https://www.asrm.org/globalassets/asrm/asrm-content/news-and-publications/ethics-committee-opinions/disparities_in_access_to_effective_treatment_for_infertility_in_the_us-pdfmembers.pdf.

38. *women implanted with eggs*: "Egg Freezing," Mayo Clinic, https://www.mayoclinic.org/tests-procedures/egg-freezing/about/pac-20384556.

39. *Nearly 60 percent of US companies*: Erin Dowling, "New Survey Finds Employers Adding Fertility Benefits to Promote DEI," Mercer, May 6, 2021, https://www.mercer.us/our-thinking/healthcare/new-survey-finds-employers-adding-fertility-benefits-to-promote-dei.html.

40. *In addition, seventeen states mandate*: "State Laws Related to Insurance Coverage for Infertility Treatment," National Conference of State Legislatures, March 12, 2021, https://www.ncsl.org/research/health/insurance-coverage-for-infertility-laws.aspx.

41. *The category is growing*: Lucy Proctor, "Why Is IVF So Popular in Denmark?," BBC News, September 21, 2018, https://www.bbc.com/news/world-europe-45512312; Naina Bajekal, "Why So Many Women Travel to Denmark for Fertility Treatments," *Time*, January 3, 2019, https://time.com/5491636/denmark-ivf-storkklinik-fertility/; Saswati Sunderam et al., "Assisted Reproductive Technology Surveillance—United States, 2016," *MMWR Surveillance Summaries* 68, no. 4 (2019): 1–23, https://www.cdc.gov/mmwr/volumes/68/ss/ss6804a1.htm.

42. *This desire to be*: Valentina Bianco et al., "Females Are More Proactive, Males Are More Reactive: Neural Basis of the Gender-Related Speed/Accuracy Trade-off in Visuo-motor Tasks," *Brain Structure and Function* 225, no. 4 (2020): 187–201, https://link.springer.com/article/10.1007%2Fs00429-019-01998-3.

43. *Building on those data*: Bonita Banducci, "Women's Philanthropic Leadership: How Is It Different?," in *The Transformative Power of Women's Philanthropy: New Diretions for Philanthropic Fundraising*, edited by Martha A. Taylor and Sondra Shaw-Hardy (New York: Jossey-Bass, 2006), updated June 2017, [added phrasing in 2017 edition on Banducci's website

www.genderwork.com are bracketed] https://img1.wsimg.com/blobby/go
/690cdf59-e053-459c-ae1b-1414ca1df3ee/downloads/Women%20in%20
Philanthropy%202019%20.pdf?ver=1572150141857.

44. *A 2016 study*: Raj Chetty et al., "The Association Between Income and
Life Expectancy in the United States, 2001–2014," *JAMA*, April 10, 2016,
https://scholar.harvard.edu/files/cutler/files/jsc160006_01.pdf.

Four: Engineering Smart Teams

1. *Around the time Deidre Willette*: Carol Dweck, "Why Do Mindsets Matter?,"
Mindset Works, 2017, https://www.mindsetworks.com/science/Impact.

2. *Studies have shown*: Hans S. Schroder et al., "Neural Evidence for Enhanced
Attention to Mistakes Among School-Aged Children with a Growth Mindset," *Developmental Cognitive Neuroscience* 24 (2017): 42–50, https://doi
.org/10.1016/j.dcn.2017.01.004.

3. *Back in the 1980s*: HBR Editors, "How Companies Can Profit from a
'Growth Mindset,'" *Harvard Business Review*, November 2014, https://hbr
.org/2014/11/how-companies-can-profit-from-a-growth-mindset.

4. *In 2017, Dweck returned*: Brooke N. Macnamara and Natasha S. Rupani,
"The Relationship Between Intelligence and Mindset," *Intelligence* 64
(2017): 52–59, https://isiarticles.com/bundles/Article/pre/pdf/156107.pdf.

5. *In fact, younger women tend*: Jack Zenger and Joseph Folkman, "How Age
and Gender Affect Self-Improvement," *Harvard Business Review*, January 5,
2016, https://hbr.org/2016/01/how-age-and-gender-affect-self-improvement.

6. *According to Dweck's best-selling book*: Carol S. Dweck, *Mindset: The New
Psychology of Success* (New York: Ballantine, 2007).

7. *One afternoon in 2009*: David Rock and Heidi Grant, "Why Diverse Teams
Are Smarter," *Harvard Business Review*, November 4, 2016, https://hbr.org
/2016/11/why-diverse-teams-are-smarter.

8. *Whatever the comforts*: Katherine W. Phillips, Katie A. Liljenquist, and Margaret A. Neale, "Is the Pain Worth the Gain? The Advantages and Liabilities of Agreeing with Socially Distinct Newcomers," *Personality and Social
Psychology Bulletin* 35, no. 3 (2008): 336–50, https://netmap.files.wordpress
.com/2009/04/liljenquist_2009_pain_worth_the_gain.pdf.

9. *As the researchers looked*: Katherine W. Phillips, Katie A. Liljenquist, and
Margaret A. Neale, "Better Decisions Through Diversity," KellogInsight,
October 1, 2010, https://insight.kellogg.northwestern.edu/article/better
_decisions_through_diversity; Phillips et al., "Is the Pain Worth the Gain?"

10. *Another study, published in* Science: Anita Williams Woolley et al.,

"Evidence for a Collective Intelligence Factor in the Performance of Human Groups," *Science* 33, no. 6004 (2010): 686–88, https://doi.org/10.1126/science.1193147.

11. *The third marker*: Ibid.

12. *Conversational turn taking*: Julia Bear and Anita Woolley, "The Role of Gender in Team Collaboration and Performance," *Interdisciplinary Science Reviews* 35, no. 2 (2011): 146–53, http://dx.doi.org/10.1179/030801811X13013181961473.

13. *by the end of 2020*: "Inclusion, Diversity, & Equity at PagerDuty," Annual Report 2020, PagerDuty, https://www.pagerduty.com/assets/report-ide-2020.pdf.

14. *(These numbers dwarf*: Eugene Kim, "Amazon's Executive Org Chart, Revealed," CNBC, January 23, 2019, https://www.cnbc.com/2019/01/23/who-are-amazons-top-executives-2019.html.

15. *Diversity has been found*: Cedric Herring, "Does Diversity Pay?: Race, Gender, and the Business Case for Diversity," *American Sociological Review* 74, no. 2 (2009): 208–24, https://doi.org/10.1177%2F000312240907400203.

16. *As discussed in the first chapter*: Vivian Hunt, Dennis Layton, and Sara Prince, "Why Diversity Matters," McKinsey & Company, January 1, 2015, https://www.mckinsey.com/business-functions/organization/our-insights/why-diversity-matters; Katrin Talke, Søren Salomo, and Alexander Kock, "Top Management Team Diversity and Strategic Innovation Orientation; The Relationship and Consequences for Innovativeness and Performance," *Journal of Product Innovation Management* 28, no. 6 (2011): 819–32, https://doi.org/10.1111/j.1540-5885.2011.00851.x; Cristina Diaz-Garcia, Angela Gonzalez-Moreno, and Francisco Jose Saez-Martinez, "Gender Diversity Within R&D Teams: Its Impact on Radicalness of Innovation," *Organization & Management* 15, no. 2 (2013): 149–60, https://doi.org/10.5172/impp.2013.15.2.149.

17. *That should benefit*: Sue Duke, "The Key to Closing the Gender Gap? Putting More Women in Charge," World Economic Forum, November 2, 2017, https://www.weforum.org/agenda/2017/11/women-leaders-key-to-workplace-equality/; Sheen S. Levine et al., "Ethnic Diversity Deflates Price Bubbles," *Proceedings of the National Academy of Sciences of the United States of America* 111, no. 52 (2014): 18524–29, https://doi.org/10.1073/pnas.1407301111.

18. *There's also evidence*: Lauren Rivera, "Hirable like Me," Kellogg Insight, April 3, 2013, https://insight.kellogg.northwestern.edu/article/hirable_like_me; Luca Flabbi, "How Do Female CEOs Affect Their Company's Gender Wage Gap?,"

World Economic Forum, April 27, 2015, https://www.weforum.org/agenda/2015/04/how-do-female-ceos-affect-their-companys-gender-wage-gap/.

19. *Plus, more than half*: McKinsey & Company/LeanIn, "Women in the Workplace," 2021, https://wiw-report.s3.amazonaws.com/Women_in_the_Workplace_2021.pdf.

20. *The need to clarify*: Donald Sull, Charles Sull, and James Yoder, "No One Knows Your Strategy—Not Even Your Top Leaders," *Sloan Management Review*, February 12, 2018, https://sloanreview.mit.edu/article/no-one-knows-your-strategy-not-even-your-top-leaders/.

21. *The data also revealed*: Cristian L. Dezs and David Gaddis Ross, "'Girl Power': Female Participation in Top Management and Firm Performance," 2007, Columbia University, https://www0.gsb.columbia.edu/mygsb/faculty/research/pubfiles/3063/girlpower.pdf.

22. *A 2017 Korn Ferry study*: "When Female CEOs Speak," Korn Ferry Institute, 2017, https://engage.kornferry.com/Global/FileLib/Women_CEOs_speak/KFI_Rockefeller_Study_Women_CEOs_Speak.pdf.

23. *A 2015 study*: Leire Gartzia and Daan van Knippenberg, "Too Masculine, Too Bad: Effects of Communion on Leaders' Promotion of Cooperation," *Group & Organization Management* 41, no. 4 (2015): 458–90, https://doi.org/10.1177%2F1059601115583580.

Five: Reforming Broken Systems

1. *The photo captured*: Sallie Krawcheck, "Career Curveballs: Doing the Job When No One Thinks You Can," LinkedIn, April 21, 2014, https://www.linkedin.com/pulse/20140421230055-174077701-career-curveballs-doing-the-job-when-no-one-thinks-you-can/.

2. *A few months after seeing*: Simon English, "Wall Street Rocked by $1.4bn Fines," *Telegraph*, December 21, 2012, https://www.telegraph.co.uk/finance/2837303/Wall-Street-rocked-by-1.4bn-fines.html.

3. *Weill wanted to reform*: Geraldine Fabrikant, "When Citi Lost Sallie," *New York Times*, November 15, 2008, https://www.nytimes.com/2008/11/16/business/16sallie.html.

4. *Wall Street was then*: Harriet Lefton, "Research Finds Female Analysts Are More Accurate, Make Bolder Calls," CNBC, March 8, 2018, https://www.cnbc.com/2018/03/08/research-finds-female-analysts-are-more-accurate-make-bolder-calls.html.

5. *(As of 2019, that number*: "Women in Financial Services (Quick Take)," Catalyst, June 29, 2020, https://www.catalyst.org/research/women-in-financial-services/.

6. *And women are in the minority*: Laura Lallos, "Women in Investing: Morningstar's View," Morningstar, March 2, 2020, https://www.morningstar.com/articles/967691/women-in-investing-morningstars-view.

7. *The higher up*: Judith Warner, Dana Boesch, and Nora Ellmann, "The Women's Leadership Gap: Women's Leadership by the Numbers," Center for American Progress, November 20, 2018, https://www.americanprogress.org/article/womens-leadership-gap-2/.

8. *Gradually, responsibilities were*: Fabrikant, "When Citi Lost Sallie."

9. *The fact that Krawcheck* : Laura Kray, Jessica Kennedy, and Gillian Ku, "Are Women More Ethical than Men?," *Greater Good Magazine*, March 8, 2017, https://greatergood.berkeley.edu/article/item/are_women_more_ethical_than_men.

10. *To explain how businesses*: Merete Wedell-Wedellsborg, "The Psychology Behind Unethical Behavior," *Harvard Business Review*, April 12, 2019, https://hbr.org/2019/04/the-psychology-behind-unethical-behavior.

11. *Perhaps because of their outsider status*: G. Franke, D. Crown, and D. F. Spake, "Gender Differences in Ethical Perceptions of Business Practices: A Social Role Theory Perspective," *Journal of Applied Psychology* 82, no. 6 (1997): 920–34, https://doi.org/10.1037/0021-9010.82.6.920.

12. *Several years earlier*: Michelle K. Ryan and S. Alexander Haslam, "The Glass Cliff: Evidence That Women Are Over-represented in Precarious Leadership Positions," *British Journal of Management* 16, no. 2 (2005): 81–90, https://doi.org/10.1111/j.1467-8551.2005.00433.x.

13. *Women customers hadn't been*: "BlackRock Annual Global Investor Pulse Survey: American Women Feeling Better About Their Financial Futures but Keen Focus on Day-to-Day Finances May Deter Longer-Term Financial Goals," BlackRock, March 7, 2016, https://ir.blackrock.com/news-and-events/press-releases/press-releases-details/2016/BlackRock-Annual-Global-Investor-Pulse-Survey-American-Women-Feeling-Better-about-Their-Financial-Futures-but-Keen-Focus-on-Day-to-Day-Finances-May-Deter-Longer-Term-Financial-Goals/default.aspx.

14. *In March 2021*: Maggie McGrath, "Sallie Krawcheck Leads Ellevest to a Landmark $1 Billion in Assets Under Management," *Forbes*, March 23, 2021, https://www.forbes.com/sites/maggiemcgrath/2021/03/23/sallie-krawcheck-grows-ellevest-to-1-billion-in-assets-under-management/?sh=5416e7322395.

15. *The positive psychological effect*: Maureen Tanner and Pabie Q. Tabo, "Ladies First: The Influence of Mobile Dating Applications on the Psychological Empowerment of Female Users," *Informing Science* 21 (2018):

289–317,http://www.inform.nu/Articles/Vol21/ISJv21p289-371Tanner4793 .pdf.

16. *in 2018, Tinder enabled*: Emily Bary, "Exclusive: Tinder Plans Women-Talk-First Option Similar to Bumble," MarketWatch, February 18, 2018, https:// www.marketwatch.com/story/exclusive-tinder-will-let-women-choose -same-rule-as-bumble-2018-02-14.

17. *In July 2019*, Forbes *published*: Angel Au-Yeung, "Exclusive Investigation: Sex, Drugs, Misogyny and Sleaze at the HQ of Bumble's Owner," *Forbes*, August 31, 2019, https://www.forbes.com/sites/angelauyeung/2019/07/08 /exclusive-investigation-sex-drugs-misogyny-and-sleaze-at-the-hq-of-bum bles-owner/#32489a6e6308.

18. *Having a different perspective*: Jeremy Kahn, "Bumble Parent Told to Implement Workplace Reforms After Sexism Allegations," *Fortune*, January 30, 2020, https://fortune.com/2020/01/30/magiclab-bumble-sexism-allegations -workplace-reforms/.

19. *It is the United States'*: John Wills, *US Environmental History: Inviting Doomsday* (Edinburgh, Scotland: Edinburgh University Press, 2013), 190.

20. *But consider this*: Steve Henn, "When Women Stopped Coding," NPR, October 21, 2014, https://www.npr.org/sections/money/2014/10/21/357629765 /when-women-stopped-coding; "Changing the Curve: Women in Computing," Berkeley School of Information, July 14, 2021, https://ischoolonline .berkeley.edu/blog/women-computing-computer-science/.

21. *A measure of whether*: Stacy L. Smith, Marc Choueiti, and Katherine Pieper, "Gender Bias Without Borders," Geena Davis Institute on Gender in Media, 2014, https://seejane.org/symposiums-on-gender-in-media/gender-bias -without-borders/.

22. *The exception was found*: "2015 Statistics," Women and Hollywood, 2015, https://womenandhollywood.com/resources/statistics/2015-statistics/; Martha M. Lauzen, "It's a Man's (Celluloid) World: Portrayals of Female Characters in the Top Grossing Films of 2019," Center for the Study of Women in Television & Film, 2020, https://womenintvfilm.sdsu.edu/wp-content /uploads/2020/01/2019_Its_a_Mans_Celluloid_World_Report_REV.pdf.

23. *In 2015, the institute*: "The Reel Truth: Women Aren't Seen or Heard: An Automated Analysis of Gender Representation in Popular Films," Geena Davis Institute on Gender in Media, September 2016, https://seejane.org /research-informs-empowers/data/.

24. *One area of cultural output*: Eric Weiner, "Why Women Read More than Men," NPR, September 5, 2007, https://www.npr.org/templates/story/story .php?storyId=14175229?storyId=14175229.

25. *Onstage she declared*: Reggie Ugwu, "Lena Waithe Made History, and She Gave an Emmys Speech for Right Now," *New York Times*, September 19, 2017, https://www.nytimes.com/2017/09/19/arts/television/lena-waithe-emmys -master-of-none.html.

26. *Nearly half of Black Americans*: Hoang Nguyen, "Representation in Film Matters to Minorities," YouGovAmerica, March 6, 2018, https://today.you gov.com/topics/entertainment/articles-reports/2018/03/06/representation -film-matters-minorities.

Six: Embracing Change

1. *"Okay, I see."*: *The Devil Wears Prada*, 20th Century Fox.

2. *Here's how the system*: "Haute Couture," Fédération de la Haute Couture et de la Mode, https://fhcm.paris/en/haute-couture-2/.

3. *And sizing at many*: Tyler McCall, "Luxury Fashion Has a Plus Size Problem," Fashionista, May 7, 2018, https://fashionista.com/2018/05/luxury -designer-plus-size-clothing-problem.

4. *In "The Piracy Paradox"*: Kal Raustiala and Christopher Jon Sprigman, "The Piracy Paradox: Innovation and Intellectual Property in Fashion Design," *Virginia Law Review* 92, no. 8 (2006): 1687–777, https://papers.ssrn .com/sol3/papers.cfm?abstract_id=878401.

5. *The constant demand*: Channon Whitehead Lohr, "5 Truths the Fast Fashion Industry Doesn't Want You to Know," HuffPost, September 19, 2014, https://www.huffpost.com/entry/5-truths-the-fast-fashion_b_5690575.

6. *Environmentalists have raised*: Dana Thomas, "Fashionopolis: The Price of Fast Fashion and the Future of Clothes," OECD Forum, December 14, 2019, https://www.oecd-forum.org/posts/57380-fashionopolis-the-price-of-fast -fashion-and-the-future-of-clothes-by-dana-thomas.

7. *On average, each piece*: Dana Thomas, "The High Price of Fast Fashion," *Wall Street Journal*, August 29, 2019, https://www.wsj.com/articles/the -high-price-of-fast-fashion-11567096637.

8. *But the 2008–2009 recession*: "Department Stores in the US—Employment Statistics 2005–2027," IBISWorld, July 13, 2021, https://www.ibisworld .com/industry-statistics/employment/department-stores-united-states/.

9. *By 2015, the situation was*: Jason Del Rey, "The Death of the Department Store and the American Middle Class," Vox, November 30, 2020, https:// www.vox.com/recode/21717536/department-store-middle-class-amazon -online-shopping-covid-19; Abha Bhattarai, "Mall Department Stores Were Struggling. The Pandemic Has Pushed Them to the Edge of Extinction,"

Washington Post, April 16, 2021, https://www.washingtonpost.com/busi
ness/2021/04/16/half-countrys-remaining-mall-based-department-stores
-are-expected-shutter-by-2025/.

10. *In a 2019 study*: Jin-Ae Kang, Glenn T. Hubbard, and Sookyeong Hong,
   "Gender and Credibility in Branded Storytelling," *Gender in Management*
   34, no. 8 (2019): 702–14, http://dx.doi.org/10.1108/GM-02-2019-0015.

11. *In 2017, MIT's Sloan*: Renee Richardson Gosline, Jeffrey Lee, and Glen
   Urban, "The Power of Consumer Stories in Digital Marketing," *MIT Sloan
   Management Review*, May 18, 2017, https://sloanreview.mit.edu/article/the
   -power-of-consumer-stories-in-digital-marketing/.

12. *Those domestic principles*: Erin Blakemore, "The Shocking River Fire That
   Fueled the Creation of the EPA," History, December 1, 2020, https://www
   .history.com/news/epa-earth-day-cleveland-cuyahoga-river-fire-clean-water
   -act.

13. *The RealReal authenticates* : "The RealReal Sets the Record Straight on Its
   Authentication Process," The RealReal, November 12, 2019, https://inves
   tor.therealreal.com/news-releases/news-release-details/realreal-sets-record
   -straight-its-authentication-process.

14. *By the time the company*: The RealReal, Inc, Form S-1, United States Se-
   curities and Exchange Commission, May 31, 2019, https://www.sec.gov
   /Archives/edgar/data/1573221/000119312519163007/d720814ds1.htm.

15. *She didn't get much*: Ibid.

16. *A rare exception was*: Dhani Mau, "Stella McCartney Wants You to Resell
   her Goods," Fashionista, October 2, 2017, https://fashionista.com/2017/10
   /stella-mccartney-the-realreal-partnership.

17. *In 2018, she became*: "The RealReal and Stella McCartney Strengthen
   Partnership," The RealReal, December 13, 2018, https://investor.thereal
   real.com/news-releases/news-release-details/realreal-and-stella-mccartney
   -strengthen-partnership.

18. *The company's lead*: "Fashion and the Circular Economy," Ellen MacArthur
   Foundation, 2017, https://www.ellenmacarthurfoundation.org/explore/fash
   ion-and-the-circular-economy.

19. *By its calculation*: "The RealReal by the Numbers," The RealReal, September 30, 2021, https://investor.therealreal.com/static-files/430255e8-f0
   c3-4073-961d-420c3713188c; Kirsi Niinimaki et al., "The Environmental Price of Fast Fashion," *Nature Reviews Earth & Environment* 1, no. 4
   (2020): 189–200, https://doi.org/10.1038/s43017-020-0039-9.

20. *After a 2018 exposé*: "Burberry and The RealReal Join Forces to Make

Fashion Circular," The RealReal, October 7, 2019, https://investor.the realreal.com/news-releases/news-release-details/burberry-and-realreal-join -forces-make-fashion-circular.

21. *In 2018, Chanel filed*: *Chanel, Inc. v. The RealReal, Inc.*, Complaint Document 1, District Court, S.D. New York, November 14, 2018, https://www .courtlistener.com/docket/8190934/1/chanel-inc-v-the-realreal-inc/.

22. *The claim (hilariously) pointed*: "Chanel Is Suing the RealReal for Allegedly Selling Counterfeit Bags," The Fashion Law, November 16, 2018, https:// www.thefashionlaw.com/chanel-is-suing-the-realreal-for-allegedly-selling -counterfeit-bags/.

23. *The RealReal filed*: "Chanel and The RealReal Both Nab Wins in Latest Round of Ongoing Counterfeit Lawsuit," The Fashion Law, March 31, 2020, https://www.thefashionlaw.com/chanel-the-realreal-both-nab-wins-in-latest -round-of-ongoing-counterfeit-lawsuit/; "Chanel, The RealReal Agree to Mediation in Escalating Counterfeiting, Antitrust Fight," The Fashion Law, April 9, 2021, https://www.thefashionlaw.com/chanel-the-realreal-agree-to -mediation-amid-escalating-counterfeiting-antitrust-fight/.

24. *As the company grew*: "The RealReal and Gucci Launch Circular Economy Partnership," The RealReal, October 5, 2020, https://investor.therealreal .com/news-releases/news-release-details/realreal-and-gucci-launch-circular -economy-partnership.

25. *Such situations are*: "The State of Women in Tech and Startups: Top Findings for 2020," Women Who Tech, 2020, https://womenwhotech.org/data -and-resources/state-women-tech-and-startups.

26. *By contrast, a department store*: "Women's Apparel Stores," Retail Owners Institute, https://retailowner.com/Benchmarks/Apparel-Accessories-Stores /Womens-Apparel-Stores.

27. *When the covid-19 pandemic hit*: Sapna Maheshwari and Ben Casselman, " 'Pretty Catastrophic' Month for Retailers, and Now a Race to Survive," *New York Times*, June 1, 2020, https://www.nytimes.com/2020/04/15/business /economy/coronavirus-retail-sales.html.

28. *In the fourth quarter*: Jinjoo Lee, "Second-Hand Luxury Still Shines at The RealReal," *Wall Street Journal*, April 7, 2020, https://www.wsj.com/articles /second-hand-luxury-still-shines-at-the-realreal-11596794580.

29. *The RealReal was part*: Oliver Chen et al., "The $86bn Re-commerce Opportunity: Leaders & Cowen's Frameworks," Cowen, March 26, 2021, https://cowen.bluematrix.com/docs/pdf/bd7cf5c5-c81d-49c9-85bd-e123 62a36e53.pdf.

30. *There's also a theory*: Pamela Oliver, "Critical Mass Theory," in *The Wiley-*

Blackwell Encyclopedia of Social and Political Movements, edited by David A. Snow et al., January 14, 2013, https://onlinelibrary.wiley.com/doi/abs/10.1002/9780470674871.wbespm059.

31. *This concept is frequently cited*: Sarah Childs and Mona Lena Krook, "Political Mass Theory and Women's Political Representation," *Political Studies* 56, no. 3 (2008): 725–36, http://mlkrook.org/pdf/childs_krook_2008.pdf.

32. *For instance, it was only*: Jay Newton-Small, "What Happens When Women Reach a Critical Mass of Influence," *Time*, November 9, 2017, https://time.com/5016735/when-women-reach-a-critical-mass-of-influence/.

33. *Researchers have found*: Vicki W. Kramer, Alison M. Konrad, and Sumru Erkut, "Critical Mass on Corporate Boards: Why Three or More Women Enhance Governance," Wellesley Centers for Women, 2006, https://www.wcwonline.org/pdf/CriticalMassExecSummary.pdf.

Seven: Managing in Crisis

1. *In fact, it illustrated*: Elena Lytkina Botelho et al., "What Sets Successful CEOs Apart," *Harvard Business Review*, May–June 2017, https://hbr.org/2017/05/what-sets-successful-ceos-apart.

2. *Several academic studies*: Mara Mather and Nichole R. Lighthall, "Risk and Reward Are Processed Differently in Decisions Made Under Stress," *Current Directions in Psychological Science* 21, no. 1 (2012): 36–41, https://doi.org/10.1177%2F0963721411429452.

3. *Three researchers at*: Ruud van den Box, Marlies Harteveld, and Hein Stoop, "Stress and Decision-Making in Humans: Performance Is Related to Cortisol Reactivity, Albeit Differently in Men and Women," *Psychoneuroendocrinology* 34, no. 10 (2009): 1449–58, https://doi.org/10.1016/j.psyneuen.2009.04.016.

4. *This is, to some extent*: Mather and Lighthall, "Risk and Reward Are Processed Differently in Decisions Made Under Stress"; Gideon Nave et al., "Single Dose Testosterone Administration Impairs Cognitive Reflection in Men," *Psychological Science* 28, no. 10 (2017): 1398–407, https://doi.org/10.1177/0956797617709592.

5. *Women, on the other hand*: Christian Schymacher, Steffen Keck, and Wenjie Tang, "Biased Interpretation of Performance Feedback: The Role of CEO Overconfidence," *Strategic Management Journal* 41, no. 6 (2020): 1139–65, https://doi.org/10.1002/smj.3138.

6. *There's also evidence*: Stuart Soroka et al., "Do Women and Men Respond Differently to Negative News?," *Politics & Gender* 12, no. 2 (2016): 344–68, https://doi.org/10.1017/S1743923X16000131.

7. *In October 2019*: "Global Health Security Index," Global Health Security Index, October 24, 2019, https://www.ghsindex.org/.

8. *New Zealand, under the leadership*: Supriya Garikipati and Uma Kambhampati,"Leading the Fight Against the Pandemic: Does Gender 'Really' Matter?," Women's Economic Imperative, June 3, 2020, https://weiforward.org/mdocs-posts/leading-the-fight-against-the-pandemic-does-gender-really-matter/.

9. *For its part, the media*: Ibid.

10. *Some posited that the tendency*: Amanda Taub, "Why Are Women-Led Nations Doing Better with Covid-19?," *New York Times*, August 13, 2020, https://www.nytimes.com/2020/05/15/world/coronavirus-women-leaders.html.

11. *Others argued that pandemic outcomes*: Helen Lewis, "The Pandemic Has Revealed the Weakness of Strongmen," *Atlantic*, May 6, 2020, https://www.theatlantic.com/international/archive/2020/05/new-zealand-germany-women-leadership-strongmen-coronavirus/611161/.

12. *These findings are echoed*: Kayla Sergent and Alexander D. Stajkovic,"Women's Leadership Is Associated with Fewer Deaths During the COVID-19 Crisis: Quantitative Analyses of United States Governors," *Journal of Applied Psychology* 105, no. 8 (2020): 771–83, https://doi.org/10.1037/apl0000577.

13. *Their confidence was expressed*: Ibid.

14. *A March 24 Facebook Live*: Taub, "Why Are Women-Led Nations Doing Better with Covid-19?"

15. *Jack Zenger and Joseph Folkman*: Jack Zenger and Joseph Folkman, "Research: Women Are Better Leaders During a Crisis," *Harvard Business Review*, December 30, 2020, https://hbr.org/2020/12/research-women-are-better-leaders-during-a-crisis.

16. *A survey of eight hundred*: Georges Desvaux, Sandrine Devillard, and Sandra Sancier-Sultan, "Women Matter: Women Leaders During and After the Crisis," McKinsey & Company, December 1, 2009, https://www.mckinsey.com/~/media/McKinsey/Business%20Functions/Organization/Our%20Insights/Women%20matter/Women_matter_dec2009_english.ashx.

17. *A separate study*: Ibid.

18 *The theory has been highly disputed*: Garikipati and Kambhampati, "Leading the Fight Against the Pandemic."

19. *With economic and social opportunities*: Anu Madgavkar et al., "COVID-19 and Gender Equality: Countering the Regressive Effects," McKinsey & Company, July 15, 2020, https://www.mckinsey.com/featured-insights/future-of-work/covid-19-and-gender-equality-countering-the-regressive-effects.

20. *That's not all*: Debbie Landis, "Gender-Based Violence (GBV) and Covid-19: The Complexities of Responding to 'The Shadow Pandemic,'" CARE International, May 2020, https://www.care-international.org/files /files/GBV_and_COVID_19_Policy_Brief_FINAL.pdf.

21. *The organization's weekly*: "Feeding America Food Bank Network Projects $1.4 Billion Shortfall Due to the COVID-19 Crisis," Feeding America, April 1, 2020, https://www.feedingamerica.org/about-us/press-room/feed ing-america-food-bank-network-projects-14-billion-shortfall-due-covid-19.

22 *Empathy, as a key part of emotional intelligence*: The Workforce Institute at UKH, "Physical Safety, Psychological Security, Job Stability: Employees Worldwide Share Top COVID-19 Concerns for the Workplace of Today and Tomorrow," Ultimate Kronos Group, September 15, 2020, https://www .kronos.com/about-us/newsroom/physical-safety-psychological-security -job-stability-employees-worldwide-share-top-covid-19-concerns.

23. *That characteristic is*: "New Research Shows Women are Better at Using Soft Skills Crucial for Effective Leadership and Superior Business Perfor-mance, Finds Korn Ferry," Korn Ferry, March 7, 2016, https://www.kornferry .com/about-us/press/new-research-shows-women-are-better-at-using-soft -skills-crucial-for-effective-leadership.

24. *As discussed in chapter 3*: John G. Vongas and Raghid Al Hajj, "The Evo-lution of Empathy and Women's Precarious Leadership Appointments," *Frontiers in Psychology* 6 (2015): article 1751, https://www.ncbi.nlm.nih.gov /pmc/articles/PMC4641904/.

25. *In fact, a 2019 study*: Yang Wang, Benjamin F. Jones, and Dashun Wang, "Early Career Failures Can Make You Stronger in the Long Run," Kellogg Insight, October 1, 2019, https://insight.kellogg.northwestern.edu/article /early-setbacks-failure-career-success.

26. *Some asked for patterns*: Emily Janoch, "Cholera to COVID19: Applying CLA in Crisis," USAID Learning Lab, April 2, 2020, https://usaidlearn inglab.org/lab-notes/cholera-covid19-applying-cla-crisis.

27. *That multifaceted approach*: Ibid.

28. *With her tax accountant understanding*: Paul Flahive, "Food Banks Across Texas, US Brace for 'Perfect Storm' of August Challenges," *Texas Standard*, July 23, 2020, https://www.texasstandard.org/stories/food-banks-across -texas-us-brace-for-perfect-storm-of-august-challenges/; Jill Ament, "Unprec-edented Demand Strains Texas Food Banks," *Texas Standard*, April 21, 2020, https://www.texasstandard.org/stories/unprecedented-demand-strains -texas-food-banks/.

29. *On April 1, the organization*: "Feeding America Food Bank Network Projects

$1.4 Billion Shortfall Due to the COVID-19 Crisis," Feeding America, April 1, 2020, https://www.feedingamerica.org/about-us/press-room/feeding-america-food-bank-network-projects-14-billion-shortfall-due-covid-19.

30. *Just days into the pandemic*: Jennifer Wong, "A New Sustainability Program with Feeding America to Reduce Waste and Rescue Food from Supply Chains," Convoy, March 19, 2020, https://convoy.com/blog/feeding-america-food-rescue/; "General Mills Announces 'Manufacture to Donate' Initiative to Address Urgent Hunger Needs," General Mills, April 17, 2020, https://www.generalmills.com/en/News/NewsReleases/Library/2020/April/General-Mills-announces-manufacture-to-donate-initiative-to-address-urgent-hunger-needs.

31. *Those efforts resulted*: "How We Fight Food Waste in the US," Feeding America, https://www.feedingamerica.org/our-work/our-approach/reduce-food-waste.

32. *One study conducted*: Curt P. Richter, "On the Phenomenon of Sudden Death in Animals and Man," *Psychosomatic Medicine* 19, no. 3 (1957): 191–98, https://www.aipro.info/wp/wp-content/uploads/2017/08/phenomena_sudden_death.pdf.

33. *The instinct to stockpile*: Inge Huijsmans et al., "A Scarcity Mindset Alters Neural Processing Underlying Consumer Decision Making," *Proceedings of the National Academy of Sciences of the United States of America* 116, no. 24 (2019): 11699–704, https://doi.org/10.1073/pnas.1818572116.

34. *Similar findings have*: Jennifer Sheehy-Skeffington and Jessica Rea, "How Poverty Affects People's Decision-Making Processes," Joseph Rowntree Foundation, February 2017, https://www.lse.ac.uk/business/consulting/assets/documents/how-poverty-affects-peoples-decision-making-processes.pdf.

35. *After that decade*: Recode Staff, "Full Transcript: Clear CEO Caryn Seidman-Becker Answers Biometric Security Questions on Too Embarassed to Ask," Vox, December 28, 2017, https://www.vox.com/2017/12/28/16826070/clear-ceo-caryn-seidman-becker-answers-biometric-security-fingerprint-iris-scan-too-embarrassed; Brad Stone, "A Rapid Security Check Could Be Revived at Airports," *New York Times*, May 3, 2010, https://www.nytimes.com/2010/05/04/technology/04secure.html.

36. *As lockdowns began*: Kashmir Hill, "The Secretive Company That Might End Privacy as We Know It," *New York Times*, January 18, 2020, https://www.nytimes.com/2020/01/18/technology/clearview-privacy-facial-recognition.html.

37. *Remarkably, despite spending*: "Monthly Travel Data Report" January 28,

2022, U.S. Travel Association, htt ps://www.ustravel.org/toolkit/covid-19 -travel-industry-research; https://ir.clearme.com/sec-filings/all-sec-filings /content/0001104659-21-088178/0001104659-21-088178.pdf, 2.

38. *In a vote of confidence*: CLEAR, "CLEAR's Latest $100mm Funding Round Fuels Expansion Strategy," PRNewswire, February 8, 2021, https://www .prnewswire.com/news-releases/clears-latest-100mm-funding-round-fuels -expansion-strategy-301223907.html.

39. *The 2005 study that coined*: Michelle K. Ryan and S. Alexander Haslam, "The Glass Cliff: Evidence That Women Are Over-represented in Precari-ous Leadership Positions," *British Journal of Management* 16, no. 2 (2005): 81–90, https://is.muni.cz/el/1423/jaro2017/VPL457/um/62145647/Ryan _Haslam_The_Glass_cliff.pdf.

40. *In 2011,* Harvard Business Review: Martin Reeves and Mike Deimler, "Adaptability: The New Competitive Advantage," *Harvard Business Review*, July–August 2011, https://hbr.org/2011/07/adaptability-the-new-competi tive-advantage.

41. *Adaptable companies are quick*: Ibid.

42. *In 2016, Korn Ferry*: "New Research Shows Women Are Better at Using Soft Skills Crucial for Effective Leadership and Superior Business Performance, Finds Korn Ferry," Korn Ferry, March 7, 2016, https://www.kornferry.com /about-us/press/new-research-shows-women-are-better-at-using-soft-skills -crucial-for-effective-leadership.

43. *In 2011,* Harvard Business Review *published*: Susanne Bruckmüller and Nyla R. Branscome, "How Women End Up on the 'Glass Cliff,'" *Harvard Business Review*, January–February 2011, https://hbr.org/2011/01/how -women-end-up-on-the-glass-cliff.

44. *This is supported*: Corinne Post, Ioana M. Latu, and Liuba Y. Belkin, "A Fe-male Leadership Trust Advantage in Times of Crisis: Under What Condi-tions?," *Psychology of Women Quarterly* 43, no. 2 (2019): 215–31, https://doi .org/10.1177%2F0361684319828292.

45. *There's a self-help strategy*: Kateri McRae et al., "Gender Differences in Emotion Regulation: An fMRI Study of Cognitive Reappraisal," *Group Processes & Intergroup Relations* 11, no. 2 (2008): 143–62, https://doi.org /10.1177%2F1368430207088035.

46. *Women have been found*: Alberto Megias-Robles, Maria Jose Gutierrez-Cobo, and Raquel Gomez-Leal, "Emotionally Intelligent People Reappraise Rather than Suppress Their Emotions," PLOS ONE 14, no. 8 (2019): 1–8, https:// doi.org/10.1371/journal.pone.0220688.

47. *We can see it clearly*: McRae et al., "Gender Differences in Emotion Regu-

lation"; Megias-Robles et al., "Emotionally Intelligent People Reappraise Rather than Suppress Their Emotions."

48. *At the end of 2020*: Leah C. Windsor et al., "Gender in the Time of COVID-19: Evaluating National Leadership and COVID-19 Fatalities," PLOS ONE 15, no. 12 (2020): e0244531, https://doi.org/10.1371/journal.pone.0244531.

49. *But they did find evidence*: Ibid.

50. *The kinds of countries*: Ibid.

51. *The study argued*: Ibid.

52. *But the study's authors*: Ibid.

Eight: Defying CEO Archetypes

1. *Today female jockeys*: Alasdair Brown and Fuyu Yang, "Does Society Underestimate Women? Evidence from the Performance of Female Jockeys in Horse Racing," *Journal of Economic Behavior & Organization* 111 (2015): 106–18, https://doi.org/10.1016/j.jebo.2014.12.031.

2. *Researchers at the University of Utah*: Lyda S. Bigelow et al., "Skirting the Issues? Experimental Evidence of Gender Bias in IPO Prospectus Evaluations," SSRN, February 2012, https://papers.ssrn.com/sol3/papers.cfm?abstract_id=1556449; J. Maureen Henderson, "Do Investors Discriminate Against Female CEOs?," *Forbes*, May 7, 2012, https://www.forbes.com/sites/jmaureenhenderson/2012/05/07/is-ipo-evaluation-a-hotbed-of-sexism/?sh=237533255771.

3. *In fact, female scarcity*: Ned Smith, "Why the Market Punishes Some Companies with Female CEOs," *Fortune*, September 28, 2016, https://fortune.com/2016/09/28/gsk-emma-walmsley-ceo-2/.

4. *The same study found*: Edward Bishop Smith, Jillian Chown, and Kevin Gaughan, "Better in the Shadows? Public Attention, Media Coverage, and Market Reactions to Female CEO Announcements," *Sociological Science* 8 (2021): 119–49, https://sociologicalscience.com/download/vol-8/may/SocSci_v8_119to149.pdf.

5. *Men in their twenties and thirties*: Jack Zenger and Joseph Folkman, "Research: Women Score Higher than Men in Most Leadership Skills," *Harvard Business Review*, June 25, 2019, https://hbr.org/2019/06/research-women-score-higher-than-men-in-most-leadership-skills; Catlin Mullen, "This Is When Confidence at Work Peaks for Women," Bizwomen, August 8, 2019, https://www.bizjournals.com/bizwomen/news/latest-news/2019/08/this-is-when-confidence-at-work-peaks-for-women.html?page=all.

6. *one study estimated*: Christopher Karpowitz, Tali Mendelberg, Lee Shaker, "Gender Inequality in Deliberative Participation," *American Political Science*

Review, 2012 106 (03): 533 https://www.cambridge.org/core/journals/ameri
can-political-science-review/article/abs/gender-inequality-in-deliberative
-participation/CE7441632EB3B0BD21CC5045C7E1AF76.

7. *Communication between the genders*: Victoria Brescoll, "Who Takes the
Floor and Why: Gender, Power, and Volubility in Organizations," *Administrative Science Quarterly* 56, no. 3 (2011): 622–41, http://citeseerx.ist.psu
.edu/viewdoc/download?doi=10.1.1.881.3353&rep=rep1&type=pdf.

8. *Other studies have found*: Adrienne B. Hancock and Benjamin A. Rubin,
"Influence of Communication Partner's Gender on Language," *Journal of
Language and Social Psychology* 34, no. 1 (2014): 46–64, https://doi.org
/10.1177%2F0261927X14533197.

9. *What is most fascinating*: Anne Cutler and Donia R. Scott, "Speaker Sex
and Perceived Apportionment of Talk," *Applied Psycholinguistics* 11, no. 3
(1990): 253–72, https://pure.mpg.de/rest/items/item_68785_7/component
/file_506904/content.

10. *There is one scenario*: Christopher F. Karpowitz, Tali Mendelberg, and Lee
Shaker, "Gender Inequality in Deliberative Participation," *American Po-
litical Science Review* 106, no. 3 (2012): 533–47, https://doi.org/10.1017
/S0003055412000329.

11. *For a woman to convince*: Monica Biernat, Kathleen Fuegen, and Diane
Kobrynowicz, "Shifting Standards and the Inference of Incompetence:
Effects of Formal and Informal Evaluation Tools," *Personality and Social Psychology Bulletin* 36, no. 7 (2010): 855–68, https://doi.org/10.11
77%2F0146167210369483; Heidi Grant Halvorson, "When You Benefit
from Being Underestimated, and When You Pay for It," *Fast Company*, October 27, 2010, https://www.fastcompany.com/1698221/when-you-benefit
-being-underestimated-and-when-you-pay-it.

12. *Many studies have also shown*: Biernat et al., "Shifting Standards and the Inference of Incompetence."

13. *One headline in response*: Gabe Delahaye, "Gwyneth Paltrow Has Just Discovered Sleep. Neat!," *Videogum*, March 4, 2010, https://www.stereogum
.com/1770988/gwyneth-paltrow-has-just-discovered-sleep-neat/videogum/.

14. *"The tearful, gushing"*: Wesley Morris, "I Love Gwyneth Paltrow. There. I
Said It," *New York Times*, September 30, 2019, https://www.nytimes.com
/2019/09/30/movies/gwyneth-paltrow.html.

15. *Inspired by Brown's work*: Anna Bruk, Sabine G. Scholl, and Herbert Bless,
"Beautiful Mess Effect: Self-Other Differences in Evaluation of Showing Vulnerability," *Journal of Personality and Social Psychology* 115, no. 2 (2018):
192–205, https://psycnet.apa.org/doi/10.1037/pspa0000120.

16. *"Every time there was"*: Taffy Brodesser-Akner, "How Goop's Haters Made Gwyneth Paltrow's Company Worth $250 Million," *New York Times Magazine*, July 25, 2018, https://www.nytimes.com/2018/07/25/magazine/big-business-gwyneth-paltrow-wellness.html.

17. *"We talk about things"*: Robyn Turk, "What Is Contextual Commerce? Gwyneth Paltrow Explains Goop at NRF," FashionUnited, January 29, 2020, https://fashionunited.com/news/business/what-is-contextual-commerce-gwyneth-paltrow-explains-goop-at-nrf/2020012931891.

18. *Paltrow's disquiet in that moment*: Anne Maass, Claudio D'Ettole, and Mara Cadinu, "Checkmate? The Role of Gender Stereotypes in the Ultimate Intellectual Sport," *European Journal of Social Psychology* 38, no. 2 (2007): 231–45, https://doi.org/10.1002/ejsp.440.

19. *And when entrepreneurship*: Vishal K. Gupta et al., "The Role of Gender Stereotypes in Perceptions of Entrepreneurs and Intentions to Become an Entrepreneur," *Entrepreneurship Theory and Practice* 33, no. 2 (2009): 397–417, https://doi.org/10.1111%2Fj.1540-6520.2009.00296.x.

20. *In 2018, three University of Wisconsin*: Wei Zheng, Olca Surgevil, and Ronit Kark, "Dancing on the Razor's Edge: How Top-Level Women Leaders Manage the Paradoxical Tensions Between Agency and Communion," *Sex Roles* 79, nos. 11–12 (2018): 633–50, https://doi.org/10.1007/s11199-018-0908-6.

21. *During that time, Goop drew*: "California Cracks Down on Goop After Tina .org Complaint," Truth in Advertising, September 4, 2018, https://www.truthinadvertising.org/california-cracks-down-on-goop-after-tina-org-complaint/.

22. *96 percent of professional women*: Kristy Wallace, "Navigating Vulnerability in the Workplace," SheSavvy, July 13, 2018, https://www.shesavvy.com/blog/navigating-vulnerability-workplace/.

23. *A study found that high levels*: Sun Hyun Park, James D. Westphal, and Ithai Stern, "Set Up for a Fall: The Insidious Effects of Flattery and Opinion Conformity Toward Corporate Leaders," *Administrative Science Quarterly* 56, no. 2 (2011): 257–302, https://doi.org/10.1177%2F0001839211429102.

24. *A study published*: Laura Guillen, "Is the Confidence Gap Between Men and Women a Myth?," *Harvard Business Review*, March 26, 2018, https://hbr.org/2018/03/is-the-confidence-gap-between-men-and-women-a-myth; Laura Guillen, Margarita Mayo, and Natalia Karelaia, "Appearing Self-confident and Getting Credit for It: Why It May Be Easier for Men than Women to Gain Influence at Work," *Human Resource Management* 57, no. 4 (2017): 839–54, https://doi.org/10.1002/hrm.21857.

25. *Academics have sought*: Samantha C. Paustian-Underdahl, Lisa Slattery

Walker, and David J. Woehr, "Gender and Perceptions of Leadership Effectiveness: A Meta-Analysis of Contextual Moderators," *Journal of Applied Psychology* 99, no. 6 (2014): 1129–45, https://www.apa.org/pubs/journals/releases/apl-a0036751.pdf.

26. *Another study found*: Adrienne Selko, "Confidence Is Top Leadership Difference Between Women and Men," IndustryWeek, March 8, 2016, https://www.industryweek.com/leadership/article/21971620/confidence-is-top-leadership-difference-between-women-and-men.

27. *A study of three hundred*: Rachel Muller-Heyndyk, "Female and Younger Leaders More Susceptible to Imposter Syndrome," *HR Magazine*, October 28, 2019, https://www.hrmagazine.co.uk/article-details/female-and-younger-leaders-more-susceptible-to-imposter-syndrome; "Women in Tech: Analyzing the Current Climate for Women in the Technology Sector," Paychex, December 3, 2018, https://www.paychex.com/articles/human-resources/women-in-technology-sector.

28. *In her book* How Women Decide: Therese Huston, *How Women Decide: What's True, What's Not, and What Strategies Spark the Best Choices* (Boston: Houghton Mifflin Harcourt, 2016), 208.

29. *One of the most comprehensive*: Katie Abouzahr et al., "Dispelling the Myths of the Gender 'Ambition Gap,'" Boston Consulting Group, April 5, 2017, https://www.bcg.com/en-us/publications/2017/people-organization-leadership-change-dispelling-the-myths-of-the-gender-ambition-gap.

Nine: Discovering Resilience

1. *George Shaheen*: Greg Sandoval, "Ex-Webvan CEO to Collect $375,000 Yearly," CNET, January 2, 2002, https://www.cnet.com/news/ex-webvan-ceo-to-collect-375000-yearly/.

2. *Webvan's COO and CFO*: Keith Regan, "Webvan CEO Lands New Job," E-commerce Times, August 1, 2001, https://www.ecommercetimes.com/story/12426.html.

3. *One by University of Alabama professor*: Vishal K. Gupta et al., "You're Fired! Gender Disparities in CEO Dismissal," *Journal of Management* 46, no. 4 (2020): 560–82, https://doi.org/10.1177%2F0149206318810415.

4. *As discussed elsewhere*: Katherine Guerard, "Analyzing Global Gender Diversity," FactSet, March 10, 2020, https://insight.factset.com/analyzing-global-gender-diversity.

5. *In a 2012 study called*: Ashleigh Selby Rosette and Robert W. Livingston, "Failure Is Not an Option for Black Women: Effects of Organizational Performance on Leaders with Single Versus Dual-Subordinate Identities," *Journal*

of Experimental Social Psychology 48, no. 5 (2012): 1162–67, https://doi.org
/10.1016/j.jesp.2012.05.002.

6. *In 2016, the Rockefeller Foundation*: "CEOs and Gender: A Media Analysis," Global Strategy Group, October 26, 2016, https://globalstrategygroup
.com/rock/; Jared Lindson, "Is the Media Partly to Blame for the CEO Gender Gap?," *Fast Company*, October 26, 2016, https://www.fastcompany.com
/3064969/is-the-media-partly-to-blame-for-the-ceo-gender-gap.

7. *Haney, for example, was skewered*: Brianna Sacks, "Outdoor Voices Became
a Staple for Millennial Cool Girls Thanks to Its Chill Aesthetic. Employees
Say They Were Drowning," BuzzFeed News, March 11, 2020, https://www
.buzzfeednews.com/article/briannasacks/outdoor-voices-ty-haney-employee
-allegations.

8. *The then thirty-one-year-old*: Zoe Schiffer, "Emotional Baggage," The
Verge, December 5, 2019, https://www.theverge.com/2019/12/5/20995453
/away-luggage-ceo-steph-korey-toxic-work-environment-travel-inclusion;
Mary Hanbury, "Here's the Full Slack Message from Away's Returning CEO
Calling a Recent Investigation into the Company 'Deliberate Lies,'" Insider,
January 13, 2020, https://www.businessinsider.com/away-ceo-calls-com
pany-investigation-deliberate-lies-2020-1.

9. *In early 2020, The Information*: Jessica E. Lessin, "The (Pink) Elephant in
the Tech Press," The Information, March 14, 2020, https://www.theinforma
tion.com/articles/the-pink-elephant-in-the-tech-press.

10. *In December 2020, Fortune*: Maria Aspan, "Female Founders Under Fire:
Are Women in the Startup World Being Unfairly Targeted?," *Fortune*, December 3, 2020, https://fortune.com/longform/female-founders-startups
-the-wing-away-outdoor-voices-ceos/.

11. *Such attacks have continued*: Melia Russell, "Spring Health CEO April Koh
on the Importance of Employees' Mental Health," Insider, December 7,
2021, https://www.businessinsider.com/spring-health-ceo-april-koh-slush
-interview-startup-culture-2021-12.

12. *It was a move*: Suzanne Lucas, "How to Lay Off Employees When Everyone
Is Remote," *Inc.*, March 31, 2020, https://www.inc.com/suzanne-lucas/how
-to-lay-off-employees-when-everyone-is-remote.html.

13. *In June 2020, Hyman addressed*: Jenn Hyman, "An Update from CEO and
Co-founder Jenn Hyman," RTR Shift, June 22, 2020, https://rtrshift.com
/update-from-renttherunway-ceo-jenn-hyman/.

14. *In the business world*: Vishal K. Gupta et al., "Do Women CEOs Face Greater
Threat of Shareholder Activism Compared to Male CEOs? A Role Congru-
ity Perspective," *Journal of Applied Psychology* 103, no. 2 (2018): 228–36,

https://scmortal.people.ua.edu/uploads/1/1/9/7/119795135/gupta_han _mortal_silveri_-_jap_2018_-_do_women_ceos_face_greater_threat_of _shareholder_activism_compared_to_male_ceos.pdf.

15. *"face more public display"*: Vishal K. Gupta, Sandra Mortal, and Daniel B. Turban, "Research: Activist Investors Are More Likely to Target Female CEOs," *Harvard Business Review*, January 22, 2018, https://hbr.org/2018 /01/research-activist-investors-are-more-likely-to-target-female-ceos.

16. *A study conducted by* Fortune: Kieran Snyder, "The abrasiveness trap: High-achieving men and women are described differently in reviews," *Fortune*, August 26, 2014, https://fortune.com/2014/08/26/performance-review-gen der-bias/.

17. *Martin Abel*: Martin Abel, "Do Workers Discriminate Against Female Bosses?," Institute of Labor Economics Discussion Paper No. 12611, September 2019, http://ftp.iza.org/dp12611.pdf.

18. *These findings are supported*: Martin Abel, "This One Unconscious Reaction May Be Holding Women Back at Work," *Fast Company*, September 19, 2020, https://www.fastcompany.com/90552194/this-one-unconscious-reac tion-may-be-holding-women-back-at-work.

19. *Yale professor Victoria Brescoll*: Victoria Brescoll and Eric Luis Uhlmann, "Can an Angry Woman Get Ahead?: Status Conferral, Gender, and Expression of Emotion in the Workplace," *Psychological Science* 19, no. 3 (2008): 268–75, https://doi.org/10.1111%2Fj.1467-9280.2008.02079.x.

20. *We've seen this play out*: Nicola Slawson, "Navratilova: BBC Pays McEnroe 10 Times More for Wimbledon Role," *Guardian*, March 18, 2018, https:// www.theguardian.com/sport/2018/mar/19/navratilova-bbc-pays-mcenroe -10-times-more-for-wimbledon-role.

21. *Serena Williams*: Alex Abad-Santos, "Serena Williams's US Open Fight with Umpire Carlos Ramos, Explained," Vox, September 10, 2018, https:// www.vox.com/2018/9/10/17837598/serena-williams-us-open-umpire -carlos-ramos.

22. *University of Arizona and*: Jon Evans et al., "Gender and the Evaluation of Humor at Work," *Journal of Applied Psychology* 104, no. 8 (2019): 1077–87, https://doi.org/10.1037/apl0000395.

23. *In 2010, Victoria Brescoll*: Victoria Brescoll, Erica Dawson, and Eric Luis Uhlmann, "Hard Won and Easily Lost: The Fragile Status of Leaders in Gender-Stereotype-Incongruent Occupations," *Psychological Science* 21, no. 11 (2010): 1640–42, https://doi.org/10.1177%2F0956797610384744.

24. *Frustratingly, women can also be penalized*: Therese Huston, "Research: We Are Way Harder on Female Leaders Who Make Bad Calls," *Harvard*

Business Review, April 21, 2016, https://hbr.org/2016/04/research-we-are
-way-harder-on-female-leaders-who-make-bad-calls.

25. *In 2020, a study*: Nicole Votolato Montgomery and Amanda P. Cowen, "How Leader Gender Influences External Audience Response to Organizational Failures," *Journal of Personality and Social Psychology: Attitudes and Social Cognition* 118, no. 4 (2020): 639–60, https://psycnet.apa.org/doi/10.1037/pspa0000176.

26. *The same study found*: Ibid.

27. *Joan Williams*: Joan C. Williams, "How Women Can Escape the Likability Trap," *New York Times*, August 16, 2019, https://www.nytimes.com/2019/08/16/opinion/sunday/gender-bias-work.html.

28. *Grossman was open*: Belinda Luscombe, "Lights, Camera, Sell: How Mindy Grossman Took the Shame Out of Home Shopping," *Time*, October 8, 2012, http://content.time.com/time/subscriber/article/0,33009,2125508-4,00.html.

29. *The United States Air Force Academy*: "Office of Diversity and Inclusion," United States Air Force Academy, https://www.usafa.edu/about/culture-climate-diversity/.

30. *Yet in the early 2000s*: Diana Jean Schemo, "Rate of Rape at Academy Is Put at 12% in Survey," *New York Times*, August 29, 2003, https://www.nytimes.com/2003/08/29/us/rate-of-rape-at-academy-is-put-at-12-in-survey.html; Pam Zubeck, "Air Force Academy Shows Improvement in Wash-out Rate," *Colorado Springs Independent*, May 22, 2018, https://web.archive.org/web/20191015025406/https://m.csindy.com/TheWire/archives/2018/05/22/air-force-academy-shows-improvement-in-wash-out-rate.

31. *Nor was it MIT*: "ORC Students," MIT Operations Research Center, https://orc.mit.edu/people/students.

32. *As she had*: Rebecca Szkutak, "Novi Raises $10.3 Million for Its B2B Marketplace of Sustainable Suppliers," *Forbes*, September 7, 2021, https://www.forbes.com/sites/rebeccaszkutak/2021/09/07/novi-raises-103-million-for-its-b2b-marketplace-of-sustainable-suppliers/?sh=21719bde6906.

33. *In fact, Stanford University*: David K. Sherman and Geoffrey L. Cohen, "The Psychology of Self-Defense: Self-Affirmation Theory," *Advances in Experimental Social Psychology* 38 (2006): 183–242, https://ed.stanford.edu/sites/default/files/self_defense.pdf.

34. *This strength Shenk found*: Robyn Fivush et al., "Family Narratives and the Development of Children's Emotional Well-Being," in *Family Stories and the Life Course: Across Time and Generations*, edited by Michael W. Pratt and Barbara H. Fiese (Mahwah, NJ: Lawrence Erlbaum Associates, 2004), 55,

76; Marshall P. Duke, "A Voyage Homeward: Fiction and Family Stories—Resilience and Rehabilitation," *Journal of Humanities in Rehabilitation*, July 8, 2015, 1–7, https://www.jhrehab.org/wp-content/uploads/2015/06/A-Voyage-Homeward_Duke_JHR.Summer2015.pdf; Marshall P. Duke, Amber Lazarus, and Robyn Fivush, "Knowledge of Family History as a Clinically Useful Index of Psychological Well-being and Prognosis: A Brief Report," *Psychotherapy: Theory, Research, Practice, Training* 45, no. 2 (2008): 268–72, https://doi.org/10.1037/0033-3204.45.2.268; Jennifer G. Bohanek et al., "Family Narratives and Self-understanding—1 Family Narrative Interaction and Children's Self-Understanding," 2004, https://doi.org/10.1111/j.1545-5300.2006.00079.x.

35. *Research by the economist*: Betsey Stevenson, "Beyond the Classroom: Using Title IX to Measure the Return to High School Sports," *Review of Economics and Statistics* 92, no. 2 (2010): 284–301, https://doi.org/10.3386/w15728.

36. *Ninety-four percent of women*: Rebecca Hinds, "The 1 Trait 94 Percent of C-Suite Women Share (And How to Get It)," *Inc.*, February 8, 2018, https://www.inc.com/rebecca-hinds/the-1-trait-94-percent-of-c-suite-women-share-and-how-to-get-it.html; Kristy Ingram, "Why a Female Athlete Should Be Your Next Leader," EY, September 23, 2020, https://www.ey.com/en_us/athlete-programs/why-female-athletes-should-be-your-next-leader.

37. *Another study identified*: Barbara Kotschwar, "Women, Sports, and Development: Does It Pay to Let Girls Play?," Peterson Institute for International Economics, March 2014, https://www.piie.com/sites/default/files/publications/pb/pb14-8.pdf.

38. *Perhaps most important*: "Why Female Athletes Make Winning Entrepreneurs," EY, May 3, 2017, https://assets.ey.com/content/dam/ey-sites/ey-com/en_gl/topics/entrepreneurship/ey-why-female-athletes-make-winning-entrepreneurs.pdf.

39. *In 2012, a group*: D. Scott Derue et al., "A Quasi-experimental Study of After-Event Reviews and Leadership Development," *Journal of Applied Psychology* 97, no. 5 (2012): 997–1015, https://ecommons.cornell.edu/bitstream/handle/1813/71444/Workman2_Quasi_experimental.pdf?sequence=1&isAllowed=y.

40. *A study by psychology*: Coren L. Apicella, Elif E. Demiral, and Johanna Mollerstrom, "No Gender Difference in Willingness to Compete When Competing Against Self," *American Economic Review* 107, no. 5 (2017): 136–40, http://dx.doi.org/10.1257/aer.p20171019.

41. *When they had a chance*: Lauren Sherman, "Target Teams with 'Who What

Wear' on Full-Fledged Fashion Line," Business of Fashion, October 13, 2015, https://www.businessoffashion.com/articles/news-analysis/target-teams -with-who-what-wear-on-full-fledged-fashion-line.

42. *In 2004, researchers gathered*: Andy Martens et al., "Combating Stereotype Threat: The Effect of Self-affirmation on Women's Intellectual Performance," *Journal of Experimental Social Psychology* 42, no. 2 (2006): 236–43, https:// doi.org/10.1016/j.jesp.2005.04.010.

Ten: Creating New Communities

1. *Studies have shown*: "Mid-career Women Networking a Lot Less than Their Male Counterparts," HR Review, February 10, 2014, https://www.hrreview .co.uk/hr-news/diversity-news/mid-career-women-networking-a-lot-less /50502.

2. *That drop-off leaves women*: Subha V. Barry, "The Gender Gap at the Top: What's Keeping Women from Leading Corporate America," Working Mother, July 2019, https://www.workingmother.com/sites/workingmother .com/files/attachments/2019/07/women_at_the_top_gender_gap_report _1.pdf.

3. *They hoped to start*: Amy Lui Abel and Rebecca Ray, "Global Executive Coaching Survey 2018," Conference Board Research Report No. 1691, 2018, https://www.executivecoachingconnections.com/sites/default/files /2018_global_executive_coaching_survey.pdf.

4. *Every year a nonprofit organization*: Shawn Achor, "Do Women's Net-working Events Move the Needle on Equality?," *Harvard Business Review*, February 13, 2018, https://hbr.org/2018/02/do-womens-networking-events -move-the-needle-on-equality.

5. *In the 2010 report*: Sylvia Ann Hewlett et al., *The Sponsor Effect: Breaking Through the Last Glass Ceiling*, Harvard Business Review Research Report, December 2010, http://wipsworkshop.weebly.com/uploads/1/4/4/5 /14458696/the_sponsor_effect_-_breaking_through_the_last_glass_ceiling .pdf.

6. *A survey given*: Ibid.

7. *"Women aren't just convinced"*: Ibid., 18.

8. *A 2019 study*: Yang Yang, Nitesh V. Chawla, and Brian Uzzi, "A Network's Gender Composition and Communication Pattern Predict Women's Leadership Success," *Proceedings of the National Academy of Sciences of the United States of America* 116, no. 6 (2019): 2033–38, https://dx.doi.org /10.1073%2Fpnas.1721438116.

9. *What helped women the most*: Brian Uzzi, "Research: Men and Women Need

Different Kinds of Networks to Succeed," *Harvard Business Review*, February 25, 2019, https://hbr.org/2019/02/research-men-and-women-need -different-kinds-of-networks-to-succeed.

10. *For women, the most*: Ibid.

11. *During the pandemic*: Rob Cross, Karen Dillon, and Danna Greenberg, "The Secret to Building Resilience," *Harvard Business Review*, January 29, 2021, https://hbr.org/2021/01/the-secret-to-building-resilience.

12. *Their mission was to colonize*: #ANGELS, "Introducing #Angels," #Angels News, March 4, 2015, https://medium.com/angels-news/angels-42e1a bb7469b.

13. *In fact, in 2016*: Dan Primack, "Top of the Morning," Axios, March 7, 2018, https://www.axios.com/newsletters/axios-pro-rata-30ed724c-d7e7-4b55 -9d69-40752b60aa2e.html.

14. *And until the late 2010s*: All Raise, "All Raise Annual Report," All Raise, 2019, https://allraise.org/assets/all-raise-annual-report-2019.pdf.

15. *In the article that first*: Reed Albergotti, "Silicon Valley Women Tell of VC's Unwanted Advances," The Information, June 22, 2017, https://www .theinformation.com/articles/silicon-valley-women-tell-of-vcs-unwanted -advances.

16. *All Raise invites people*: "About," Founders for Change, https://www.founder sforchange.org/about.

17. *In 2018, they published*: #ANGELS, "#TheGapTable," Medium, February 28, 2018, https://medium.com/angels-news/thegaptable-9982230d923a.

18. *women earned 82 cents*: "The State of the Gender Pay Gap in 2021," Pay-Scale, 2022, https://www.payscale.com/data/gender-pay-gap.

19. *In its first report*: #ANGELS, "Silicon Valley's Equity Gap: Women Own Just 9%," Medium, September 18, 2018, https://medium.com/angels-news /silicon-valleys-equity-gap-women-own-just-9-29159f40a17.

20. *Carta issued updated*: "2020: A Study Analyzing Equity Distribution By Gender, Race & Ethnicity, & Geography," Carta Equity Summit, December 8, 2021, https://www.cartaequitysummit.com/2020-a-study-analyz ing-equity-distribution-by-gender-race-ethnicity-geography-carta-equity summit/.

21. *The equity gap in 2018*: "Explaining Trends in the Gender Wage Gap," Council of Economic Advisers, June 1998, https://clintonwhitehouse4 .archives.gov/WH/EOP/CEA/html/gendergap.html; Jordan Weissmann, "Why Are Women Paid Less?," *Atlantic*, October 17, 2012, https://www.the atlantic.com/business/archive/2012/10/why-are-women-paid-less/263776/.

22. *A 2005 study*: Hannah Riley Bowles, Linda Babcock, and Kathleen L.

McGinn, "Constraints and Triggers: Situational Mechanics of Gender in Negotiation," *Journal of Personality and Social Psychology* 89, no. 6 (2005): 951–65, https://projects.iq.harvard.edu/files/hbowles/files/situational_mechanics.pdf.

23. *One opportunity to study*: Steffen Andersen et al., "Gender Differences in Negotiation: Evidence from Real Estate Transactions," *Economic Journal* 131, no. 638 (2021): 2304–32, https://sites.pitt.edu/~vester/wp_realestate_10172018.pdf; Jens Mazei et al., "A Meta-analysis on Gender Differences in Negotiation Outcomes and Their Moderators," *Psychological Bulletin* 141, no. 1 (2015): 85–104, https://www.apa.org/pubs/journals/releases/bul-a0038184.pdf.

24. *In 2016, digitalundivided*: Onezero, "An Exclusive Club of Black Women Is Disrupting Silicon Valley," Angel, February 25, 2020, https://angel.co/today/stories/an-exclusive-club-of-black-women-is-disrupting-silicon-valley-12558.

25. *Oh, and that year*: "Startups That Failed in 2016," Crunchbase, 2016, https://www.crunchbase.com/hub/startups-that-failed-in-2016.

26. *By 2018, thirty-four Black women*: Emma Hinchliffe, "The Number of Black Female Founders Who Have Raised More than $1 Million Has Nearly Tripled Since 2018," *Fortune*, December 2, 2020, https://fortune.com/2020/12/02/black-women-female-founders-venture-capital-funding-vc-2020-project-diane/; "The State of Black & Latinx Female Founders," digitalundivided, 2021, https://www.projectdiane.com/.

27. *But consider that in 2020*: Samara Lynn, "Digitalundivided Founder Talks Black Women and Tech Funding," Black Enterprise, February 9, 2016, https://www.blackenterprise.com/digitalundivided-founder-talks-black-women-and-tech-funding; Gené Teare, "A Decade of Supergiants: Rounds Above $100M Dominate in 2020," Crunchbase, November 24, 2020, https://news.crunchbase.com/news/a-decade-of-supergiants/.

28. *This pattern was discovered*: Nilanjana Dasgupta, Melissa McManus Scircle, and Matthew Hunsinger, "Female Peers in Small Work Groups Enhance Women's Motivation, Verbal Participation, and Career Aspirations in Engineering," *Proceedings of the National Academy of Sciences of the United States of America* 112, no. 16 (2015): 4988–93, https://doi.org/10.1073/pnas.1422822112.

29. *And women may be*: David G. Rand et al., "Social Heuristics and Social Roles: Intuition Favors Altruism for Women but Not for Men," *Journal of Experimental Psychology* 145, no. 4 (2016): 389–96, https://doi.org/10.1037/xge0000154.

30. *In 2016, a decade after*: Julia B. Bear and Linda Babcock, "Negotiating Femininity: Gender-Relevant Primes Improve Women's Economic Performance in Gender Role Incongruent Negotiations," *Psychology of Women Quarterly* 41, no. 2 (3016): 163–74, https://doi.org/10.1177%2F0361684316679652.

Eleven: Defeating Bias with Data

1. *The twins have*: Robert Hackett, "Uber's CEO Comes from What May Be the World's Most Techie Family," *Fortune*, November 17, 2017, https://fortune.com/2017/11/17/uber-ceo-dara-khosrowshahi/.

2. *Though they soon returned*: Ali Partovi, "Immigrants Are Humans," LinkedIn, June 24, 2020, https://www.linkedin.com/pulse/immigrants-humans-ali-partovi/.

3. *Though his parents had*: David Gelles, "Hadi Partovi Was Raised in a Revolution. Today He Teaches Kids to Code," *New York Times*, January 17, 2019, https://www.nytimes.com/2019/01/17/business/hadi-partovi-code-org-corner-office.html.

4. *As of February 2022*: "We Invest in People, Which Begins with Investing Our Time," Neo, https://neo.com/portfolio.

5. *Much ink has been spilled*: Lincoln Quillian et al., "Meta-analysis of Field Experiments Shows No Change in Racial Discrimination in Hiring over Time," *Proceedings of the National Academy of Sciences of the United States of America* 114, no. 41 (2017): 10870–75, https://doi.org/10.1073/pnas.1706255114.

6. *Pymetrics now works*: Marie Baldauf-Lenschen, "Evaluate for the Long Term with Soft Skill Data," Pymetrics, September 17, 2020, https://www.pymetrics.ai/pygest/evaluate-for-the-long-term-with-soft-skill-data.

7. *That's why, she said*: Christo Wilson et al., "Building and Auditing Fair Algorithms: A Case Study in Candidate Screening," Conference: FAccT (2021): ACM Conference on Fairness, Accountability, and Transparency, https://evijit.github.io/docs/pymetrics_audit_FAccT.pdf.

8. *Google released its*: Laszlo Bock, "Getting to Work on Diversity at Google," Google, May 28, 2014, https://blog.google/outreach-initiatives/diversity getting-to-work-on-diversity-at-google/.

9. *VanPutten found the BlendScore*: Tracy Jan, Jena McGregor, and Meghan Hoyer, "Corporate America's $50 Billion Promise," *Washington Post*, August 24, 2021, https://www.washingtonpost.com/business/interactive/2021/george-floyd-corporate-america-racial-justice/.

10. *Not only did they*: Mitch and Freada Kapor, "Dear Investors: So You Want to Take Diversity Seriously (Part 1)," Kapor Center, February 18, 2016, https://

medium.com/kapor-the-bridge/dear-investors-so-you-want-to-take-diversity
-seriously-part-1-777972b5450c.

11. *So far, their thesis*: "Kapor Capital Impact Report," Kapor Capital, May 8, 2019, https://impact.kaporcapital.com/wp-content/uploads/2019/05/2019 -Kapor-Impact-Report.pdf.

12. *By 2020, it had trained*: "Bitwise Industries Hires Laura Maristany to Advance Workforce Diversity and Inclusion," Bitwise Industries, April 5, 2021, https://bitwiseindustries.com/media/bitwise-industries-hires-laura -maristany-to-advance-workforce-diversity-and-inclusion/.

13. *By early 2021, Bitwise's employee base*: Kristin Stoller, "California Tech Hub Bitwise Industries Raises $50 Million in Quest to Diversify the Workforce," *Forbes*, February 24, 2021, https://www.forbes.com/sites/kristinstoller/2021 /02/24/california-tech-hub-bitwise-industries-raises-50-million-in-quest-to -diversify-the-workforce/?sh=62c72d35582d.

14. *Coed founding teams*: Gené Teare, "Global VC Funding to Female Founders Dropped Dramatically This Year," Crunchbase, December 21, 2020, https:// news.crunchbase.com/news/global-vc-funding-to-female-founders/.

15. *Recent studies have found*: Marjolein Dennissen, Yvonne Benschop, and Marieke van den Brink, "Rethinking Diversity Management: An Intersectional Analysis of Diversity Networks," *Organization Studies* 41, no. 2 (2018): 219–40, https://journals.sagepub.com/doi/full/10.1177/01708406 18800103.

16. *It's well documented*: Courtney Connley, "How Corporate America's Diversity Initiatives Continue to Fail Black Women," CNBC, January 12, 2021, https://www.cnbc.com/2020/07/01/how-corporate-americas-diversity -initiatives-continue-to-fail-black-women.html.

17. *And the percentage of women*: Alexandra Kalev, Frank Dobbin, and Erin Kelly, "Best Practices or Best Guesses? Assessing the Efficacy of Corporate Affirmative Action and Diversity Policies," *American Sociological Review* 2, no. 71 (2006): 589–617, https://scholar.harvard.edu/files/dobbin/files/2006 _asr_kalev.pdf.

18. *They polled more than two hundred*: Trae Vassallo et al., "Elephant in the Valley," 2017, https://www.elephantinthevalley.com/.

19. *A 2010 study, however*: Emilio J. Castilla and Stephen Benard, "The Paradox of Meritocracy in Organizations," *Administrative Science Quarterly* 55, no. 4 (2010): 543–676, https://doi.org/10.2189%2Fasqu.2010.55.4.543.

20. *The program, they discovered*: Project Include, "Startup Include Report on our First Cohort," Medium, August 7, 2017, https://medium.com/project include/startup-include-report-on-our-first-cohort-55412485b2b0.

21. *Moskovitz has written about*: Dustin Moskovitz, "Building a Diverse and Inclusive Workplace: Q and A with Dustin Moskovitz," Asana, November 7, 2018, https://blog.asana.com/2018/11/asana-diversity-project-include/; David Rock and Heidi Grant, "Why Diverse Teams Are Smarter," *Harvard Business Review*, November 4, 2016, https://hbr.org/2016/11/why-diverse-teams-are-smarter.

22. *Their instincts tended*: Scott Austin, Stephanie Stamm, and Rolfe Winkler, "Uber Jackpot: Inside One of the Greatest Startup Investments of All Time," *Wall Street Journal*, May 10, 2019, https://www.wsj.com/articles/uber-jackpot-inside-one-of-the-greatest-startup-investments-of-all-time-11557496421.

23. *Some interesting trends emerged*: "First Round 10 Year Project," First Round, 2015, http://10years.firstround.com.

24. *Then, in 2020, he read*: Cliff Worley, "So You Want to Fund Black Founders," Kapor Capital, December 14, 2020, https://www.kaporcapital.com/so-you-want-to-fund-black-founders/.

25. *According to McKinsey's calculation*: Kweilin Ellingrud et al., "The Power of Parity: Advancing Women's Equality in the United States," McKinsey & Company, April 7, 2016, https://www.mckinsey.com/featured-insights/employment-and-growth/the-power-of-parity-advancing-womens-equality-in-the-united-states#.

Index of Names

Abel, Martin/Middlebury College, 274–275
Achor, Shawn/researcher, 305–306, 306n
Ahmad, Asima/Carrot Fertility, 109
Ajayi, Toyin/CityBlock Health, 82–89, 90, 94–101, 112, 113–117, 126, 361, 363, 364, 366, 369
Allen, Sheena/CapWay, 60–63, 74, 81
Anderson, Steve/Baseline Ventures, 191, 366
Anderson, Tracy/Tracy Anderson Method, 250, 253
Andreev, Andrey/Badoo, 153, 155–156
Annis, Barbara/Gender Intelligence Group, 85, 92
Ardern, Jacinda/New Zealand, 206, 207, 232
Arnell, Peter, 251

Babcock, Linda/Carnegie Mellon University, 324
Babineaux-Fontenot, Claire/Feeding America, 211–214, 220–225, 229, 230, 231, 363, 364
Baker, Erica Joy/Project Include, 348
Banducci, Bonita/Santa Clara University, 112, 134
Baron-Cohen, Simon/professor, 96
Bartasi, Gina/Kindbody, 110–112, 117
Bartz, Carol/Autodesk, 113
Bdeir, Ayah/littleBits, 279–280, 286, 292

Becker, Gail/CAULIPOWER, 122–124, 334
Blakely, Sara/Spanx, 10, 369
Bowie, David, 255–256, 262
Brescoll, Victoria/Yale School of Management, 244, 275, 276–277
Brown, Alasdair/professor, 237–238
Brown, Brené/author, 253

Caldbeck, Justin/Lightspeed Venture Partners, 192, 313
Caldwell, Nick, Twitter, 330
Chekroud, Adam/Spring Health, 91–93, 366
Chernin, Peter/Otter Media, 161
Childers, Caroline/Chief, 297–299, 301, 308
Cohen, Stephanie/Goldman Sachs, 302, 353
Collins, Julia/Planet FWD; Zume, 76–80, 363
Conferences for Women, 305–306

David, Grainger/*Fortune* magazine, 4
Defries, Tony, 255
DeSteno, David/Northeastern University, 75–76
Drexler, Mickey/J.Crew, 5
Dufu, Tiffany/The Cru, 301–303, 307–309
Dweck, Carol/professor, 120–122

Ellison, Larry/Oracle, 3
Emmons, Robert/University of California Davis, 75

The Female Quotient, 296, 305, 372
Fields, Debbi/Mrs. Fields Cookies, 10
Folkman, Joseph/Zenger/Folkman, 208
Fowler, Susan/Uber, 109, 313

Gadde, Vijaya/#ANGELS, 311-312
Gallardo, Karla/Cuyana, 34-40, 47, 51, 74
Gelman, Audrey/The Wing, 304
Gielan, Michelle/researcher, 305
Gold, Jim/Neiman Marcus, 176
Graham, Paul/Y Combinator, 34
Green, Diane/VMware, 93
Green, Kirsten/Forerunner Ventures, 272, 277-278, 281
Grossman, Mindy/WW, 281-282
Gupta, Vishal/University of Alabama, 270

Haney, Tyler/Outdoor Voices, 271-272
Hanna, Linda/Mahmee, 102-105, 112, 117
Hanna, Melissa/Mahmee, 102-105, 112, 117
Harden, Sarah/HelloSunshine, 160-164, 168
Hartz, Julia/Eventbrite, 93
Hartz, Kevin/Eventbrite, 93
Hastings, Reed/Netflix, 7
Hewlett, Sylvia Ann/economist, 306
Holmgren/Jennifer/LanzaTech, 9, 74, 240-244, 246-249, 264-265, 266, 361-362
Huang, Laura/Harvard Business School, 54
Huffington, Arianna/Huffington Post, 10
Hunsicker, Christine/CaaStle, 287-288, 292, 361
Huston, Therese/cognitive psychologist, 263-264
Hyman, Jennifer/Rent the Runway, 10-11, 12, 173-180, 187, 188, 189-190, 192, 196, 198-200, 273, 278, 366, 368

Ibrahim, Maha/Canaan Ventures, 39, 41, 42
Iger, Bob/Walt Disney Company, 7

Jenkins, Christina/Portfolia FemTech Fund, 106

Kanze, Dana, 372
Kaplan, Lindsay/Chief, 297-299, 301

Kapor, Mitch/Kapor Capital, 342-344
Kapor Klein, Freada/Kapor Capital, 342-344
Kardashian, Kim/ShoeDazzle, 36
Kazi, Rousseau/Threads, 318
Kerr, Hillary/Who What Wear, 290
Khosrowshahi, Dara/Uber, 327
Kimmelman, Jay, 330
Koh, April/Spring Health, 11, 90-94, 96, 117, 272, 366, 368, 369
Kopelman, Josh/First Round Capital, 350-352
Korey, Steph/Away, 271, 272
Kostka, Pam/All Raise, 46-47, 314-315
Krawcheck, Sallie/Ellevest, 10, 141-151, 168, 169, 361

Lake, Katrina/Stitch Fix, 188-201, 313, 361, 366
Lampkin, Stephanie/Blendoor, 320, 335
Lauder, Estée/Estée Lauder, 10
Lee, Aileen/All Raise, 10, 312-314
Lee, Matthew/INSEAD, 54
Levesque, Ravi/The RealReal, 182-183
Loomis, Carol/*Fortune* magazine, 3

Ma, Shan-Lyn/Zola, 38, 44, 245, 352
Mackey, John/Whole Foods, 5
Maillian, Lauren/digitalundivided, 321-322
Master, Robert/Commonwealth Care Alliance, 100
Mather, Mara/University of California Davis, 203, 206
McCartney, Stella/Stella McCartney, 185, 186, 186n, 251, 361, 366
McCormick, Elizabeth, 116
McEnroe, John, 276
McPhee, John/Princeton University, 2
Merkel, Angela/Germany, 232
Messerschmidt, Jana/#ANGELS, 311, 315, 317-318
Morris, Wesley, 252
Moseley, Christine/Full Harvest, 55-60, 68, 74, 81
Moskovitz, Dustin/Asana, 349
Mullainathan, Sendhil/University of Chicago Booth School of Business, 92

Nunn, Michelle/CARE USA, 209-211, 216-219, 224-225, 229, 230, 231, 363, 364

Olguin, Irma Jr./Bitwise Industries, 338–342, 344–346

Paknad, Daryoush/WorkBoard, 130, 132–133
Paknad, Deidre/WorkBoard, 130–137, 286, 365
Paltrow, Gwyneth/Goop, 249–262, 264–266, 361
Pao, Ellen/Project Include, 347–348
Partovi, Ali/Neo, 327–331, 334
Partovi, Hadi/Code.org, 327, 328
Perkins, Sonja/Broadway Angels, 41, 42, 49–50
Polli, Frida/Pymetrics, 332–334, 343
Power, Katherine/Clique Media; Versed; Avaline Wine, 289–291, 361

Renfrew, Gregg/Beautycounter, 13–14, 15, 18, 19, 155, 368–369
Richter, Kurt/Harvard University, 223
Rivera, Miriam/Ulu Ventures, 60, 148
Romm, Iyah/CityBlock Health, 101, 113–114, 361, 366
Rosenblum, Mendel/VMware, 93

Sandberg, Sheryl/LeanIn, 9, 304
Sankaran, Meena/Ketos, 68–74, 81
Sarnoff, Ann/WarnerMedia Studios and Networks Group, 16–17
Seidman-Becker, Caryn/Clear, 202–203, 224–229, 230, 231, 361
Serwer, Andy/*Fortune* magazine, 5
Settle, Dana/Greycroft, 51, 52, 154, 261, 262
Shah, Shilpa/Cuyana, 38–40, 44, 47, 51
Shaheen, George/Webvan, 268–269
Shenk, Kimberly/Novi, 282–286, 292
Siroya, Shivani/Tala, 10, 63–68, 74, 81, 365
Sladden, Chloe/#ANGELS, 311–312
Small, Deborah/University of Pennsylvania, 60
Soberal, Jake, 341–342, 344, 346
Solomon, Andrew, 91
Stanton, Katie/#ANGELS, 311–312
Stevenson, Betsey/economist, 286

Stewart, Martha, 10, 254, 257, 261
Sun, Tammy/Carrot Fertility, 108–110, 112, 117
Swan, Bob/Webvan, 269

Tannen, Deborah/Georgetown University, 97
Taylor, Kimberly/Cluster, 275, 280, 281, 286, 364
Taylor, Tanya/designer, 180
Tejada, Jennifer/PagerDuty, 74, 127–130, 134–137, 248–249, 286, 361, 365

Uhlmann, Eric Luis/INSEAD, 275
Underwood, April/#ANGELS, 311–312

VanPutten, Stephanie (Lampkin), /Blendoor, 320, 335
Verrilli, Jessica/#ANGELS, 311, 315, 317

Wainwright, Julie/The RealReal, 11, 180–187, 184n, 188, 196, 197, 200, 201, 269, 273, 286, 292, 361, 366
Waithe, Lena/Hillman Grad Productions, 165–168, 169
Wedell-Wedellsborg, Merete/psychologist, 145
Williams, Joan/University of California Hastings College of Law, 280
Williams, Serena, 276
Winblad, Ann/venture capitalist, 180, 182
Winfrey, Oprah, 10, 250, 251, 259, 369
Witherspoon, Reese/HelloSunshine, 158–164, 168, 169, 369
Wojcicki, Anne/23andMe, 112
Wolfe Herd, Whitney/Bumble, 9, 74, 151–157, 168, 169, 195, 304n, 369

Yang, Fuyu/professor, 238

Zacharia, Snejina/Insurify, 28–34, 43, 51, 52, 93
Zalis, Shelley/The Female Quotient, 296, 305, 372
Zenger, Jack/Zenger/Folkman, 208

⊖ Index of Concepts and Skills

Abrasiveness trap, 17–18

Abundance mentality/scarcity mindset, 220, 223

Adaptability, 224–225, 229–230, 233

After-event reviews, 288, 361

Age, 122, 148, 167, 201, 242

Aggressiveness, 9, 99, 154, 167, 224, 289, 291, 319, 368

Ambition, 32, 89, 113, 134, 264–265, 277, 291, 302, 303, 322

Anger, 275

Archetypes, 157, 240, 264–266, 329

Artificial intelligence, 78, 184

Asking for help, 303, 306, 307, 314

Authentic authorship, 163, 164, 169

"Beautiful mess effect," 253

Bechdel test, 158–159

Bias, 4, 18, 26–27, 40, 43, 45, 49, 54–55, 279, 292

Black women, 26–27, 41, 62, 77–80, 99, 163, 165, 167, 168, 270–271, 303–304, 304n, 317, 319–320, 322, 330, 335–337, 336, 345–348, 353, 356n, 358, 363

"Bright girl effect," 121–122

Business school, 28, 30–31, 35, 36, 57, 161, 173, 174, 176, 189, 190, 332, 336

Cap table gap, 310–311, 317

"Centeredness," 245n

Circular economy, 180–187

Coed founding teams, 27, 32, 33, 50, 55n, 346, 350

Cognitive reappraisal, 231

Collective intelligence, 124, 126, 126n

Communal (collaborative) leadership, 137–138, 280, 365

Communication between genders, 29, 32, 39, 44, 48, 51, 97, 103, 113, 123, 129n, 135–137, 204, 207, 228, 231n, 244–245, 277, 279, 286, 291, 321, 323, 360, 362–363

Companies with only-male founders, 46, 272, 274, 284, 314, 315, 318

Competition, 32, 54, 69, 88, 175, 176, 183, 185, 289, 291, 300, 341, 349

Confidence, 3, 9, 39, 44, 48, 51, 103, 123, 135–137, 204, 207, 231n, 242, 243n, 258, 260, 262–265, 277, 279, 286, 291, 321, 323, 360, 362–363

Confirmatory standard, 247–248, 257

"Contextual commerce," 251

Contextual thinking, 86, 116

Convergent thinking, 87

Covid-19 pandemic, 20, 59, 110, 124, 196–199, 202–207, 206n, 211, 211n, 212, 227–228, 231, 232–233, 261–262, 308

Critical mass theory and scarcity impact, 200–201, 223–224

Criticism, 18, 99, 210, 254, 256, 271, 273, 275, 292, 360

Cultural numbness, 141, 145, 151, 169

Decentralized decision making, 211

Decision making, 15, 34, 40, 47, 48, 55, 98, 129n, 144, 145, 202–204, 208–209, 211, 218, 219, 223–224, 232, 233, 245, 256, 260, 262, 263, 273–274, 312, 333, 349, 359, 362

Dismissiveness (patronizing), 238, 266–267

"Distance traveled," 342

Divergent thinking, 86

Diversity and inclusion, 41–43, 49, 52, 98n, 128–130, 129n, 130n, 163, 168, 210, 264–265, 282, 296, 304, 313–315, 320, 321, 326, 330, 334, 335, 337, 343, 345–349, 350n, 352, 354–355, 372

Doing more with less, 47–50

Double standards, 10, 20, 178, 272–274, 277, 279, 280, 285, 292, 323, 363, 372

E-commerce and internet, 38, 91, 190, 269

Emotional quotient/emotional intelligence, 96, 214, 229, 230

Emotional reaction, 75, 76, 96, 97, 204, 214, 255, 256, 275–276, 284, 339–342, 369

Empathy, 19, 82, 95–99, 116, 117, 207, 214, 215, 229, 233, 280

Environmental, social, and governance (ESG) funds, 59, 59n

Equity ownership gap, 45, 45n, 316–317

Ethical behavior, 145

Expectations—minimum and confirmatory standards, 247–249, 257

Female archetypes, 15, 237–267, 327

Female-dominated microenvironments, 322, 325, 366

Female government leaders, 205–209, 232–233

Female leadership advantage, 20, 206–208, 230–231, 351

Female participation effect, 135–136

Femtech, 102–112

Funding gap, 11, 26, 45–46, 55n, 284, 320, 322, 331, 363, 368

Gender discrimination, 284

Gender equity, 9, 16, 19, 20–21, 42, 50, 168, 354

Gender gap, 26, 45, 143, 147, 297, 316, 319

Gender incongruity, 276–277

Gender intelligence, 86, 93

Gender judo, 280, 282

Gender ratio, 350–351, 350n

Glass cliff, 146, 229, 233, 274

Gratitude-driven leadership, 16, 19, 69, 74–77, 79, 80–81, 302

Great man theory, 208–209

Growth mindset/mindset theory, 20, 118–124, 127, 137, 223–224, 225, 302, 315, 362

Hispanic/Latinx women, 27, 62, 163, 168, 249, 319–321, 322, 330, 336, 340, 342, 344, 346, 353

Hope experiment, 233

Humility, 68, 75, 137, 148, 192, 245n, 362

Identity, 4, 6–8, 99, 226–228, 255–257, 269, 271, 285–293, 346, 357

Impact of showing emotion, 75, 76, 96, 97, 214, 255, 256, 275, 284, 292, 339–342, 369

Impact of warmth on bias, 55

Imposter syndrome, 262–263

Improving outlook, 122–124

Intersectionality, 346–349

Introversion, 245, 264

"Jugaad" (Hindi for "hack"), 85, 94

Leadership, 15–16, 20, 48, 60, 68, 74–75, 81, 98n, 130n, 137–138, 146, 150, 206, 208, 214, 229–233, 231n, 237, 240, 244–246, 245n, 248, 260, 262, 265, 266, 270, 274, 278, 280, 288, 304n, 309, 359, 360–361, 365, 367, 369

Learning from failure, 187, 217, 230, 258, 269, 287

LGBTQ+, 110, 345

Male gaze, 158

Media coverage, 152, 239, 271

"Mega" financing round ($100m plus), 45–46

Mentorship, 5, 25, 49, 62, 70, 75, 130, 167, 180, 230, 297, 299, 301, 302–303, 315, 322, 329, 366

Meritocracy myth, 348

Microaggression, 167

Microaudiences, 161

minorities, 27, 34, 41, 42, 49, 51, 128, 167, 200, 248–249, 304n, 314, 330, 336, 351, 367

Motivation, 48, 54, 67, 136n, 246, 286

Negotiating power, 44, 309, 318, 319, 323–325, 368

Networking, 31, 146, 153, 296–310, 320–322, 347, 367

"Out-group" (outside) advantage, 127–130

Pattern matching, 33–40, 50, 60, 266, 279, 332, 359

Personal questions, 29, 32, 33, 278

Personalized follow-up, 177, 178

Power structures, 310–313

Preparing for the worst, 203, 204, 225, 361

Proactive thinking (or "fire prevention"), 113, 135

Proximity-impact on investing and founding, 60–63

Purpose-oriented companies, 55, 56, 59, 115

Racially diverse founding teams, 49, 127–128, 129, 130, 135, 326, 349, 352, 365

Radical trust, 67

Reading the mind through the eyes test, 96–97

Realistic projections vs. bluster, 43–45, 265

Recognition, 306–307

Rejection, 28, 150, 153–154, 192, 286

Resilience, 12, 20, 232, 233, 268–293, 310

Resumes, 332–335

Risk taking, 15, 36, 42, 48, 146–149, 203, 206, 208, 212, 225, 230, 261, 271, 289, 321, 329, 333, 363

Rooney rule, 128, 248–249

Scarcity impact, 223, 224

Seed round, 26, 32, 33, 46, 46n, 66

Self-doubt, 263

Servant leadership, 68, 81

Sexual harassment, 2, 3, 6, 7, 130, 151, 152, 192, 200, 313

Shifting the power dynamic, 2, 9, 115, 153, 219, 245, 361, 367

Social-impact framing, 55, 59, 60, 164

"Social infertility," 110

Social media/internet, 150, 152–153, 161, 162, 173, 221, 251, 308

Social sensitivity, 97, 125–126

Soft skills, 334, 342

Speech (voice), 29, 99, 143, 243, 244–245, 276

Startup failure rate, 136, 230, 233, 277, 368

Stereotypes, 55, 248, 257–258, 270, 275–277, 279, 291–292, 293, 319, 322–323, 325, 359, 367

Talent magnet, 361

Token theory, 270

Transparency, 130–135, 260, 284, 310, 314, 315, 318, 319, 325, 337, 361

Unconscious bias, 4, 43, 45, 335

Venture capital, 11, 12, 13, 25–28, 32–33, 34, 40–47

Venture capital homogeneity, 43

Volubility and interruption, 100, 125, 135, 244, 244n, 275

Vulnerability, 15–16, 20, 76, 249, 253–254, 260, 264, 265, 359, 362

Women labeled aggressive, 99, 289, 319, 368

Women-led countries, 205–209, 232–233

YPO (Young President's Organization), 295–296

◉ About the Author

Julia Boorstin is CNBC's Senior Media & Tech correspondent; she reports and conducts CEO interviews across CNBC programming. Boorstin also plays a key role on CNBC's bicoastal tech-focused franchise *TechCheck*, delivering reporting, analysis, and interviews around streaming, social, and the convergence of media and technology. She joined CNBC in May 2006 as a general assignment reporter and in 2007 moved to Los Angeles to cover media before adding social media and technology to her beat. In 2013, Boorstin created and launched the CNBC *Disruptor 50*, an annual list she oversees, highlighting the private companies transforming the economy and challenging companies in established industries. Additionally, she reported a documentary on the future of television for the network, *Stay Tuned . . . The Future of TV*. She also helped launch CNBC's *Closing the Gap* initiative, covering the people and companies closing gender gaps, and leads CNBC's coverage of studies on this topic. In October 2023 she launched a new list and franchise for CNBC, *Changemakers: Women Transforming Business*, which will highlight women who have had a meaningful impact on the business and nonprofit world in the prior year.

Boorstin joined CNBC from *Fortune* magazine, where she was a writer and reporter since 2000. During that time she was also a contributor to "Street Life," a live market wrap-up segment on CNN Headline News. In 2003, 2004, and 2006, *The Journalist and Financial Reporting* newsletter named Boorstin to the "TJFR 30 under 30" list of the most promising business journalists under thirty years old. She was an intern for the State Department's delegation to the Organization for Economic

Co-operation and Development and for Vice President Gore's domestic policy office.

She graduated with honors from Princeton University with a BA in history. She was also an editor of *The Daily Princetonian*. She lives in Los Angeles with her husband, her two sons, and their two cats.

When
Women
Lead

Julia Boorstin

This reading group guide for When Women Lead *includes an introduction and discussion questions with author Julia Boorstin. The suggested questions are intended to provoke interesting and lively discussions in your reading group. We hope that these ideas will inspire connection with the women profiled in these pages, self-reflection, and goal setting.*

Dear Readers,

In *When Women Lead* I lay out a new, inclusive vision for leadership. My goal in writing this book was to showcase a diverse set of new leadership icons to inspire people of any gender. I intended for the varied leadership styles and approaches to problem solving of the women in these pages to prompt readers to examine their own traits and how they can be reframed and leveraged as superpowers. We are at a moment when women's leadership—their empathetic, communal, and purpose-driven approach—is more important than ever.

I hope you will use this book as a guide to defying odds yourself—just like all the women in these pages have. As I've traveled the country on my book tour I've heard about how both women and men have suffered from insufficient role models to set new patterns in which they could follow. The stories of the women in my book can serve as a beacon, and the data outlining the underlying value of their approach can serve as a blueprint. I've seen in my experience and heard from hundreds of women how a lack of understanding about the nature of deep-seated societal biases has prevented success. I hope you will find all the data empowering, and can use the explanation of phenomena, from confirmatory bias to pattern matching, to navigate your own challenges.

Despite all the gender gaps and bias revealed in my reporting and research, I remain more optimistic than ever. I have seen hundreds of times how women have been able to tap into their own authentic leadership styles to thrive and achieve success on their own terms. A key way women find and pursue their own path is through community. Please strip away any socially imposed concerns that it would be inappropriate to talk about money, lay out audacious goals, or discuss your weaknesses.

Don't try to fit any stereotype of leadership, but rather figure out what you really want, what drives you, and how your differences can be your superpowers. I know we all have them.

Please use a conversation about my book, and the thoughts and feelings it prompts about your own experiences and dreams, as a way to connect with a group, class, or community. Use these conversations to identify people who would be a valuable addition to your personal board of advisors. Remember the power in vulnerability—it invites collaboration. And know that no one is born a leader but everyone can become one. I hope the questions posed on the following pages inspire self-reflection, goal setting, and inspiration.

Julia Boorstin

Topics & Questions for Discussion

1. *When Women Lead* tells a series of stories spotlighting women who have managed to defy the odds to found and run successful companies. Which women's stories resonated most with you? Are there women who remind you of yourself or a peer? Which of their traits are familiar? Which characteristics or skills that contributed to success were most surprising and counterintuitive to you?

2. The book explains the strategies and skills used to achieve success with a range of research studies and social science experiments. Were there any concepts—like token theory, social sensitivity, or beautiful mess effect—that were exciting or validating? Which studies changed your perception of your experience in the workplace? Discuss the study about jockeys that identified how people who are rare in certain roles are underestimated. Did the idea that people are harder on themselves than they are on others resonate? Share your reaction to the sorority and fraternity members solving a murder mystery; does it make sense that the addition of an outsider made the original members of the group smarter?

3. *When Women Lead* opens with the author recalling how, when she was a teenager, her mother was optimistic that women would be equally

represented in leadership positions, and how disappointed she was to see the reality of inequality. How did your family and upbringing frame your expectations of your own opportunity? What do you wish you'd known when you were starting your career that you know now?

4. Have you ever felt underestimated in your professional or personal life? Perhaps both? Share your experiences in the group and discuss the commonalities or differences.
    a. Bonus question: Have you ever been able to leverage being underestimated to your advantage? Have you ever been able to surprise people with your skills?
    b. Bonus question: Feeling like an outsider can be hard, but have you ever been able to tap into the value of that outsider perspective?

5. Think about the concepts introduced in *When Women Lead* that explain bias—pattern matching, token theory, the glass cliff, minimum and confirmatory standards, etc. Have you experienced any of those concepts in your work or life? How did you navigate around them? Does learning about these concepts give you ideas about how to better manage them in the future?

6. What are some ways you've experienced bias because of your gender or identity? Have you ever directly confronted or rejected stereotypes placed on you? What was the result? Did you face backlash? Did you earn more respect? Bonus question: Talk about a time when you caught yourself applying pattern matching or stereotypes to others or yourself.

7. One theme in this book is how having a purpose beyond just a financial profit helps people and companies succeed and that women face less bias when embracing social or environmental goals. Purpose-

driven companies have an advantage in hiring and retaining talent and founders and leaders can draw on their greater purpose to push through challenging times. What do you feel is your purpose beyond succeeding at work? How can you tap into what you're most passionate about—mentoring people, helping the environment, etc.—to drive your success with work?

8. Make a list of what you consider to be your strengths and your weaknesses. Now, dig into your weaknesses category. Are you being too critical of yourself? Are there ways to reframe those traits you see as negative? Is there any way to think of them as superpowers?

   a. Bonus question: Do you think that the way you saw your shortcomings would be different if you were a different gender or had a different identity? How would you recategorize your traits if your identity matched that of people who have traditionally held positions of authority?

9. Have you ever felt like your ability to achieve a particular goal was limited because of a part of your identity? Have you felt like something core to who you are, like your gender or race, prevented you from succeeding?

   a. If you struggled with a limitation, but *were* still able to succeed, what enabled you to overcome those obstacles? Make a list of the steps you took to navigate those challenges and identify which of those strategies you can deploy again.

   b. If you have *not* been able to overcome challenges tied to your identity, list what you think is preventing your progress. Are there any structural disadvantages laid out in this book, like pattern matching or the confirmatory standard, that are hindering your progress? Are people judging you more harshly because people with an identity like yours are rare in a particular role? Looking at your list of obstacles, refer back to *When Women Lead*. Are any of your challenges similar to those faced by the women in the book? How might you be able to emulate their strategies?

10. One of the core messages of *When Women Lead* is that diversity can drive success. How can you think about the value in bringing in different perspectives to your work? Thinking about intersectionality: Can you broaden your definition of diversity beyond simply gender and race? Can you reframe your company's approach to investing in diversity from something that's a nice thing to do to something that provides a financial advantage?

11. Between the studies and the stories, which were some of the most useful lessons that you took from *When Women Lead*? How can you apply these new tools to navigate adversity or pursue success in your work and life?

12. *When Women Lead* notes that women are less likely than men to network and pursue audacious professional goals. Do you have a dream job, a fantasy of starting a company, or just a bold personal goal? Write down your ideal position or outcome for yourself in ten years. Then think about how to make this dream a reality. Break down the steps it would take to achieve your most audacious goal over time. Set yourself long-term goals for the next year or two, along with some near-term targets. What would you like to achieve this month? What's the target you want to stretch and reach for this year?

   a. Make a list of all the people you can call upon—friends, colleagues, work contacts—to talk about your goals. Share your dream with them, ask them for advice, and to hold you accountable. Create your own personal board of advisors to help and push you on your journey. You can do it!